WRITER
ZEB WELLS

ART
LEONARD KIRK
WITH **ANDREW CURRIE**

COLORS
GURU eFX

LETTERS
VC'S JOE CARAMAGNA
WITH **CHRIS ELIOPOULOS**

COVER ART
DAVE WILKINS

ASSISTANT EDITOR
JAKE THOMAS

ASSOCIATE EDITOR
DANIEL KETCHUM

EDITOR
NICK LOWE

NEW MUTANTS

FALL OF THE NEW MUTANTS

COLLECTION EDITOR: JENNIFER GRÜNWALD

EDITORIAL ASSISTANTS: JAMES EMMETT & JOE HOCHSTEIN

ASSISTANT EDITORS: ALEX STARBUCK & NELSON RIBEIRO

EDITOR, SPECIAL PROJECTS: MARK D. BEAZLEY

SENIOR EDITOR, SPECIAL PROJECTS: JEFF YOUNGQUIST

SENIOR VICE PRESIDENT OF SALES: DAVID GABRIEL

SVP OF BRAND PLANNING & COMMUNICATIONS: MICHAEL PASCIULLO

BOOK DESIGN: JEFF POWELL

EDITOR IN CHIEF: AXEL ALONSO

CHIEF CREATIVE OFFICER: JOE QUESADA

PUBLISHER: DAN BUCKLEY

EXECUTIVE PRODUCER: ALAN FINE

NEW MUTANTS VOL. 3: FALL OF THE NEW MUTANTS. Contains material originally published in magazine form as NEW MUTANTS #15-21. First printing 2011. ISBN# 978-0-7851-4584-4. Published by MARVEL WORLDWIDE, INC., a subsidiary of MARVEL ENTERTAINMENT, LLC. OFFICE OF PUBLICATION: 135 West 50th Street, New York, NY 10020. $19.99 per copy in the U.S. and $21.99 in Canada (GST #R127032852); Canadian Agreement #40668537. **Printed in the U.S.A.** ALAN FINE, EVP - Office of the President, Marvel Worldwide, Inc. and EVP & CMO Marvel Characters B.V.; DAN BUCKLEY, Publisher & President - Print, Animation & Digital Divisions; JOE QUESADA, Chief Creative Officer; JIM SOKOLOWSKI, Chief Operating Officer; DAVID BOGART, SVP of Business Affairs & Talent Management; TOM BREVOORT, SVP of Publishing; C.B. CEBULSKI, SVP of Creator & Content Development; DAVID GABRIEL, SVP of Publishing Sales & Circulation; MICHAEL PASCIULLO, SVP of Brand Planning & Communications; JIM O'KEEFE, VP of Operations & Logistics; DAN CARR, Executive Director of Publishing Technology; SUSAN CRESPI, Editorial Operations Manager; ALEX MORALES, Publishing Operations Manager; STAN LEE, Chairman Emeritus. For information regarding advertising in Marvel Comics or on Marvel.com, please contact John Dokes, SVP Integrated Sales and Marketing, at jdokes@marvel.com. For Marvel subscription inquiries, please call 800-217-9158. **Manufactured between 8/17/2011 and 9/5/2011 by R.R. DONNELLEY, INC., SALEM, VA, USA.**

10 9 8 7 6 5 4 3 2 1

PREVIOUSLY...

When the mutant-slaying cyborg Bastion made his final bid to exterminate mutantkind, Cyclops tasked New Mutant Cannonball and his team with crippling Bastion's reinforcements. While the team succeeded in subduing Bastion's lieutenant, Cameron Hodge, victory came at a price: Karma lost her leg. Warlock was forced to compromise his principles and destroy sentient organic life. And Magik, shot into the hell dimension of Limbo by Bastion's troops, barely escaped execution at the hands of Limbo's demonic forces.

With Bastion defeated, the New Mutants and mutantkind turn their eyes to the future. But, unbeknownst to the X-Men, Magik is not the only one who's recently returned from Limbo...

CANNONBALL
Sam Guthrie
Explosive blast field

MAGIK
Illyana Rasputin
Teleportation, Soulsword

SUNSPOT
Roberto Da Costa
Solar energy aborption and manipulation

KARMA
Xi'an (Shan) Coy Manh
Telepathic mind control

MAGMA
Amara Aquilla
Control over fire and molten earth

DANI MOONSTAR
De-powered

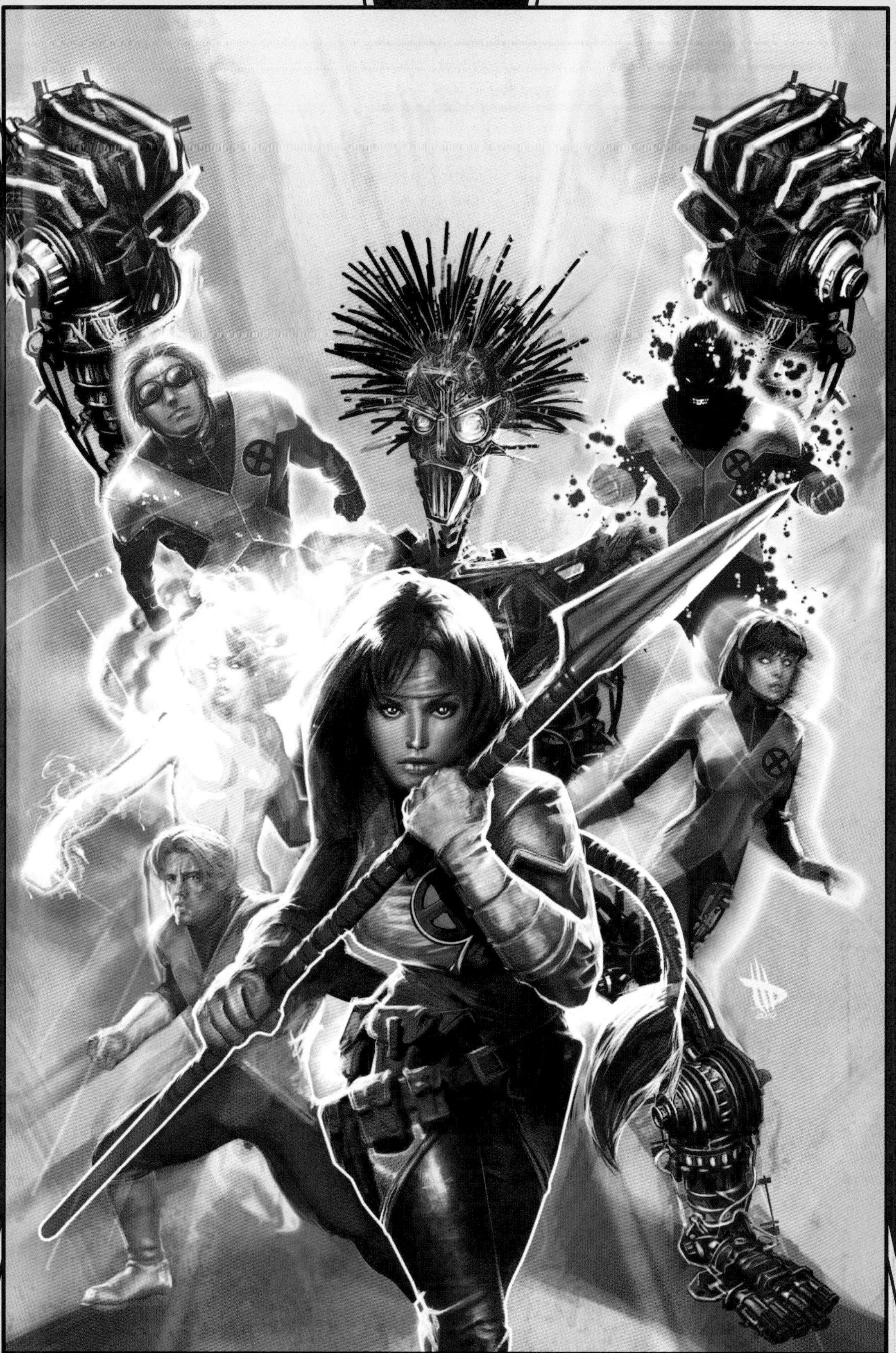

15

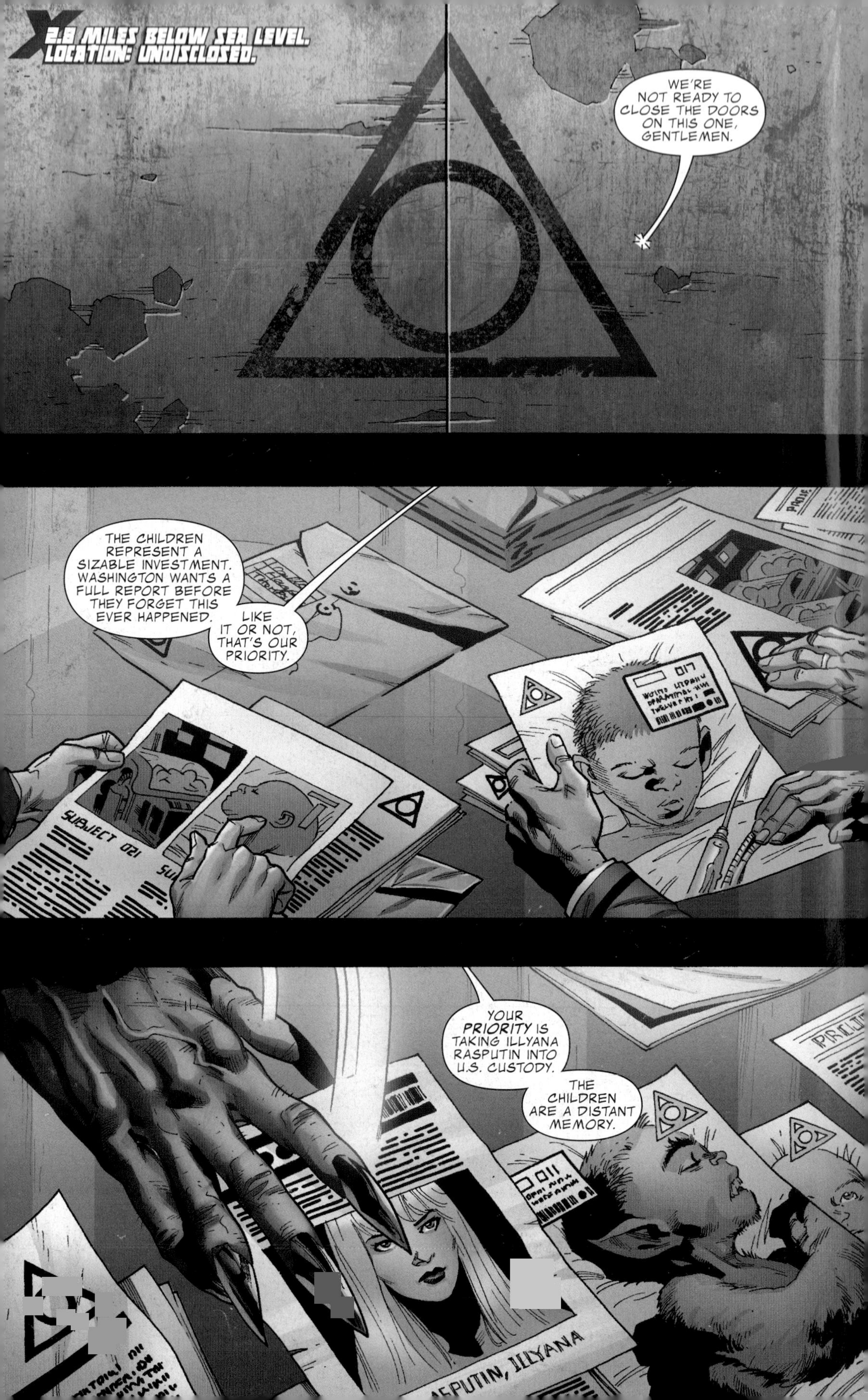
2.8 MILES BELOW SEA LEVEL. LOCATION: UNDISCLOSED.
WE'RE NOT READY TO CLOSE THE DOORS ON THIS ONE, GENTLEMEN.
THE CHILDREN REPRESENT A SIZABLE INVESTMENT. WASHINGTON WANTS A FULL REPORT BEFORE THEY FORGET THIS EVER HAPPENED.
LIKE IT OR NOT, THAT'S OUR PRIORITY.
SUBJECT 021
YOUR PRIORITY IS TAKING ILLYANA RASPUTIN INTO U.S. CUSTODY.
THE CHILDREN ARE A DISTANT MEMORY.

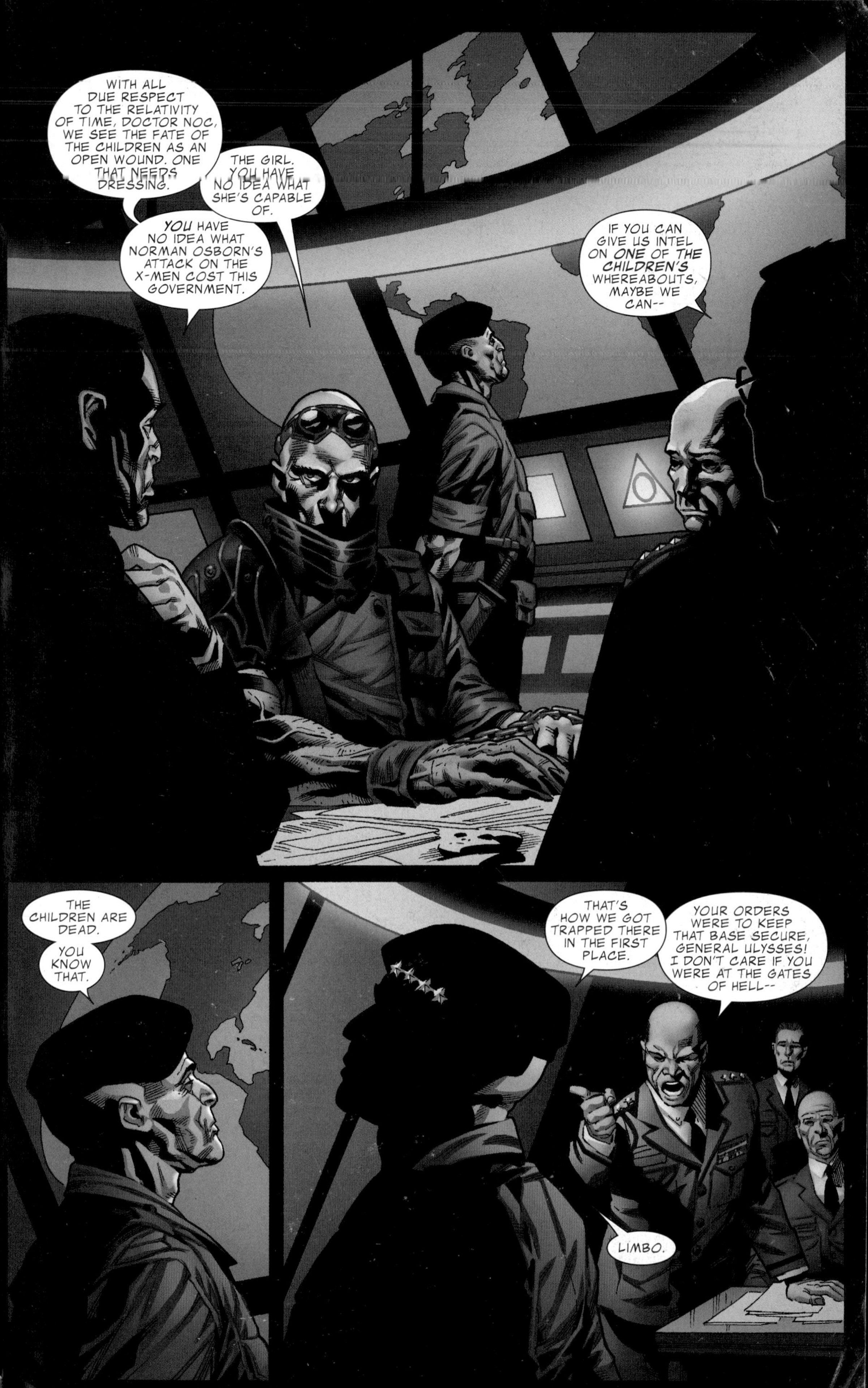
WITH ALL DUE RESPECT TO THE RELATIVITY OF TIME, DOCTOR NOC, WE SEE THE FATE OF THE CHILDREN AS AN OPEN WOUND. ONE THAT NEEDS DRESSING.
THE GIRL. YOU HAVE NO IDEA WHAT SHE'S CAPABLE OF.
YOU HAVE NO IDEA WHAT NORMAN OSBORN'S ATTACK ON THE X-MEN COST THIS GOVERNMENT.
IF YOU CAN GIVE US INTEL ON ONE OF THE CHILDREN'S WHEREABOUTS, MAYBE WE CAN--
THE CHILDREN ARE DEAD.
YOU KNOW THAT.
YOUR ORDERS WERE TO KEEP THAT BASE SECURE, GENERAL ULYSSES! I DON'T CARE IF YOU WERE AT THE GATES OF HELL--
THAT'S HOW WE GOT TRAPPED THERE IN THE FIRST PLACE.
LIMBO.

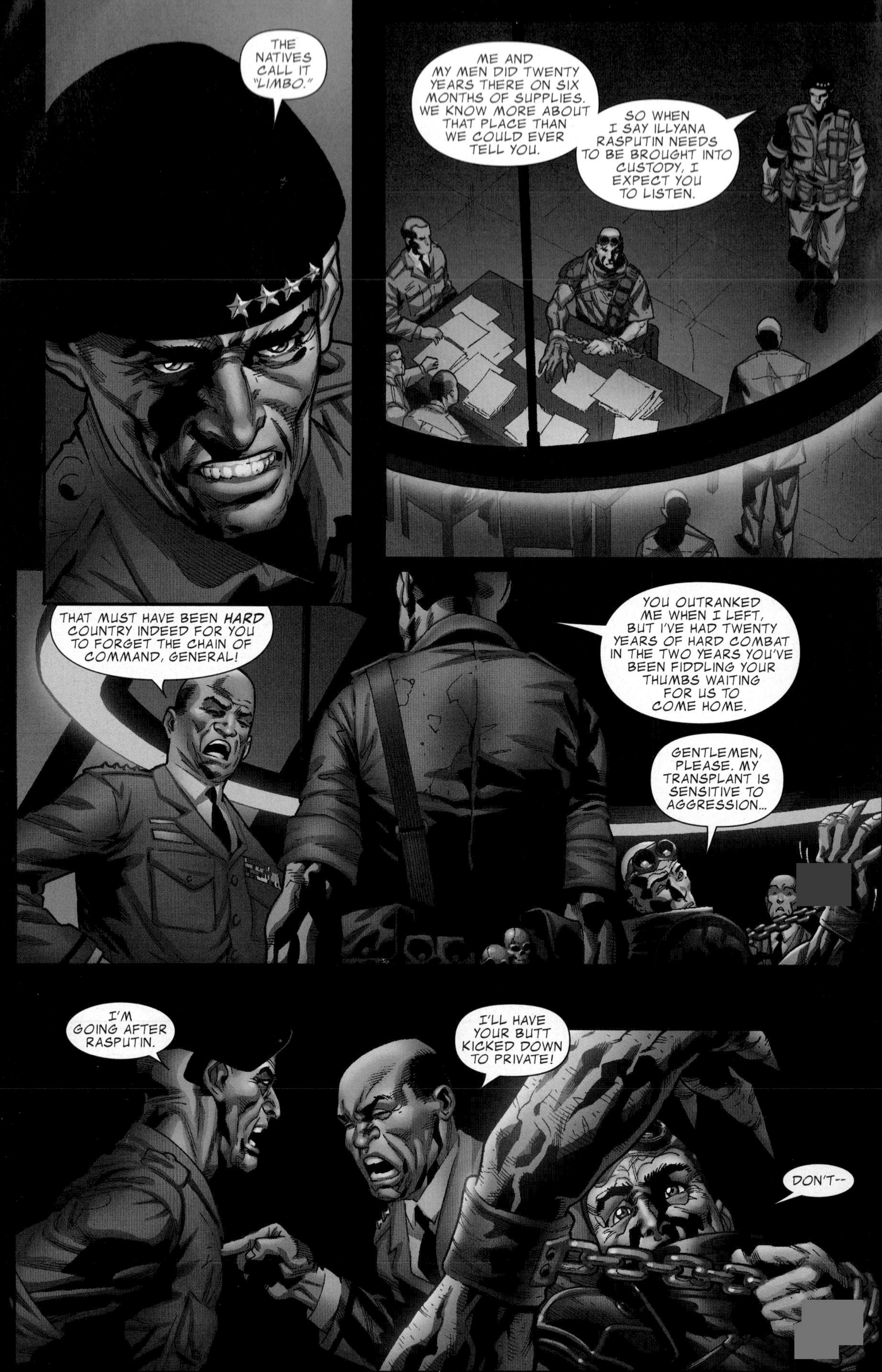
THE NATIVES CALL IT "LIMBO."
ME AND MY MEN DID TWENTY YEARS THERE ON SIX MONTHS OF SUPPLIES. WE KNOW MORE ABOUT THAT PLACE THAN WE COULD EVER TELL YOU.
SO WHEN I SAY ILLYANA RASPUTIN NEEDS TO BE BROUGHT INTO CUSTODY, I EXPECT YOU TO LISTEN.
THAT MUST HAVE BEEN HARD COUNTRY INDEED FOR YOU TO FORGET THE CHAIN OF COMMAND, GENERAL!
YOU OUTRANKED ME WHEN I LEFT, BUT I'VE HAD TWENTY YEARS OF HARD COMBAT IN THE TWO YEARS YOU'VE BEEN FIDDLING YOUR THUMBS WAITING FOR US TO COME HOME.
GENTLEMEN, PLEASE. MY TRANSPLANT IS SENSITIVE TO AGGRESSION...
I'M GOING AFTER RASPUTIN.
I'LL HAVE YOUR BUTT KICKED DOWN TO PRIVATE!
DON'T--

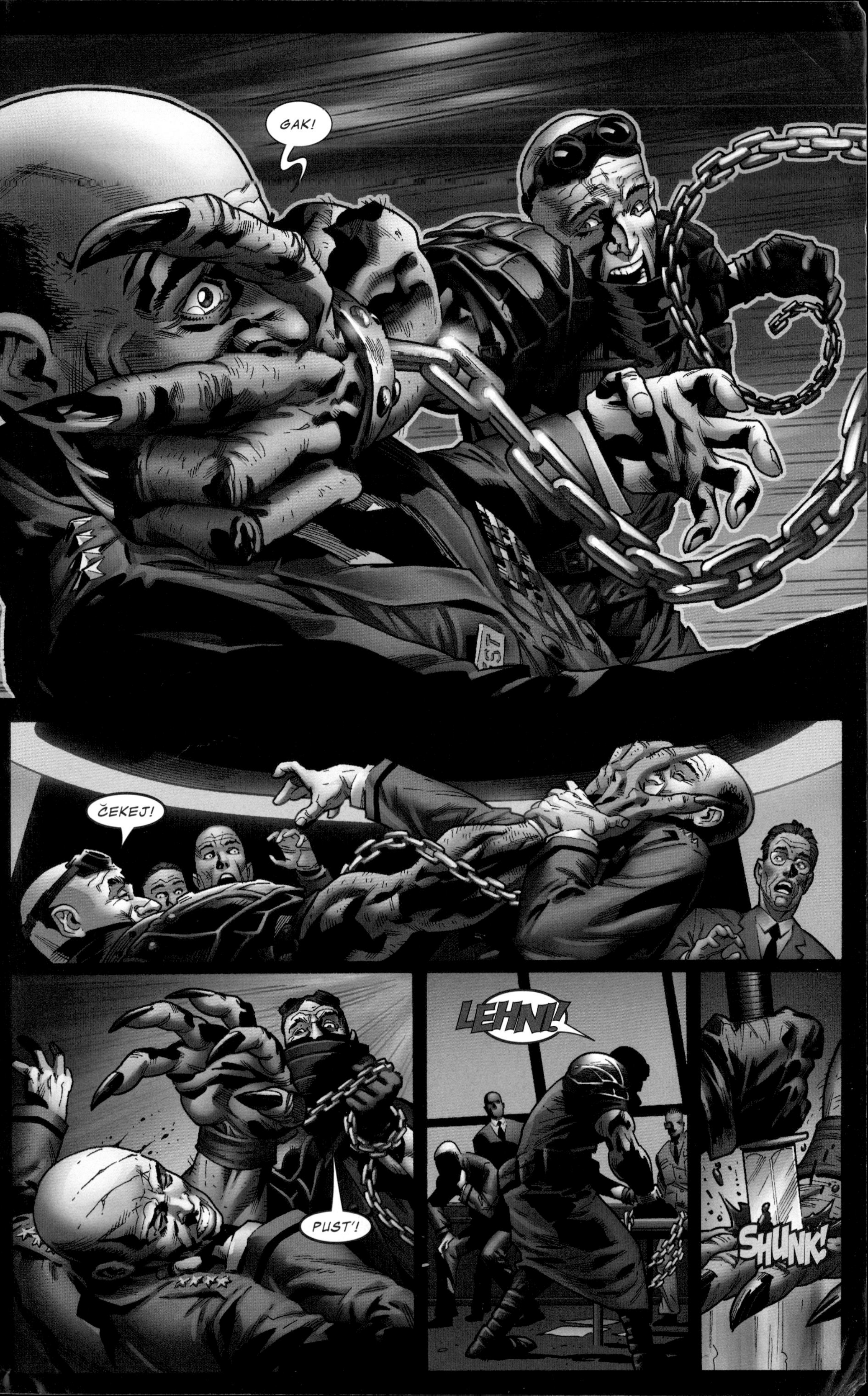
GAK!
ČEKEJ!
PUST'!
LEHNI!
SHUNK!

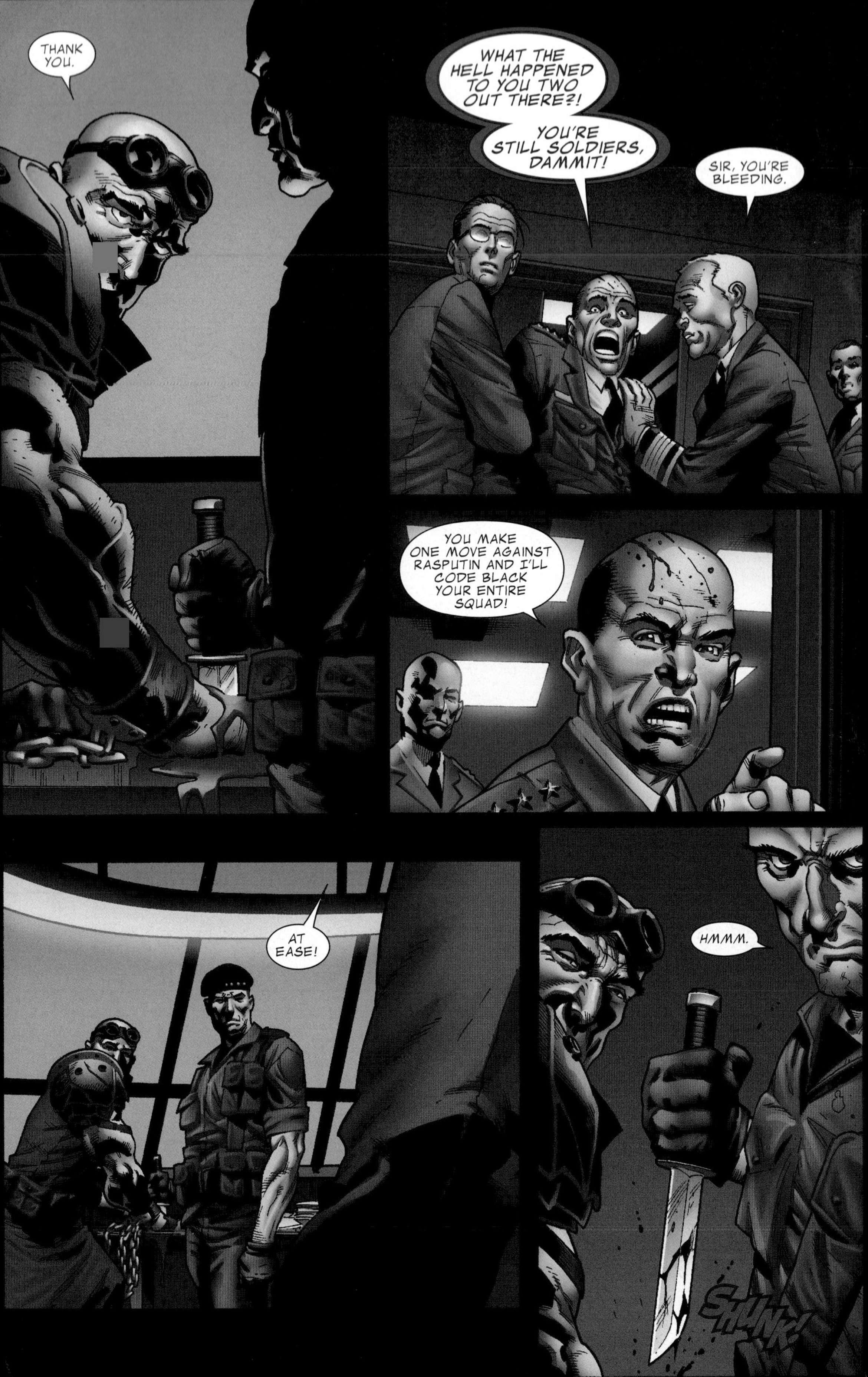
THANK YOU.
WHAT THE HELL HAPPENED TO YOU TWO OUT THERE?!
YOU'RE STILL SOLDIERS, DAMMIT!
SIR, YOU'RE BLEEDING.
YOU MAKE ONE MOVE AGAINST RASPUTIN AND I'LL CODE BLACK YOUR ENTIRE SQUAD!
AT EASE!
HMMM.
SHUNK!

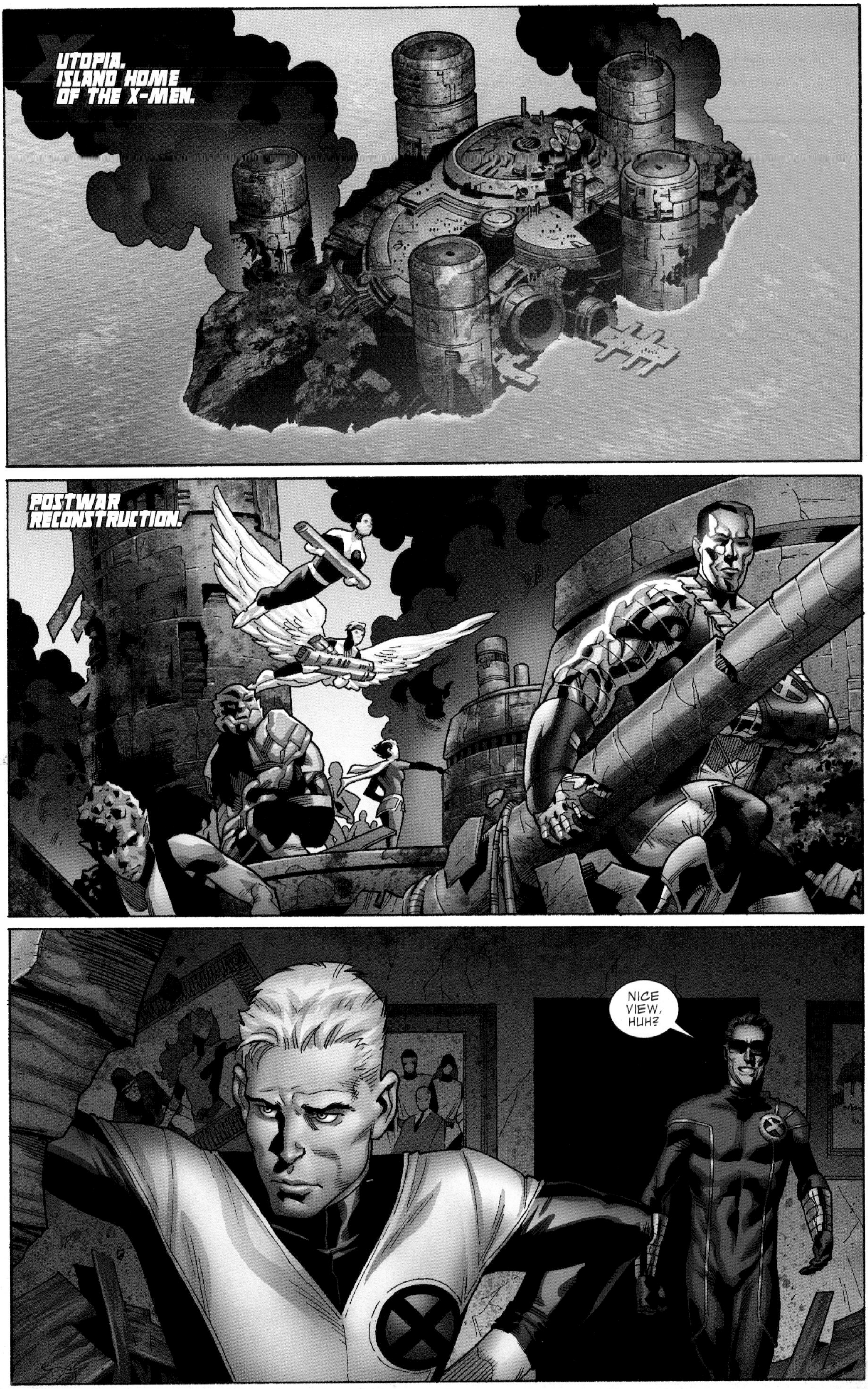
UTOPIA. ISLAND HOME OF THE X-MEN.
POSTWAR RECONSTRUCTION.
NICE VIEW, HUH?

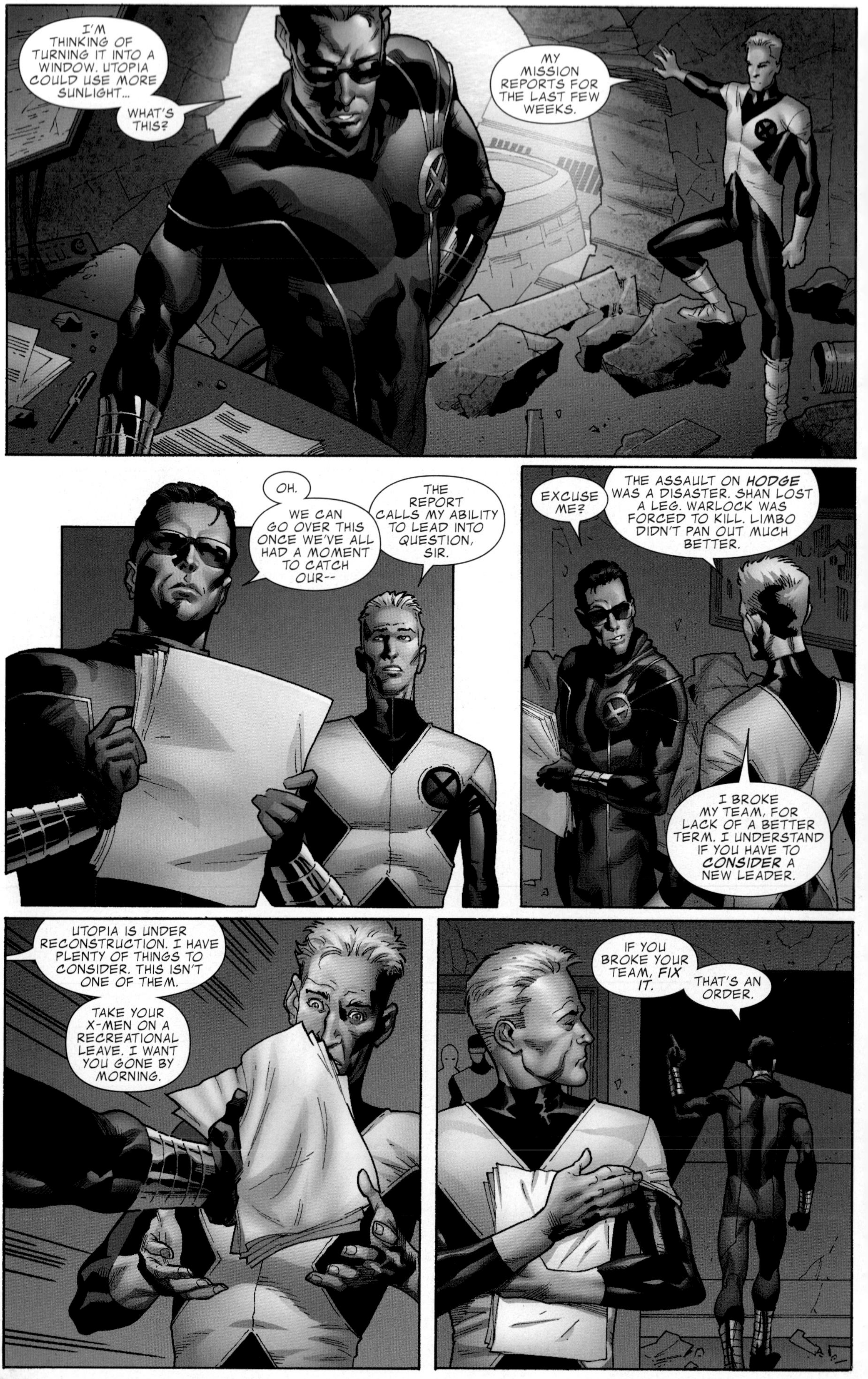

I'M THINKING OF TURNING IT INTO A WINDOW. UTOPIA COULD USE MORE SUNLIGHT...
WHAT'S THIS?
MY MISSION REPORTS FOR THE LAST FEW WEEKS.
OH.
WE CAN GO OVER THIS ONCE WE'VE ALL HAD A MOMENT TO CATCH OUR--
THE REPORT CALLS MY ABILITY TO LEAD INTO QUESTION, SIR.
EXCUSE ME?
THE ASSAULT ON HODGE WAS A DISASTER. SHAN LOST A LEG. WARLOCK WAS FORCED TO KILL. LIMBO DIDN'T PAN OUT MUCH BETTER.
I BROKE MY TEAM, FOR LACK OF A BETTER TERM. I UNDERSTAND IF YOU HAVE TO CONSIDER A NEW LEADER.
UTOPIA IS UNDER RECONSTRUCTION. I HAVE PLENTY OF THINGS TO CONSIDER. THIS ISN'T ONE OF THEM.
TAKE YOUR X-MEN ON A RECREATIONAL LEAVE. I WANT YOU GONE BY MORNING.
IF YOU BROKE YOUR TEAM, FIX IT.
THAT'S AN ORDER.

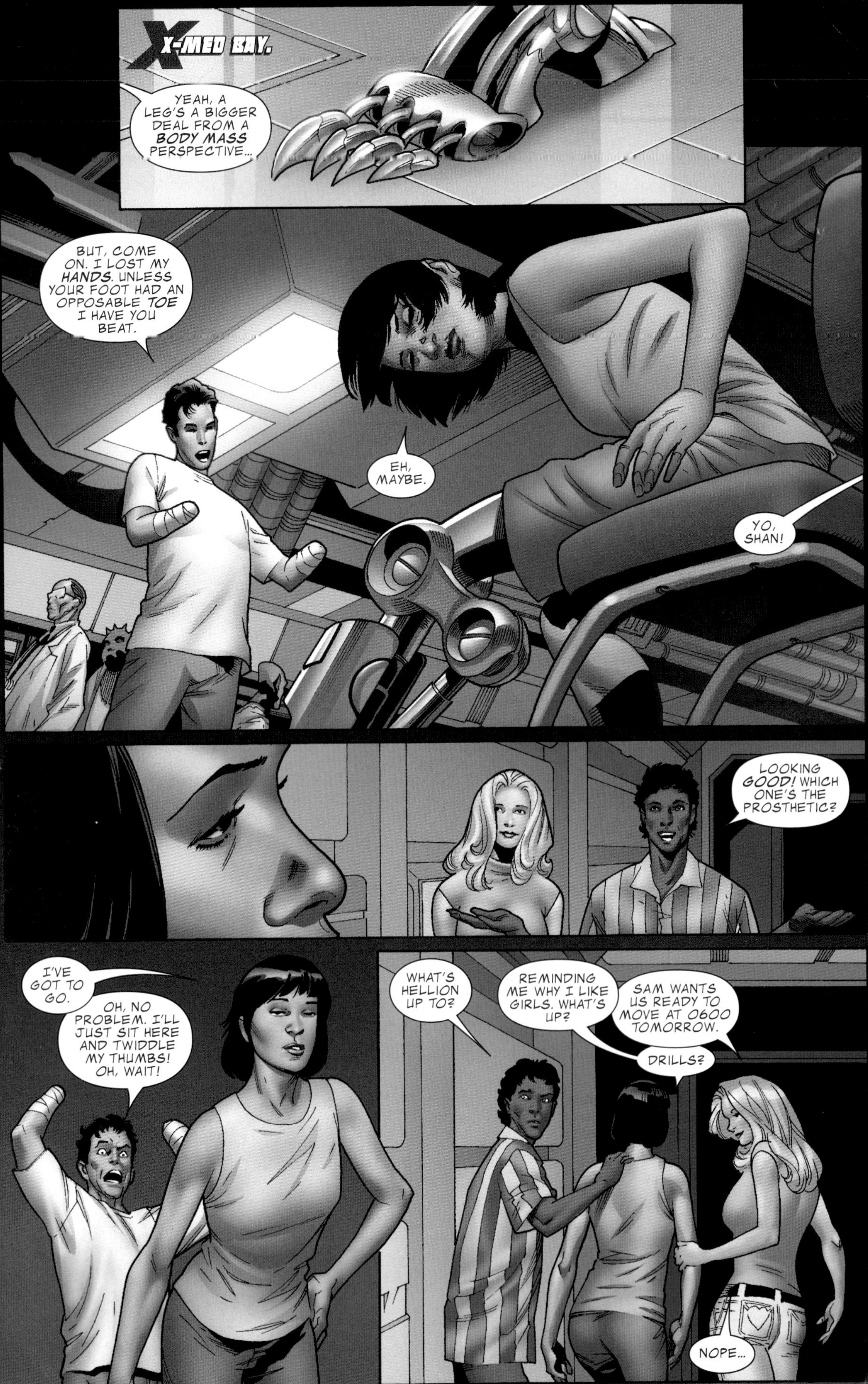
X-MED BAY.
YEAH, A LEG'S A BIGGER DEAL FROM A BODY MASS PERSPECTIVE...
BUT, COME ON. I LOST MY HANDS. UNLESS YOUR FOOT HAD AN OPPOSABLE TOE I HAVE YOU BEAT.
EH, MAYBE.
YO, SHAN!
LOOKING GOOD! WHICH ONE'S THE PROSTHETIC?
I'VE GOT TO GO.
OH, NO PROBLEM. I'LL JUST SIT HERE AND TWIDDLE MY THUMBS! OH, WAIT!
WHAT'S HELLION UP TO?
REMINDING ME WHY I LIKE GIRLS. WHAT'S UP?
SAM WANTS US READY TO MOVE AT 0600 TOMORROW.
DRILLS?
NOPE...

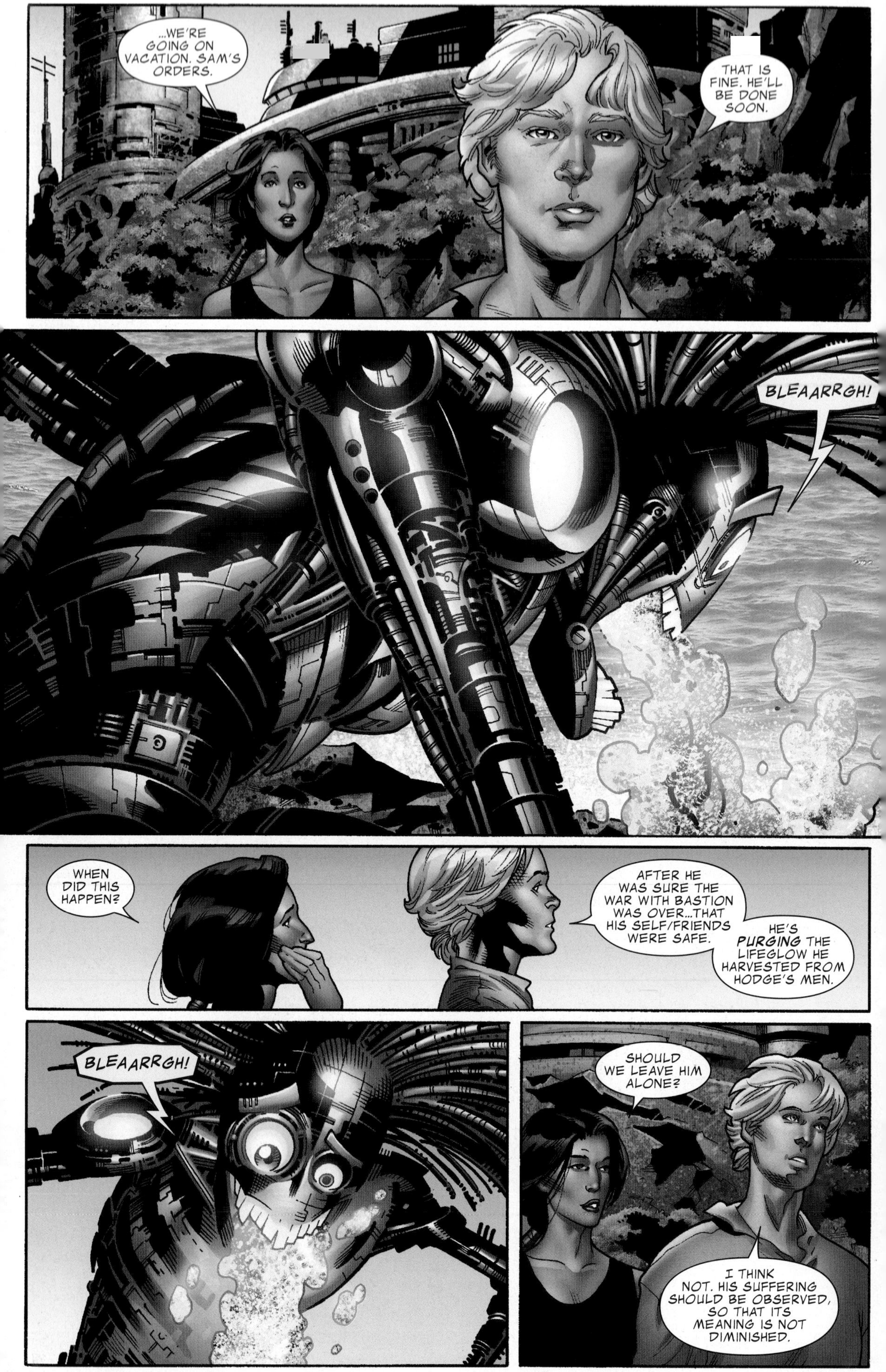
...WE'RE GOING ON VACATION. SAM'S ORDERS.
THAT IS FINE. HE'LL BE DONE SOON.
BLEAARRGH!
WHEN DID THIS HAPPEN?
AFTER HE WAS SURE THE WAR WITH BASTION WAS OVER...THAT HIS SELF/FRIENDS WERE SAFE.
HE'S PURGING THE LIFEGLOW HE HARVESTED FROM HODGE'S MEN.
BLEAARRGH!
SHOULD WE LEAVE HIM ALONE?
I THINK NOT. HIS SUFFERING SHOULD BE OBSERVED, SO THAT ITS MEANING IS NOT DIMINISHED.

I CAN FEEL YOU WATCHING ME.

I DON'T WANT TO HURT YOUR FEELINGS, BUT I STILL DON'T CONSIDER YOU ONE OF MY "POP-IN" FRIENDS.

YOU'RE LEAVING?

I'M GRABBING SOME R & R, JUST LIKE YOU GUYS. DIDN'T YOU HEAR? THE WAR'S OVER. WE WON.

MY WAR HASN'T BEGUN YET. BUT SOON, MEGAN...AND I MAY HAVE USE FOR YOUR AID.

YOU'RE ASKING ME FOR HELP? THE FIRST TIME THIS HAPPENED YOU WARPED A PIECE OF MY SOUL INTO A BLOODSTONE.

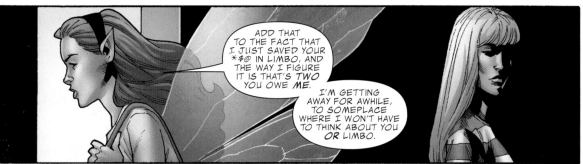

ADD THAT TO THE FACT THAT I JUST SAVED YOUR *$@ IN LIMBO, AND THE WAY I FIGURE IT IS THAT'S TWO YOU OWE ME.

I'M GETTING AWAY FOR AWHILE, TO SOMEPLACE WHERE I WON'T HAVE TO THINK ABOUT YOU OR LIMBO.

TRY TO RETURN THE FAVOR.

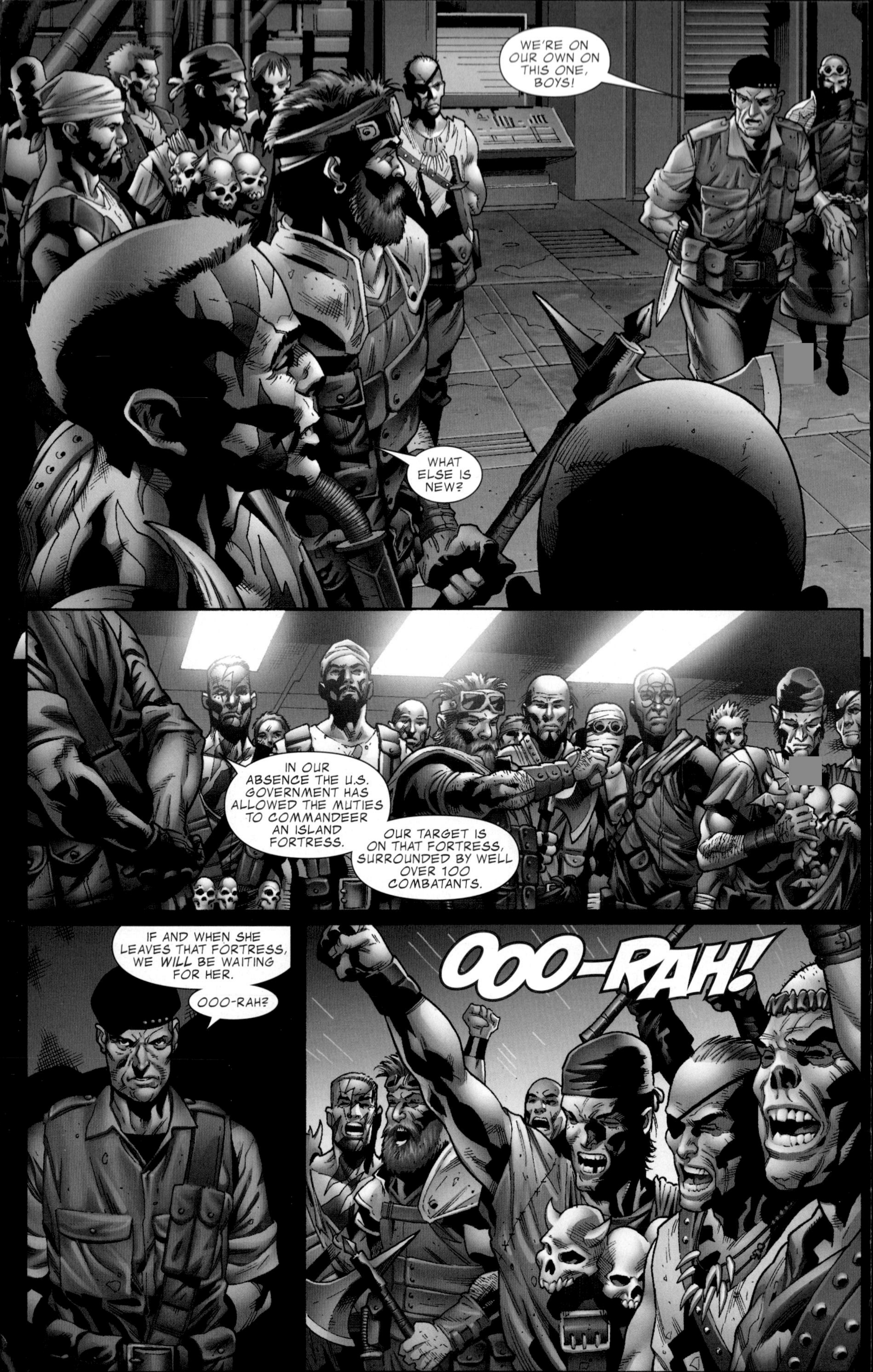
WE'RE ON OUR OWN ON THIS ONE, BOYS!
WHAT ELSE IS NEW?
IN OUR ABSENCE THE U.S. GOVERNMENT HAS ALLOWED THE MUTIES TO COMMANDEER AN ISLAND FORTRESS.
OUR TARGET IS ON THAT FORTRESS, SURROUNDED BY WELL OVER 100 COMBATANTS.
IF AND WHEN SHE LEAVES THAT FORTRESS, WE WILL BE WAITING FOR HER.
OOO-RAH?
OOO-RAH!

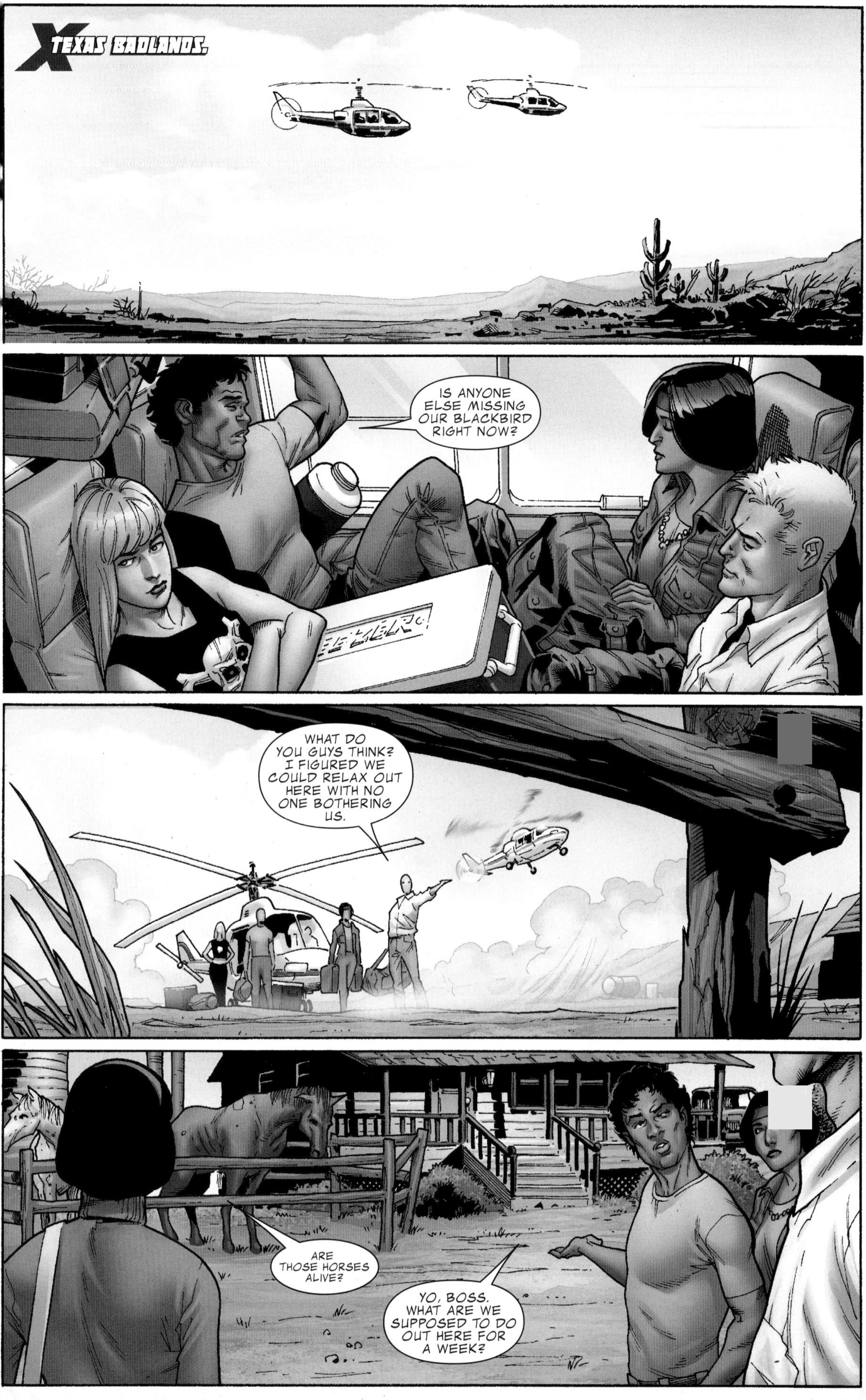
TEXAS BADLANDS.
IS ANYONE ELSE MISSING OUR BLACKBIRD RIGHT NOW?
WHAT DO YOU GUYS THINK? I FIGURED WE COULD RELAX OUT HERE WITH NO ONE BOTHERING US.
ARE THOSE HORSES ALIVE?
YO, BOSS. WHAT ARE WE SUPPOSED TO DO OUT HERE FOR A WEEK?

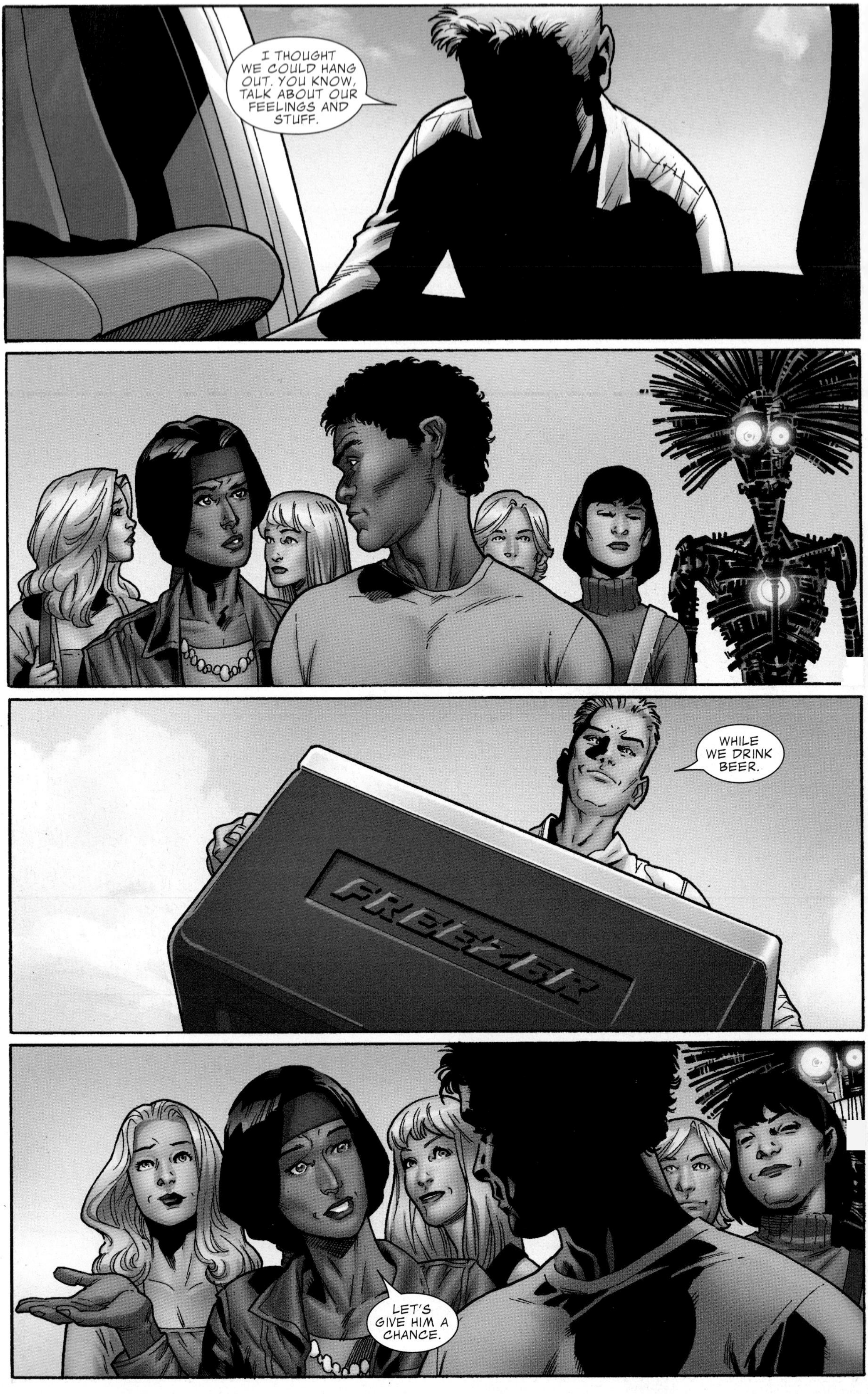
I THOUGHT WE COULD HANG OUT. YOU KNOW, TALK ABOUT OUR FEELINGS AND STUFF.
WHILE WE DRINK BEER.
FREEZER
LET'S GIVE HIM A CHANCE.

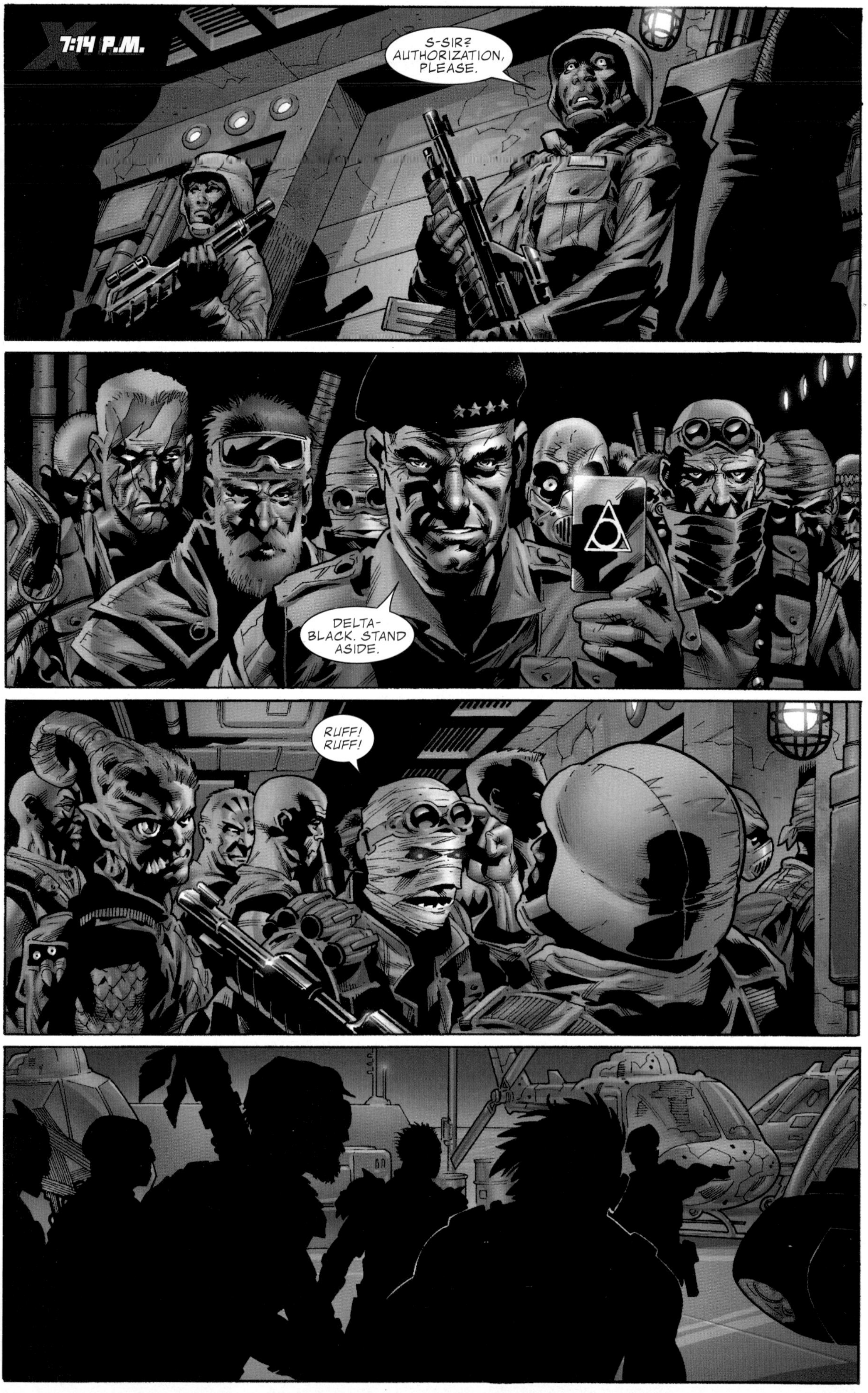
7:14 P.M.
S-SIR? AUTHORIZATION, PLEASE.
DELTA-BLACK. STAND ASIDE.
RUFF! RUFF!

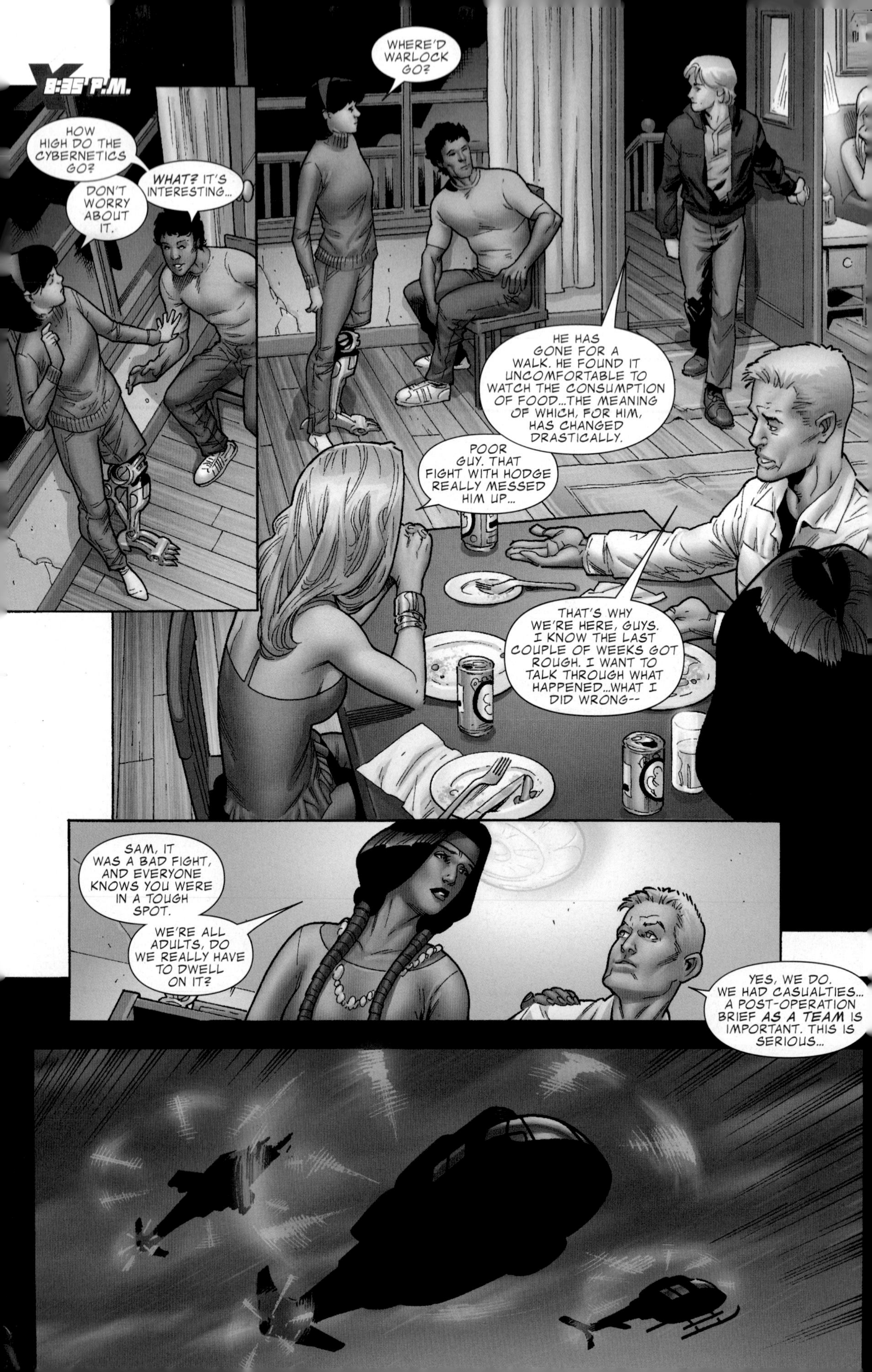
8:35 P.M.
HOW HIGH DO THE CYBERNETICS GO?
DON'T WORRY ABOUT IT.
WHAT? IT'S INTERESTING...
WHERE'D WARLOCK GO?
HE HAS GONE FOR A WALK. HE FOUND IT UNCOMFORTABLE TO WATCH THE CONSUMPTION OF FOOD...THE MEANING OF WHICH, FOR HIM, HAS CHANGED DRASTICALLY.
POOR GUY. THAT FIGHT WITH HODGE REALLY MESSED HIM UP...
THAT'S WHY WE'RE HERE, GUYS. I KNOW THE LAST COUPLE OF WEEKS GOT ROUGH. I WANT TO TALK THROUGH WHAT HAPPENED...WHAT I DID WRONG--
SAM, IT WAS A BAD FIGHT, AND EVERYONE KNOWS YOU WERE IN A TOUGH SPOT.
WE'RE ALL ADULTS, DO WE REALLY HAVE TO DWELL ON IT?
YES, WE DO. WE HAD CASUALTIES... A POST-OPERATION BRIEF AS A TEAM IS IMPORTANT. THIS IS SERIOUS...

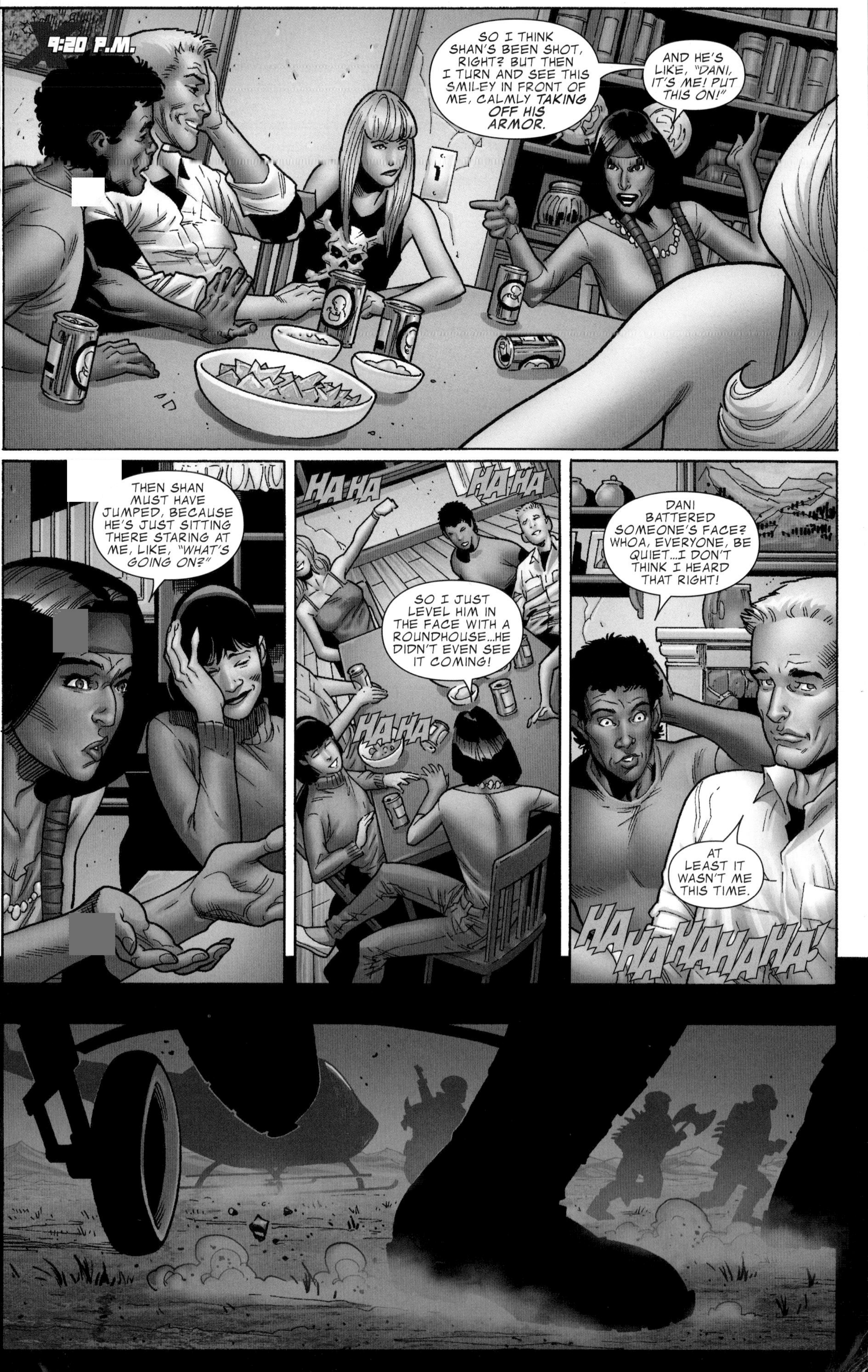
9:20 P.M.
SO I THINK SHAN'S BEEN SHOT, RIGHT? BUT THEN I TURN AND SEE THIS SMILEY IN FRONT OF ME, CALMLY TAKING OFF HIS ARMOR.
AND HE'S LIKE, "DANI, IT'S ME! PUT THIS ON!"
THEN SHAN MUST HAVE JUMPED, BECAUSE HE'S JUST SITTING THERE STARING AT ME, LIKE, "WHAT'S GOING ON?"
HA HA
HA HA
SO I JUST LEVEL HIM IN THE FACE WITH A ROUNDHOUSE...HE DIDN'T EVEN SEE IT COMING!
HA HA
DANI BATTERED SOMEONE'S FACE? WHOA, EVERYONE, BE QUIET...I DON'T THINK I HEARD THAT RIGHT!
AT LEAST IT WASN'T ME THIS TIME.
HA HA HA HA HA HA!

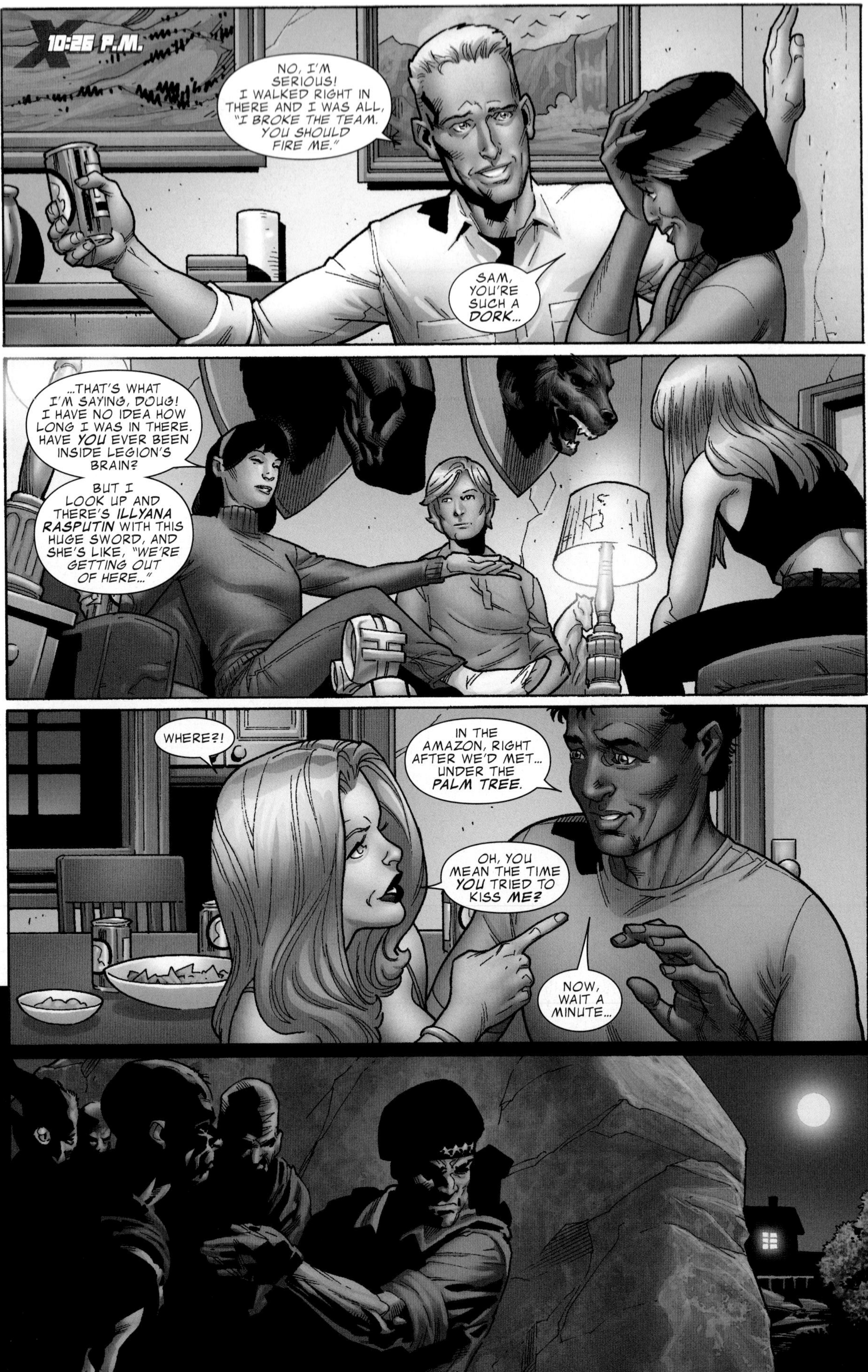
10:26 P.M.
NO, I'M SERIOUS! I WALKED RIGHT IN THERE AND I WAS ALL, "I BROKE THE TEAM. YOU SHOULD FIRE ME."
SAM, YOU'RE SUCH A DORK...
...THAT'S WHAT I'M SAYING, DOUG! I HAVE NO IDEA HOW LONG I WAS IN THERE. HAVE YOU EVER BEEN INSIDE LEGION'S BRAIN?
BUT I LOOK UP AND THERE'S ILLYANA RASPUTIN WITH THIS HUGE SWORD, AND SHE'S LIKE, "WE'RE GETTING OUT OF HERE..."
WHERE?!
IN THE AMAZON, RIGHT AFTER WE'D MET... UNDER THE PALM TREE.
OH, YOU MEAN THE TIME YOU TRIED TO KISS ME?
NOW, WAIT A MINUTE...

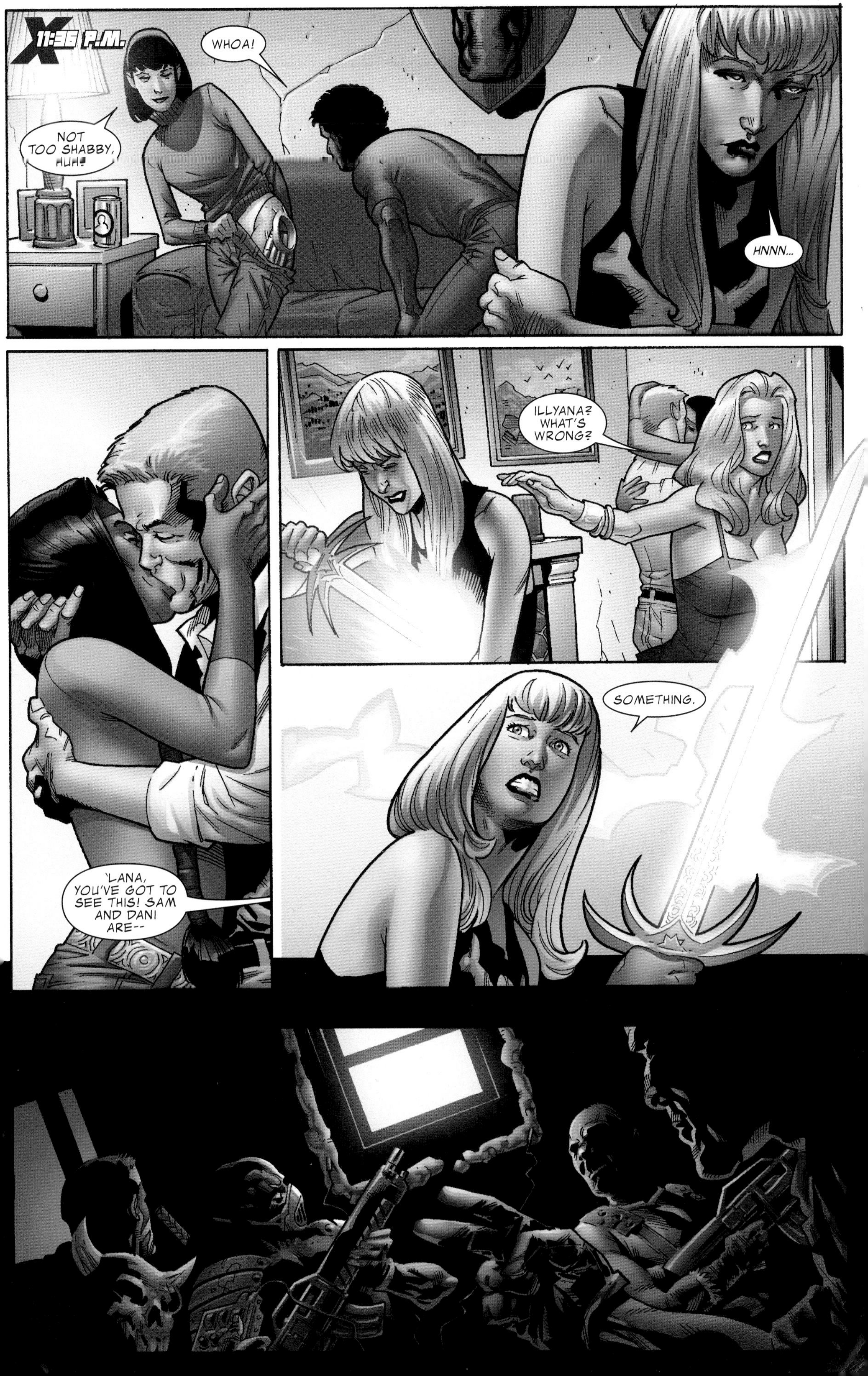
11:36 P.M.
WHOA!
NOT TOO SHABBY, HUH?
HNNN...
'LANA, YOU'VE GOT TO SEE THIS! SAM AND DANI ARE--
ILLYANA? WHAT'S WRONG?
SOMETHING.

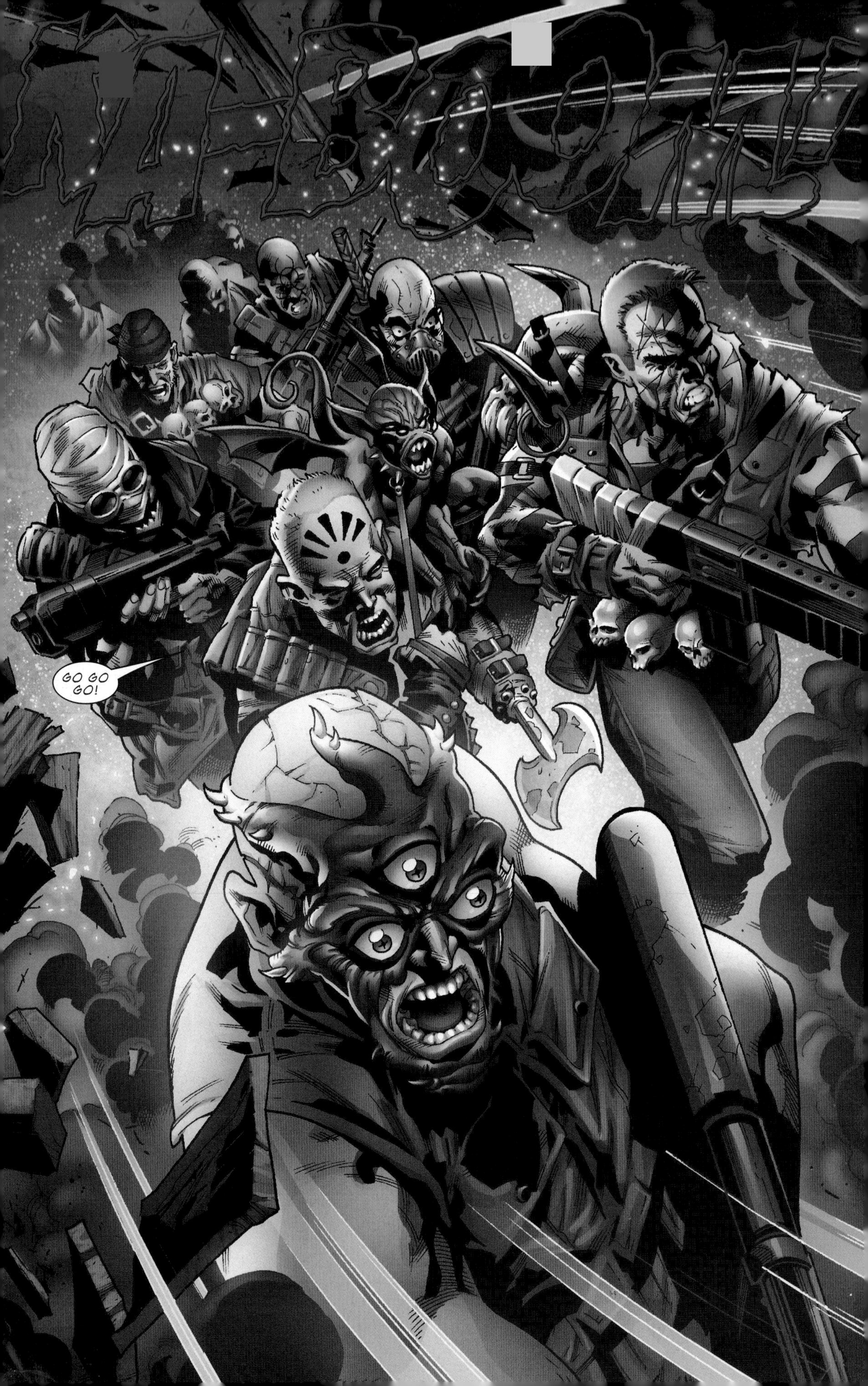
GO GO GO!

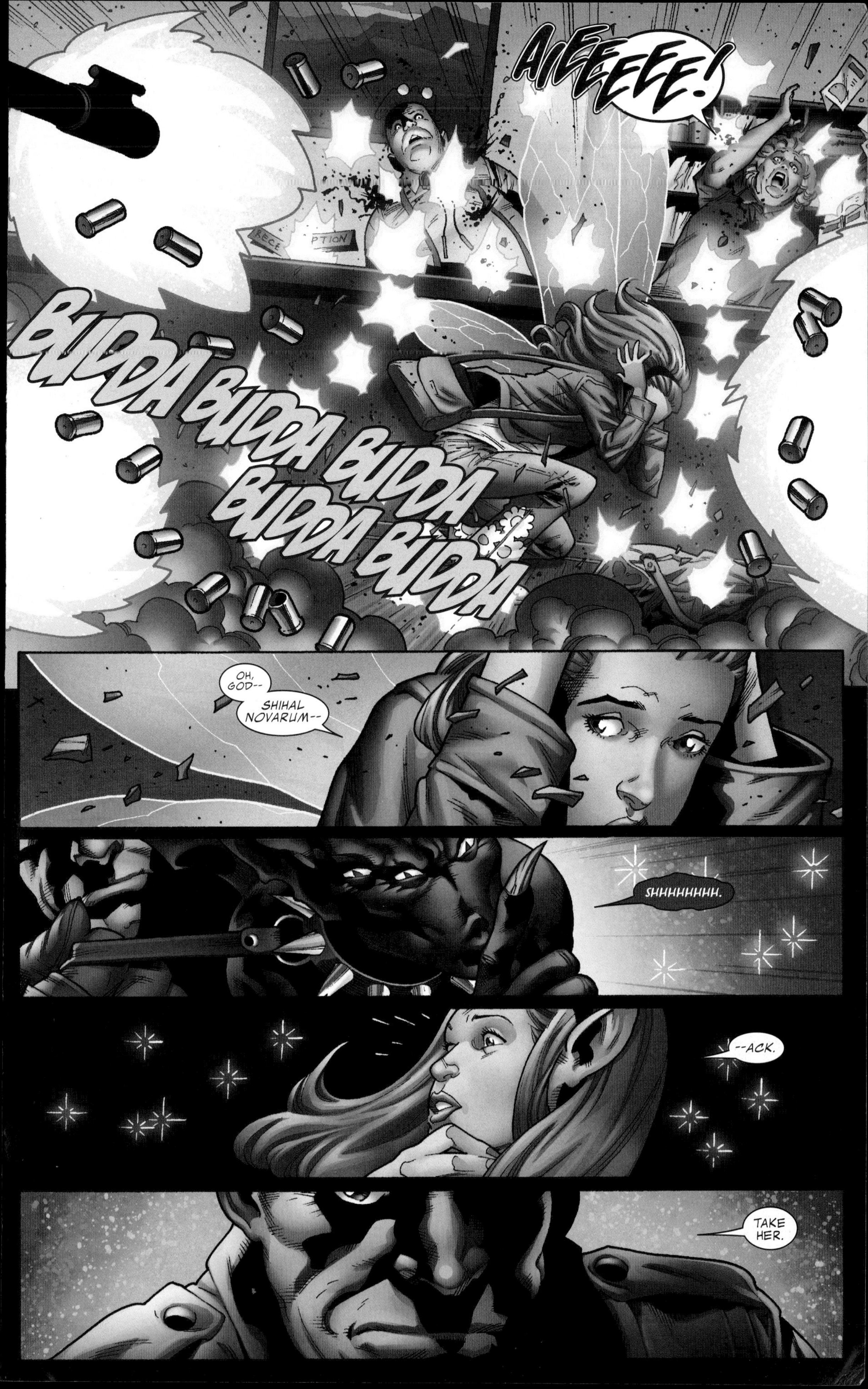
AIEEEEEE!
RECE PTION
BUDDA BUDDA BUDDA
BUDDA BUDDA BUDDA
OH, GOD--
SHIHAL NOVARUM--
SHHHHHHHH.
--ACK.
TAKE HER.

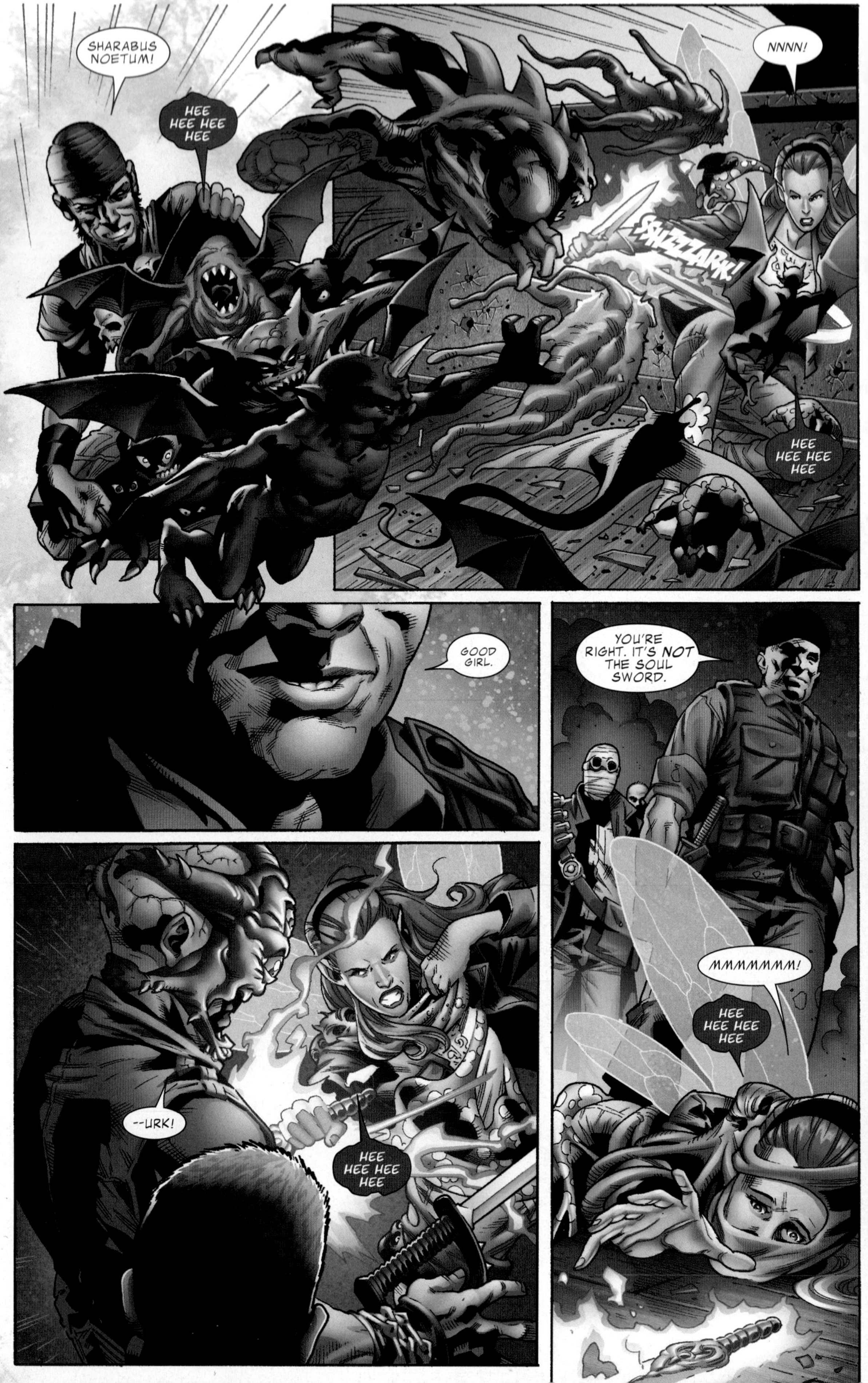
SHARABUS NOETUM!
HEE HEE HEE HEE
NNNN!
SHZZZARK!
HEE HEE HEE HEE
GOOD GIRL.
YOU'RE RIGHT. IT'S NOT THE SOUL SWORD.
--URK!
HEE HEE HEE HEE
MMMMMMM!
HEE HEE HEE HEE

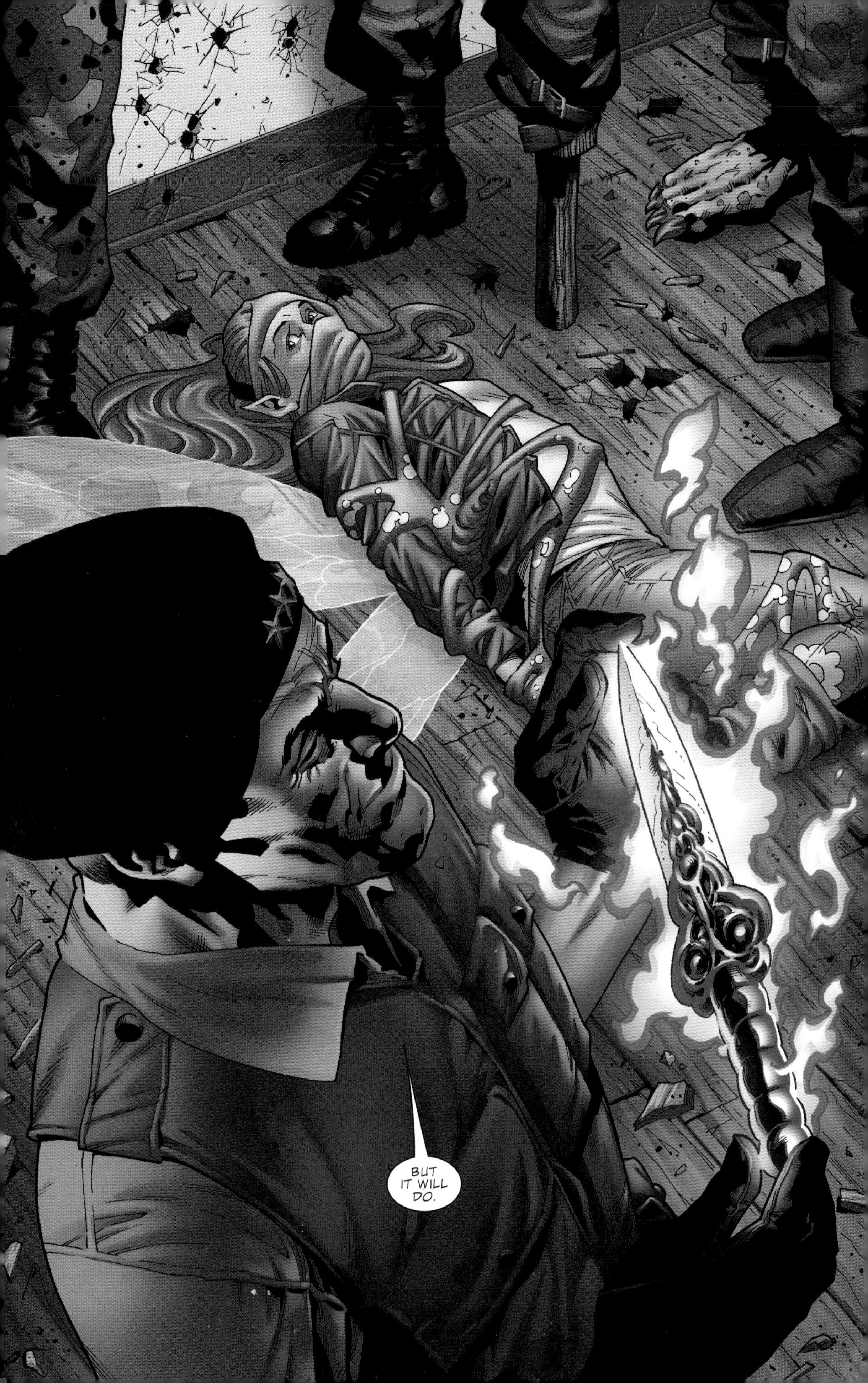
BUT IT WILL DO.

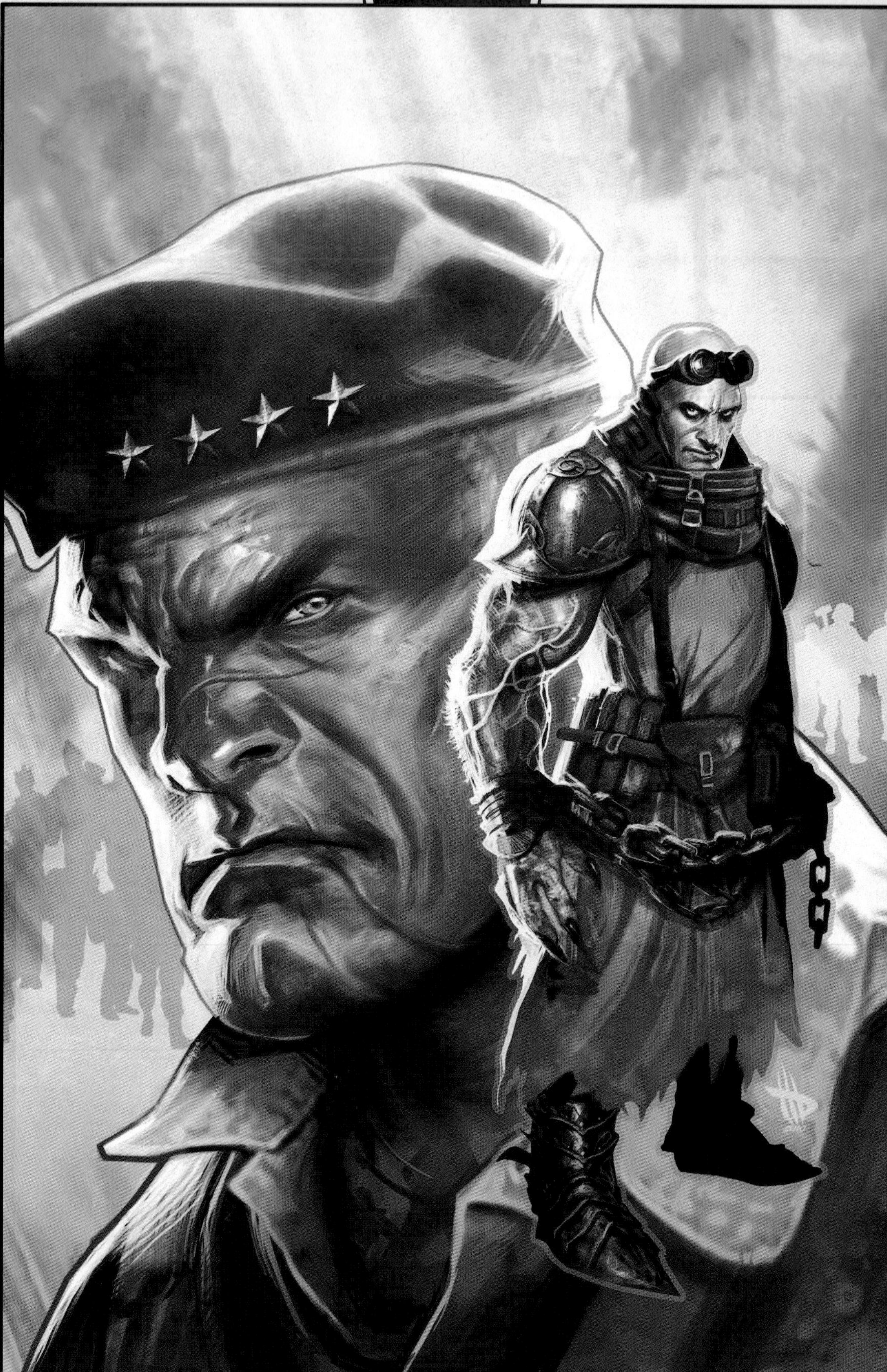

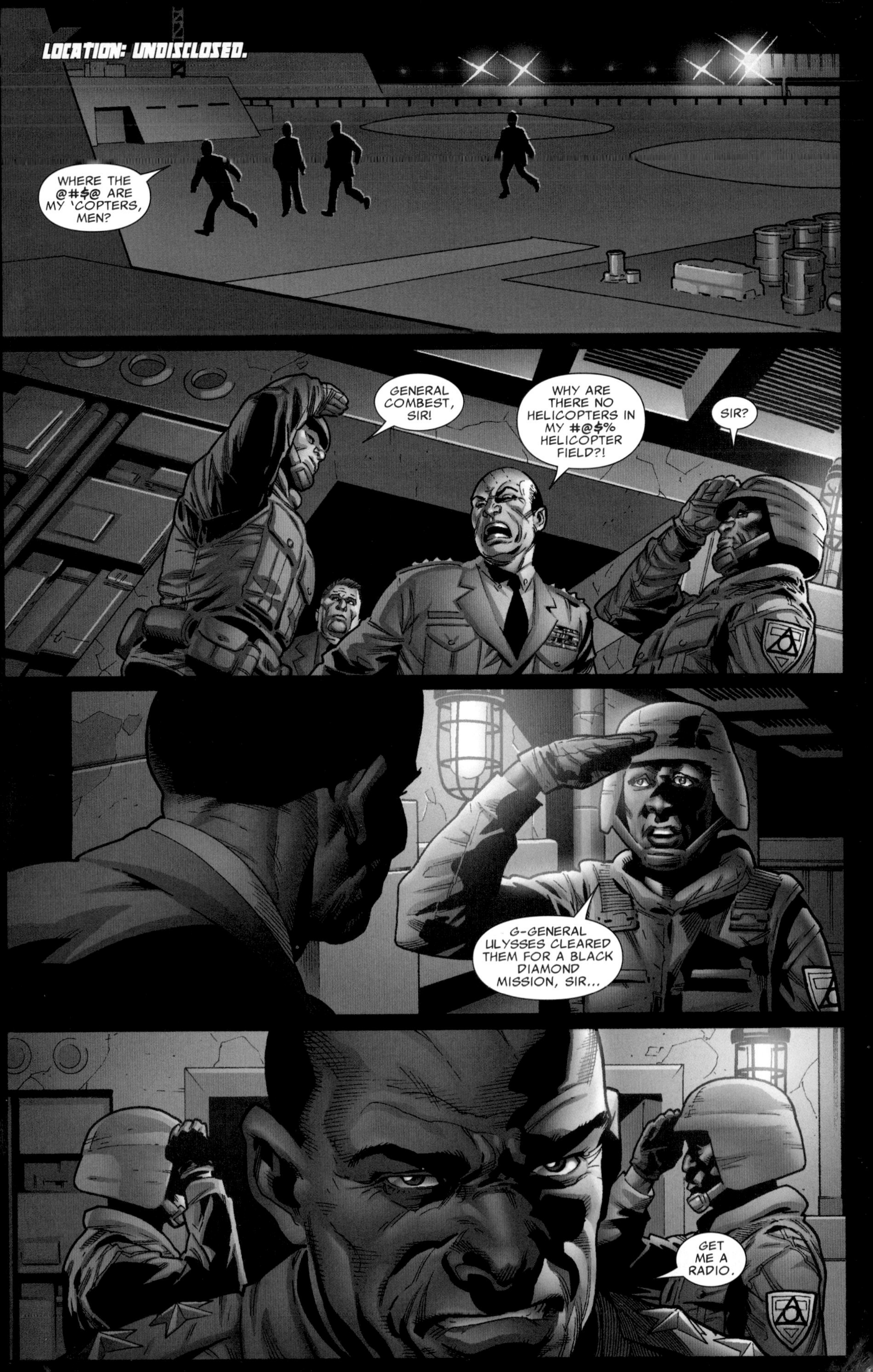
LOCATION: UNDISCLOSED.
WHERE THE @#$@ ARE MY 'COPTERS, MEN?
GENERAL COMBEST, SIR!
WHY ARE THERE NO HELICOPTERS IN MY #@$% HELICOPTER FIELD?!
SIR?
G-GENERAL ULYSSES CLEARED THEM FOR A BLACK DIAMOND MISSION, SIR...
GET ME A RADIO.

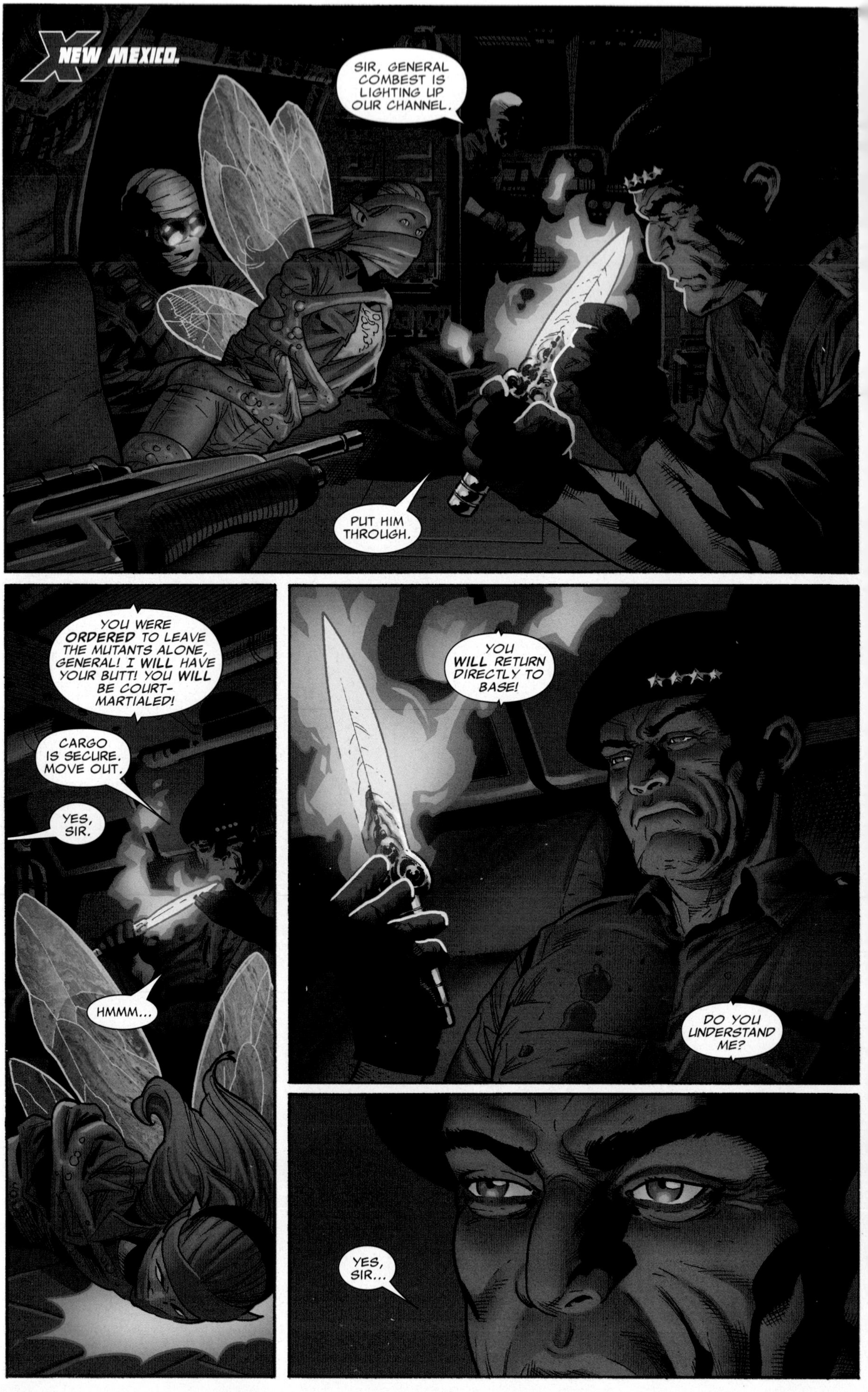
NEW MEXICO.
SIR, GENERAL COMBEST IS LIGHTING UP OUR CHANNEL.
PUT HIM THROUGH.
YOU WERE ORDERED TO LEAVE THE MUTANTS ALONE, GENERAL! I WILL HAVE YOUR BUTT! YOU WILL BE COURT-MARTIALED!
CARGO IS SECURE. MOVE OUT.
YES, SIR.
HMMM...
YOU WILL RETURN DIRECTLY TO BASE!
DO YOU UNDERSTAND ME?
YES, SIR...

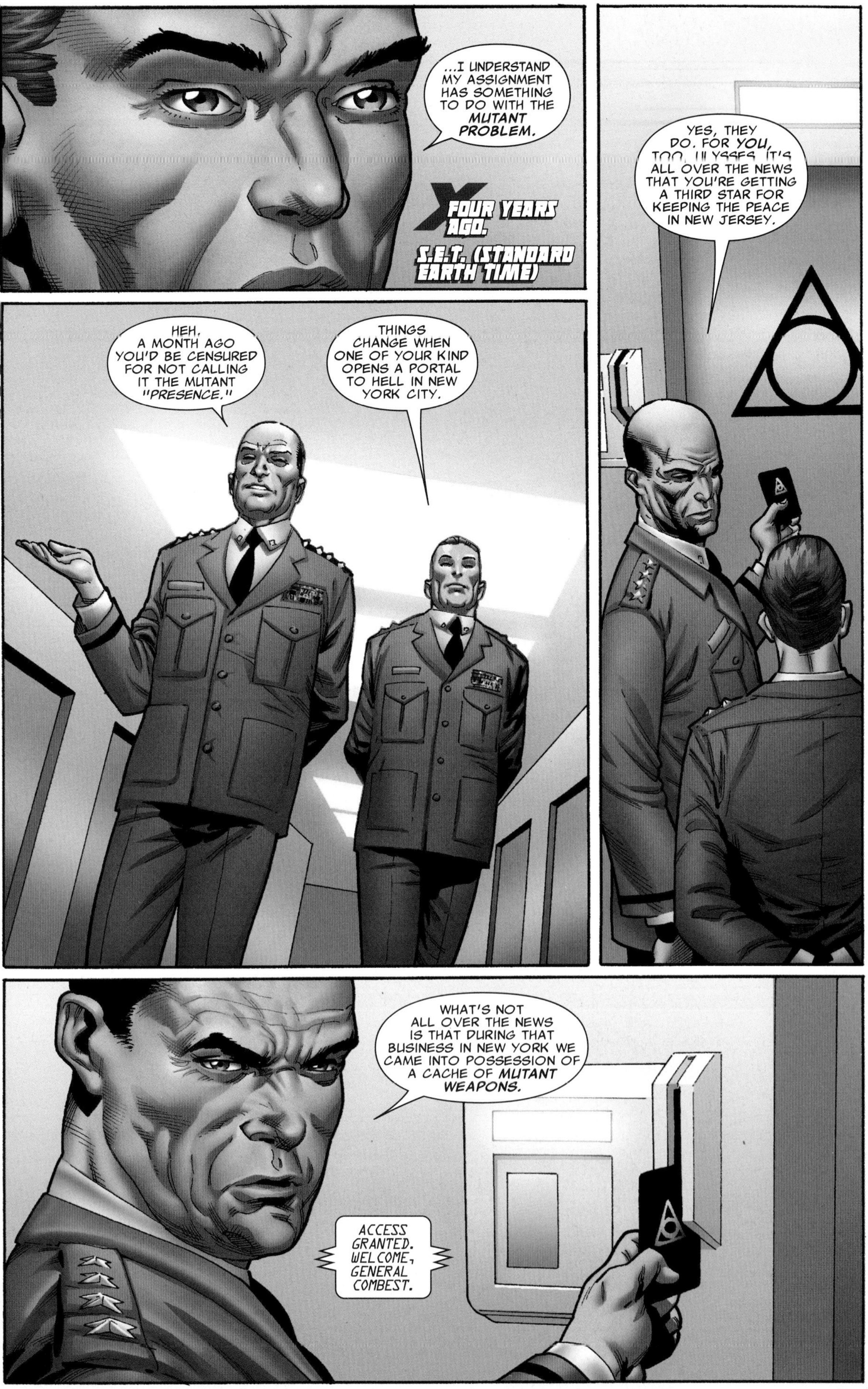
...I UNDERSTAND MY ASSIGNMENT HAS SOMETHING TO DO WITH THE MUTANT PROBLEM.
FOUR YEARS AGO.
S.E.T. (STANDARD EARTH TIME)
HEH. A MONTH AGO YOU'D BE CENSURED FOR NOT CALLING IT THE MUTANT "PRESENCE."
THINGS CHANGE WHEN ONE OF YOUR KIND OPENS A PORTAL TO HELL IN NEW YORK CITY.
YES, THEY DO. FOR YOU, TOO, ULYSSES. IT'S ALL OVER THE NEWS THAT YOU'RE GETTING A THIRD STAR FOR KEEPING THE PEACE IN NEW JERSEY.
WHAT'S NOT ALL OVER THE NEWS IS THAT DURING THAT BUSINESS IN NEW YORK WE CAME INTO POSSESSION OF A CACHE OF MUTANT WEAPONS.
ACCESS GRANTED. WELCOME, GENERAL COMBEST.

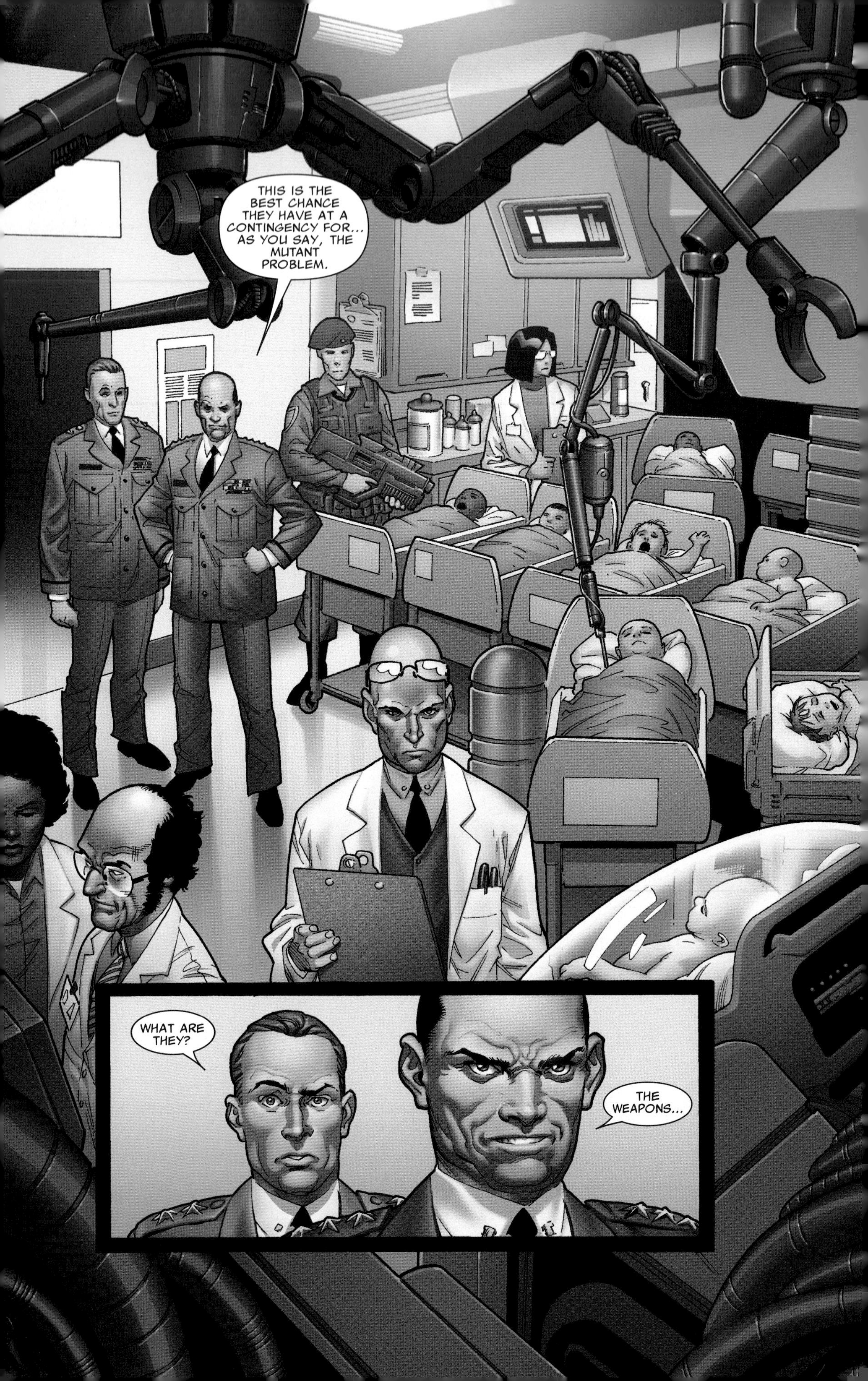
THIS IS THE BEST CHANCE THEY HAVE AT A CONTINGENCY FOR... AS YOU SAY, THE MUTANT PROBLEM.
WHAT ARE THEY?
THE WEAPONS...

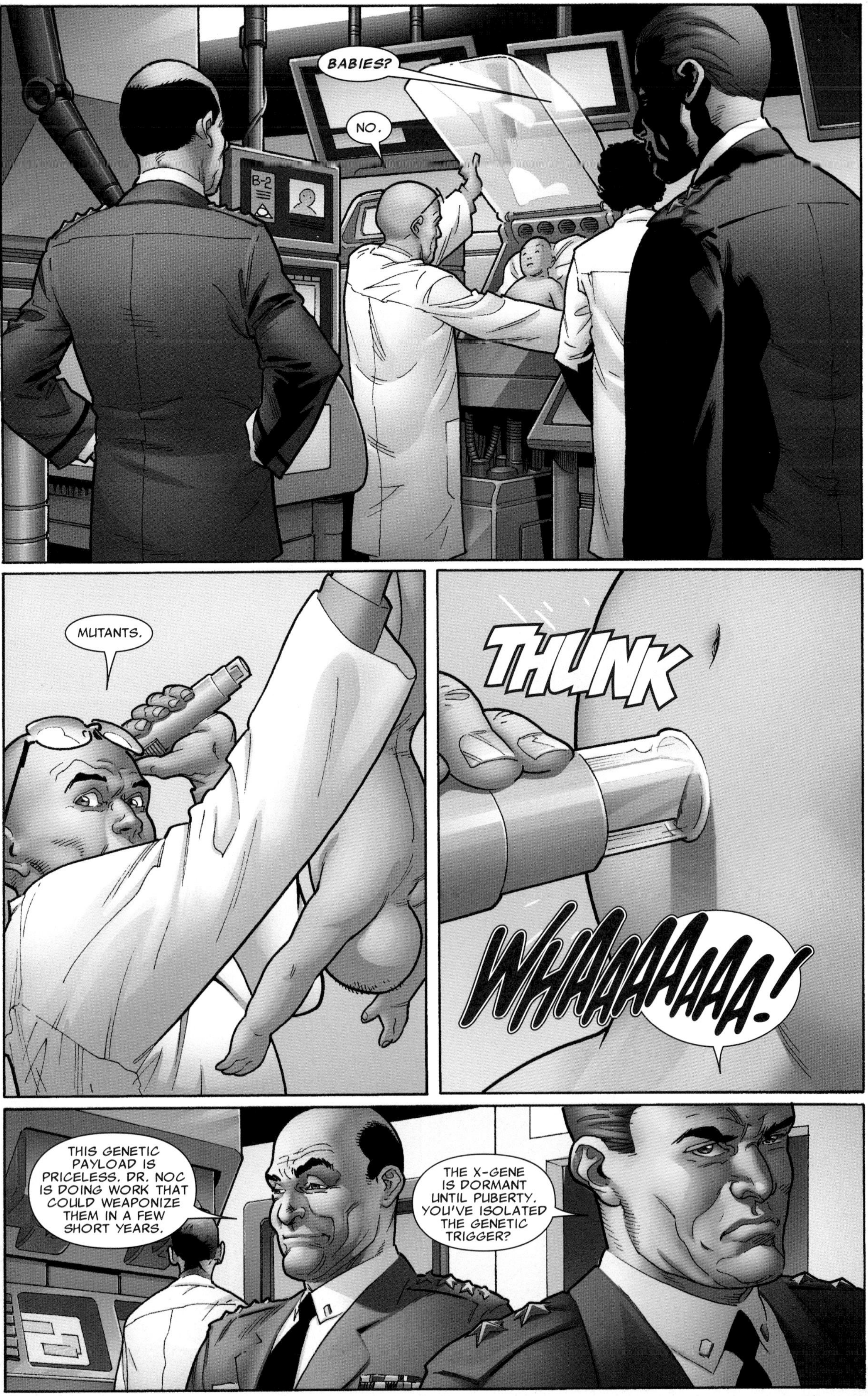
BABIES?
NO.
MUTANTS.
THUNK
WHAAAAAAAA!
THIS GENETIC PAYLOAD IS PRICELESS. DR. NOC IS DOING WORK THAT COULD WEAPONIZE THEM IN A FEW SHORT YEARS.
THE X-GENE IS DORMANT UNTIL PUBERTY. YOU'VE ISOLATED THE GENETIC TRIGGER?

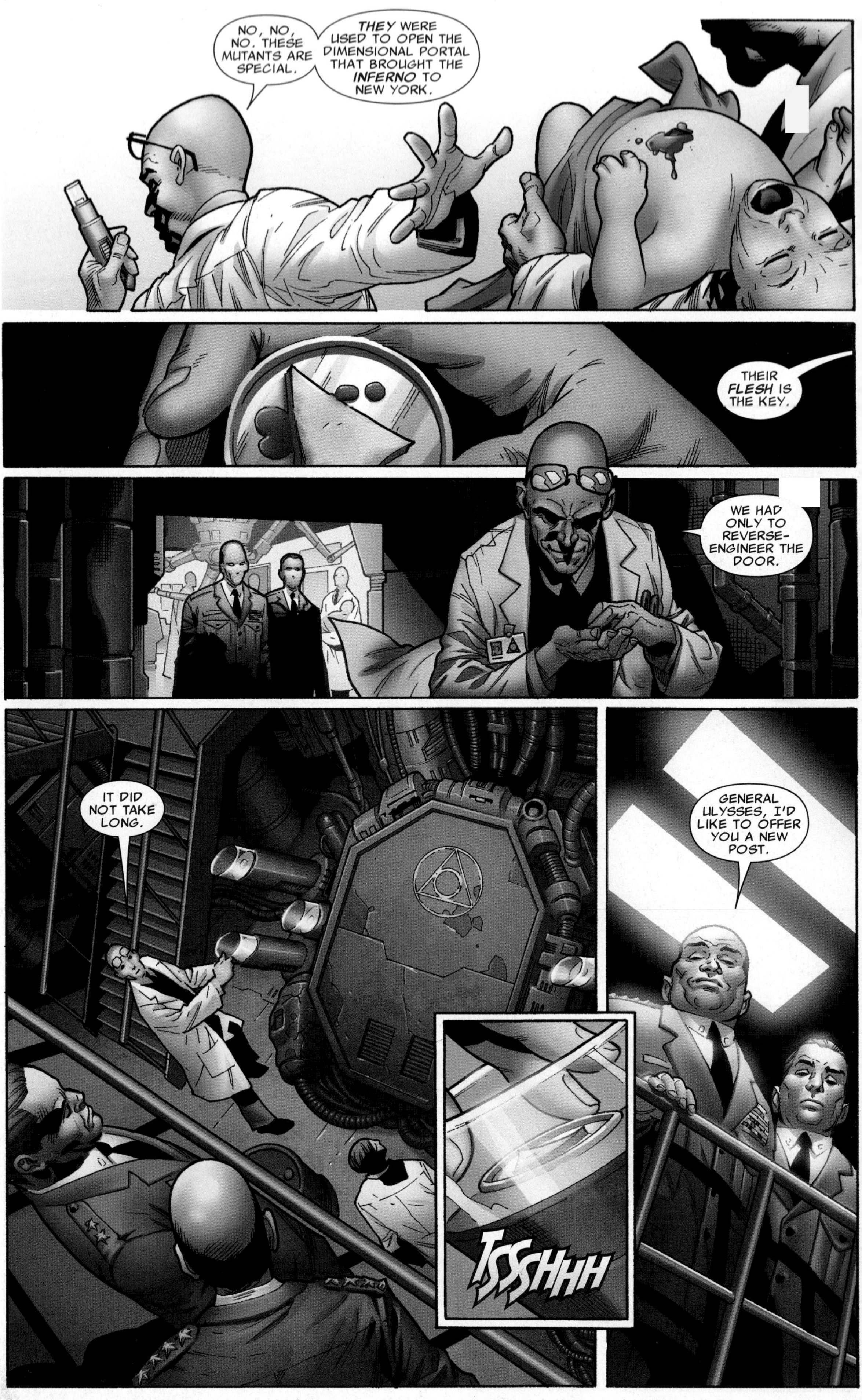
NO, NO, NO. THESE MUTANTS ARE SPECIAL.
THEY WERE USED TO OPEN THE DIMENSIONAL PORTAL THAT BROUGHT THE INFERNO TO NEW YORK.
THEIR FLESH IS THE KEY.
WE HAD ONLY TO REVERSE-ENGINEER THE DOOR.
IT DID NOT TAKE LONG.
TSSHHH
GENERAL ULYSSES, I'D LIKE TO OFFER YOU A NEW POST.

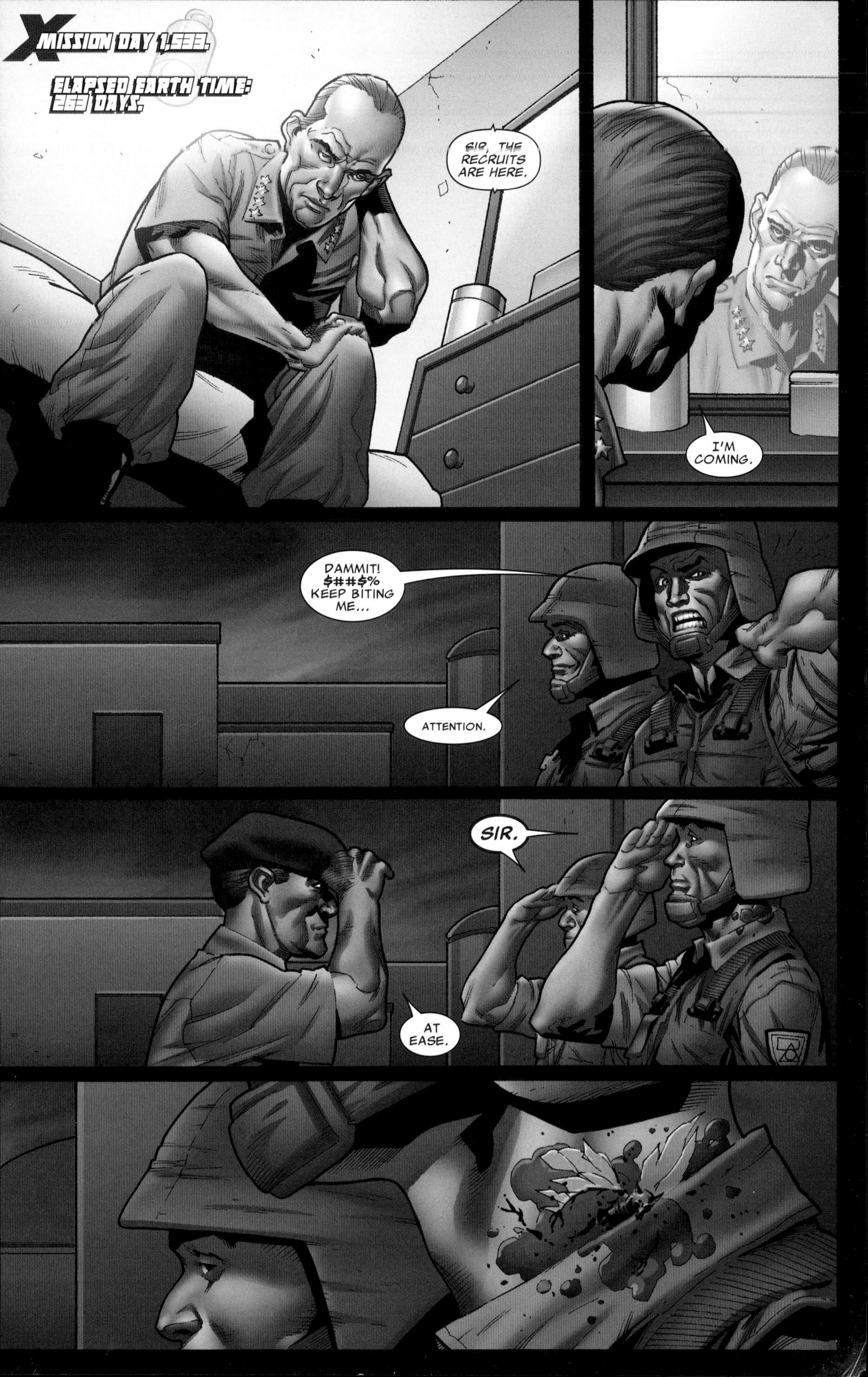
MISSION DAY 1,533.
ELAPSED EARTH TIME: 263 DAYS.
SIR, THE RECRUITS ARE HERE.
I'M COMING.
DAMMIT! $#%$% KEEP BITING ME...
ATTENTION.
SIR.
AT EASE.

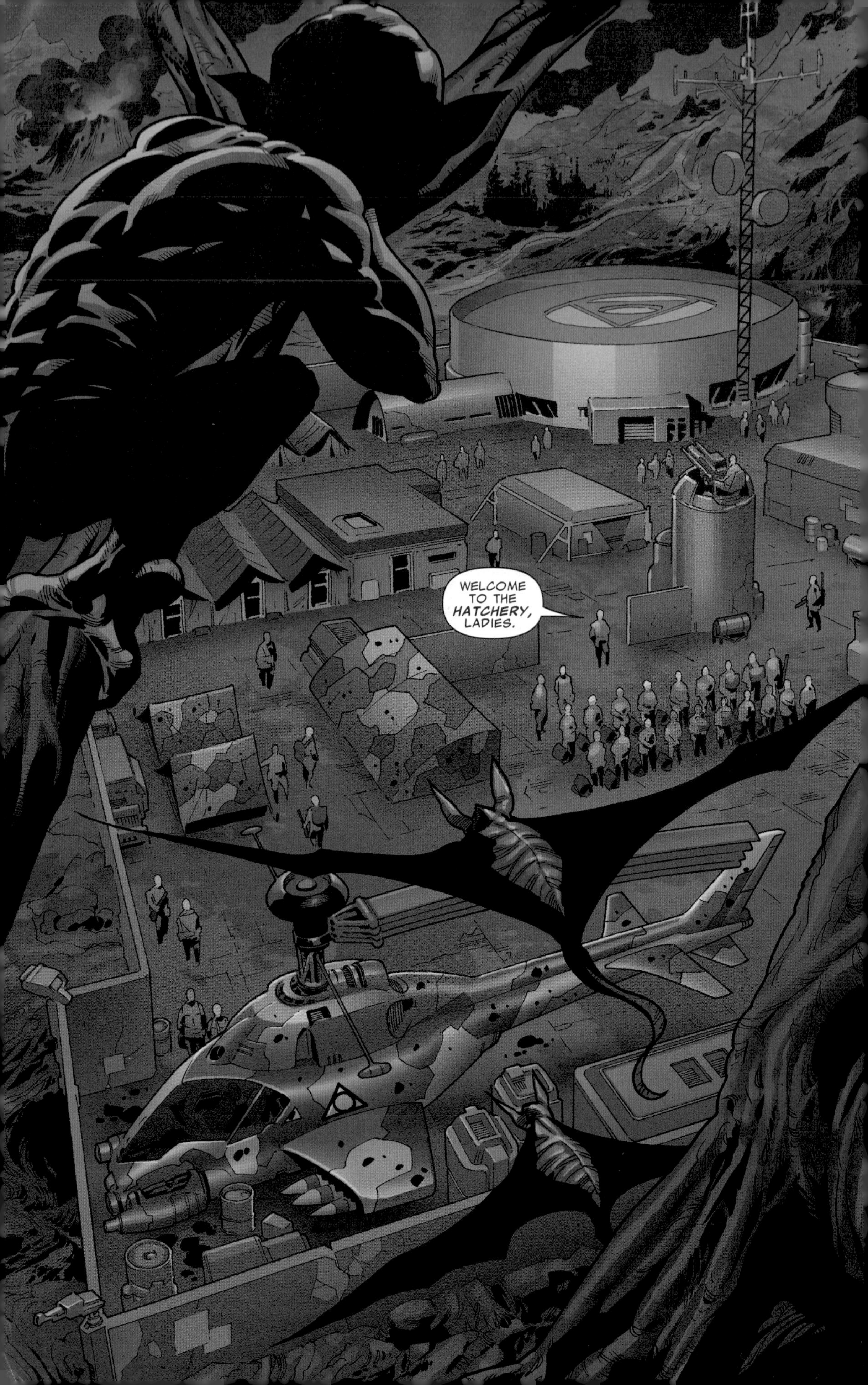
WELCOME TO THE HATCHERY, LADIES.

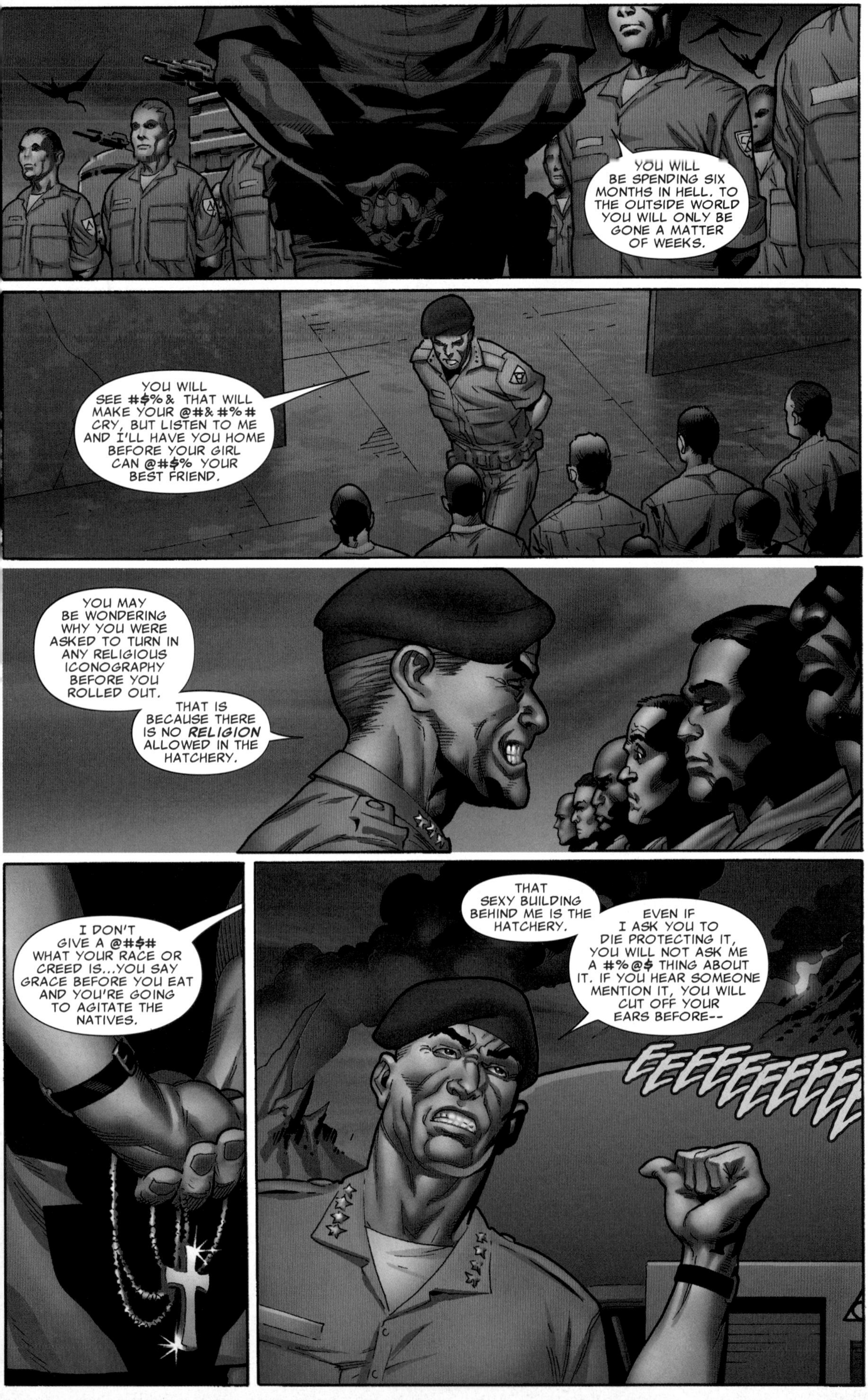
YOU WILL BE SPENDING SIX MONTHS IN HELL. TO THE OUTSIDE WORLD YOU WILL ONLY BE GONE A MATTER OF WEEKS.
YOU WILL SEE #$%& THAT WILL MAKE YOUR @#&#%# CRY, BUT LISTEN TO ME AND I'LL HAVE YOU HOME BEFORE YOUR GIRL CAN @#$% YOUR BEST FRIEND.
YOU MAY BE WONDERING WHY YOU WERE ASKED TO TURN IN ANY RELIGIOUS ICONOGRAPHY BEFORE YOU ROLLED OUT.
THAT IS BECAUSE THERE IS NO RELIGION ALLOWED IN THE HATCHERY.
I DON'T GIVE A @#$# WHAT YOUR RACE OR CREED IS...YOU SAY GRACE BEFORE YOU EAT AND YOU'RE GOING TO AGITATE THE NATIVES.
THAT SEXY BUILDING BEHIND ME IS THE HATCHERY.
EVEN IF I ASK YOU TO DIE PROTECTING IT, YOU WILL NOT ASK ME A #%@$ THING ABOUT IT. IF YOU HEAR SOMEONE MENTION IT, YOU WILL CUT OFF YOUR EARS BEFORE--
EEEEEEEEEE

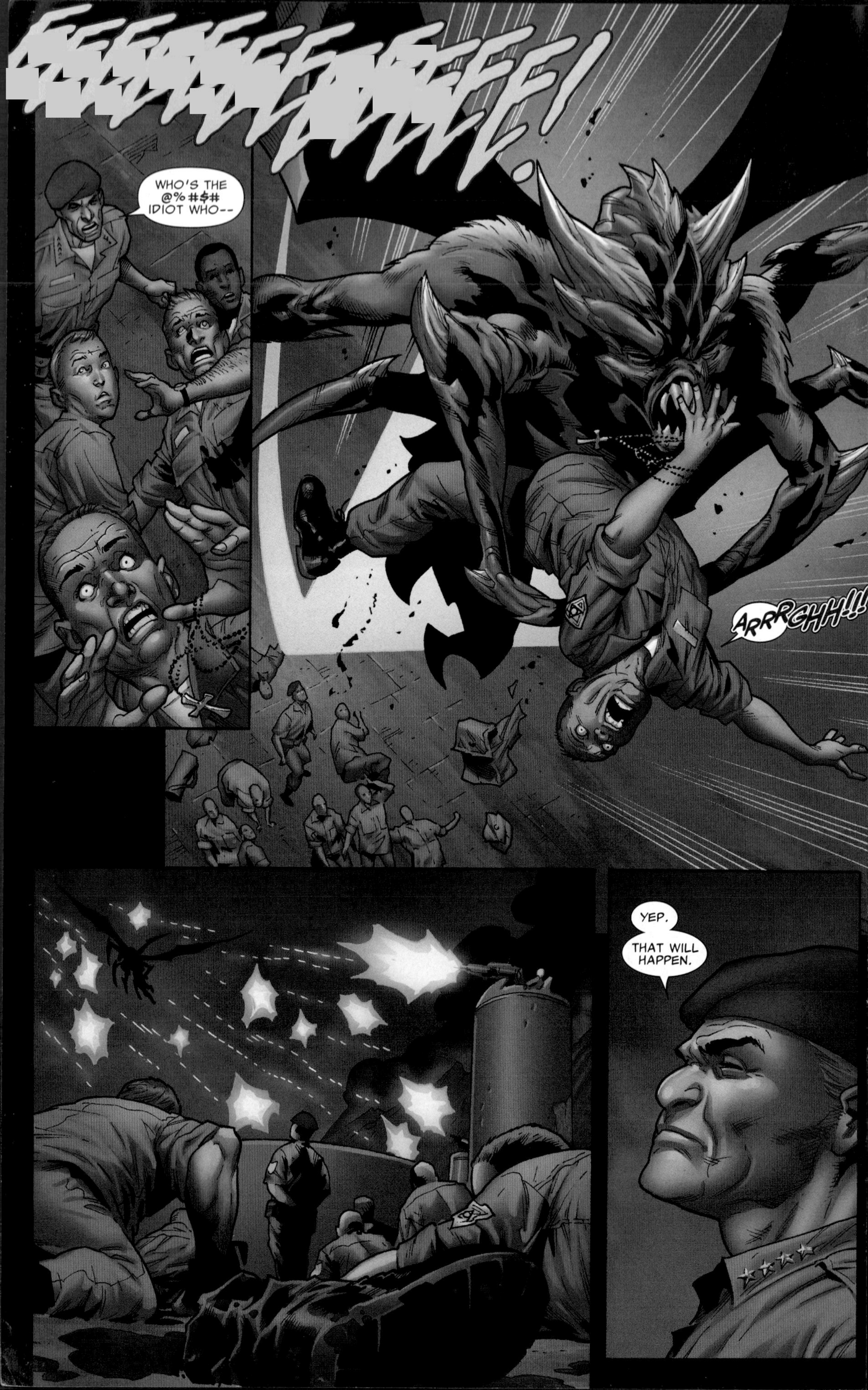
WHO'S THE @%#$# IDIOT WHO--
ARRRGHH!!!
YEP.
THAT WILL HAPPEN.

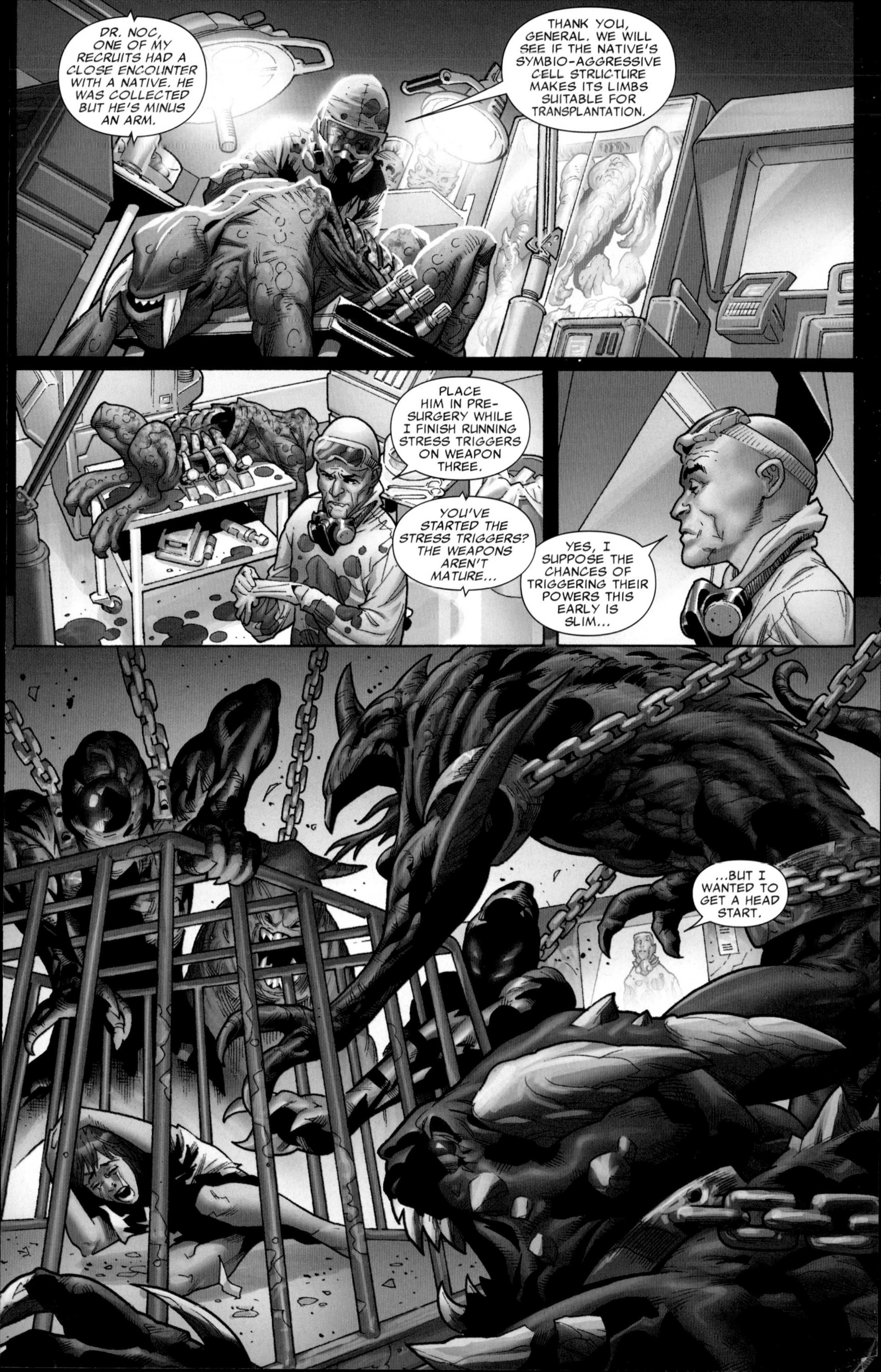
DR. NOC, ONE OF MY RECRUITS HAD A CLOSE ENCOUNTER WITH A NATIVE. HE WAS COLLECTED BUT HE'S MINUS AN ARM.
THANK YOU, GENERAL. WE WILL SEE IF THE NATIVE'S SYMBIO-AGGRESSIVE CELL STRUCTURE MAKES ITS LIMBS SUITABLE FOR TRANSPLANTATION.
PLACE HIM IN PRE-SURGERY WHILE I FINISH RUNNING STRESS TRIGGERS ON WEAPON THREE.
YOU'VE STARTED THE STRESS TRIGGERS? THE WEAPONS AREN'T MATURE...
YES, I SUPPOSE THE CHANCES OF TRIGGERING THEIR POWERS THIS EARLY IS SLIM...
...BUT I WANTED TO GET A HEAD START.

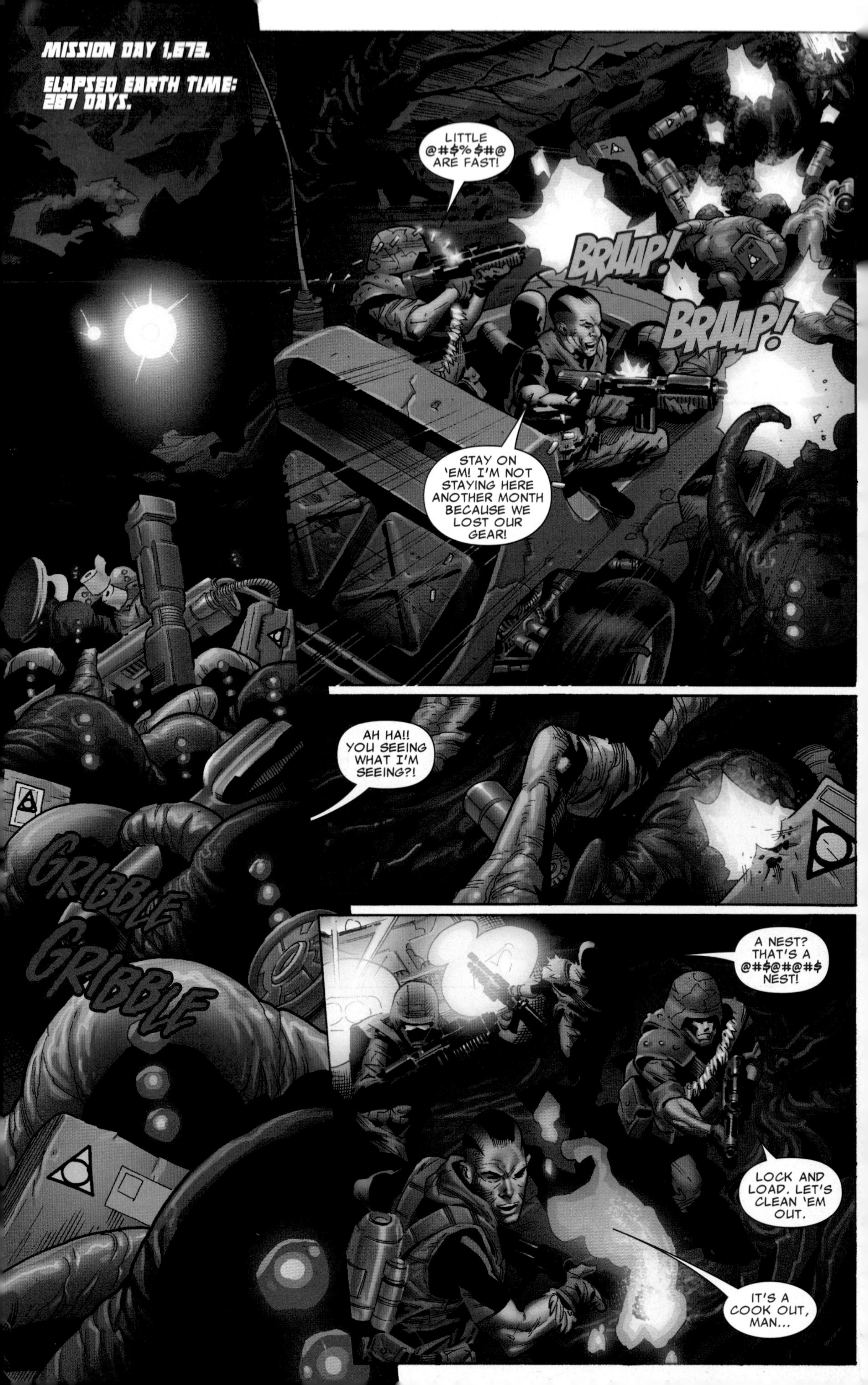
MISSION DAY 1,673.
ELAPSED EARTH TIME: 287 DAYS.
LITTLE @#$%$#@ ARE FAST!
BRAAP!
BRAAP!
STAY ON 'EM! I'M NOT STAYING HERE ANOTHER MONTH BECAUSE WE LOST OUR GEAR!
AH HA!! YOU SEEING WHAT I'M SEEING?!
GRIBBLE GRIBBLE
A NEST? THAT'S A @#$@#@#$ NEST!
LOCK AND LOAD. LET'S CLEAN 'EM OUT.
IT'S A COOK OUT, MAN...

FWWOOOOOOOOSHHH!!!

EEEEEE!

EEEEEE!

FWWOOOOOSHHH!!!

BRAP!
BRAP!

HEY... HEY!! HOLD IT...

WHERE DO YOU THINK THEY GOT HER?

I... I DON'T KNOW...

YEAH, WELL @#$@ IT. SHE DOESN'T NEED *THAT* ANYMORE.

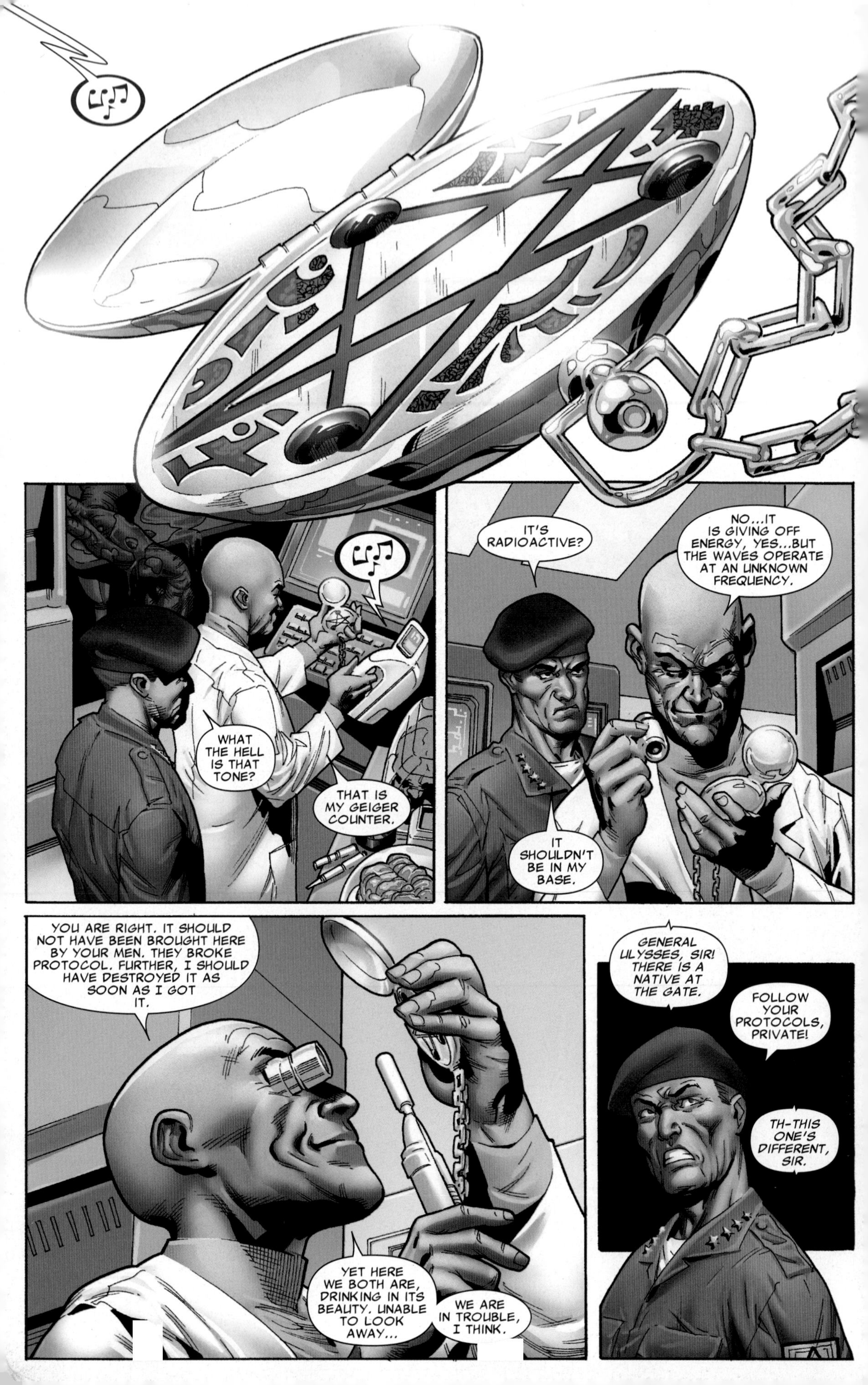
♪♫
♪♫
WHAT THE HELL IS THAT TONE?
THAT IS MY GEIGER COUNTER.
IT'S RADIOACTIVE?
NO...IT IS GIVING OFF ENERGY, YES...BUT THE WAVES OPERATE AT AN UNKNOWN FREQUENCY.
IT SHOULDN'T BE IN MY BASE.
YOU ARE RIGHT. IT SHOULD NOT HAVE BEEN BROUGHT HERE BY YOUR MEN. THEY BROKE PROTOCOL. FURTHER, I SHOULD HAVE DESTROYED IT AS SOON AS I GOT IT.
YET HERE WE BOTH ARE, DRINKING IN ITS BEAUTY. UNABLE TO LOOK AWAY...
WE ARE IN TROUBLE, I THINK.
GENERAL ULYSSES, SIR! THERE IS A NATIVE AT THE GATE.
FOLLOW YOUR PROTOCOLS, PRIVATE!
TH-THIS ONE'S DIFFERENT, SIR.

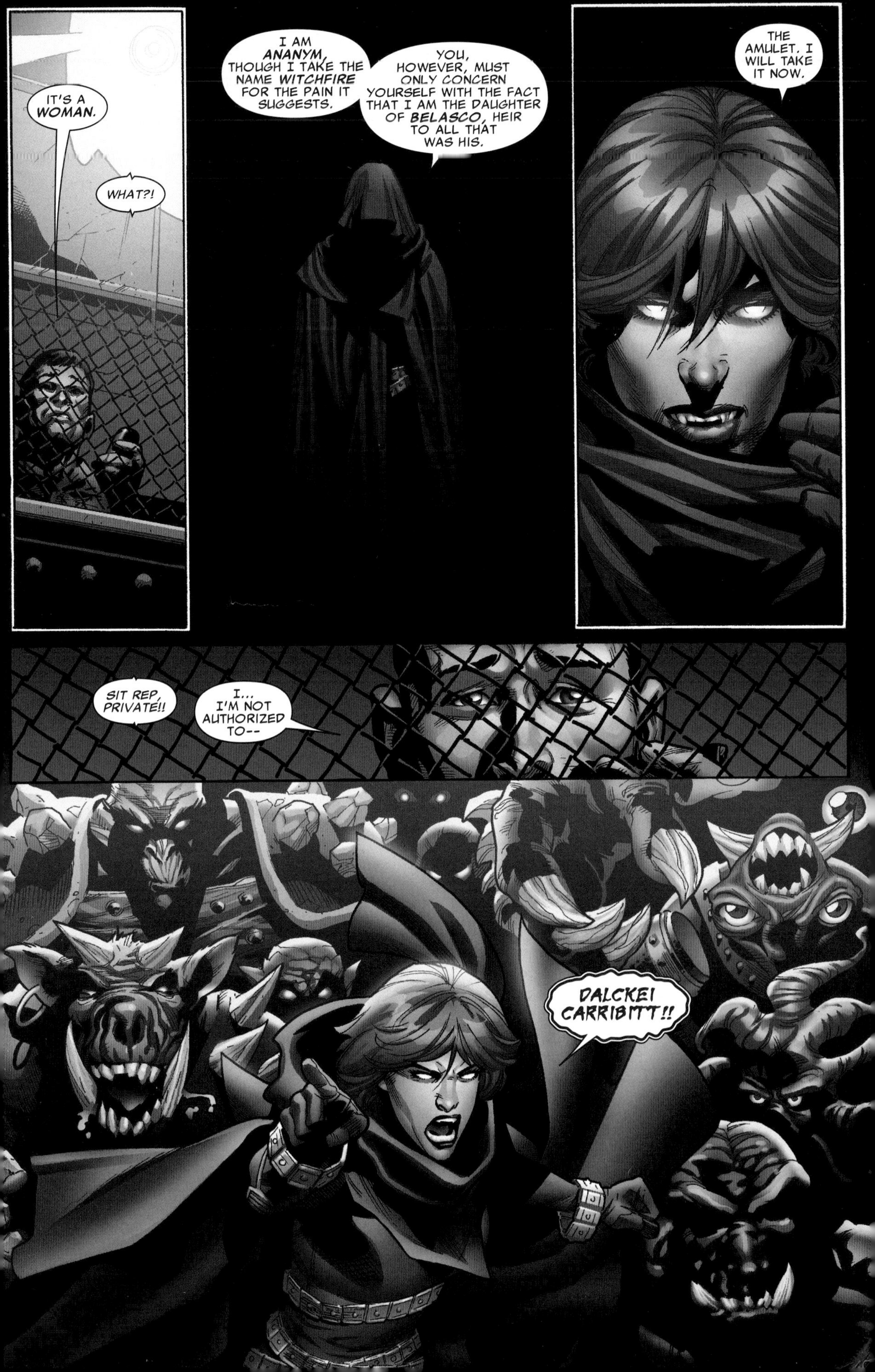
IT'S A WOMAN.
WHAT?!
I AM ANANYM, THOUGH I TAKE THE NAME WITCHFIRE FOR THE PAIN IT SUGGESTS.
YOU, HOWEVER, MUST ONLY CONCERN YOURSELF WITH THE FACT THAT I AM THE DAUGHTER OF BELASCO, HEIR TO ALL THAT WAS HIS.
THE AMULET. I WILL TAKE IT NOW.
SIT REP, PRIVATE!!
I... I'M NOT AUTHORIZED TO--
DALCKEI CARRIBITT!!

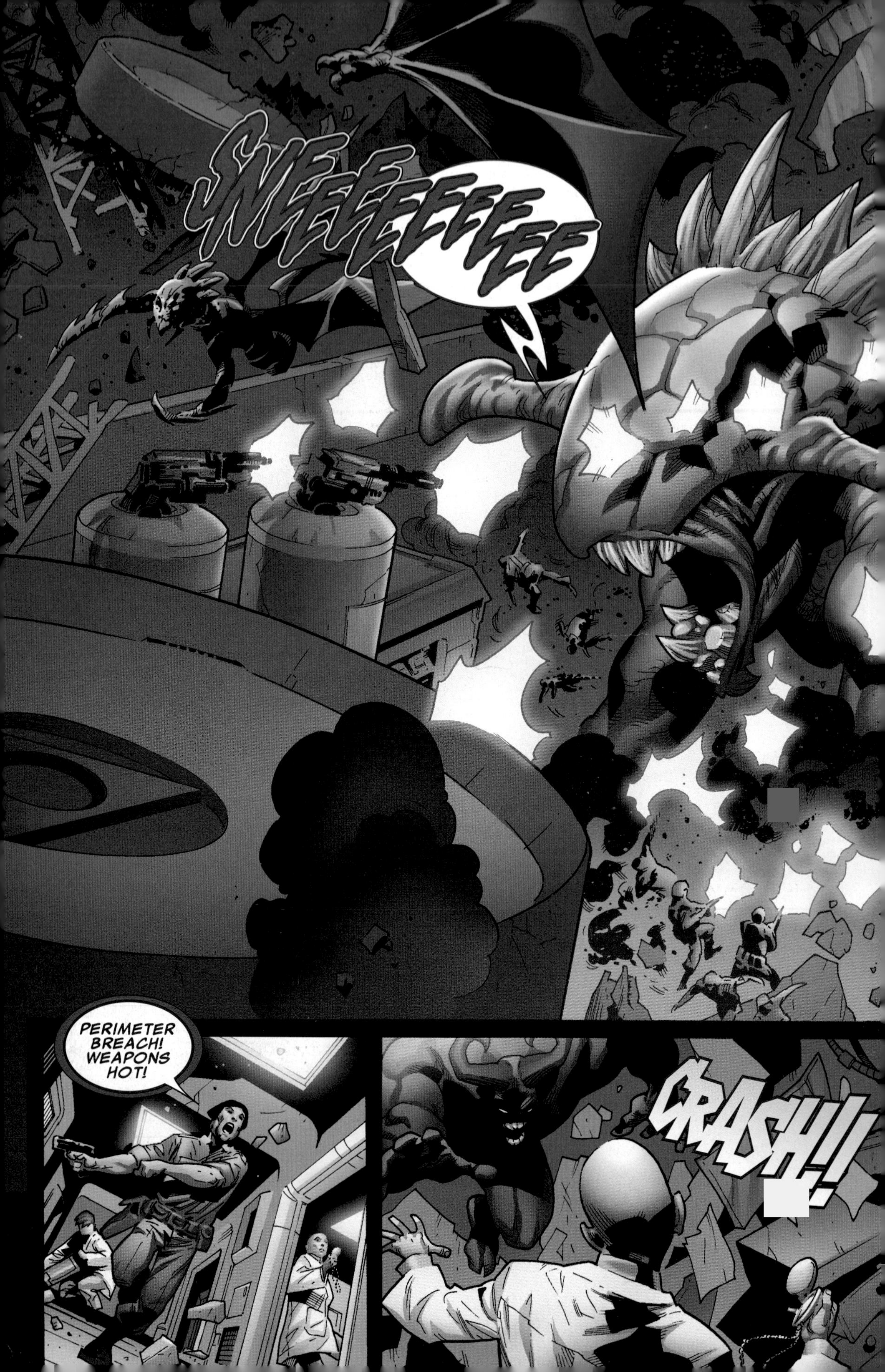
SNEEEEEEEEE
PERIMETER BREACH! WEAPONS HOT!
CRASH!!

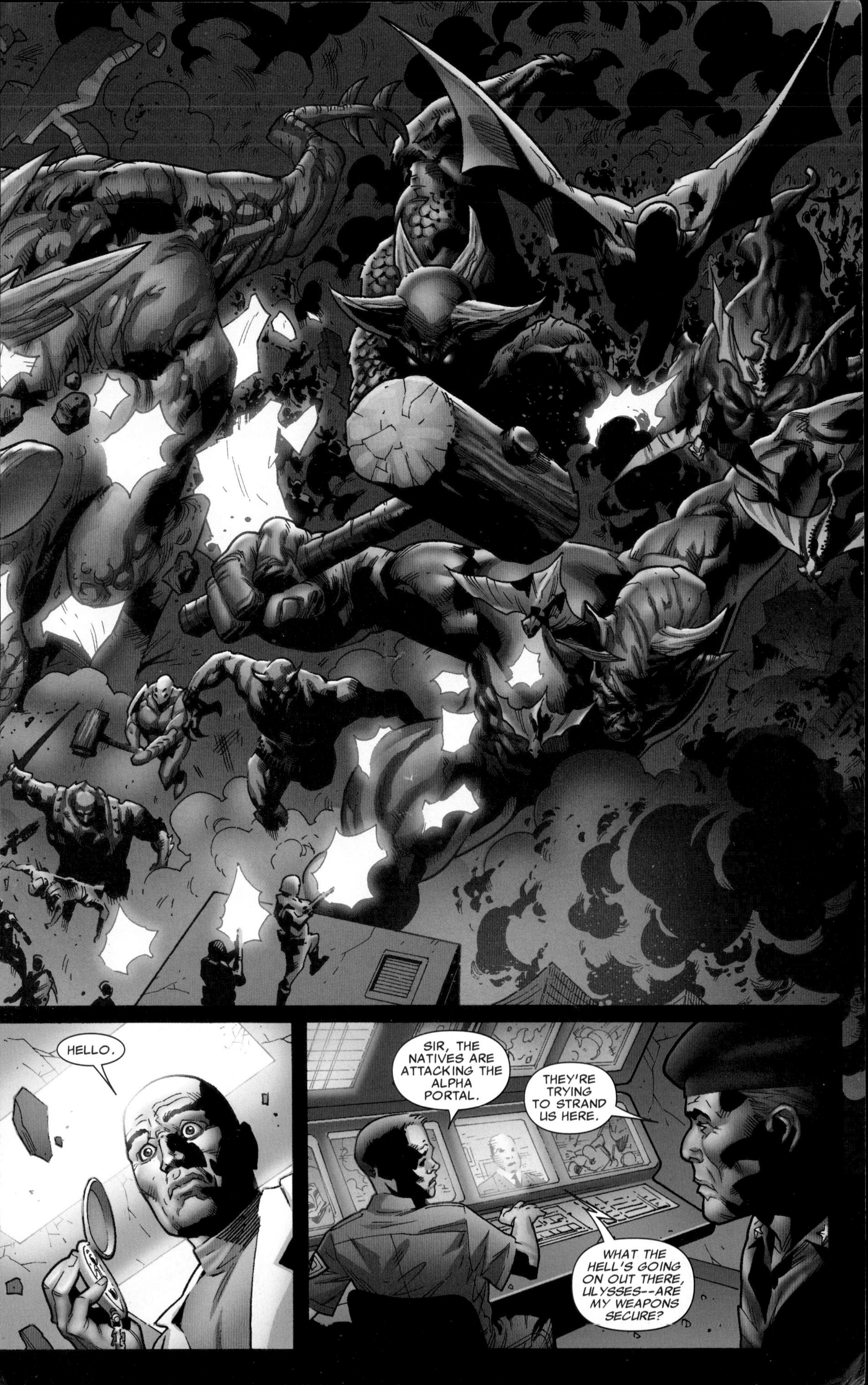
HELLO.
SIR, THE NATIVES ARE ATTACKING THE ALPHA PORTAL.
THEY'RE TRYING TO STRAND US HERE.
WHAT THE HELL'S GOING ON OUT THERE, ULYSSES--ARE MY WEAPONS SECURE?

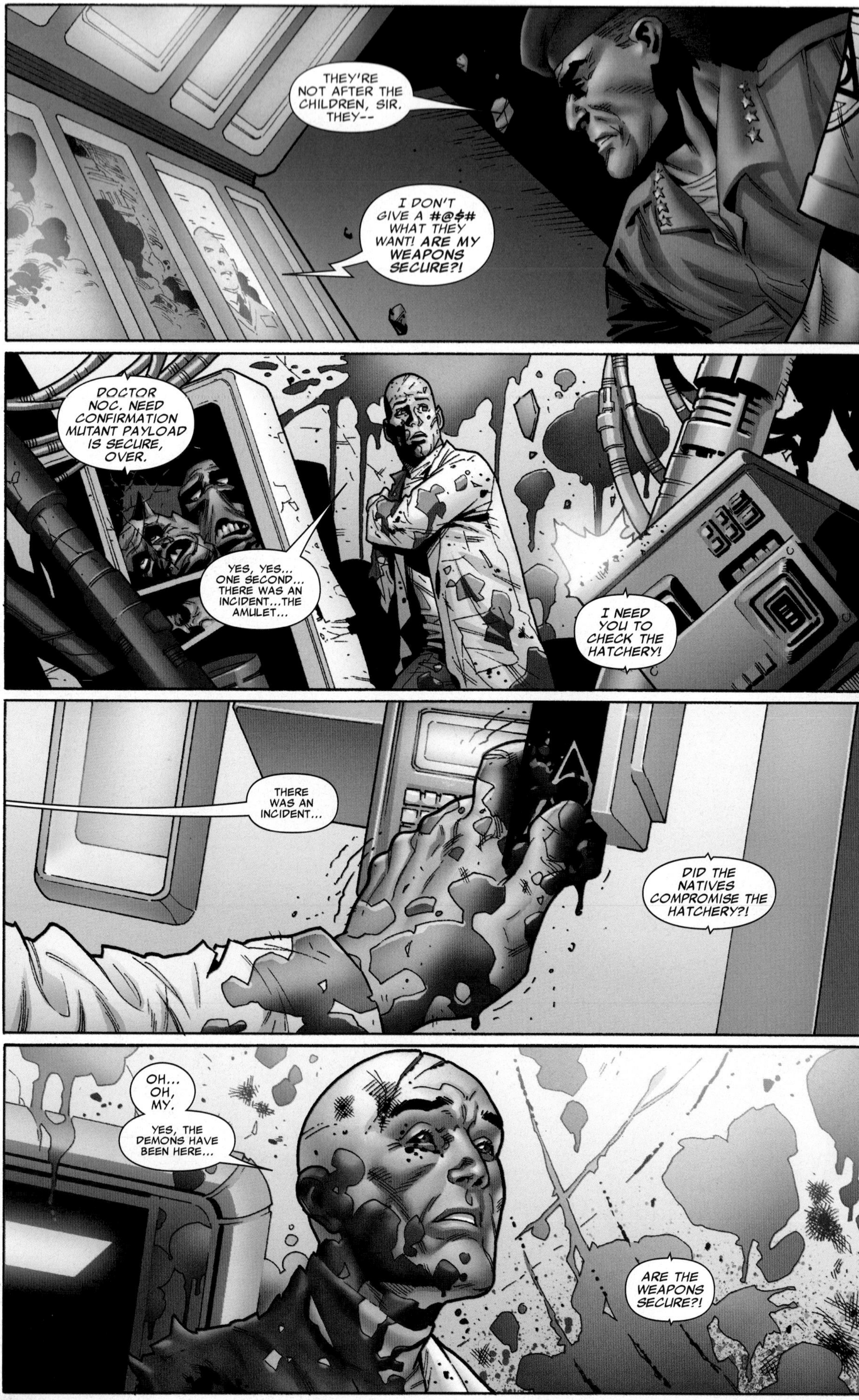
THEY'RE NOT AFTER THE CHILDREN, SIR. THEY--
I DON'T GIVE A #@$# WHAT THEY WANT! ARE MY WEAPONS SECURE?!
DOCTOR NOC. NEED CONFIRMATION MUTANT PAYLOAD IS SECURE, OVER.
YES, YES... ONE SECOND... THERE WAS AN INCIDENT...THE AMULET...
I NEED YOU TO CHECK THE HATCHERY!
THERE WAS AN INCIDENT...
DID THE NATIVES COMPROMISE THE HATCHERY?!
OH... OH, MY.
YES, THE DEMONS HAVE BEEN HERE...
ARE THE WEAPONS SECURE?!

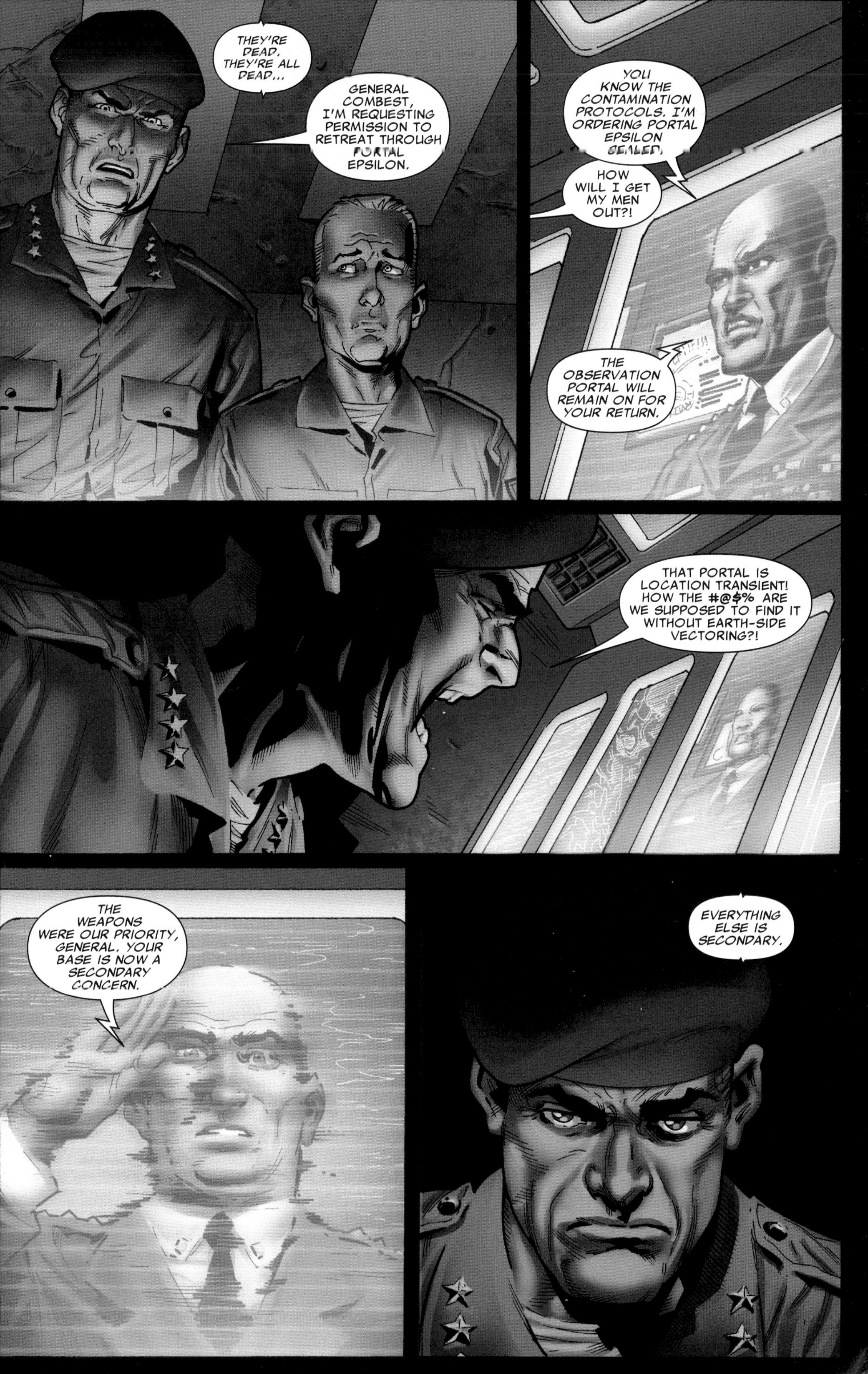
THEY'RE DEAD. THEY'RE ALL DEAD...
GENERAL COMBEST, I'M REQUESTING PERMISSION TO RETREAT THROUGH PORTAL EPSILON.
YOU KNOW THE CONTAMINATION PROTOCOLS. I'M ORDERING PORTAL EPSILON SEALED.
HOW WILL I GET MY MEN OUT?!
THE OBSERVATION PORTAL WILL REMAIN ON FOR YOUR RETURN.
THAT PORTAL IS LOCATION TRANSIENT! HOW THE #@$% ARE WE SUPPOSED TO FIND IT WITHOUT EARTH-SIDE VECTORING?!
THE WEAPONS WERE OUR PRIORITY, GENERAL. YOUR BASE IS NOW A SECONDARY CONCERN.
EVERYTHING ELSE IS SECONDARY.

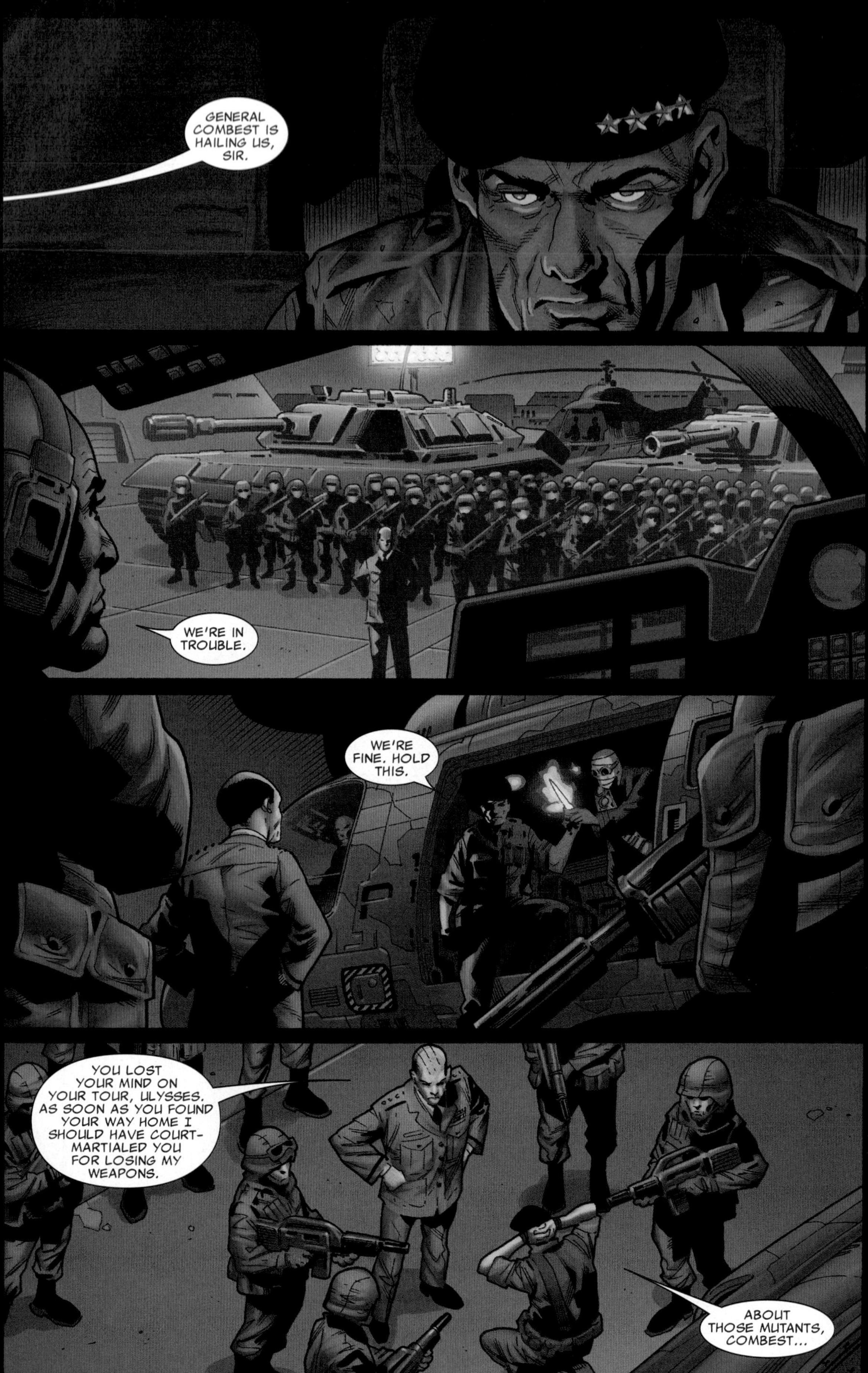
GENERAL COMBEST IS HAILING US, SIR.
WE'RE IN TROUBLE.
WE'RE FINE. HOLD THIS.
YOU LOST YOUR MIND ON YOUR TOUR, ULYSSES. AS SOON AS YOU FOUND YOUR WAY HOME I SHOULD HAVE COURT-MARTIALED YOU FOR LOSING MY WEAPONS.
ABOUT THOSE MUTANTS, COMBEST...

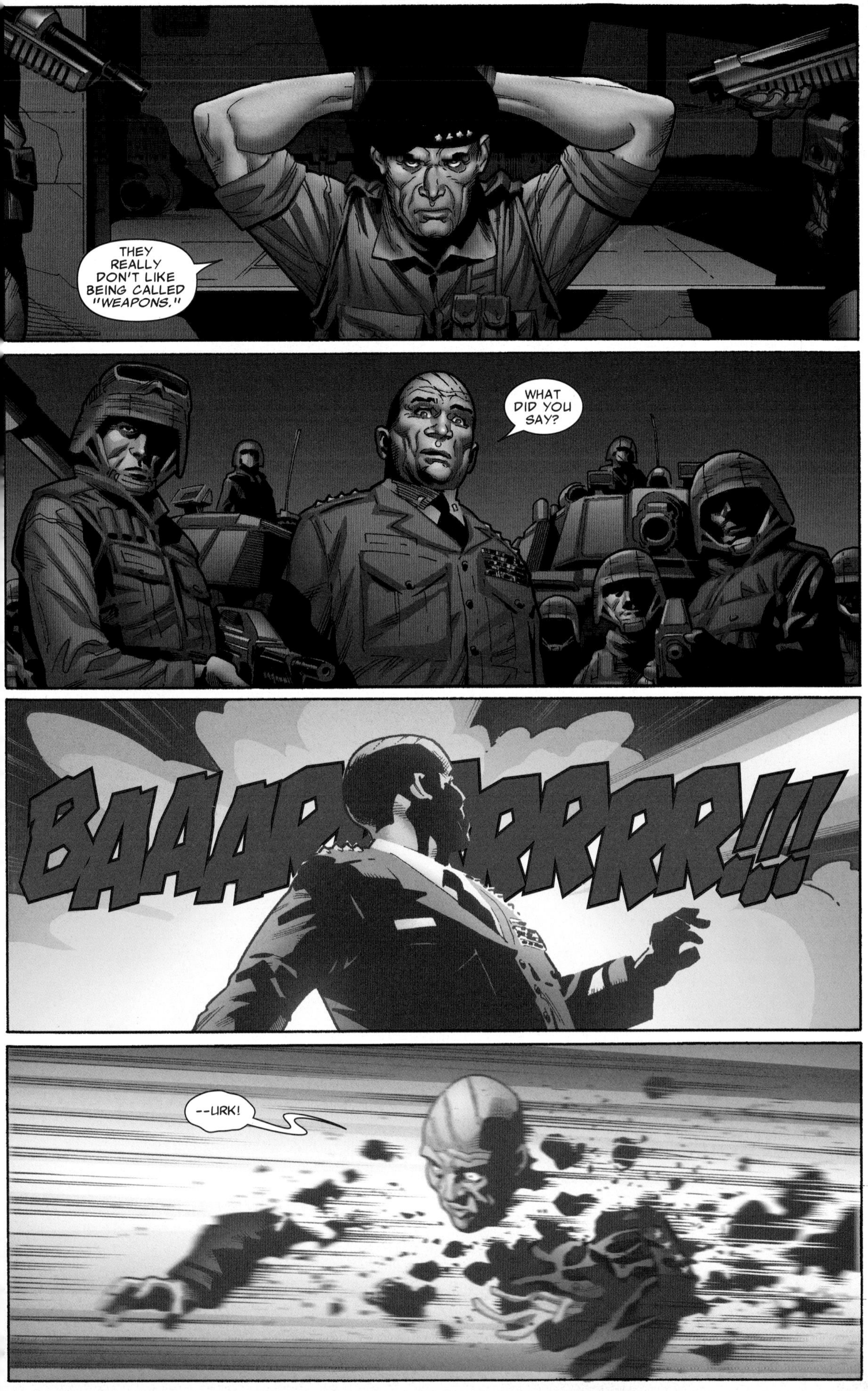
THEY REALLY DON'T LIKE BEING CALLED "WEAPONS."
WHAT DID YOU SAY?
BAAARRRRRRR!!!
--URK!

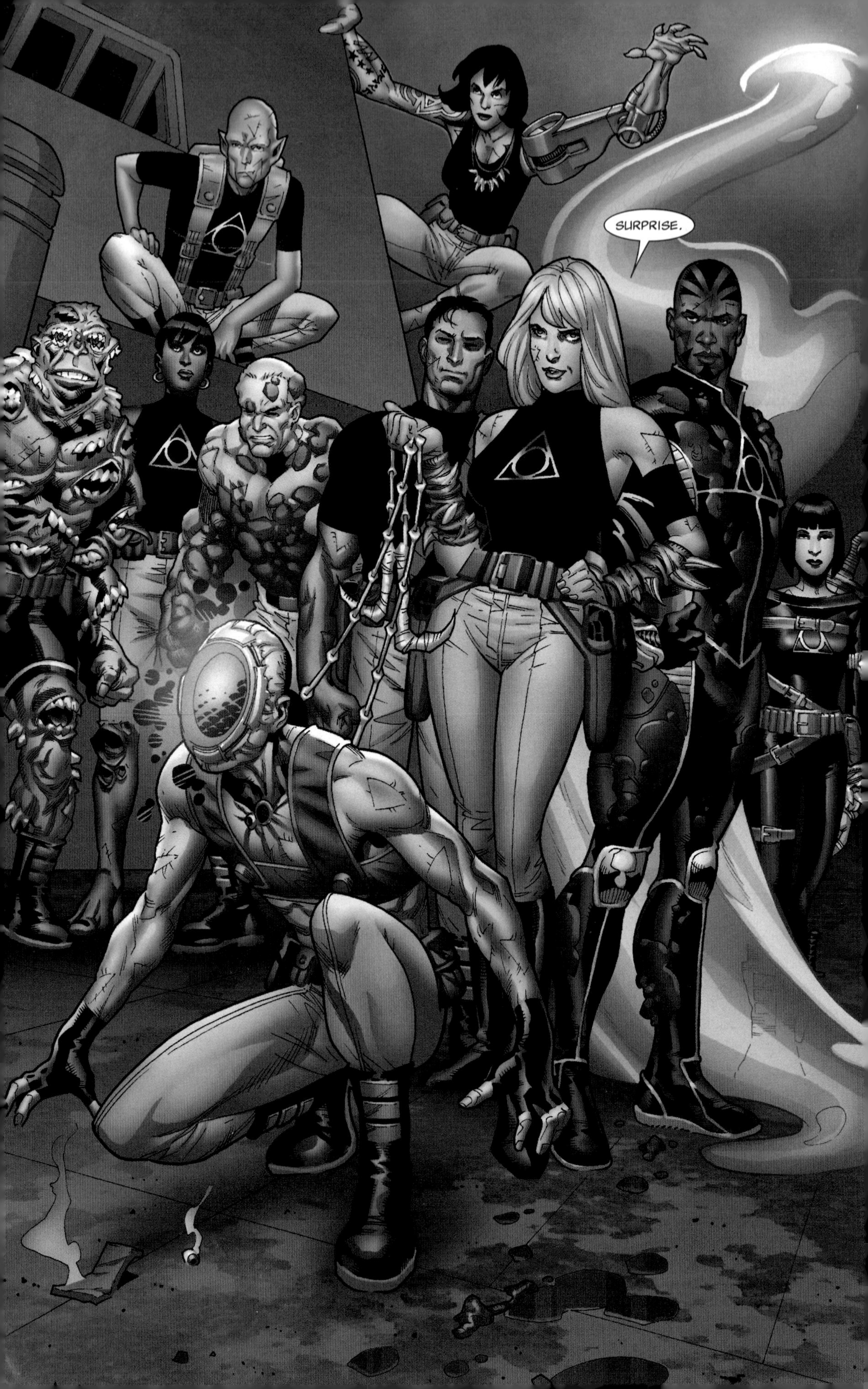
SURPRISE.

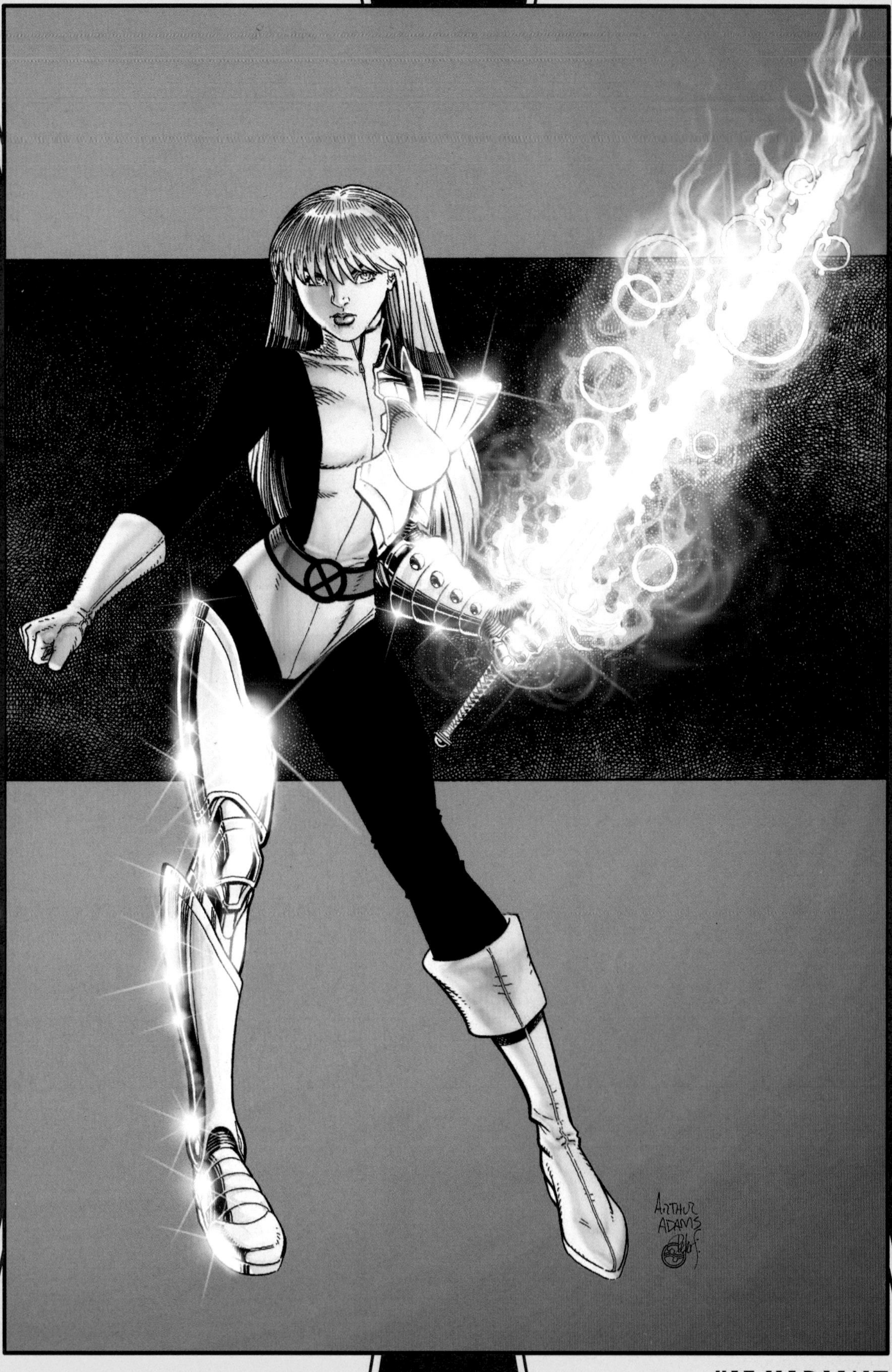
ARTHUR ADAMS

#15 VARIANT

BY ARTHUR ADAMS & PETER STEIGERWALD

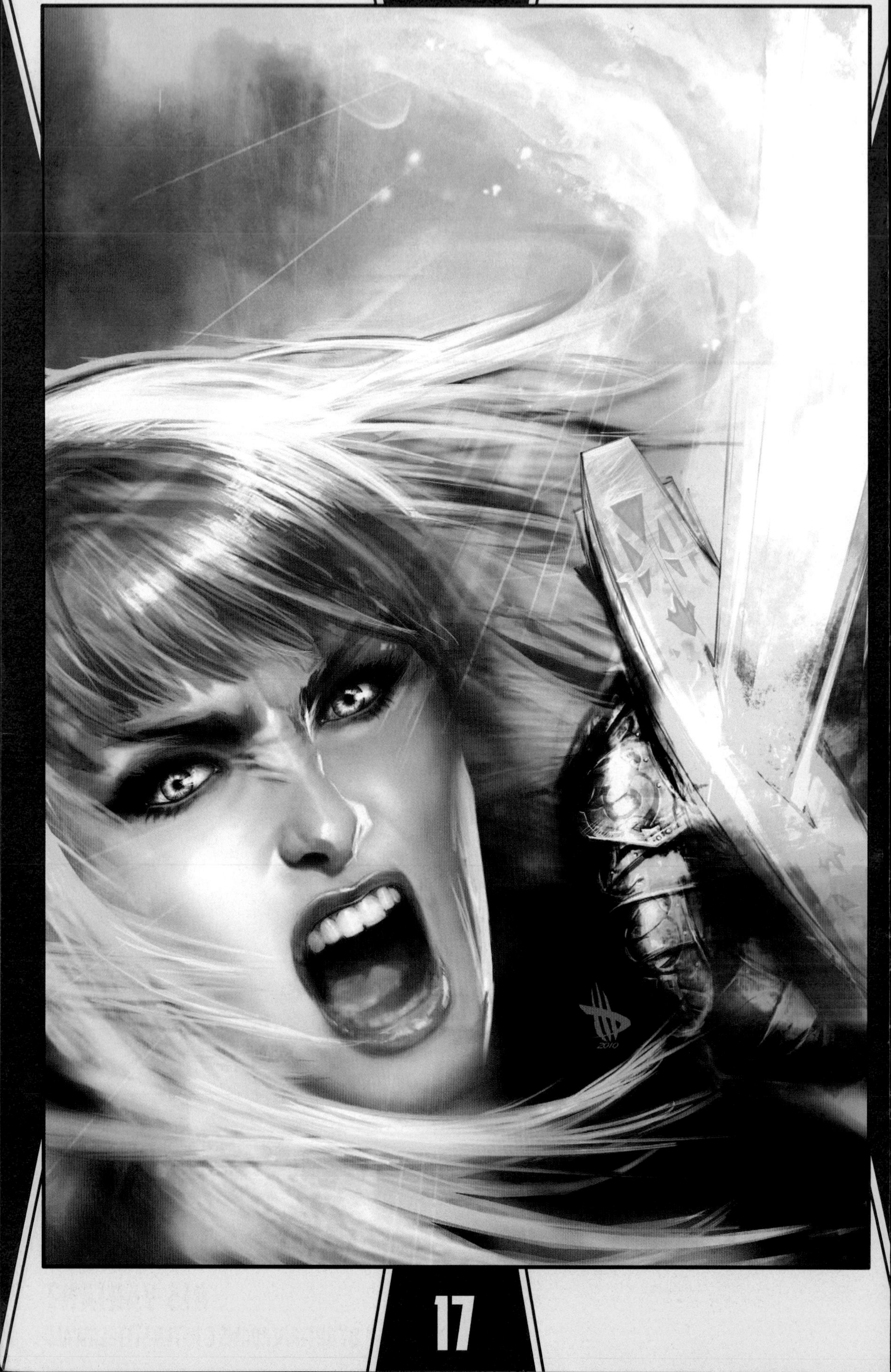

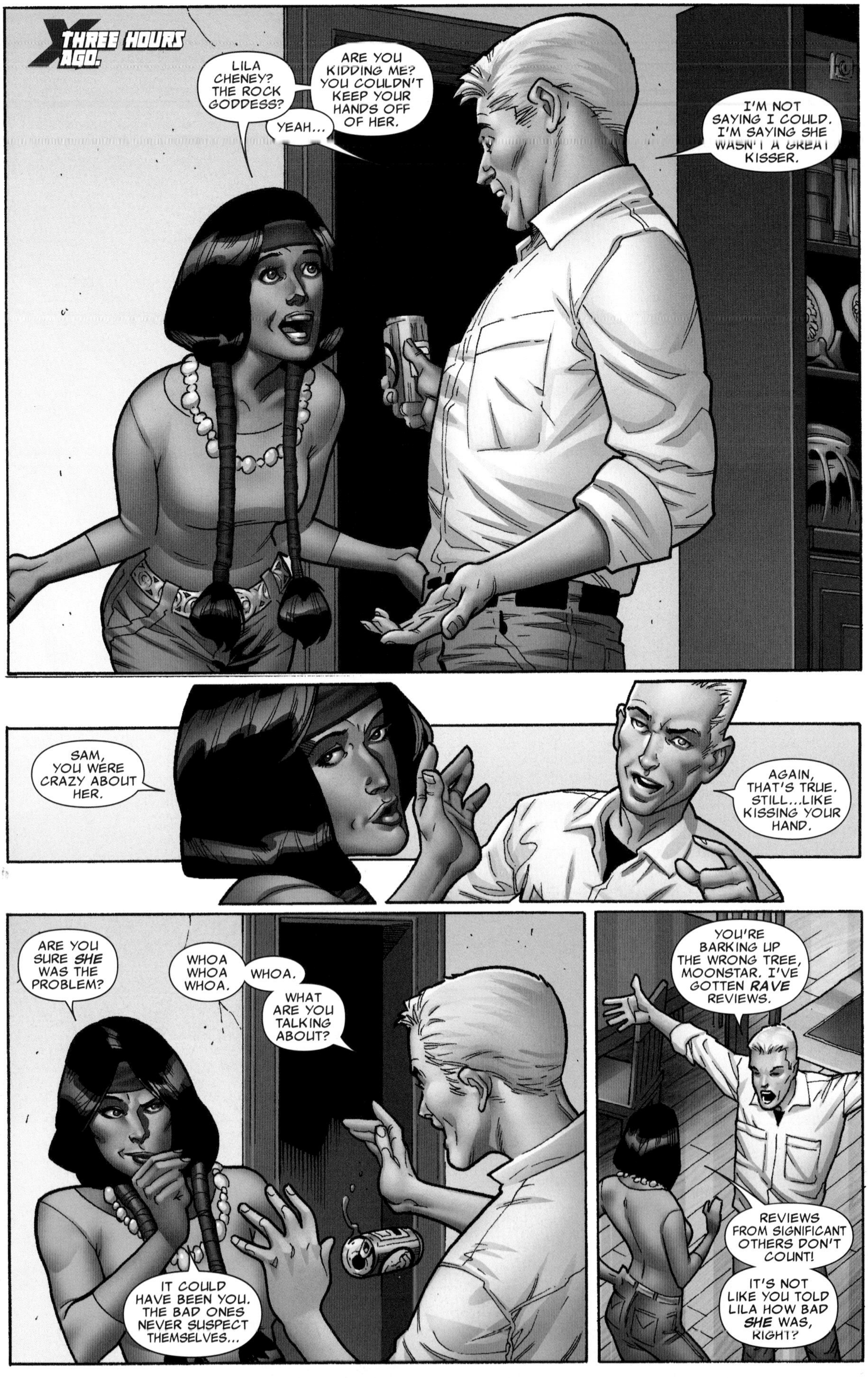
THREE HOURS AGO.
LILA CHENEY? THE ROCK GODDESS?
YEAH...
ARE YOU KIDDING ME? YOU COULDN'T KEEP YOUR HANDS OFF OF HER.
I'M NOT SAYING I COULD. I'M SAYING SHE WASN'T A GREAT KISSER.
SAM, YOU WERE CRAZY ABOUT HER.
AGAIN, THAT'S TRUE. STILL...LIKE KISSING YOUR HAND.
ARE YOU SURE SHE WAS THE PROBLEM?
WHOA WHOA WHOA.
WHOA.
WHAT ARE YOU TALKING ABOUT?
IT COULD HAVE BEEN YOU. THE BAD ONES NEVER SUSPECT THEMSELVES...
YOU'RE BARKING UP THE WRONG TREE, MOONSTAR. I'VE GOTTEN RAVE REVIEWS.
REVIEWS FROM SIGNIFICANT OTHERS DON'T COUNT!
IT'S NOT LIKE YOU TOLD LILA HOW BAD SHE WAS, RIGHT?

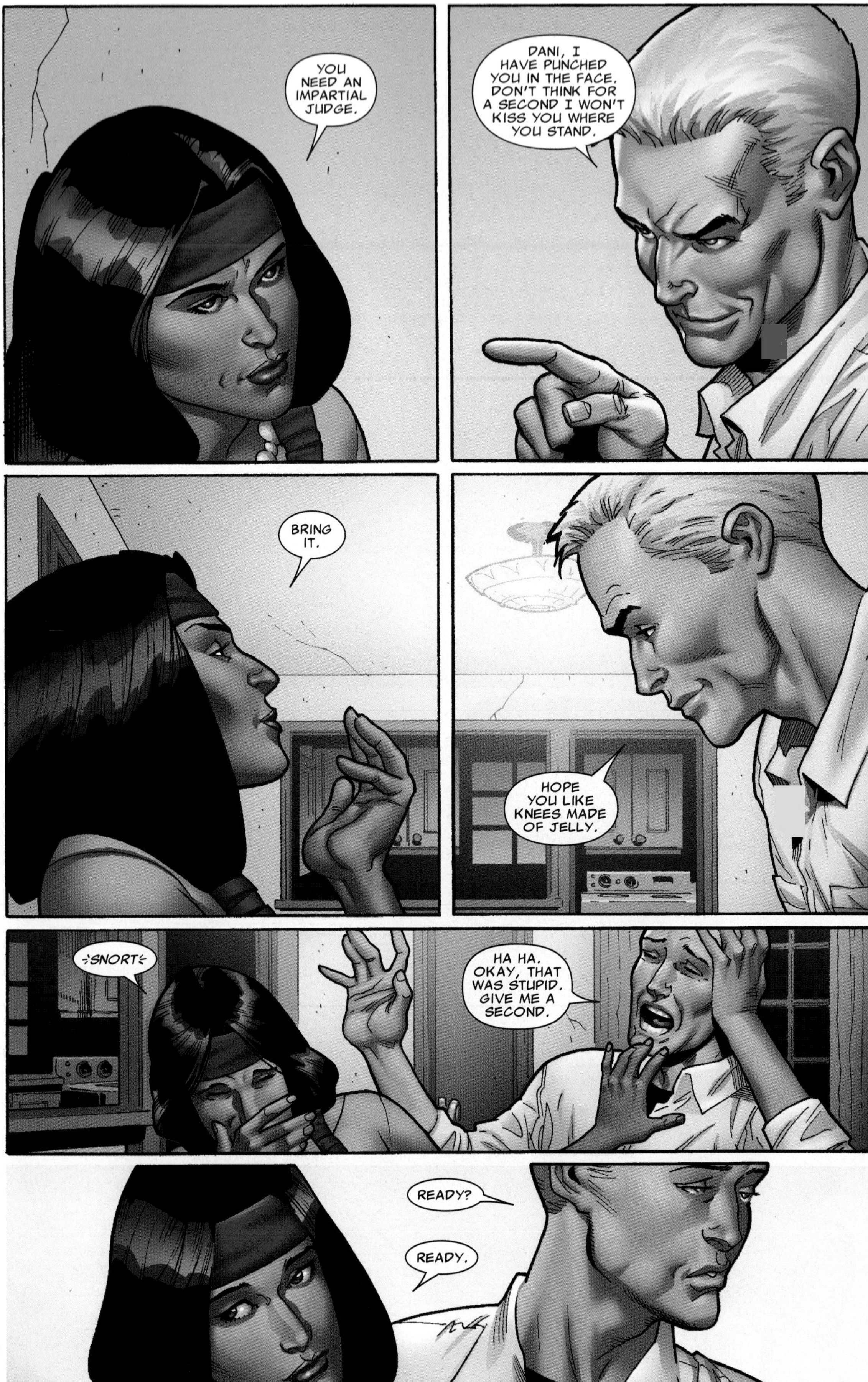
YOU NEED AN IMPARTIAL JUDGE.
DANI, I HAVE PUNCHED YOU IN THE FACE. DON'T THINK FOR A SECOND I WON'T KISS YOU WHERE YOU STAND.
BRING IT.
HOPE YOU LIKE KNEES MADE OF JELLY.
SNORT
HA HA. OKAY, THAT WAS STUPID. GIVE ME A SECOND.
READY?
READY.

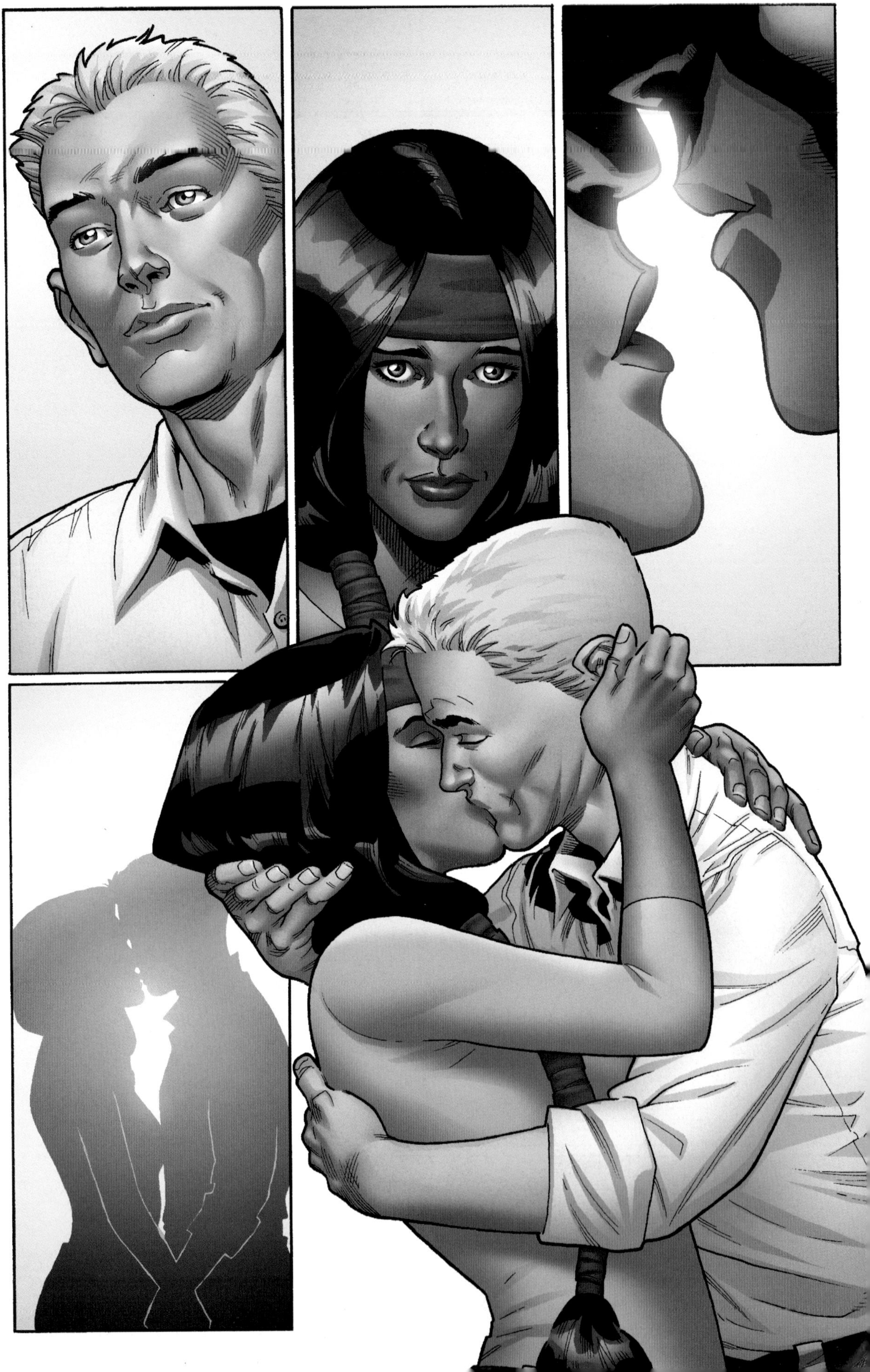

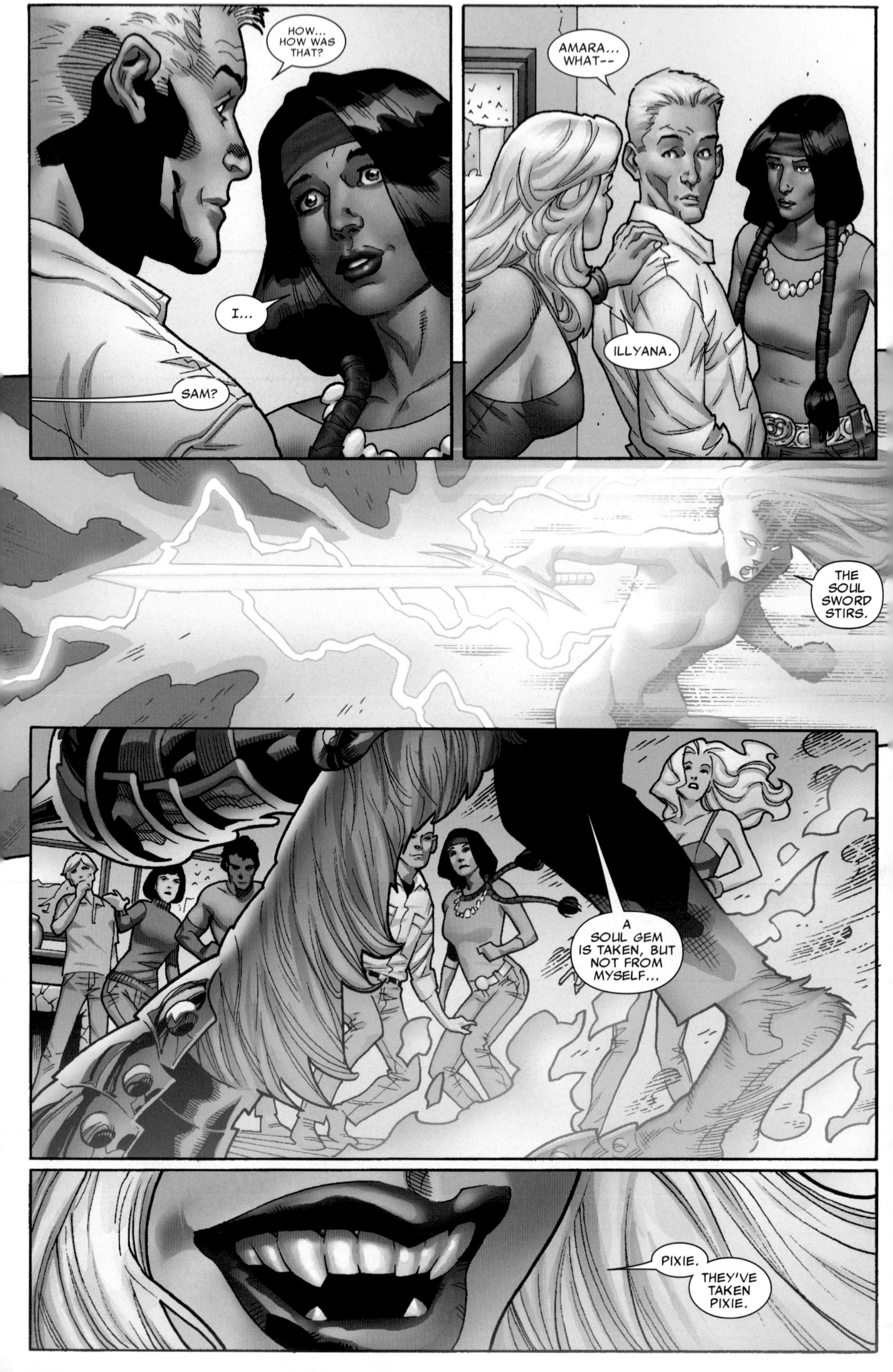
HOW... HOW WAS THAT?
I...
SAM?
AMARA... WHAT--
ILLYANA.
THE SOUL SWORD STIRS.
A SOUL GEM IS TAKEN, BUT NOT FROM MYSELF...
PIXIE.
THEY'VE TAKEN PIXIE.

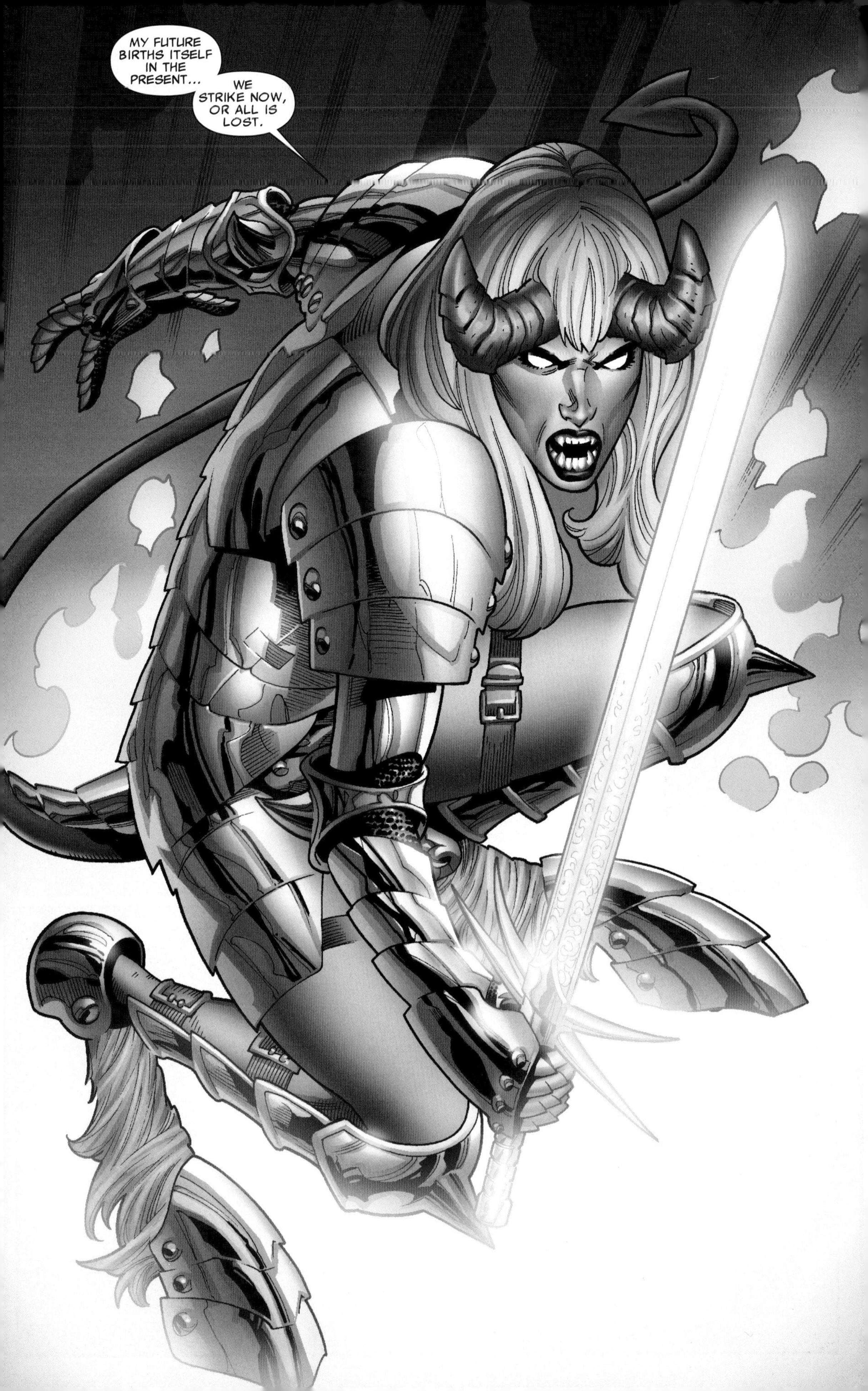
MY FUTURE BIRTHS ITSELF IN THE PRESENT...
WE STRIKE NOW, OR ALL IS LOST.

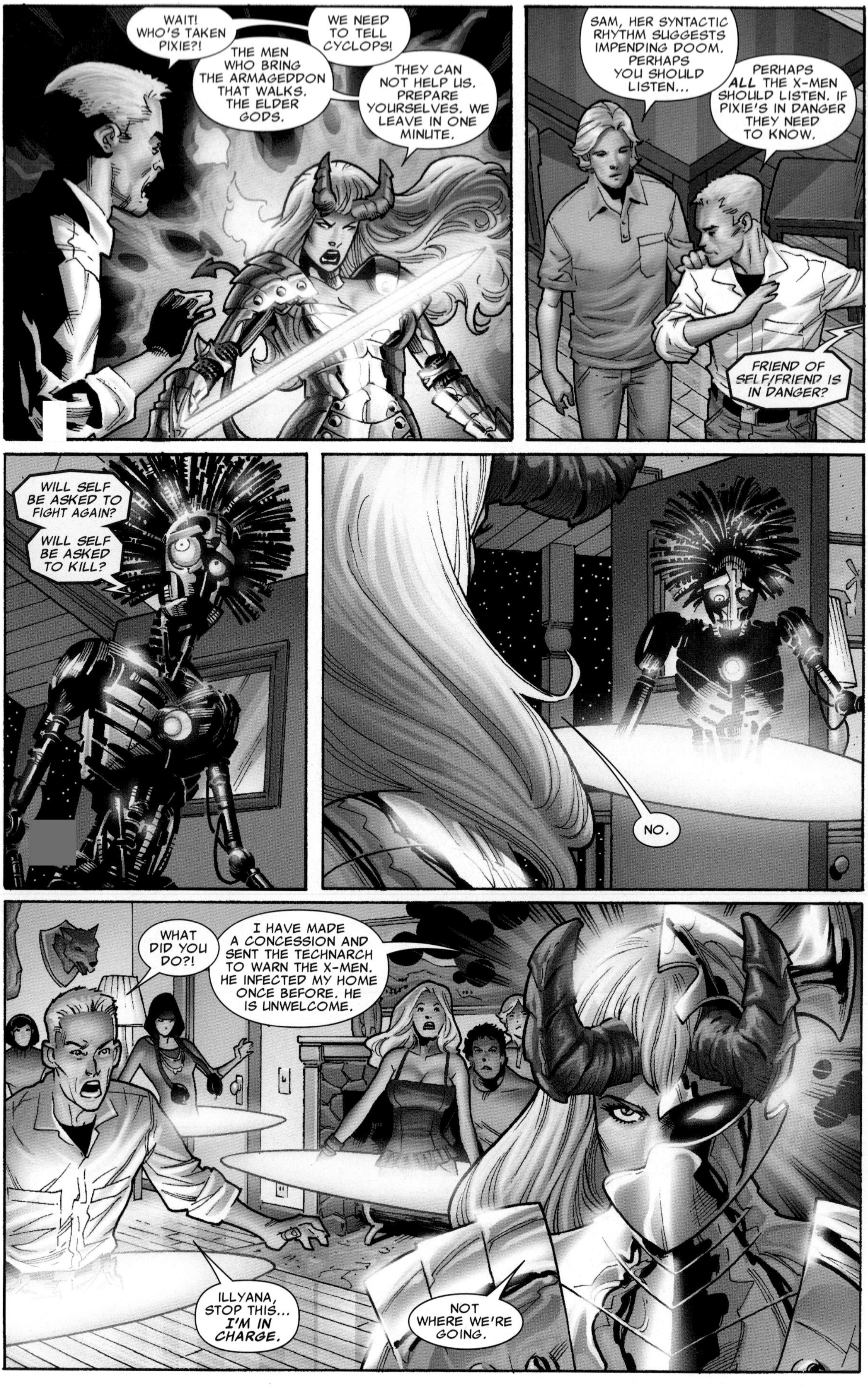
WAIT! WHO'S TAKEN PIXIE?!
WE NEED TO TELL CYCLOPS!
THE MEN WHO BRING THE ARMAGEDDON THAT WALKS. THE ELDER GODS.
THEY CAN NOT HELP US. PREPARE YOURSELVES. WE LEAVE IN ONE MINUTE.
SAM, HER SYNTACTIC RHYTHM SUGGESTS IMPENDING DOOM. PERHAPS YOU SHOULD LISTEN...
PERHAPS ALL THE X-MEN SHOULD LISTEN. IF PIXIE'S IN DANGER THEY NEED TO KNOW.
FRIEND OF SELF/FRIEND IS IN DANGER?
WILL SELF BE ASKED TO FIGHT AGAIN?
WILL SELF BE ASKED TO KILL?
NO.
WHAT DID YOU DO?!
I HAVE MADE A CONCESSION AND SENT THE TECHNARCH TO WARN THE X-MEN. HE INFECTED MY HOME ONCE BEFORE. HE IS UNWELCOME.
ILLYANA, STOP THIS... I'M IN CHARGE.
NOT WHERE WE'RE GOING.

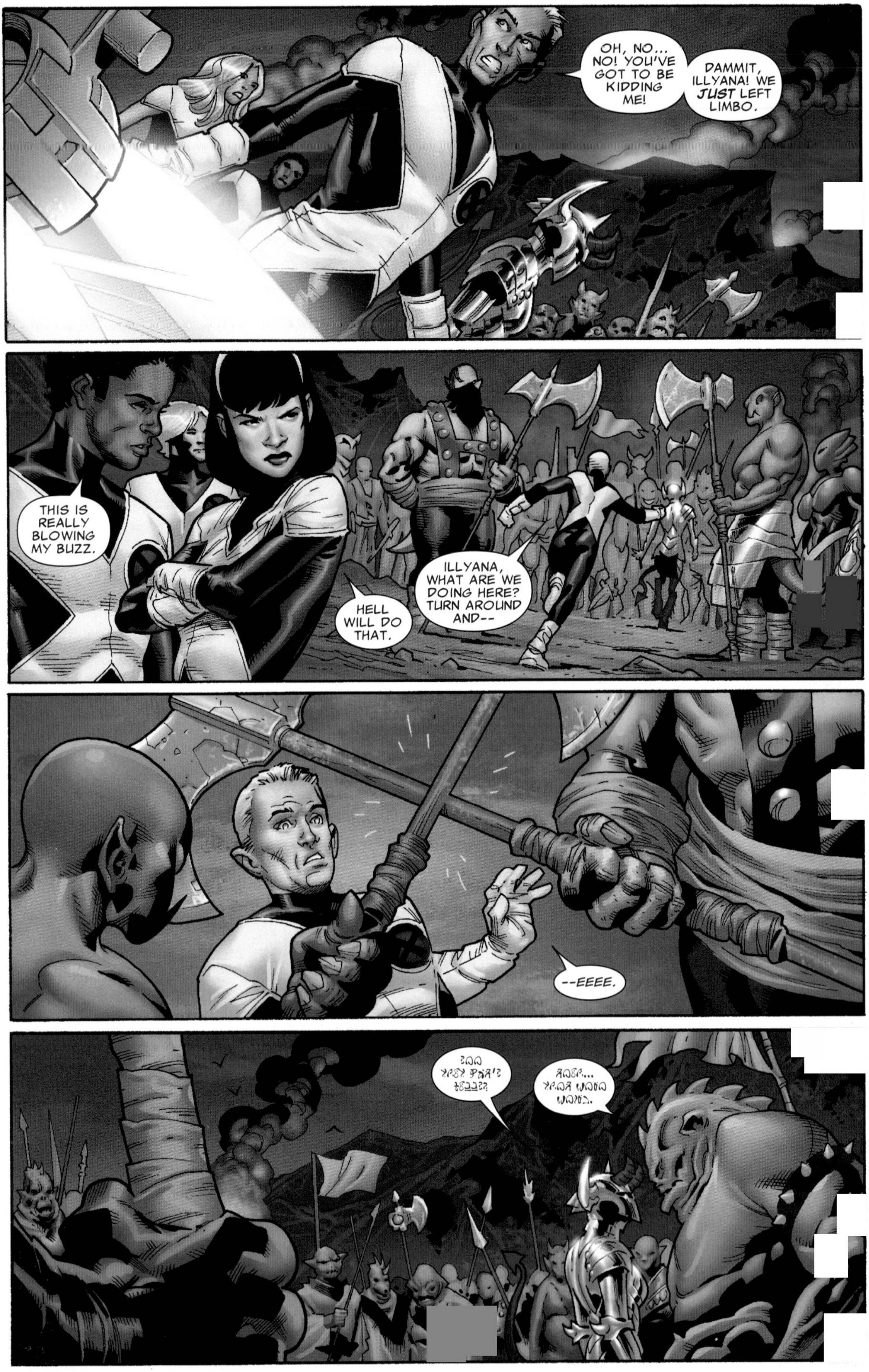
OH, NO... NO! YOU'VE GOT TO BE KIDDING ME!
DAMMIT, ILLYANA! WE JUST LEFT LIMBO.
THIS IS REALLY BLOWING MY BUZZ.
ILLYANA, WHAT ARE WE DOING HERE? TURN AROUND AND--
HELL WILL DO THAT.
--EEEE.

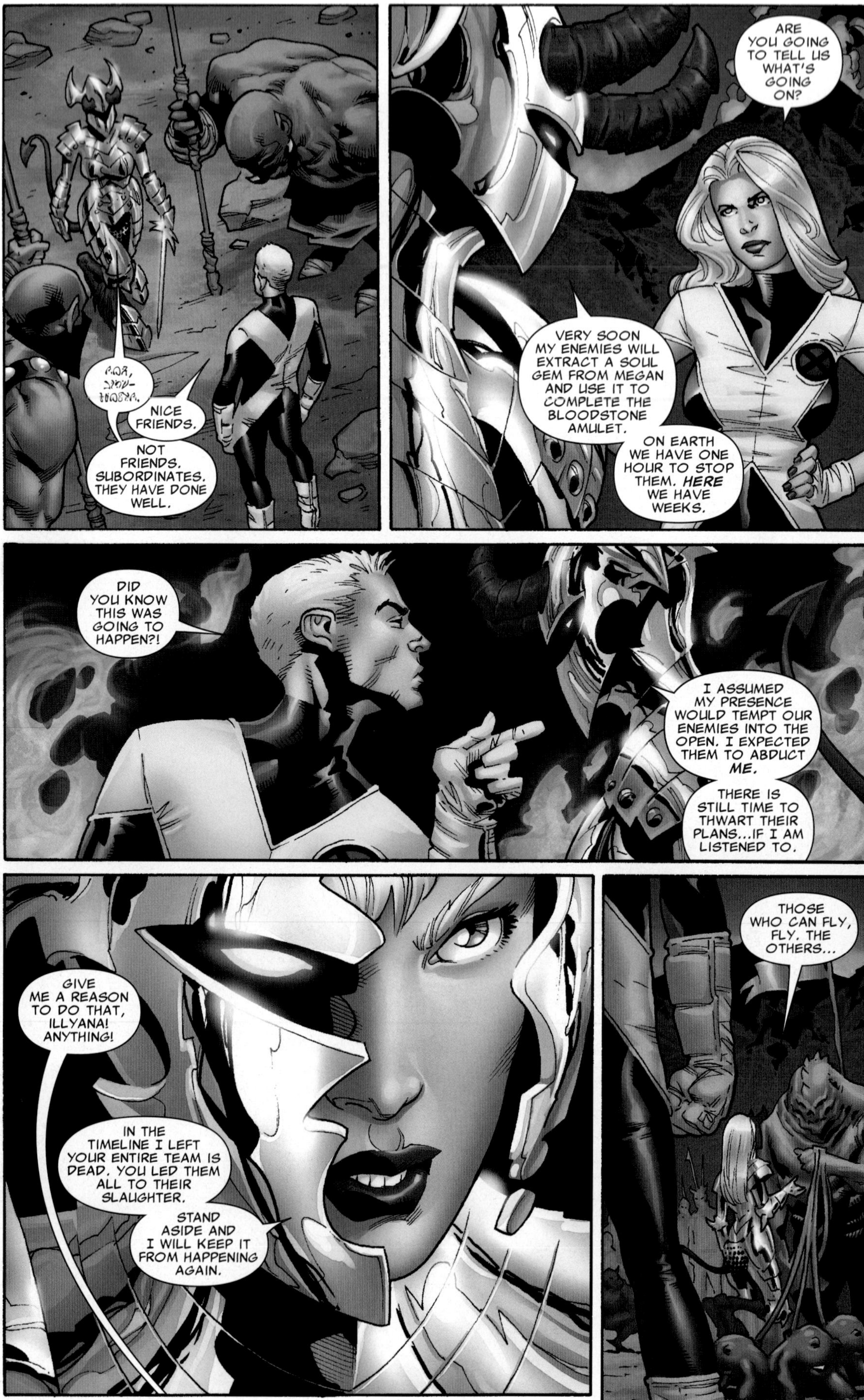
NICE FRIENDS.
NOT FRIENDS. SUBORDINATES. THEY HAVE DONE WELL.
ARE YOU GOING TO TELL US WHAT'S GOING ON?
VERY SOON MY ENEMIES WILL EXTRACT A SOUL GEM FROM MEGAN AND USE IT TO COMPLETE THE BLOODSTONE AMULET.
ON EARTH WE HAVE ONE HOUR TO STOP THEM. *HERE* WE HAVE WEEKS.
DID YOU KNOW THIS WAS GOING TO HAPPEN?!
I ASSUMED MY PRESENCE WOULD TEMPT OUR ENEMIES INTO THE OPEN. I EXPECTED THEM TO ABDUCT *ME.*
THERE IS STILL TIME TO THWART THEIR PLANS...IF I AM LISTENED TO.
GIVE ME A REASON TO DO THAT, ILLYANA! ANYTHING!
IN THE TIMELINE I LEFT YOUR ENTIRE TEAM IS DEAD. YOU LED THEM ALL TO THEIR SLAUGHTER.
STAND ASIDE AND I WILL KEEP IT FROM HAPPENING AGAIN.
THOSE WHO CAN FLY, FLY. THE OTHERS...

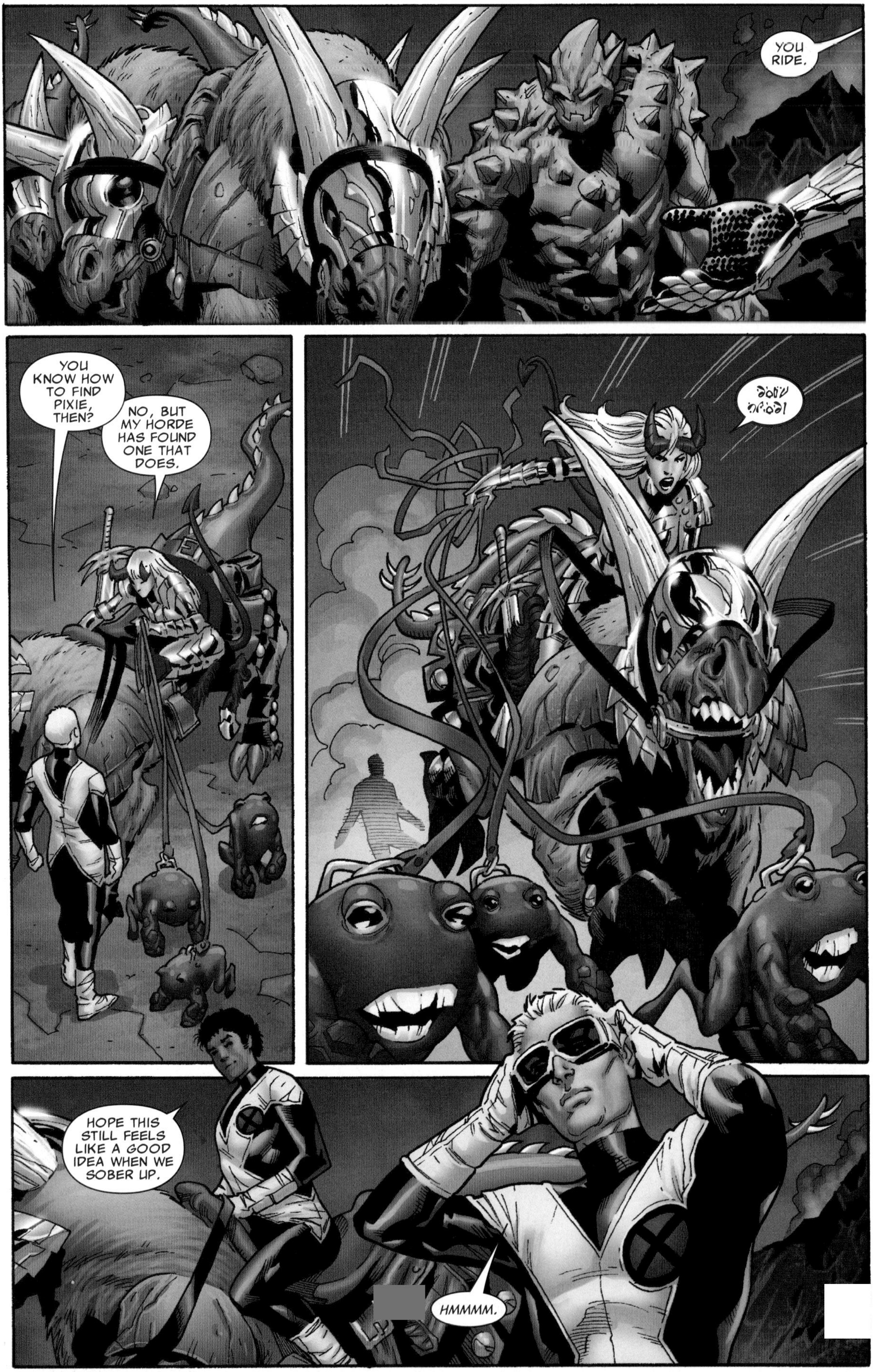
YOU RIDE.
YOU KNOW HOW TO FIND PIXIE, THEN?
NO, BUT MY HORDE HAS FOUND ONE THAT DOES.
HOPE THIS STILL FEELS LIKE A GOOD IDEA WHEN WE SOBER UP.
HMMMM.

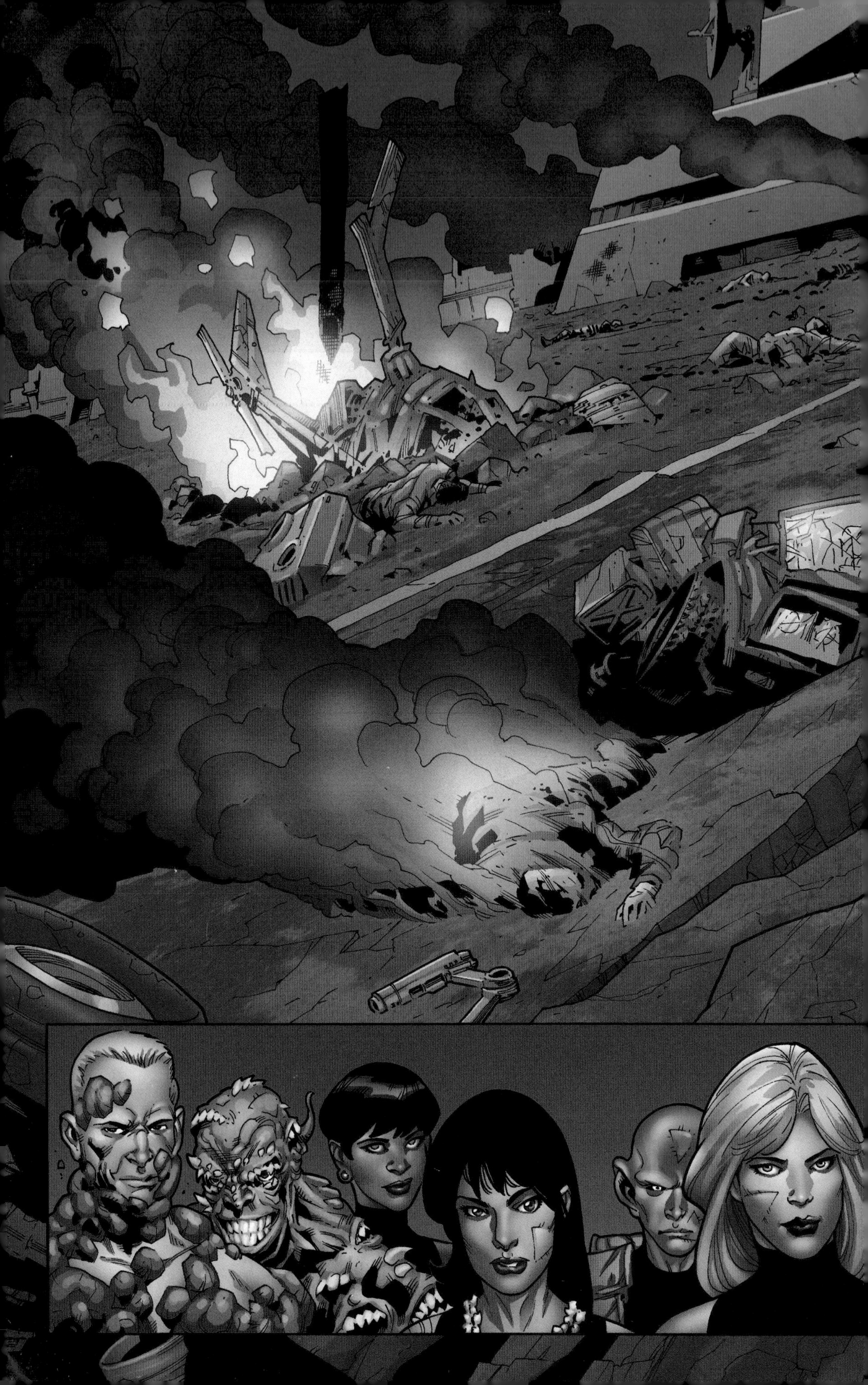

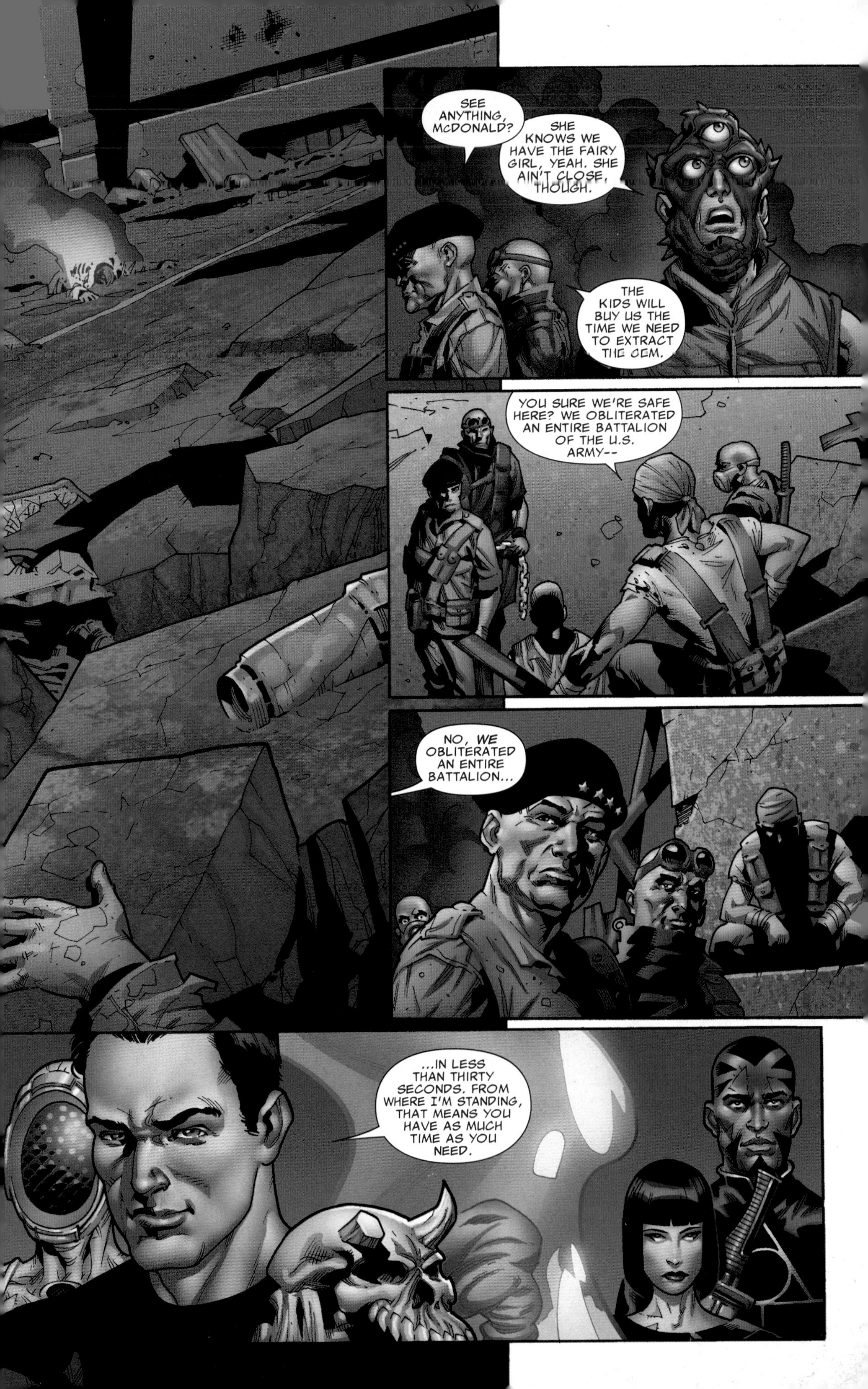
SEE ANYTHING, McDONALD?
SHE KNOWS WE HAVE THE FAIRY GIRL, YEAH. SHE AIN'T CLOSE, THOUGH.
THE KIDS WILL BUY US THE TIME WE NEED TO EXTRACT THE GEM.
YOU SURE WE'RE SAFE HERE? WE OBLITERATED AN ENTIRE BATTALION OF THE U.S. ARMY--
NO, WE OBLITERATED AN ENTIRE BATTALION...
...IN LESS THAN THIRTY SECONDS. FROM WHERE I'M STANDING, THAT MEANS YOU HAVE AS MUCH TIME AS YOU NEED.

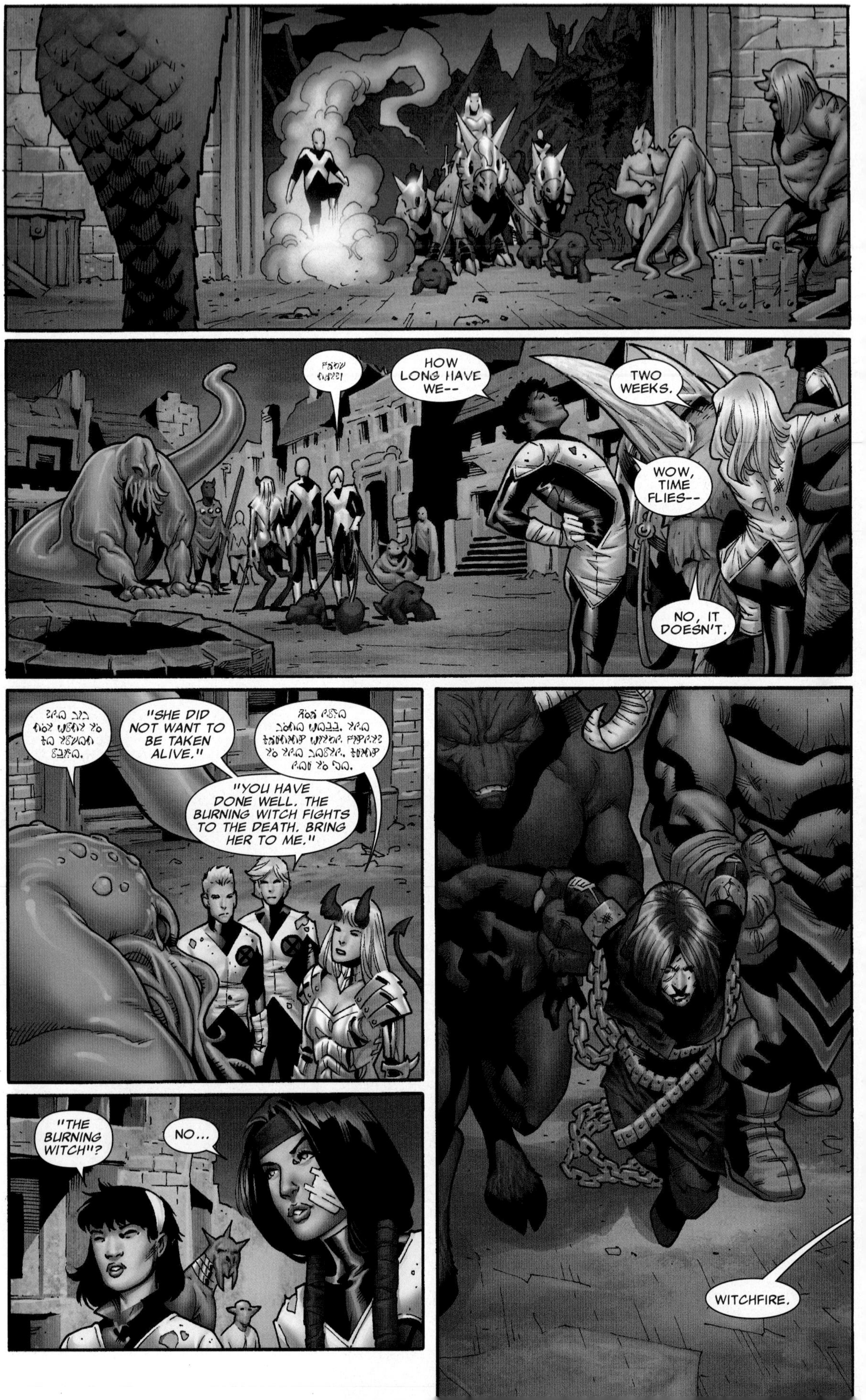
HOW LONG HAVE WE--
TWO WEEKS.
WOW, TIME FLIES--
NO, IT DOESN'T.
"SHE DID NOT WANT TO BE TAKEN ALIVE."
"YOU HAVE DONE WELL. THE BURNING WITCH FIGHTS TO THE DEATH. BRING HER TO ME."
"THE BURNING WITCH"?
NO...
WITCHFIRE.

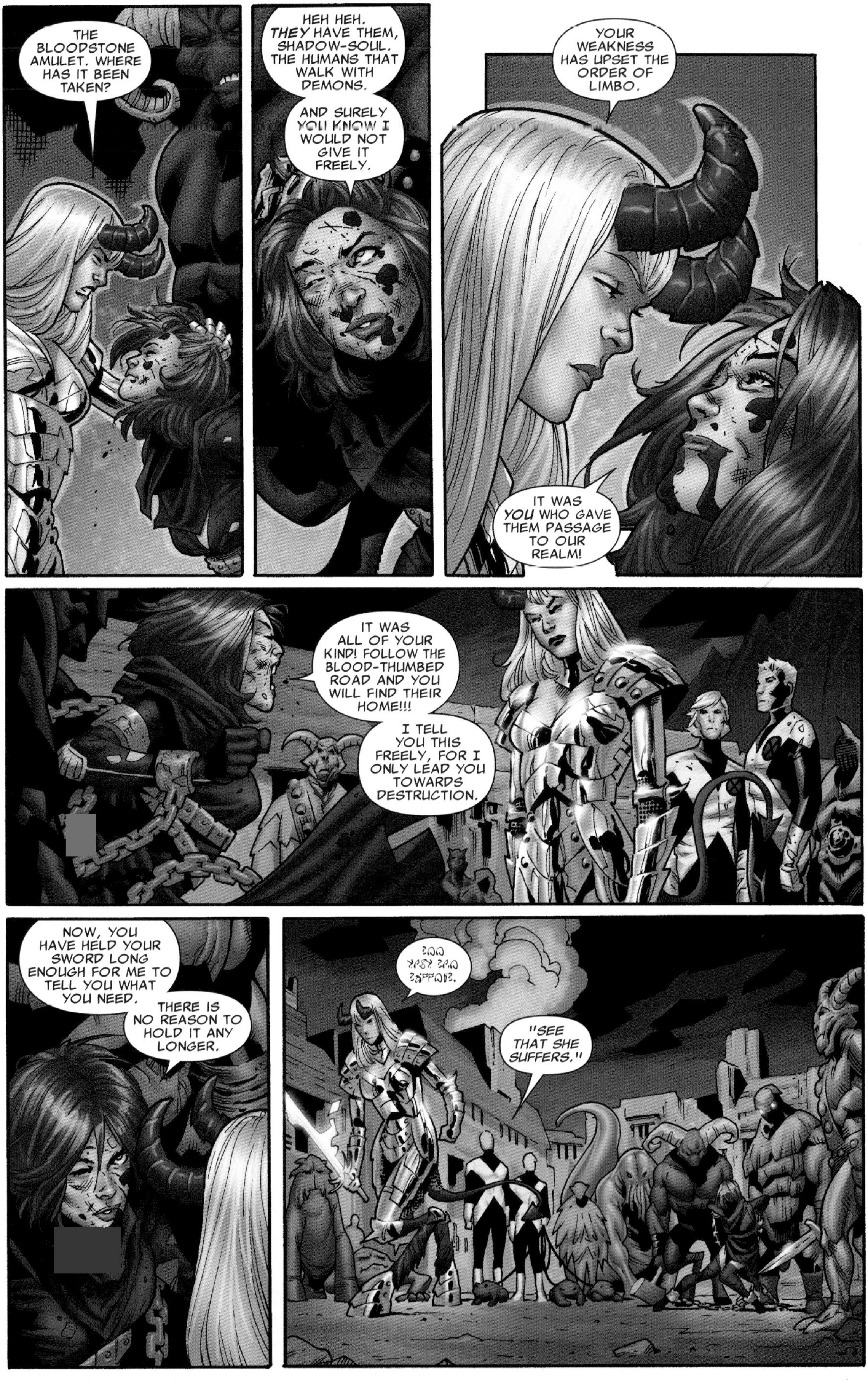
THE BLOODSTONE AMULET. WHERE HAS IT BEEN TAKEN?
HEH HEH. THEY HAVE THEM, SHADOW-SOUL. THE HUMANS THAT WALK WITH DEMONS.
AND SURELY YOU KNOW I WOULD NOT GIVE IT FREELY.
YOUR WEAKNESS HAS UPSET THE ORDER OF LIMBO.
IT WAS YOU WHO GAVE THEM PASSAGE TO OUR REALM!
IT WAS ALL OF YOUR KIND! FOLLOW THE BLOOD-THUMBED ROAD AND YOU WILL FIND THEIR HOME!!!
I TELL YOU THIS FREELY, FOR I ONLY LEAD YOU TOWARDS DESTRUCTION.
NOW, YOU HAVE HELD YOUR SWORD LONG ENOUGH FOR ME TO TELL YOU WHAT YOU NEED.
THERE IS NO REASON TO HOLD IT ANY LONGER.
"SEE THAT SHE SUFFERS."

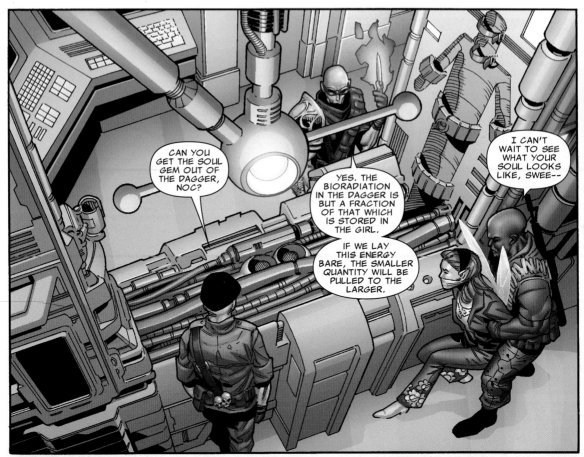

CAN YOU GET THE SOUL GEM OUT OF THE DAGGER, NOC?

YES. THE BIORADIATION IN THE DAGGER IS BUT A FRACTION OF THAT WHICH IS STORED IN THE GIRL.

IF WE LAY THIS ENERGY BARE, THE SMALLER QUANTITY WILL BE PULLED TO THE LARGER.

I CAN'T WAIT TO SEE WHAT YOUR SOUL LOOKS LIKE, SWEE--

FLUTTER

HAK!

BEES... SCARY BEES...

AM I HOLDING A LEPRECHAUN?

NO.

HALLUCINOGENIC?

I'M AFRAID SO. IT'S QUITE HARMLESS, THOUGH. IF WE JUST--

STING THIS, YOU HONEY BEE #@$%-@$% S!!!

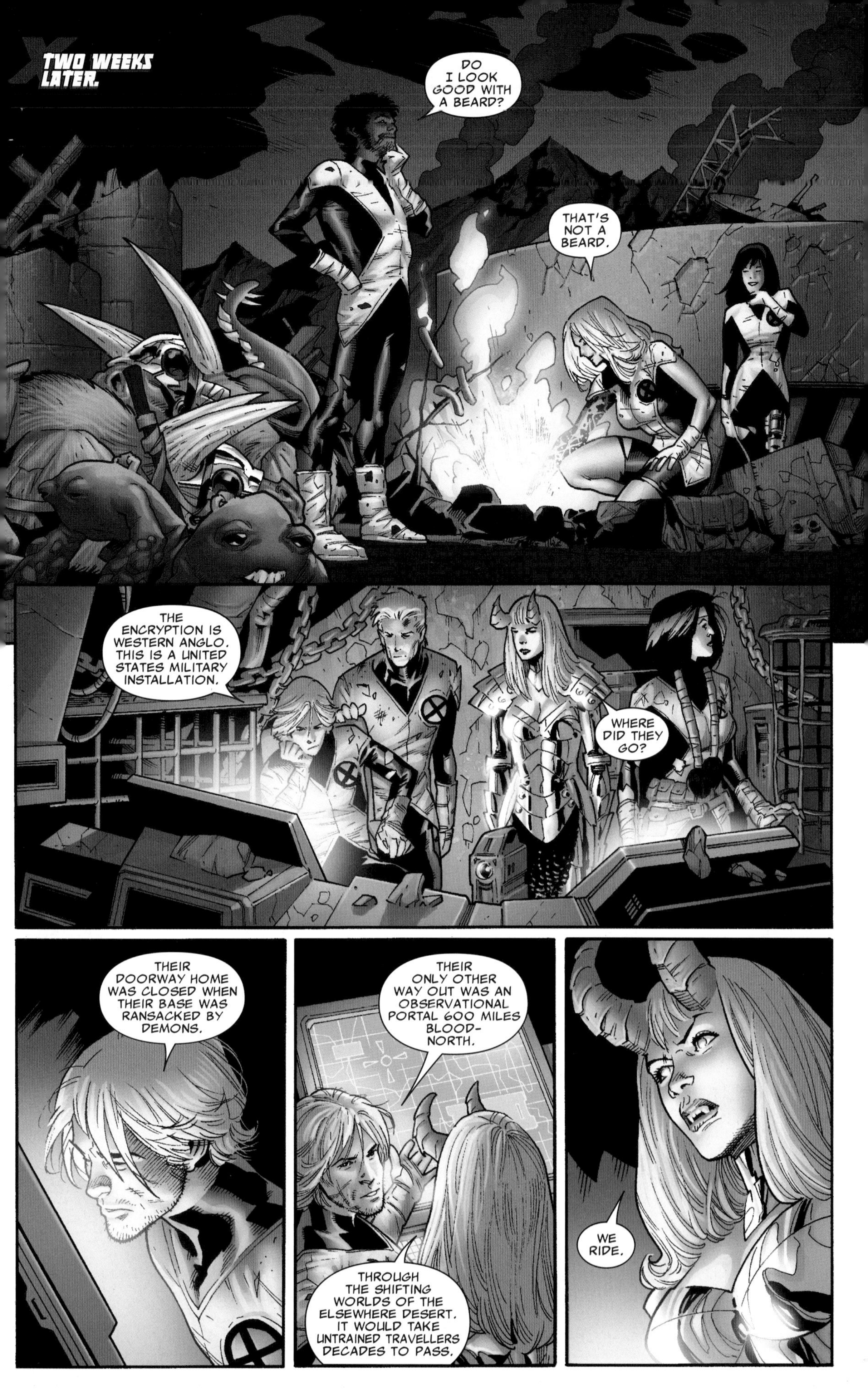
TWO WEEKS LATER.
DO I LOOK GOOD WITH A BEARD?
THAT'S NOT A BEARD.
THE ENCRYPTION IS WESTERN ANGLO. THIS IS A UNITED STATES MILITARY INSTALLATION.
WHERE DID THEY GO?
THEIR DOORWAY HOME WAS CLOSED WHEN THEIR BASE WAS RANSACKED BY DEMONS.
THEIR ONLY OTHER WAY OUT WAS AN OBSERVATIONAL PORTAL 600 MILES BLOOD-NORTH.
THROUGH THE SHIFTING WORLDS OF THE ELSEWHERE DESERT. IT WOULD TAKE UNTRAINED TRAVELLERS DECADES TO PASS.
WE RIDE.

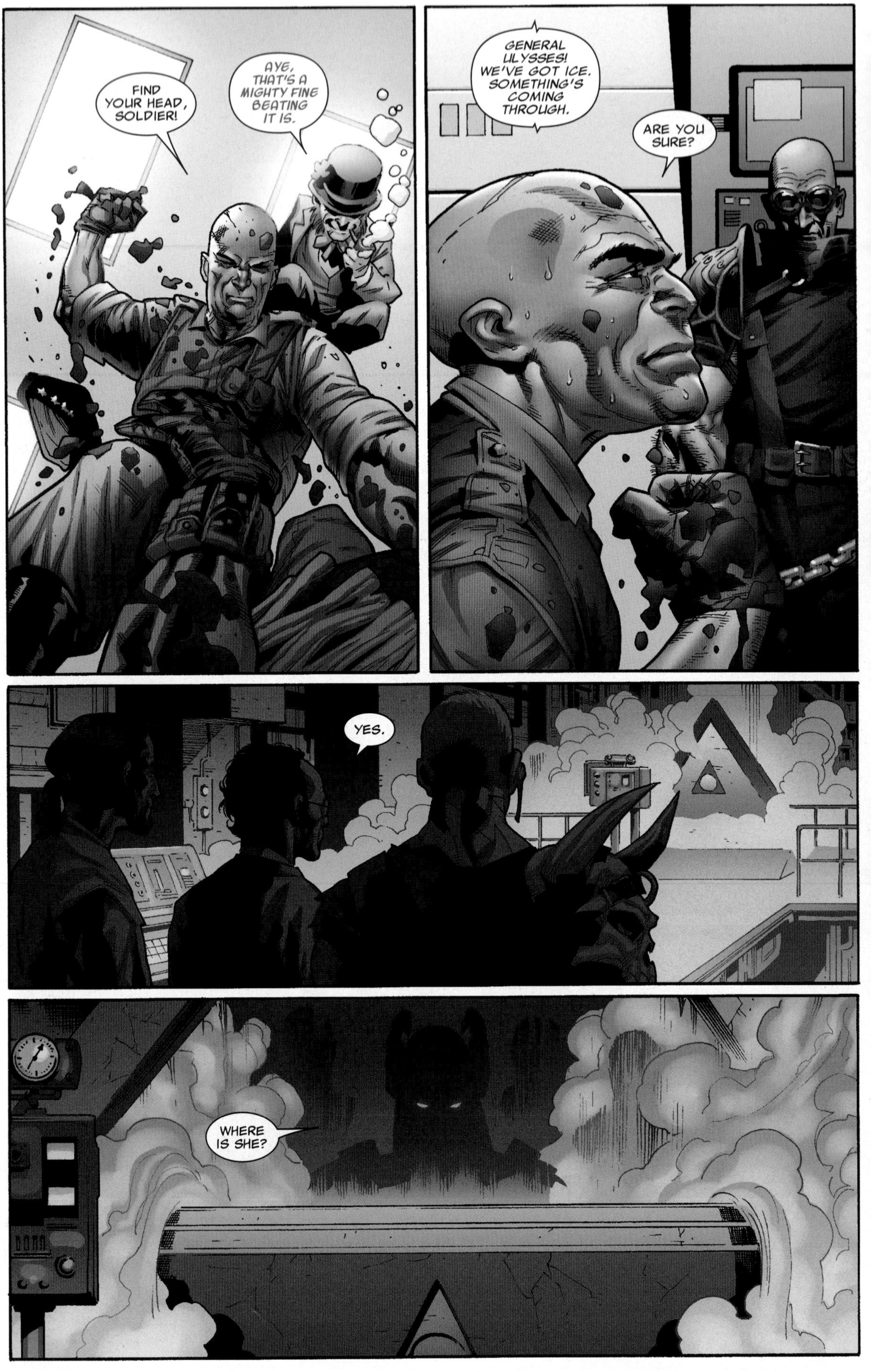
FIND YOUR HEAD, SOLDIER!
AYE, THAT'S A MIGHTY FINE BEATING IT IS.
GENERAL ULYSSES! WE'VE GOT ICE. SOMETHING'S COMING THROUGH.
ARE YOU SURE?
YES.
WHERE IS SHE?

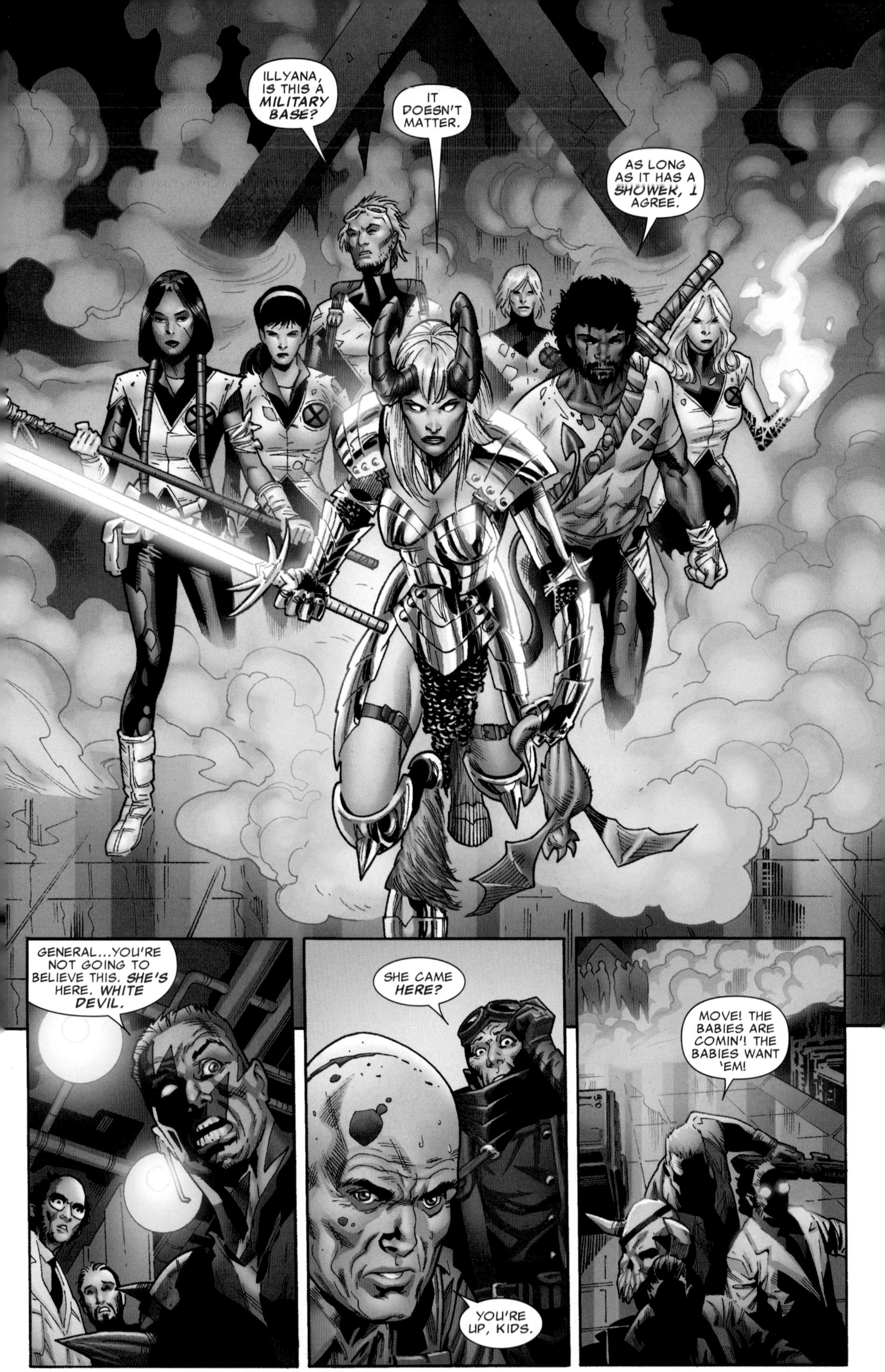
ILLYANA, IS THIS A MILITARY BASE?
IT DOESN'T MATTER.
AS LONG AS IT HAS A SHOWER, I AGREE.
GENERAL...YOU'RE NOT GOING TO BELIEVE THIS. SHE'S HERE. WHITE DEVIL.
SHE CAME HERE?
YOU'RE UP, KIDS.
MOVE! THE BABIES ARE COMIN'! THE BABIES WANT 'EM!

THE
BABIES?

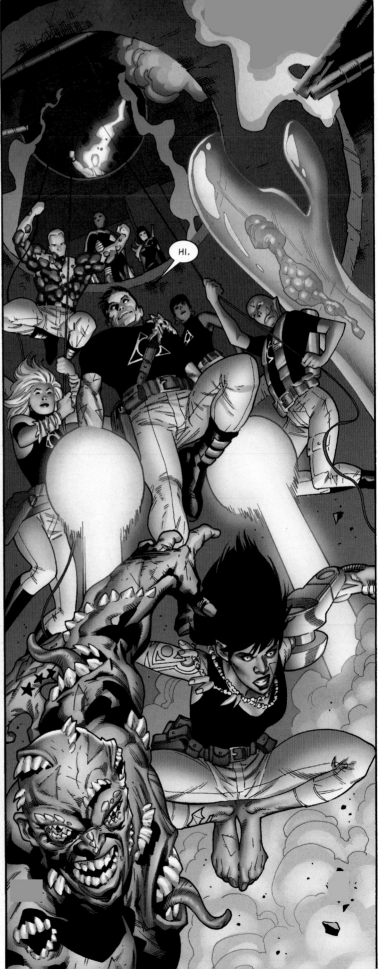

HI.

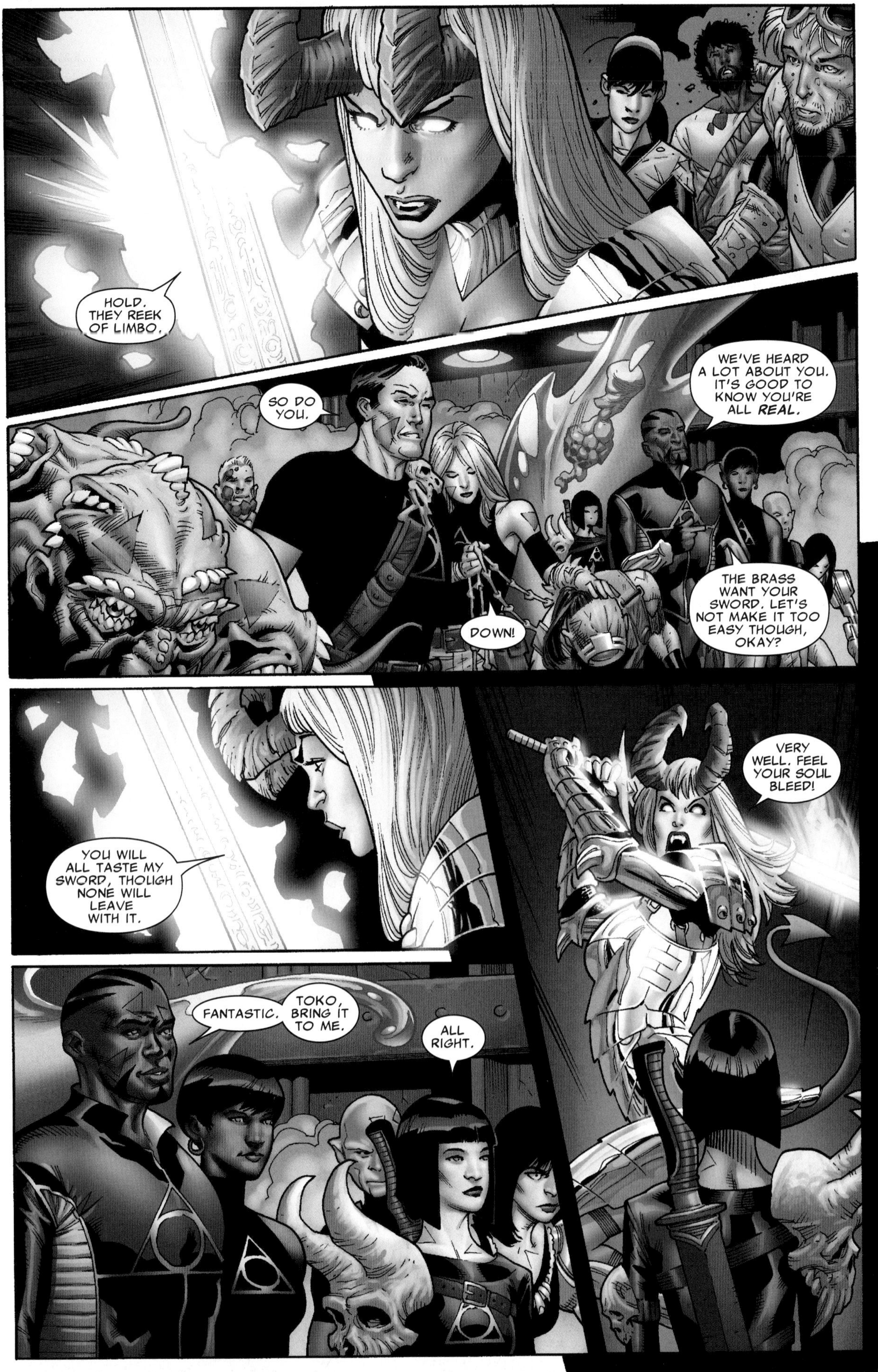
HOLD. THEY REEK OF LIMBO.
SO DO YOU.
WE'VE HEARD A LOT ABOUT YOU. IT'S GOOD TO KNOW YOU'RE ALL REAL.
DOWN!
THE BRASS WANT YOUR SWORD. LET'S NOT MAKE IT TOO EASY THOUGH, OKAY?
YOU WILL ALL TASTE MY SWORD, THOUGH NONE WILL LEAVE WITH IT.
VERY WELL. FEEL YOUR SOUL BLEED!
FANTASTIC.
TOKO, BRING IT TO ME.
ALL RIGHT.

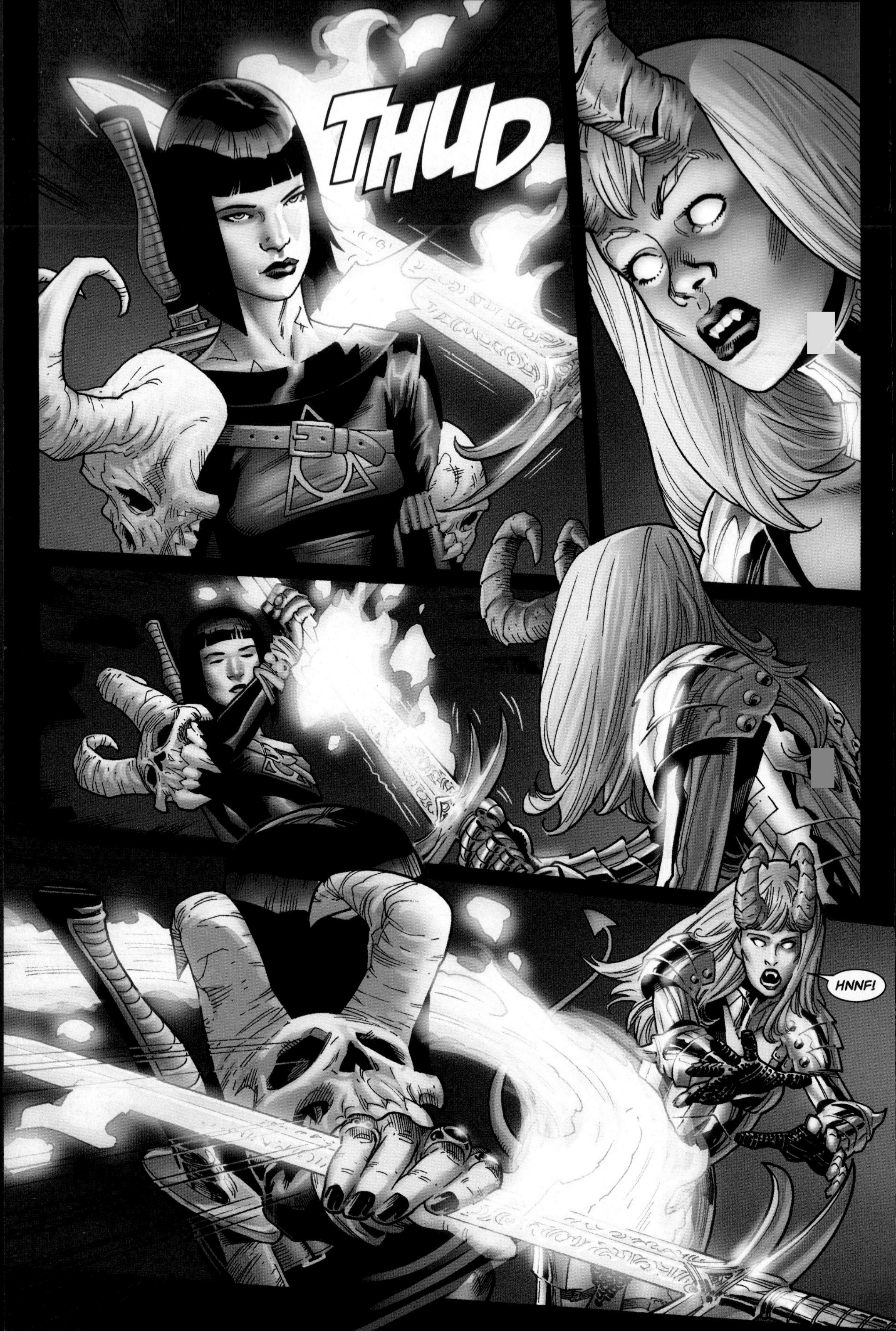
THUD
HNNF!

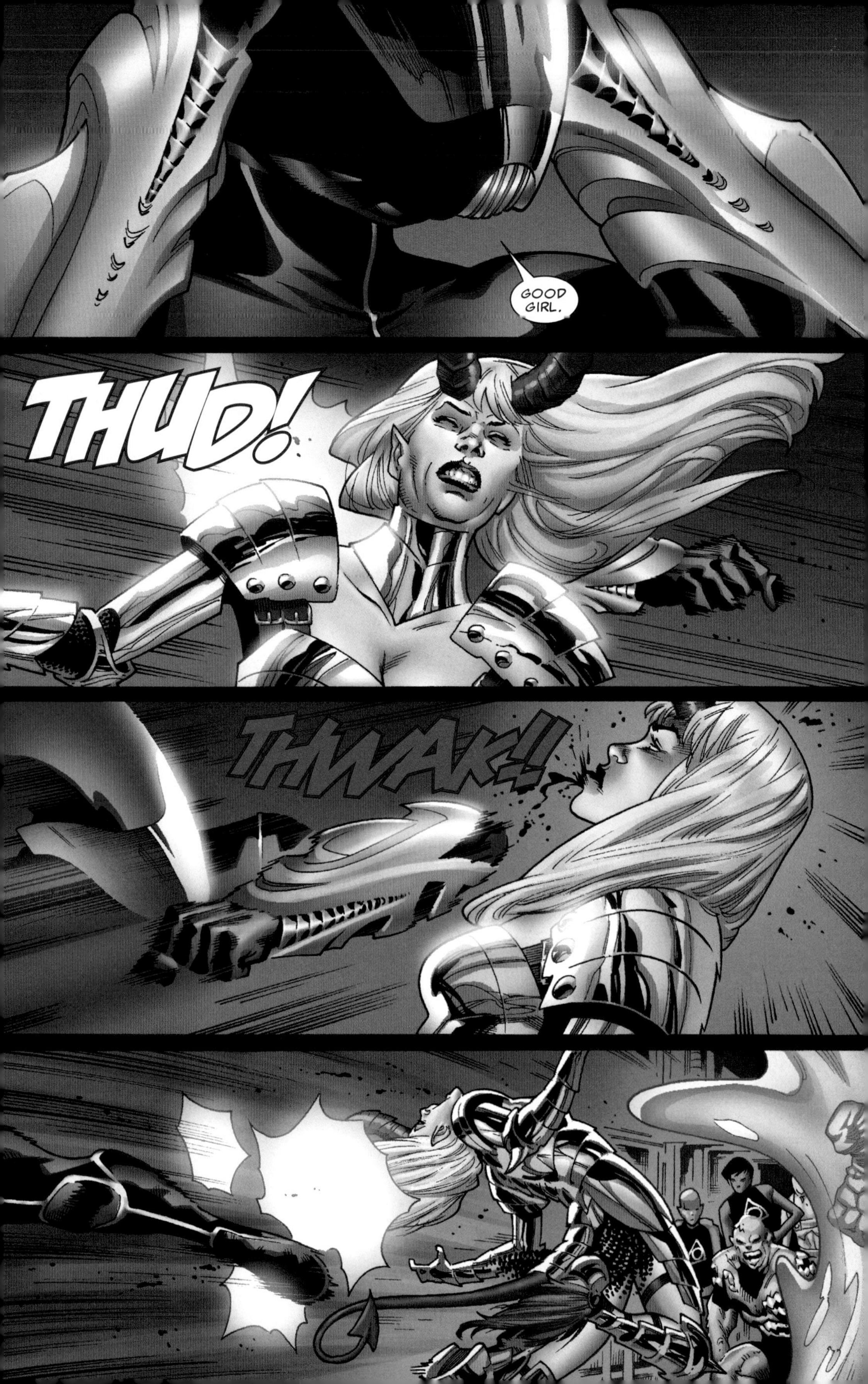
GOOD GIRL.
THUD!
THWAK!!

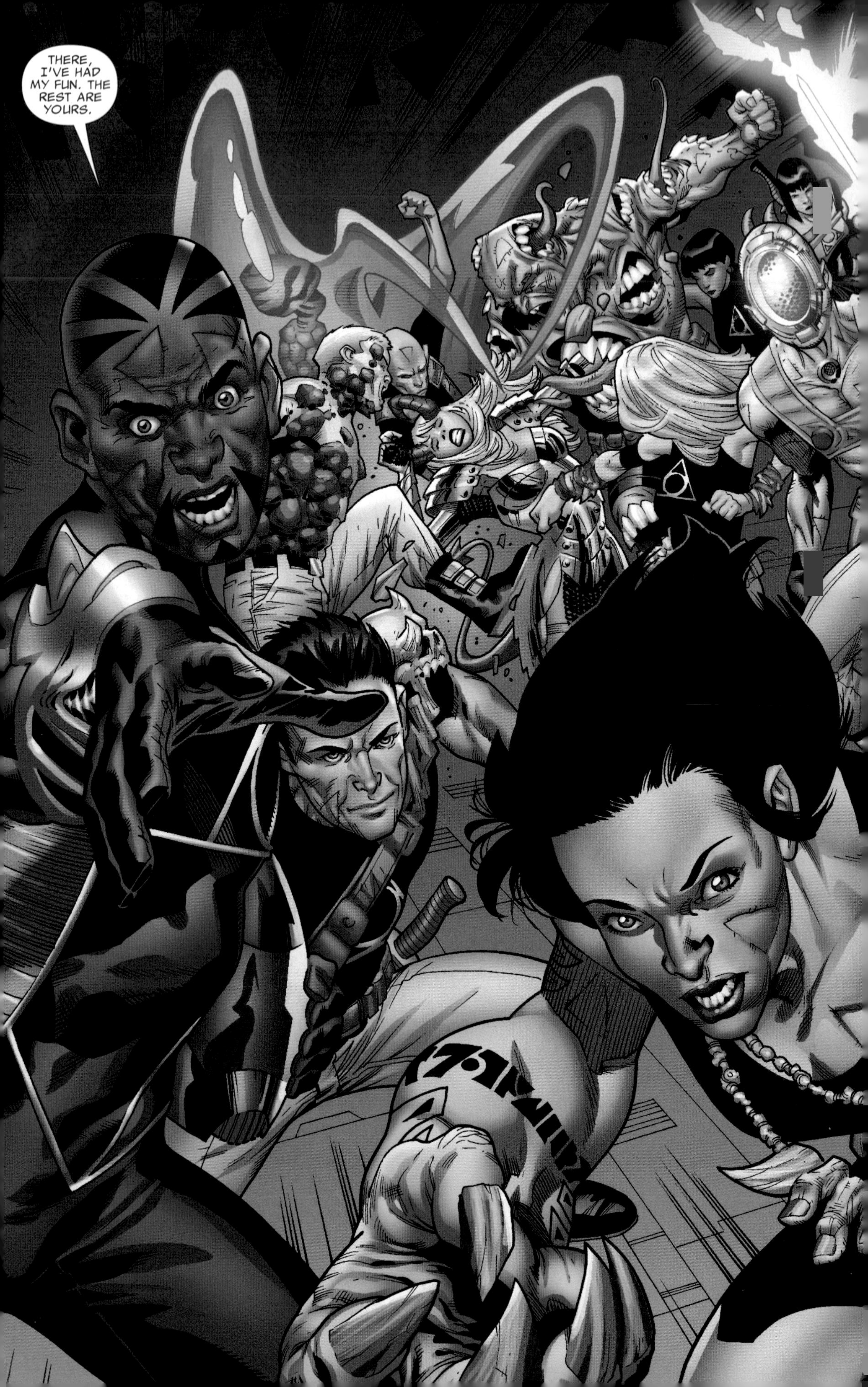
THERE, I'VE HAD MY FUN. THE REST ARE YOURS.

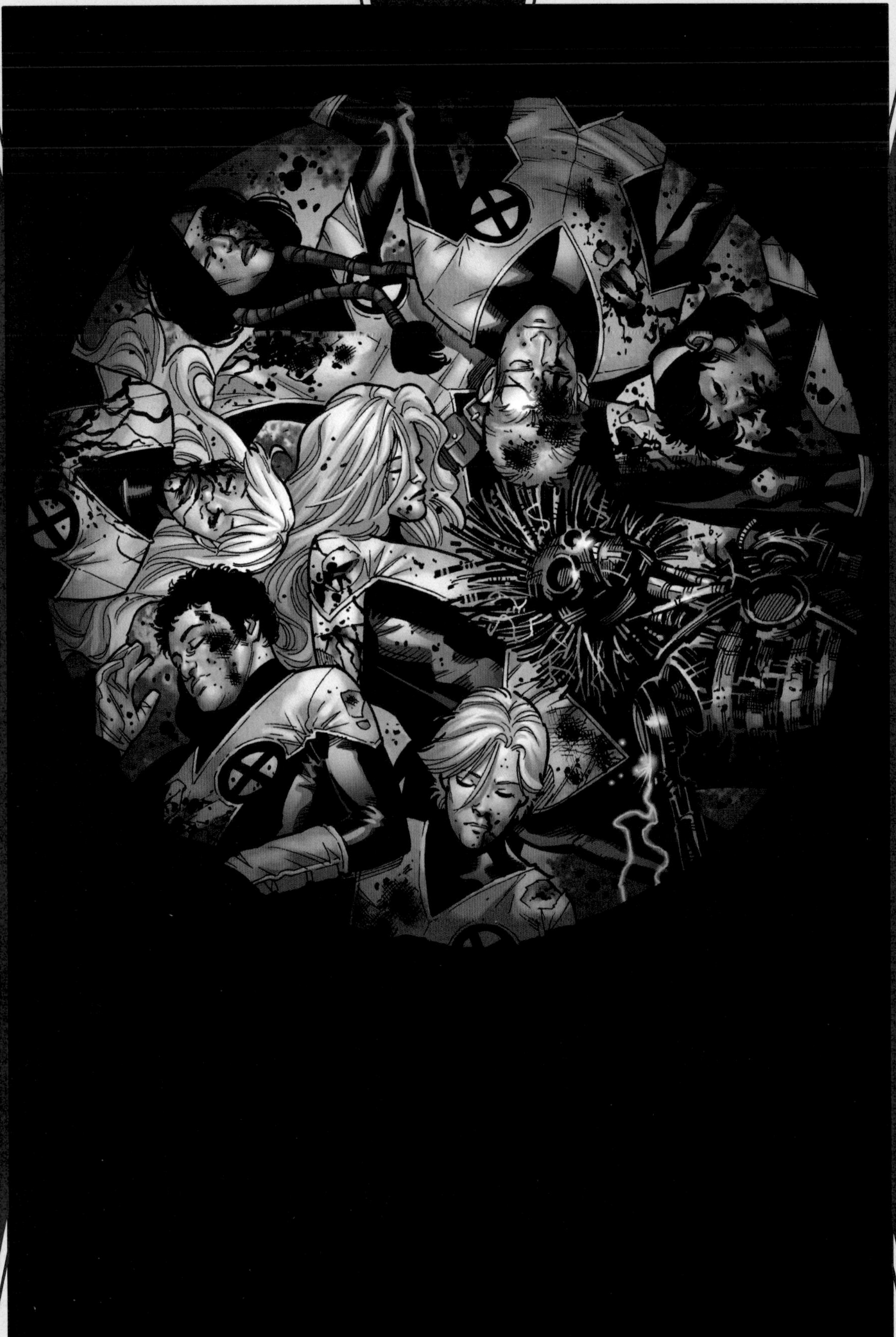

PROMOTIONAL ART
BY LEONARD KIRK & BRIAN REBER

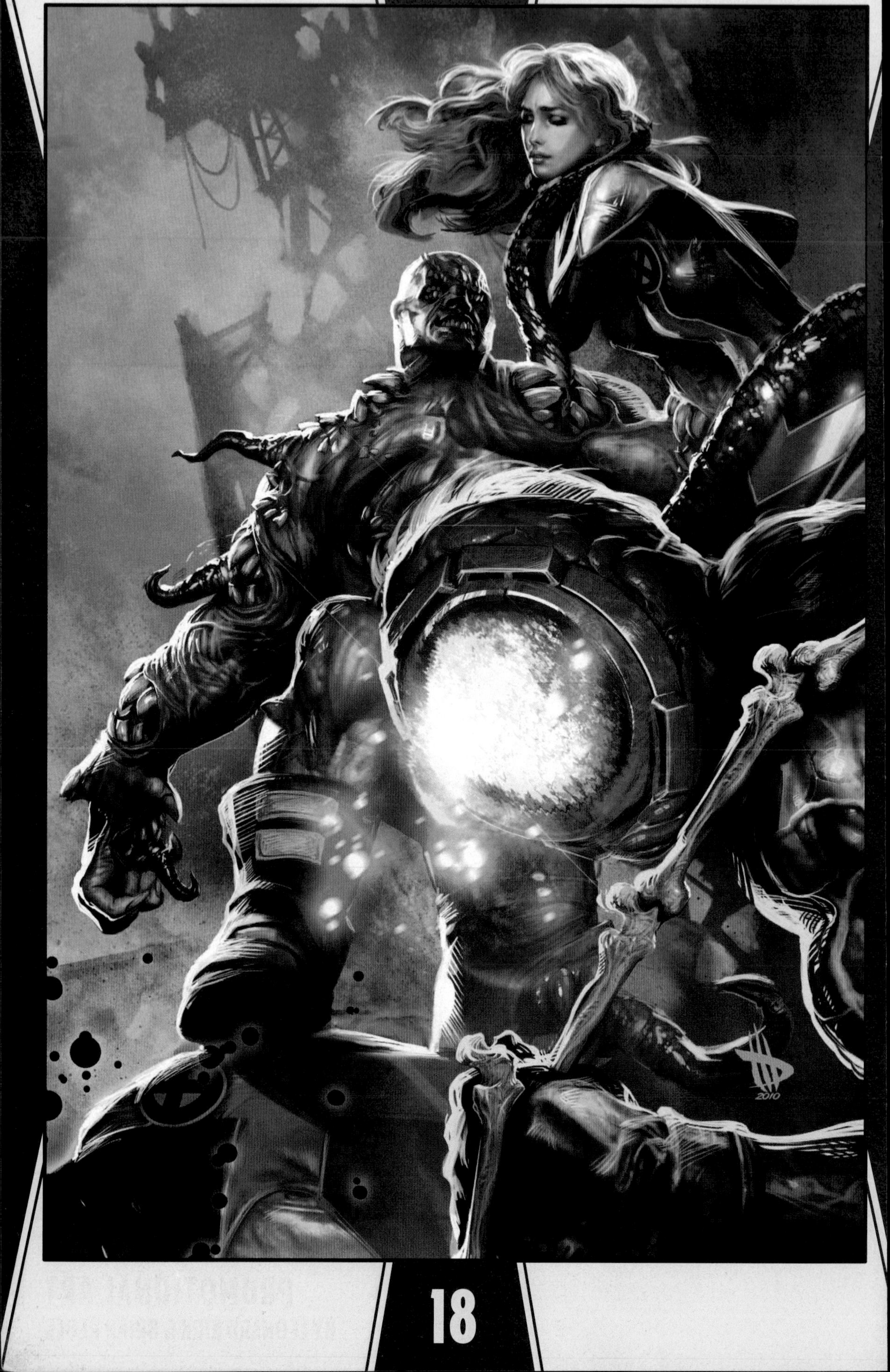

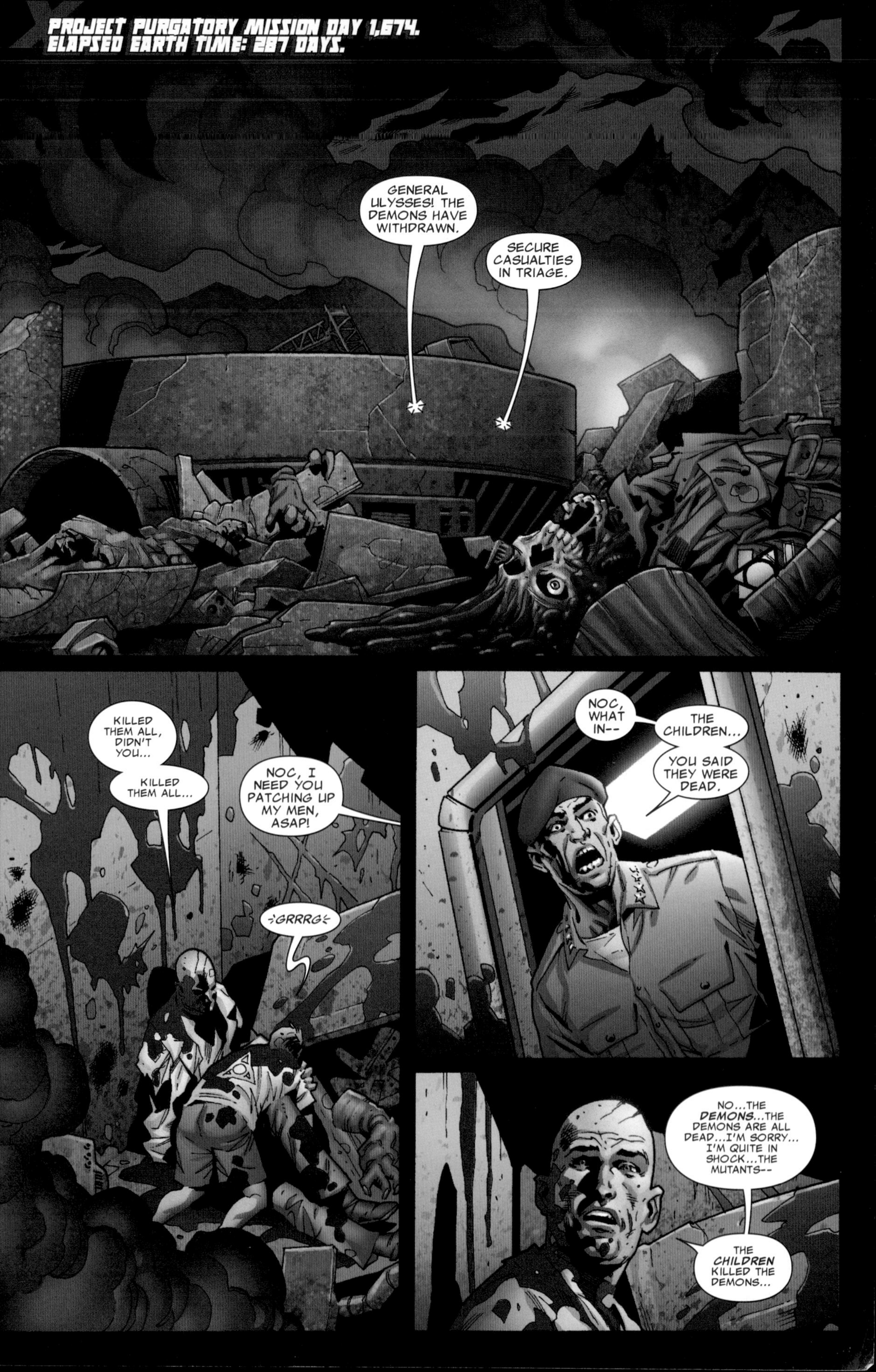
PROJECT PURGATORY MISSION DAY 1,674.
ELAPSED EARTH TIME: 287 DAYS.
GENERAL ULYSSES! THE DEMONS HAVE WITHDRAWN.
SECURE CASUALTIES IN TRIAGE.
KILLED THEM ALL, DIDN'T YOU...
KILLED THEM ALL...
NOC, I NEED YOU PATCHING UP MY MEN, ASAP!
GRRRG
NOC, WHAT IN--
THE CHILDREN...
YOU SAID THEY WERE DEAD.
NO...THE DEMONS...THE DEMONS ARE ALL DEAD...I'M SORRY... I'M QUITE IN SHOCK...THE MUTANTS--
THE CHILDREN KILLED THE DEMONS...

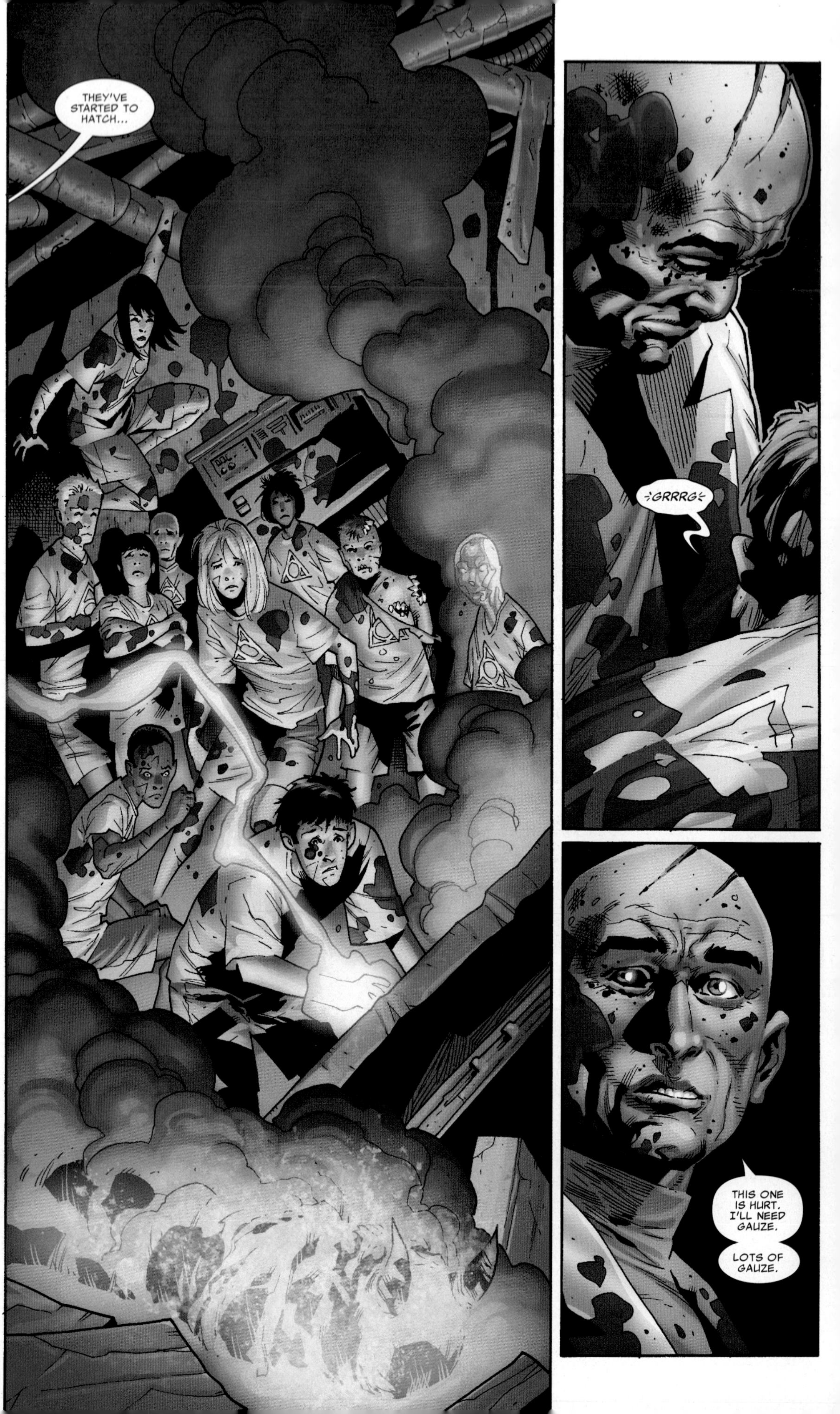
THEY'VE STARTED TO HATCH...
GRRRG
THIS ONE IS HURT. I'LL NEED GAUZE.
LOTS OF GAUZE.

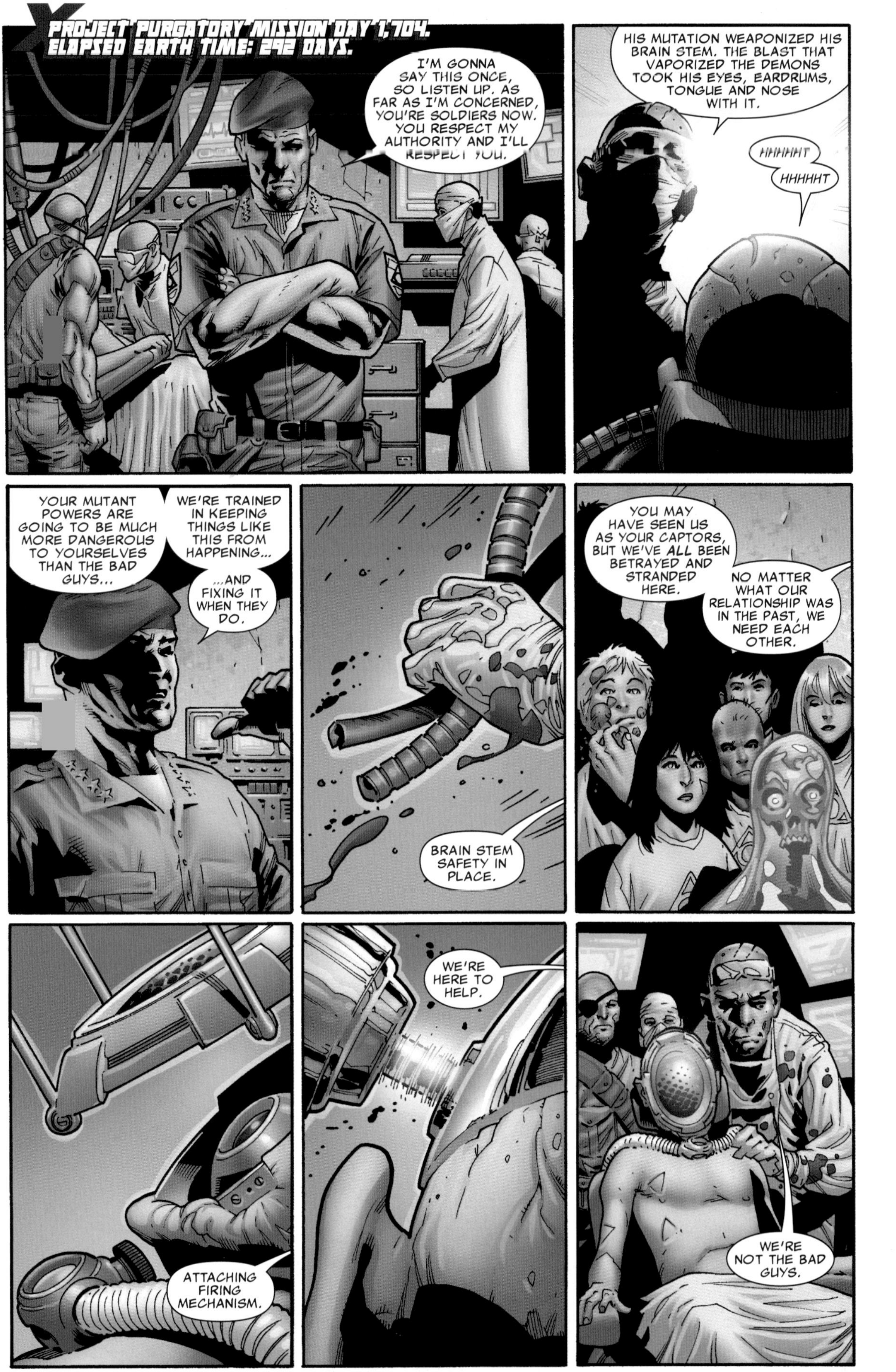
PROJECT PURGATORY MISSION DAY 1,704.
ELAPSED EARTH TIME: 292 DAYS.
I'M GONNA SAY THIS ONCE, SO LISTEN UP. AS FAR AS I'M CONCERNED, YOU'RE SOLDIERS NOW. YOU RESPECT MY AUTHORITY AND I'LL RESPECT YOU.
HIS MUTATION WEAPONIZED HIS BRAIN STEM. THE BLAST THAT VAPORIZED THE DEMONS TOOK HIS EYES, EARDRUMS, TONGUE AND NOSE WITH IT.
HHHHHHT
HHHHHT
YOUR MUTANT POWERS ARE GOING TO BE MUCH MORE DANGEROUS TO YOURSELVES THAN THE BAD GUYS...
WE'RE TRAINED IN KEEPING THINGS LIKE THIS FROM HAPPENING...
...AND FIXING IT WHEN THEY DO.
BRAIN STEM SAFETY IN PLACE.
YOU MAY HAVE SEEN US AS YOUR CAPTORS, BUT WE'VE ALL BEEN BETRAYED AND STRANDED HERE.
NO MATTER WHAT OUR RELATIONSHIP WAS IN THE PAST, WE NEED EACH OTHER.
ATTACHING FIRING MECHANISM.
WE'RE HERE TO HELP.
WE'RE NOT THE BAD GUYS.

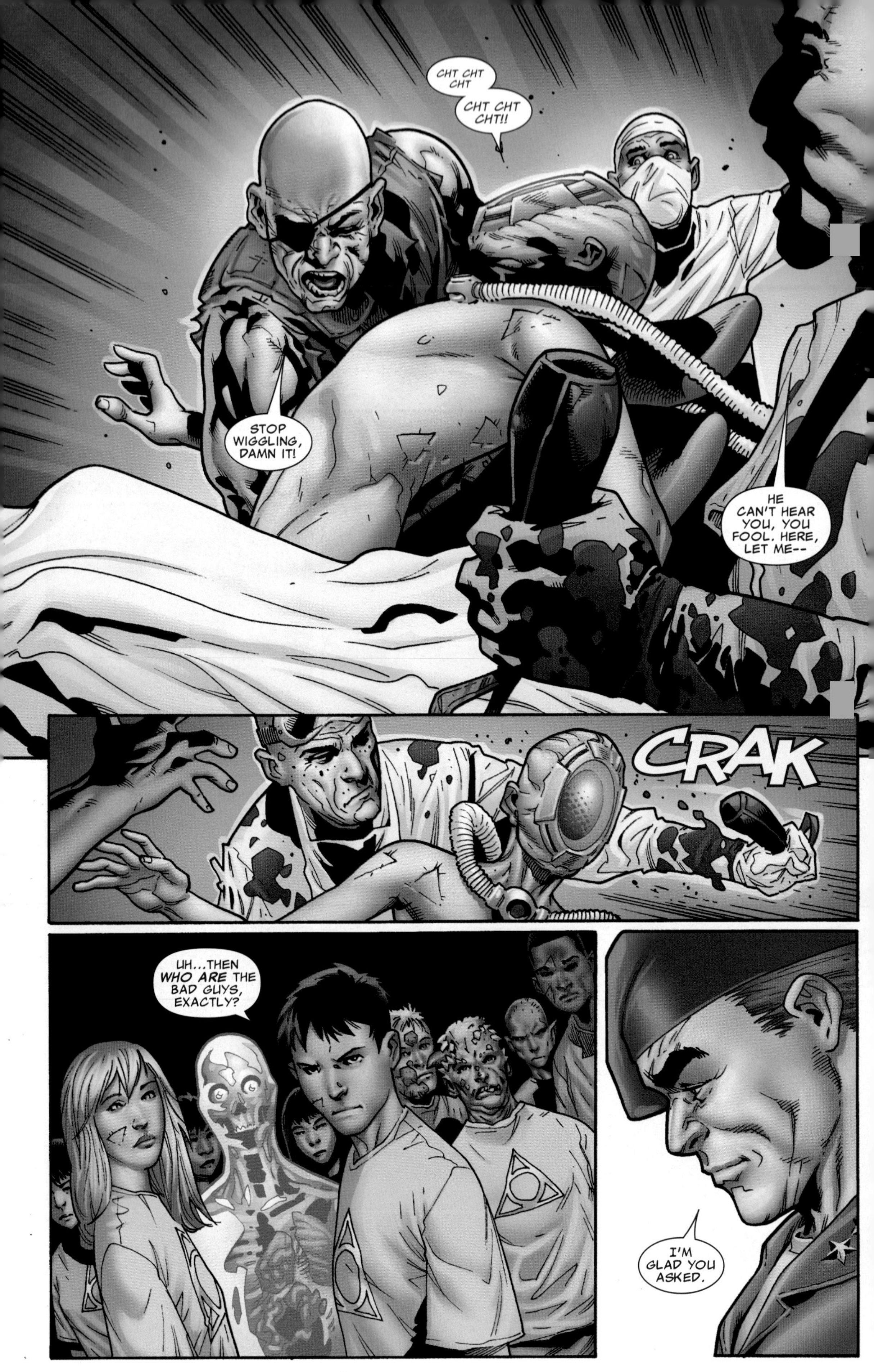
CHT CHT CHT
CHT CHT CHT!!
STOP WIGGLING, DAMN IT!
HE CAN'T HEAR YOU, YOU FOOL. HERE, LET ME--
CRAK
UH...THEN WHO ARE THE BAD GUYS, EXACTLY?
I'M GLAD YOU ASKED.

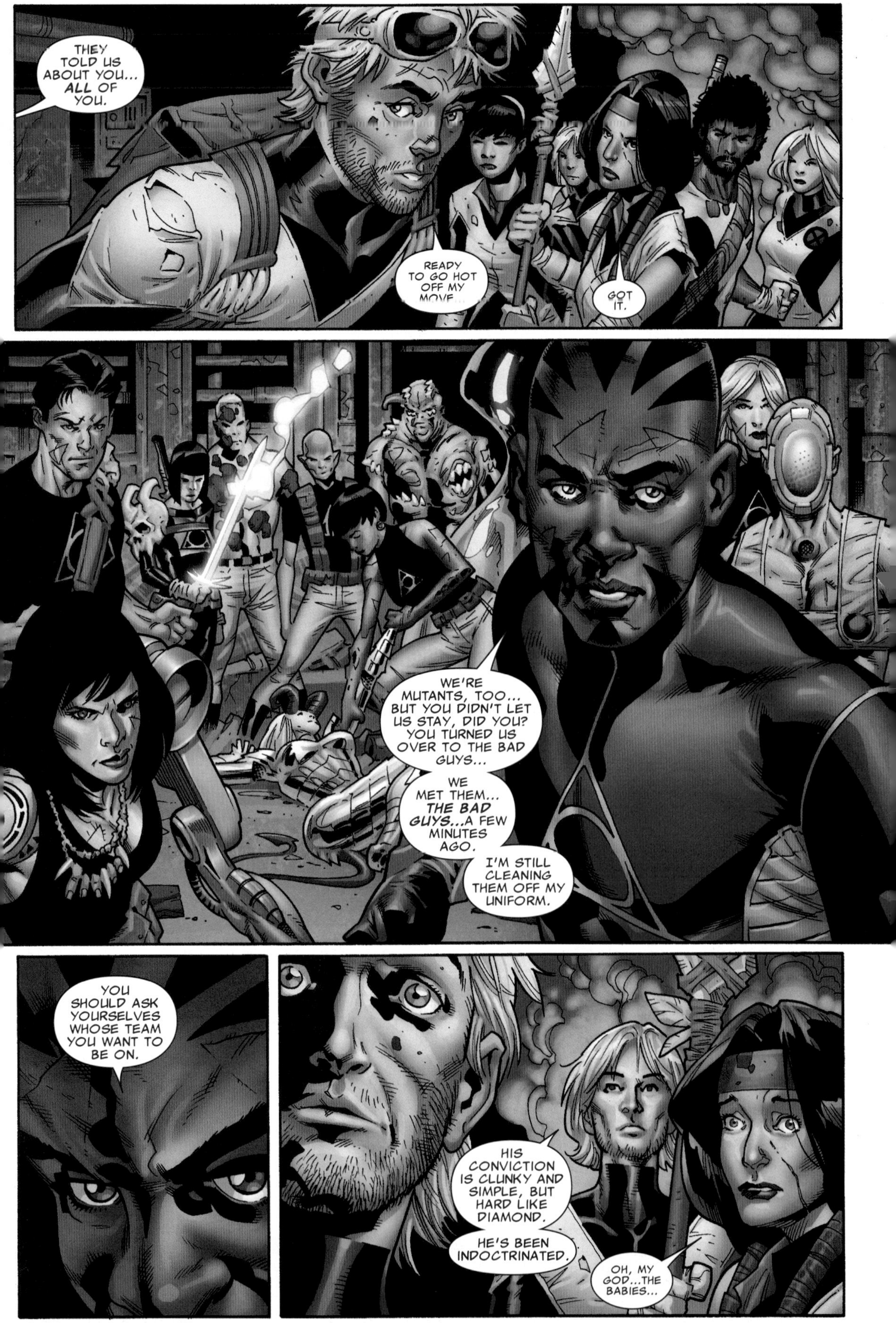
THEY TOLD US ABOUT YOU... ALL OF YOU.
READY TO GO HOT OFF MY MOVE...
GOT IT.
WE'RE MUTANTS, TOO... BUT YOU DIDN'T LET US STAY, DID YOU? YOU TURNED US OVER TO THE BAD GUYS...
WE MET THEM... THE BAD GUYS...A FEW MINUTES AGO.
I'M STILL CLEANING THEM OFF MY UNIFORM.
YOU SHOULD ASK YOURSELVES WHOSE TEAM YOU WANT TO BE ON.
HIS CONVICTION IS CLUNKY AND SIMPLE, BUT HARD LIKE DIAMOND.
HE'S BEEN INDOCTRINATED.
OH, MY GOD...THE BABIES...

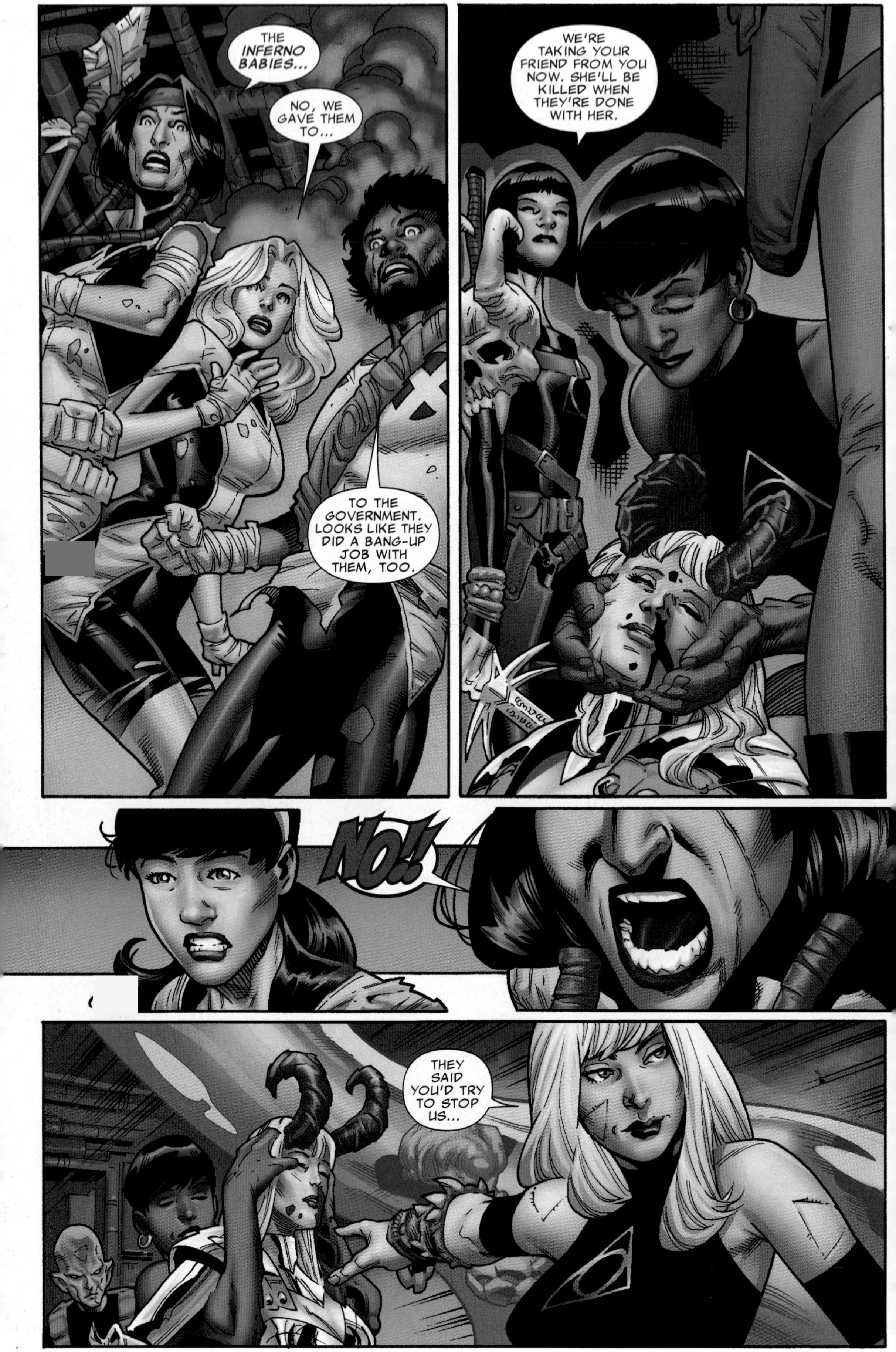
THE INFERNO BABIES...
NO, WE GAVE THEM TO...
TO THE GOVERNMENT. LOOKS LIKE THEY DID A BANG-UP JOB WITH THEM, TOO.
WE'RE TAKING YOUR FRIEND FROM YOU NOW. SHE'LL BE KILLED WHEN THEY'RE DONE WITH HER.
NO!!
THEY SAID YOU'D TRY TO STOP US...

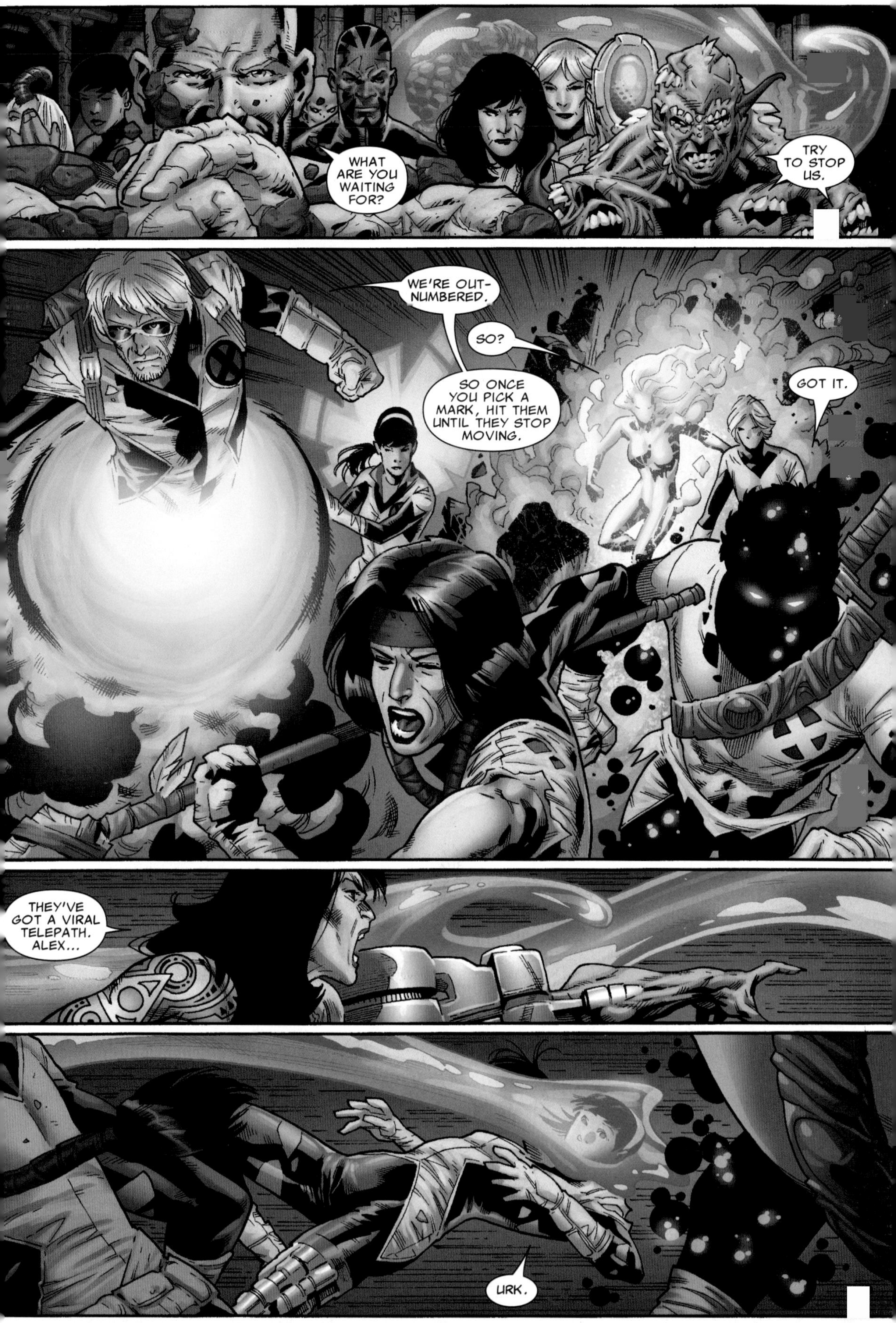
WHAT ARE YOU WAITING FOR?
TRY TO STOP US.
WE'RE OUT-NUMBERED.
SO?
SO ONCE YOU PICK A MARK, HIT THEM UNTIL THEY STOP MOVING.
GOT IT.
THEY'VE GOT A VIRAL TELEPATH. ALEX...
URK.

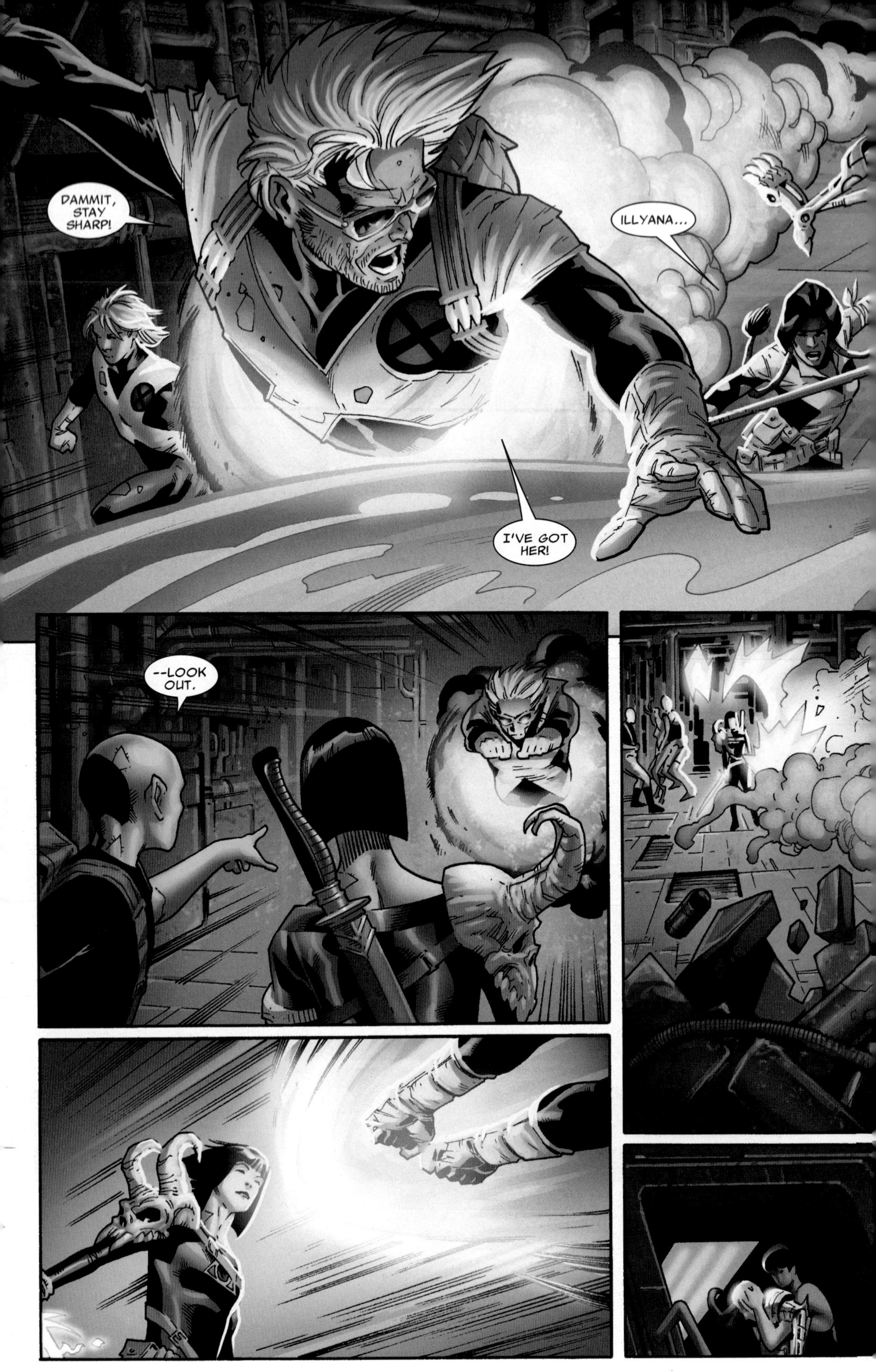

DAMMIT, STAY SHARP!
ILLYANA...
I'VE GOT HER!
--LOOK OUT.

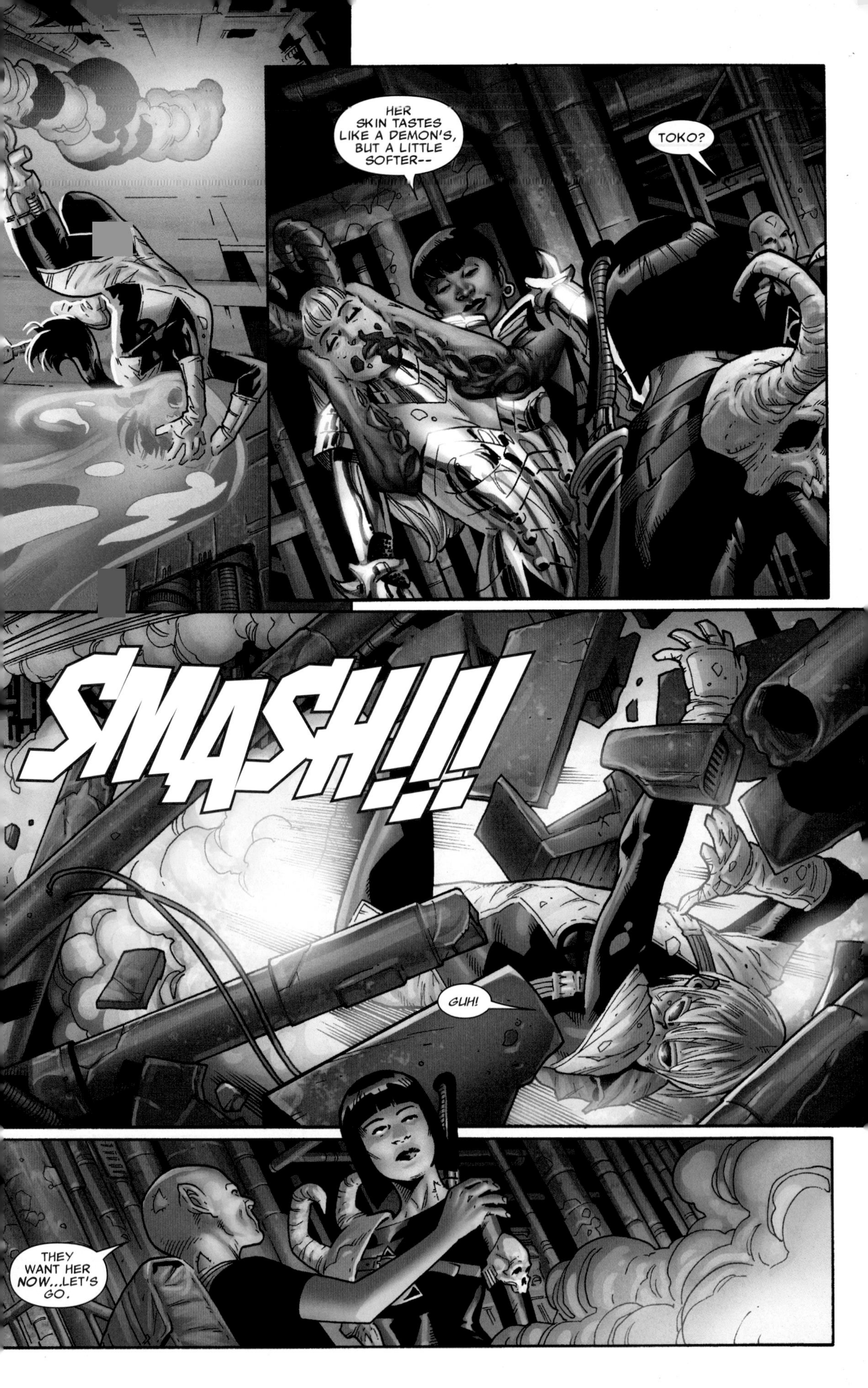
HER SKIN TASTES LIKE A DEMON'S, BUT A LITTLE SOFTER--
TOKO?
SMASH!!!
GUH!
THEY WANT HER NOW...LET'S GO.

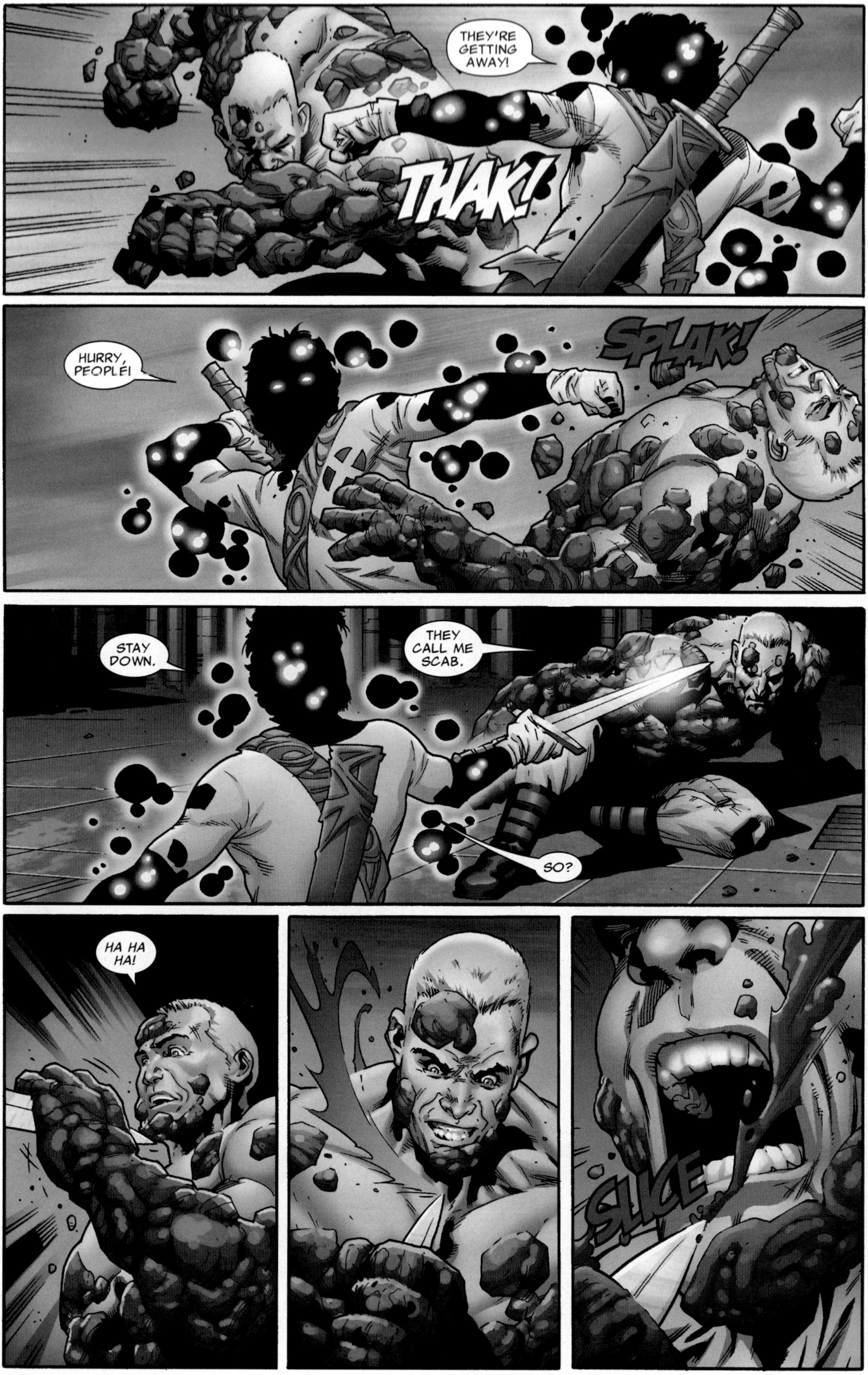
THEY'RE GETTING AWAY!
THAK!
HURRY, PEOPLE!
SPLAK!
STAY DOWN.
THEY CALL ME SCAB.
SO?
HA HA HA!
SLICE

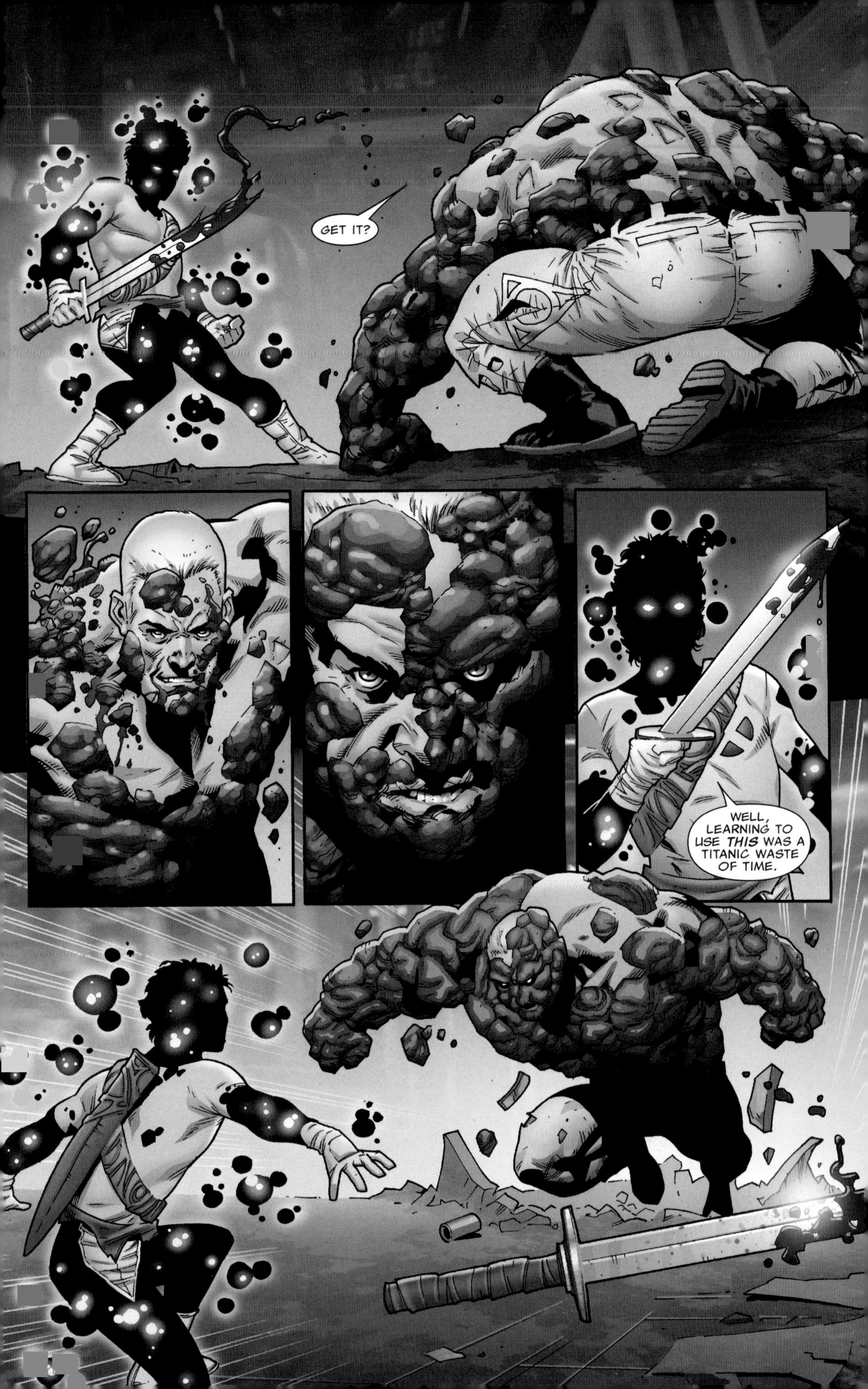
GET IT?
WELL, LEARNING TO USE *THIS* WAS A TITANIC WASTE OF TIME.

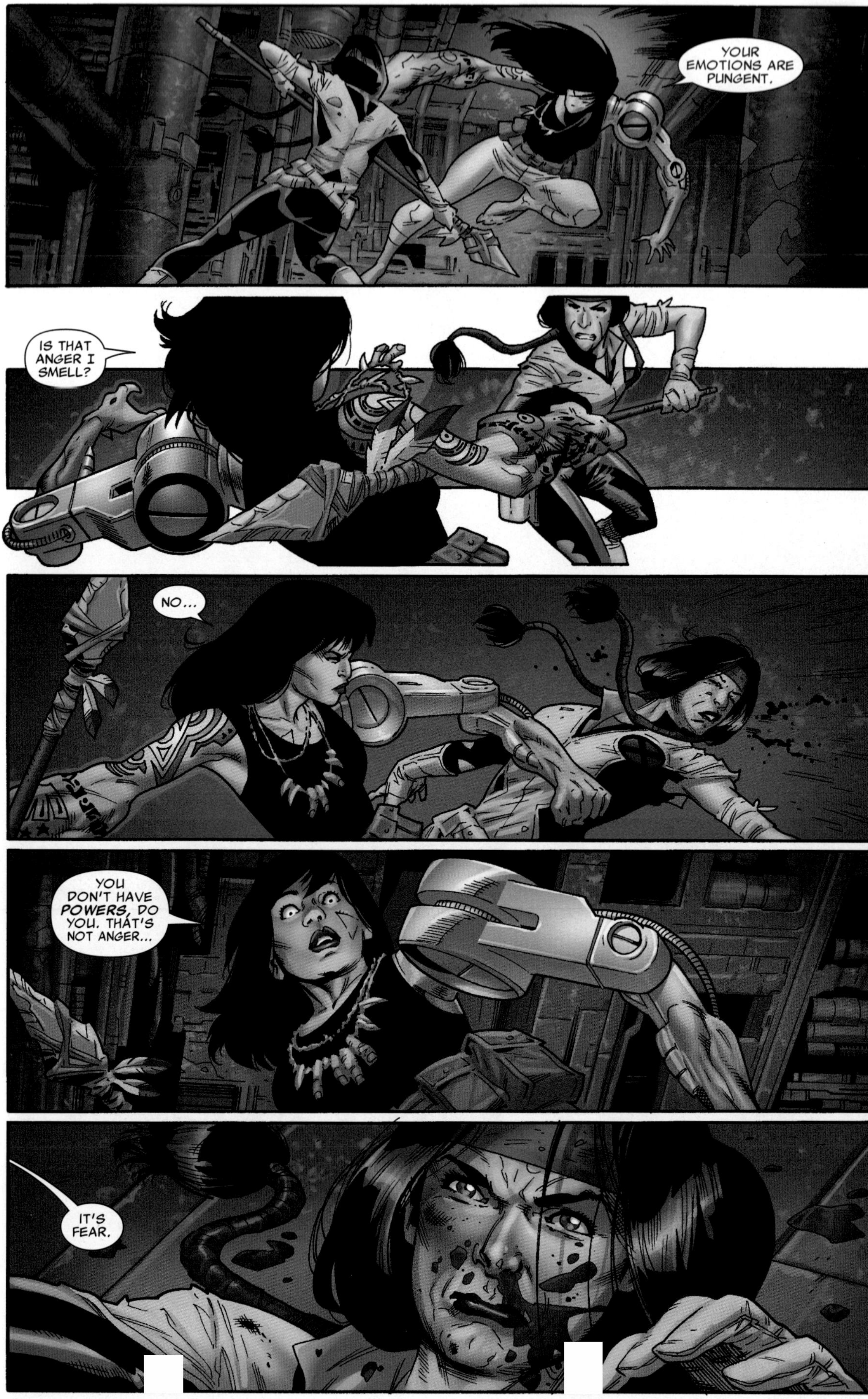
YOUR EMOTIONS ARE PUNGENT.
IS THAT ANGER I SMELL?
NO...
YOU DON'T HAVE POWERS, DO YOU. THAT'S NOT ANGER...
IT'S FEAR.

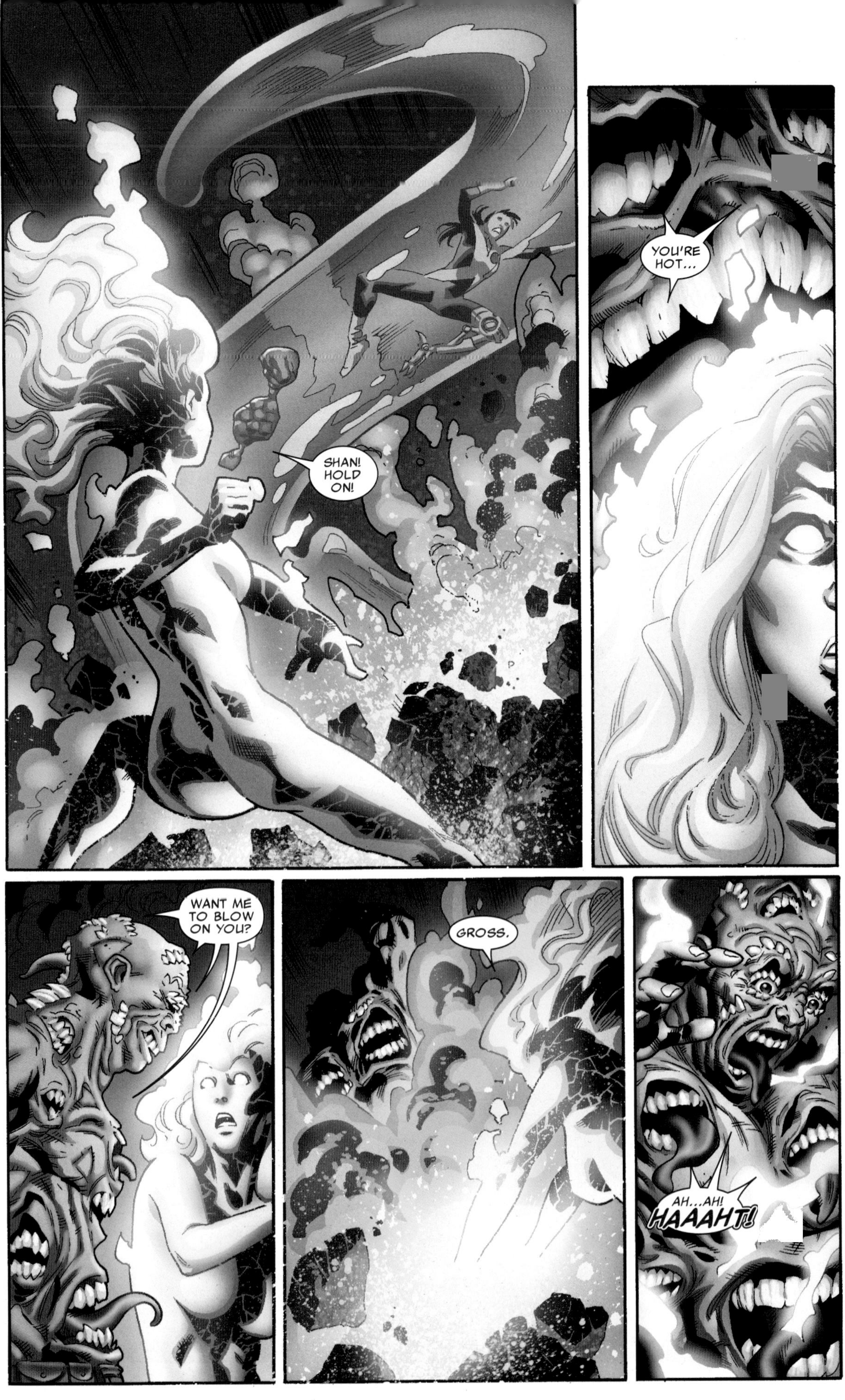
SHAN! HOLD ON!
YOU'RE HOT...
WANT ME TO BLOW ON YOU?
GROSS.
AH...AH! HAAAHT!

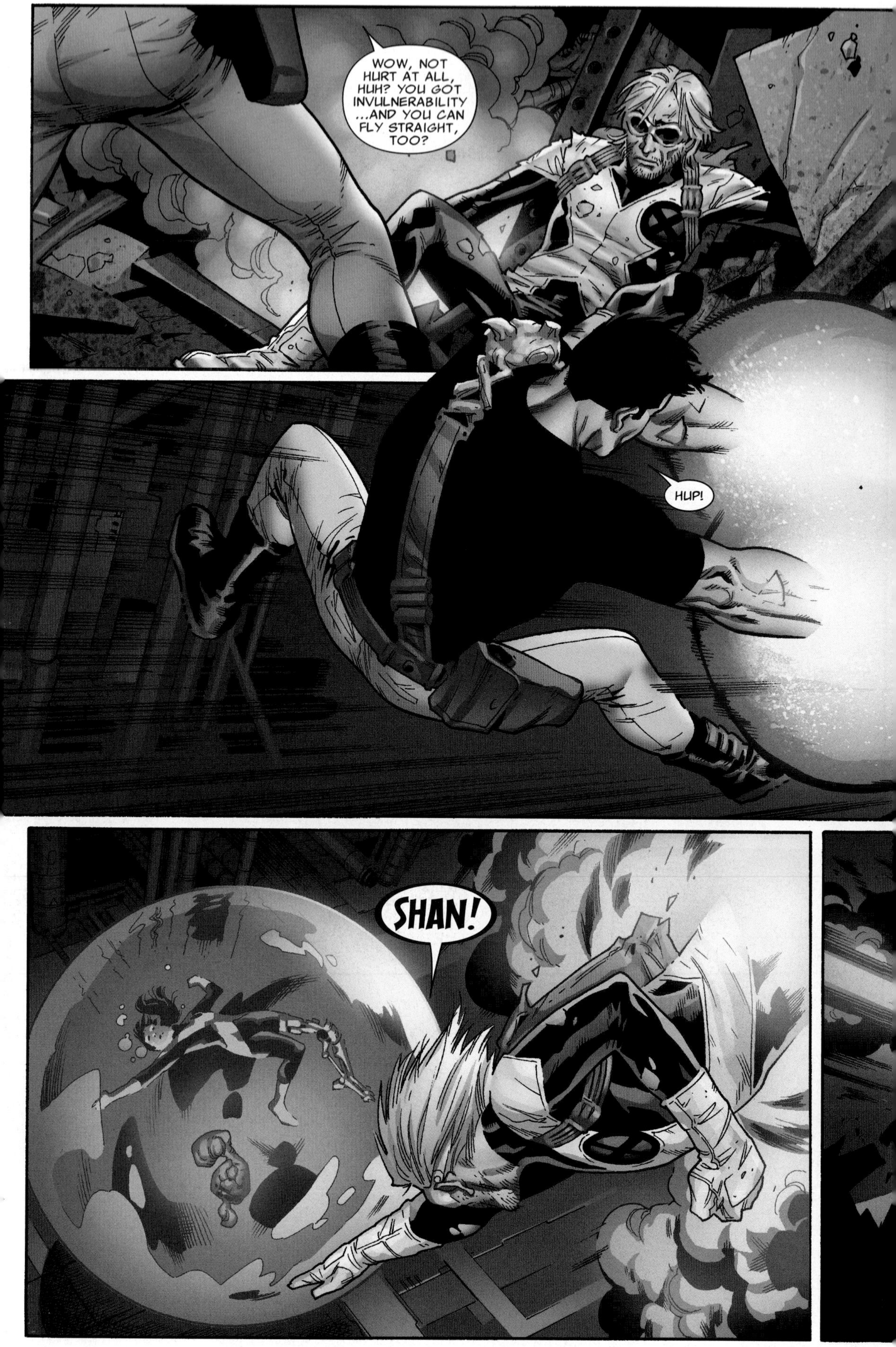
WOW, NOT HURT AT ALL, HUH? YOU GOT INVULNERABILITY ...AND YOU CAN FLY STRAIGHT, TOO?
HUP!
SHAN!

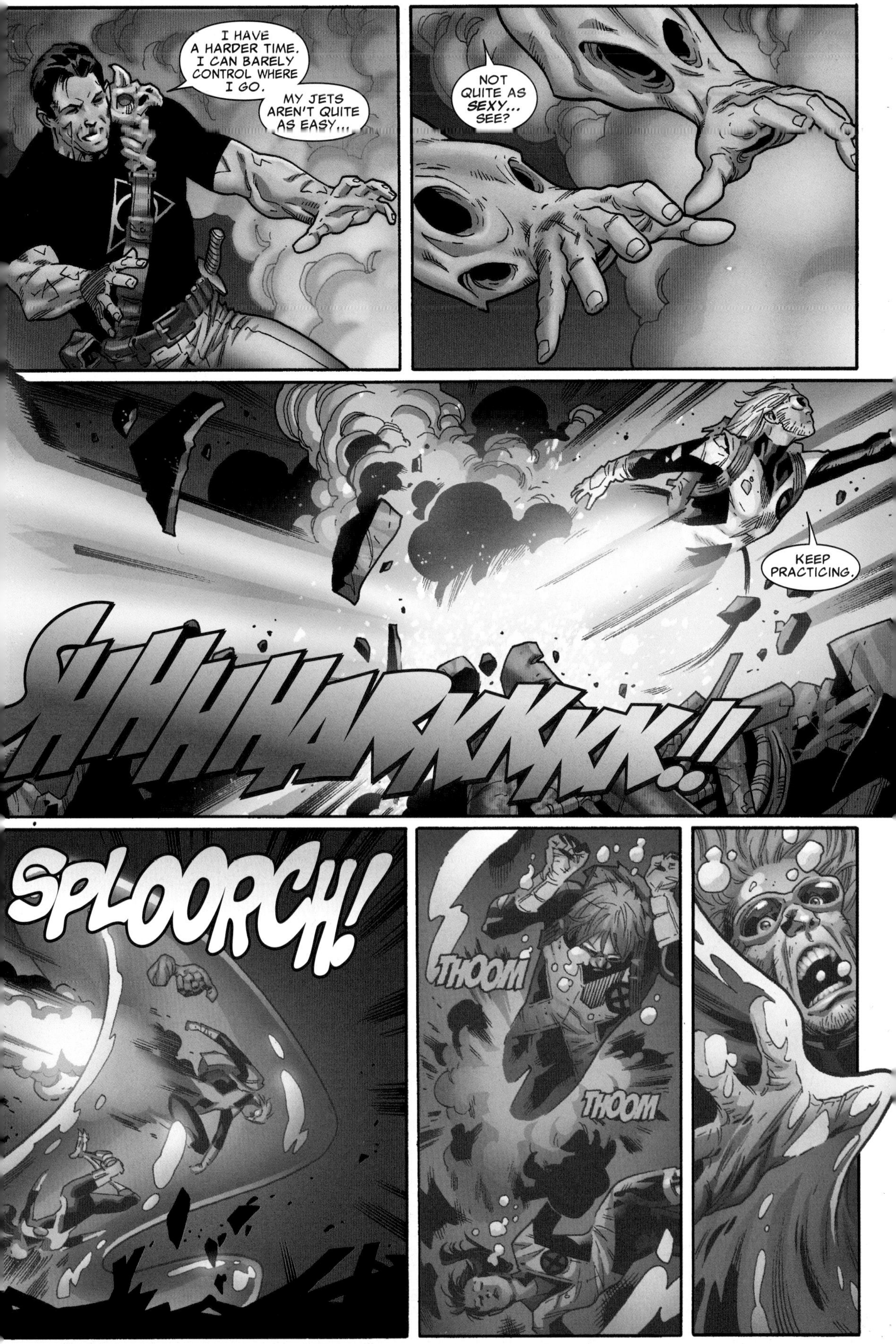

I HAVE A HARDER TIME. I CAN BARELY CONTROL WHERE I GO.
MY JETS AREN'T QUITE AS EASY...
NOT QUITE AS SEXY... SEE?
KEEP PRACTICING.
SHHHAKKKKK!!
SPLOORCH!
THOOM
THOOM

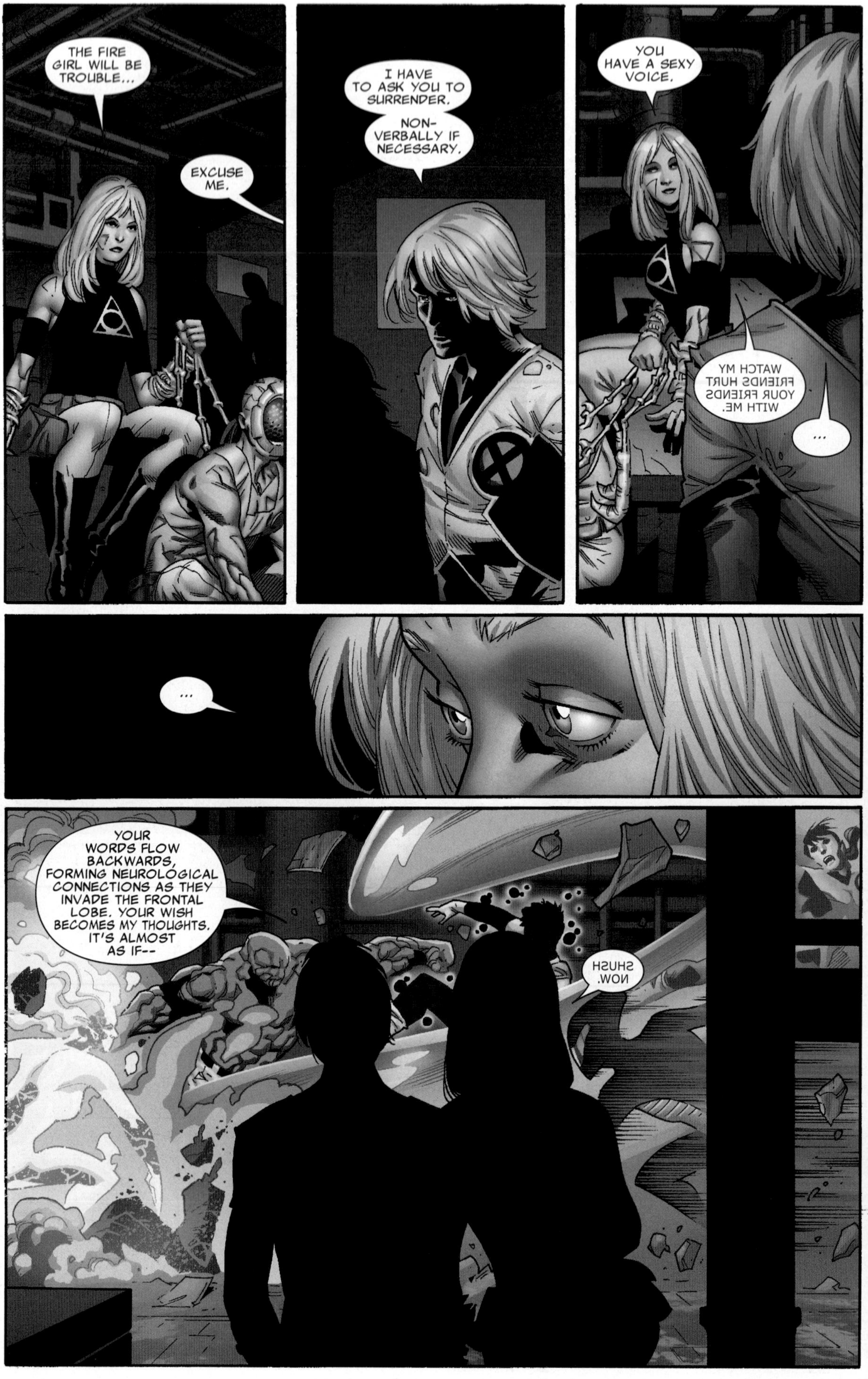
THE FIRE GIRL WILL BE TROUBLE...
EXCUSE ME.
I HAVE TO ASK YOU TO SURRENDER.
NON-VERBALLY IF NECESSARY.
YOU HAVE A SEXY VOICE.
WATCH MY FRIENDS HURT YOUR FRIENDS WITH ME.
...
...
YOUR WORDS FLOW BACKWARDS, FORMING NEUROLOGICAL CONNECTIONS AS THEY INVADE THE FRONTAL LOBE. YOUR WISH BECOMES MY THOUGHTS. IT'S ALMOST AS IF--
SHUSH NOW.

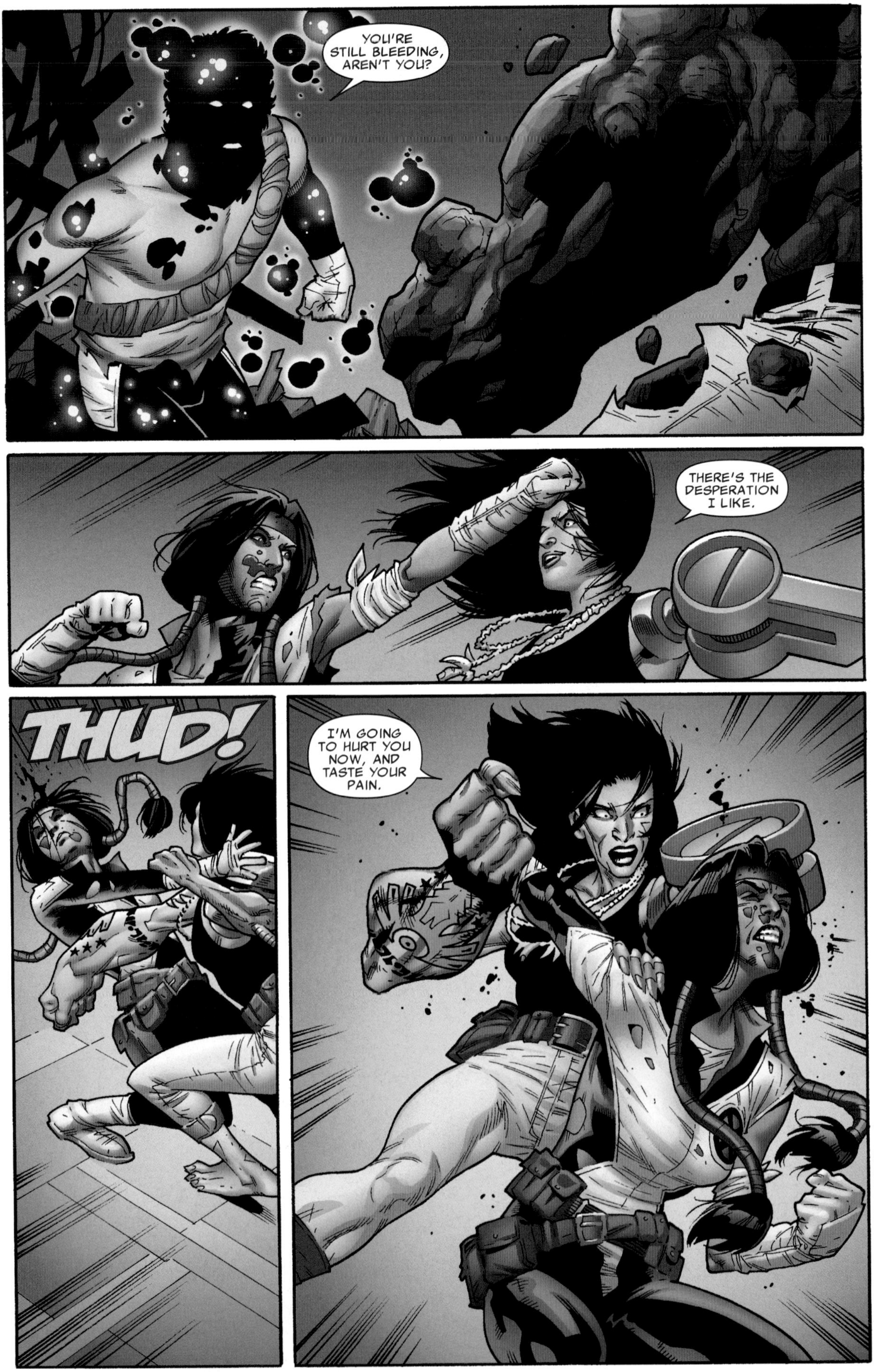
YOU'RE STILL BLEEDING, AREN'T YOU?
THERE'S THE DESPERATION I LIKE.
THUD!
I'M GOING TO HURT YOU NOW, AND TASTE YOUR PAIN.

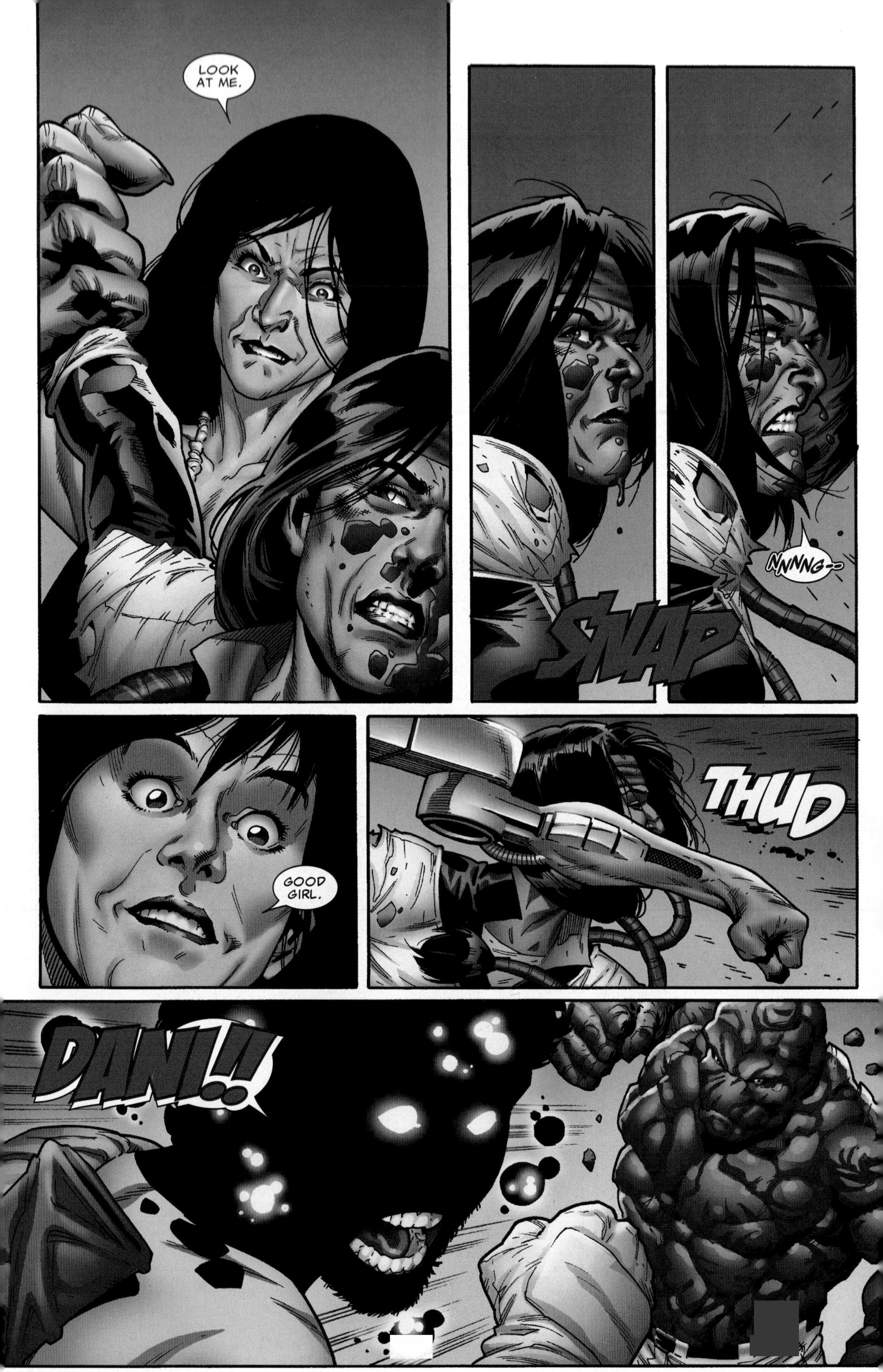
LOOK AT ME.
SNAP
NNNNG--
GOOD GIRL.
THUD
DANI!!

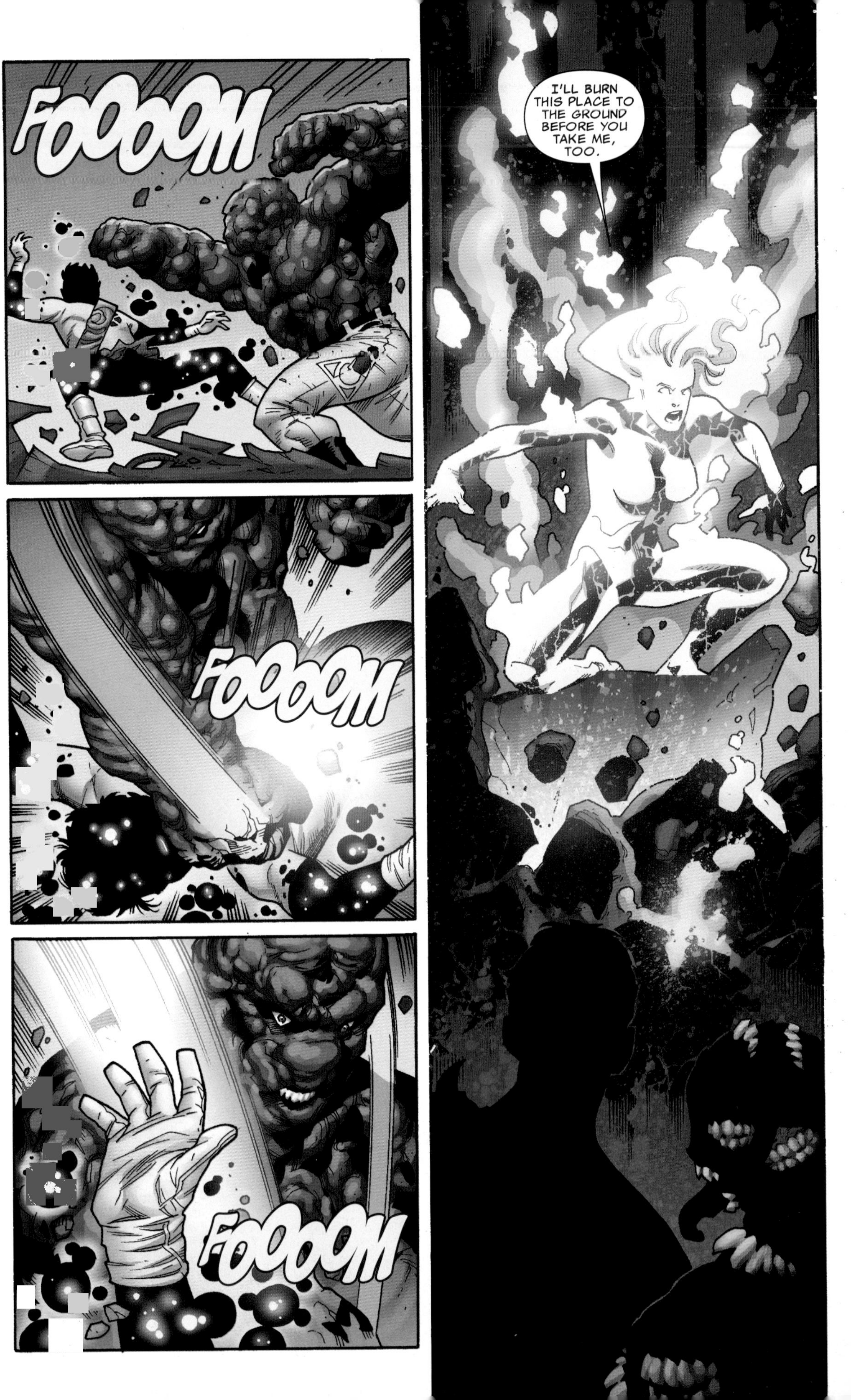
FOOOOM
FOOOOM
FOOOOM
I'LL BURN THIS PLACE TO THE GROUND BEFORE YOU TAKE ME, TOO.

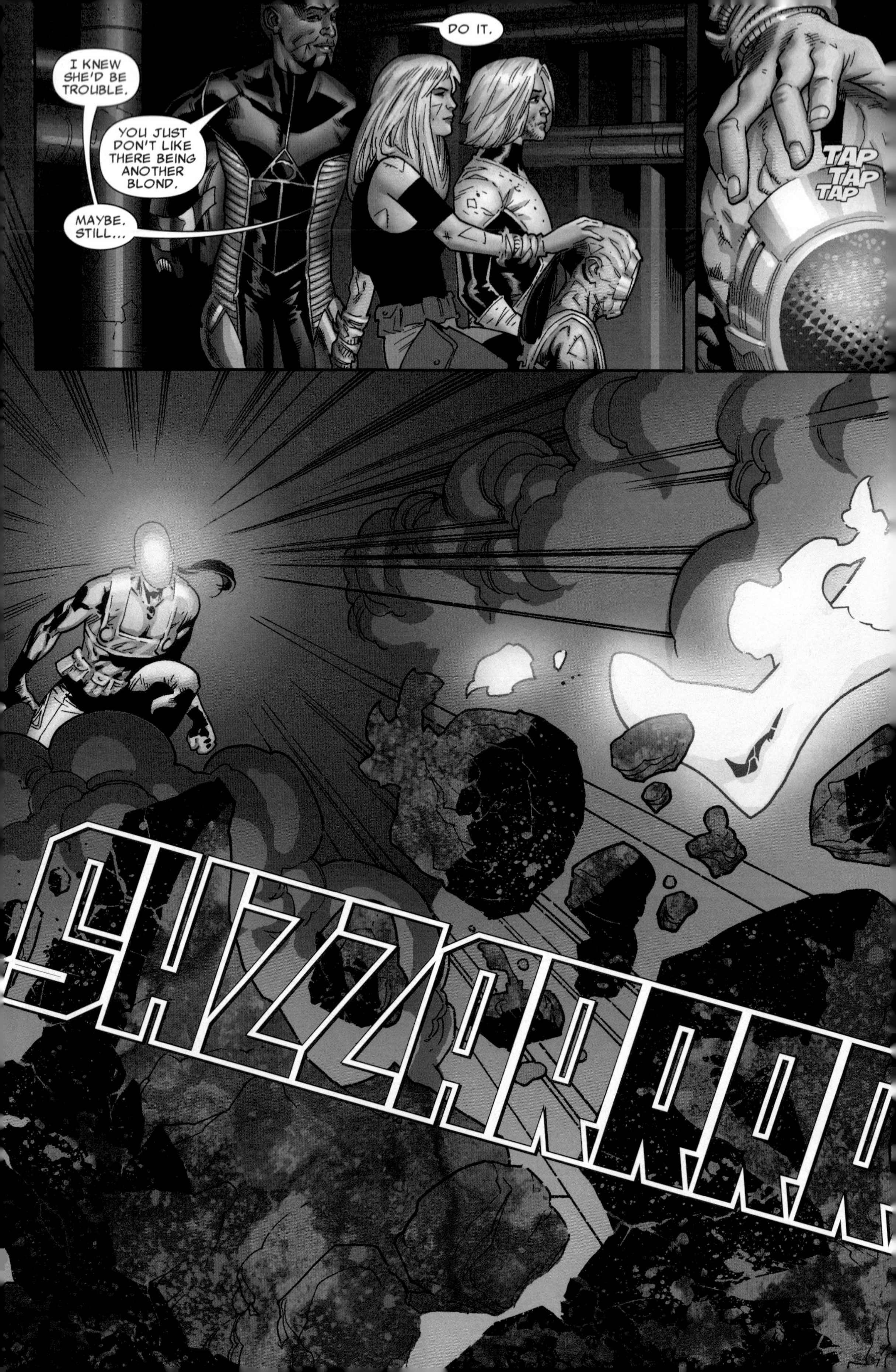
I KNEW SHE'D BE TROUBLE.
YOU JUST DON'T LIKE THERE BEING ANOTHER BLOND.
MAYBE. STILL...
DO IT.
TAP TAP TAP

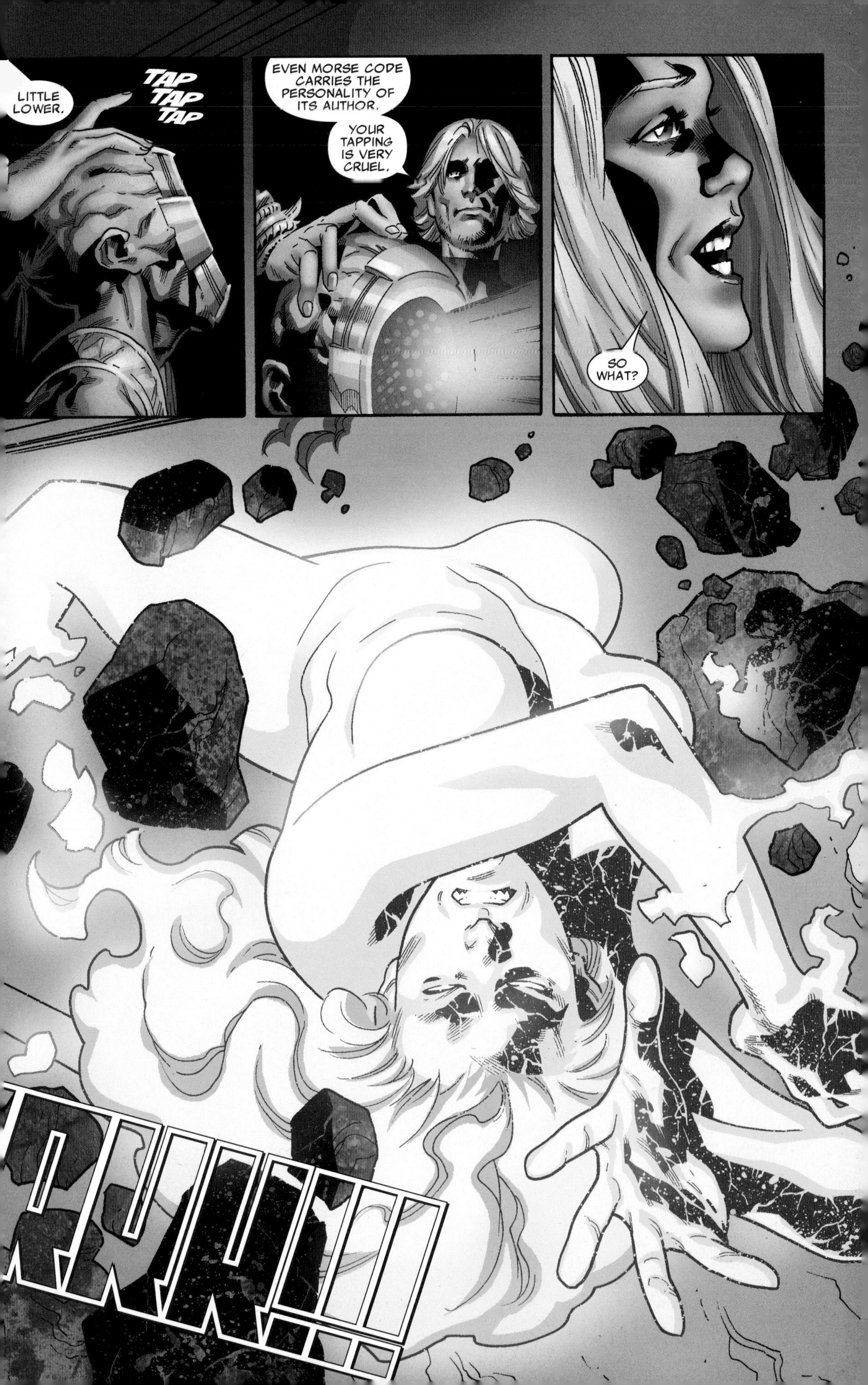
LITTLE LOWER.
TAP TAP TAP
EVEN MORSE CODE CARRIES THE PERSONALITY OF ITS AUTHOR.
YOUR TAPPING IS VERY CRUEL.
SO WHAT?

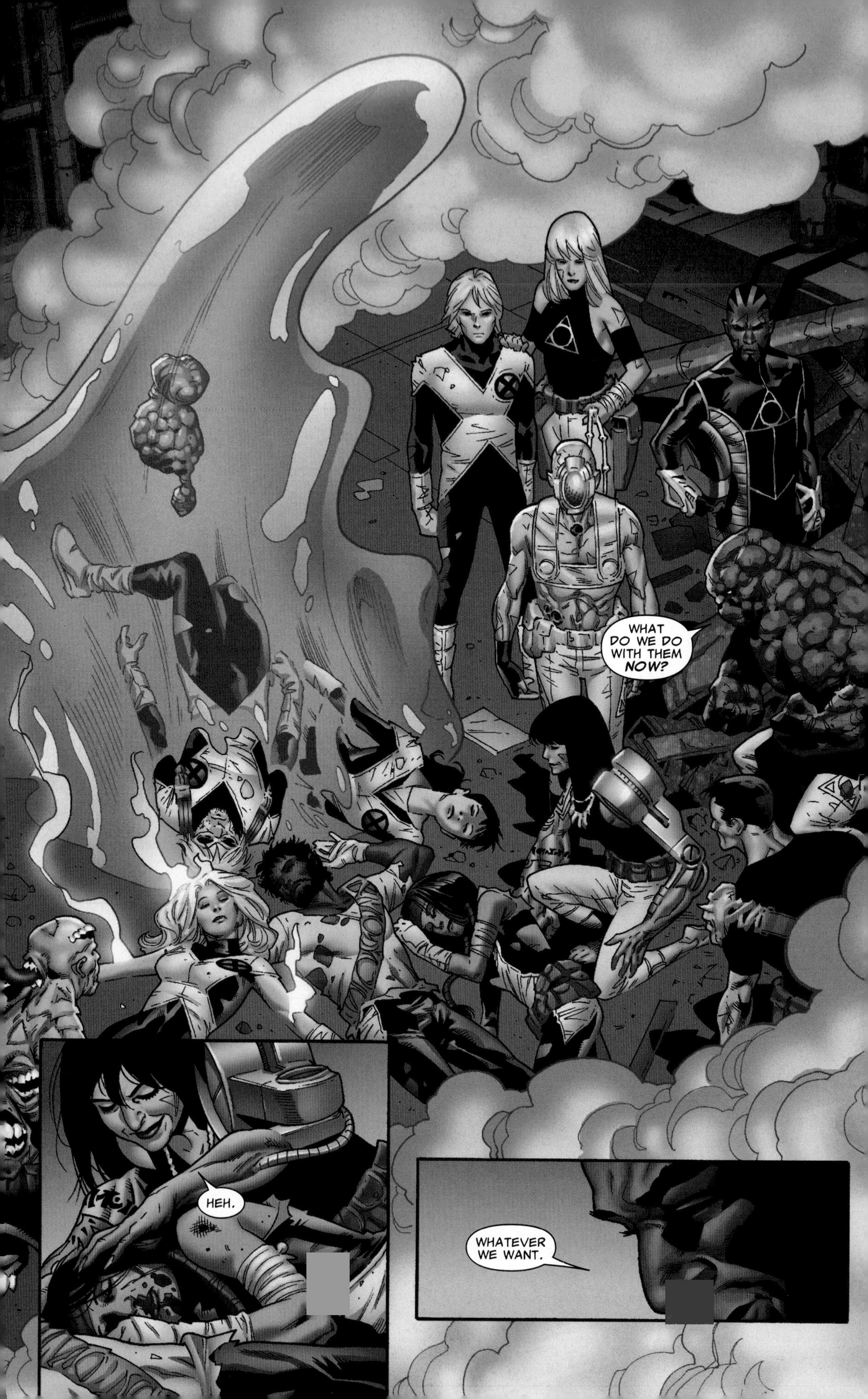
WHAT DO WE DO WITH THEM NOW?
HEH.
WHATEVER WE WANT.

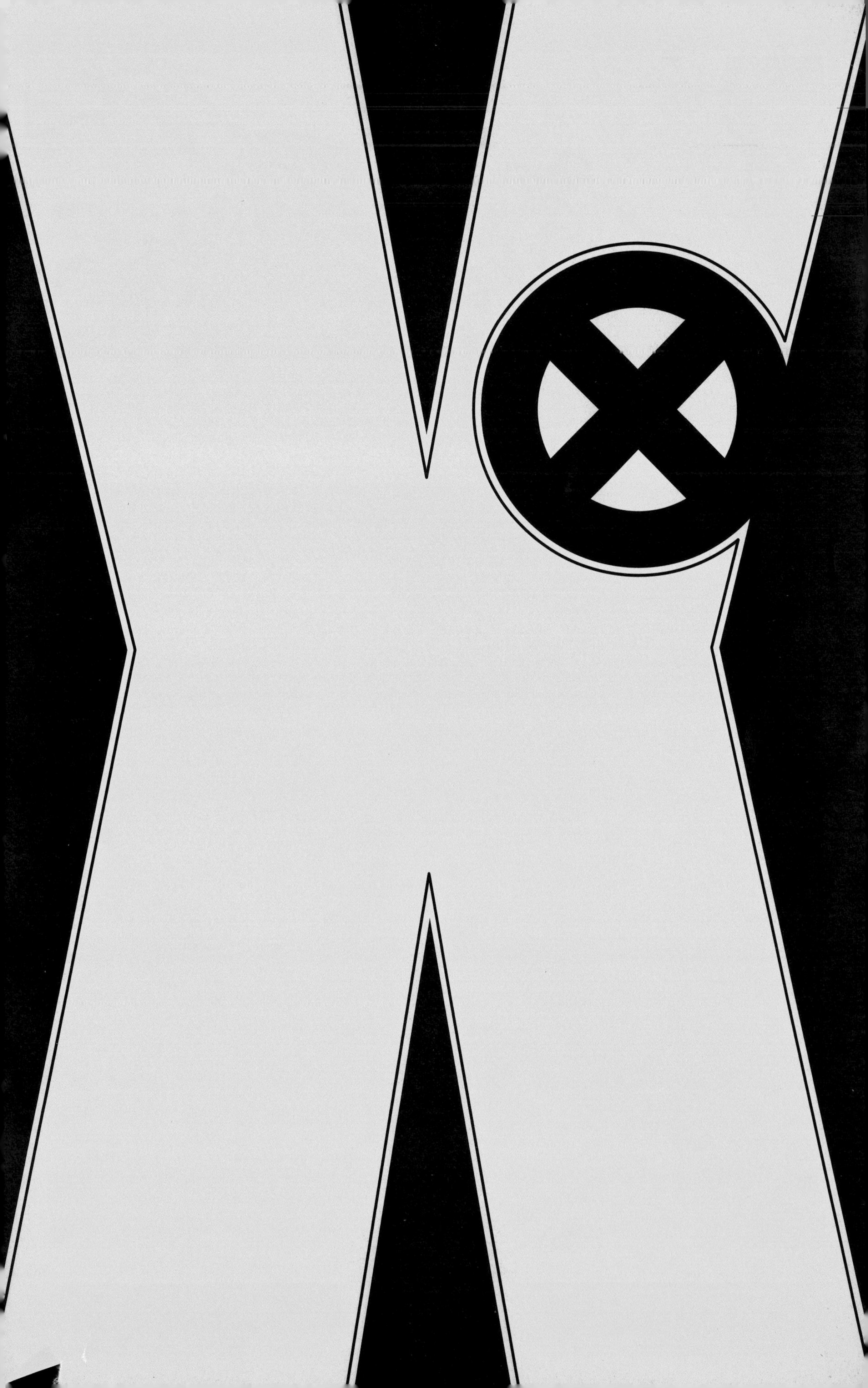

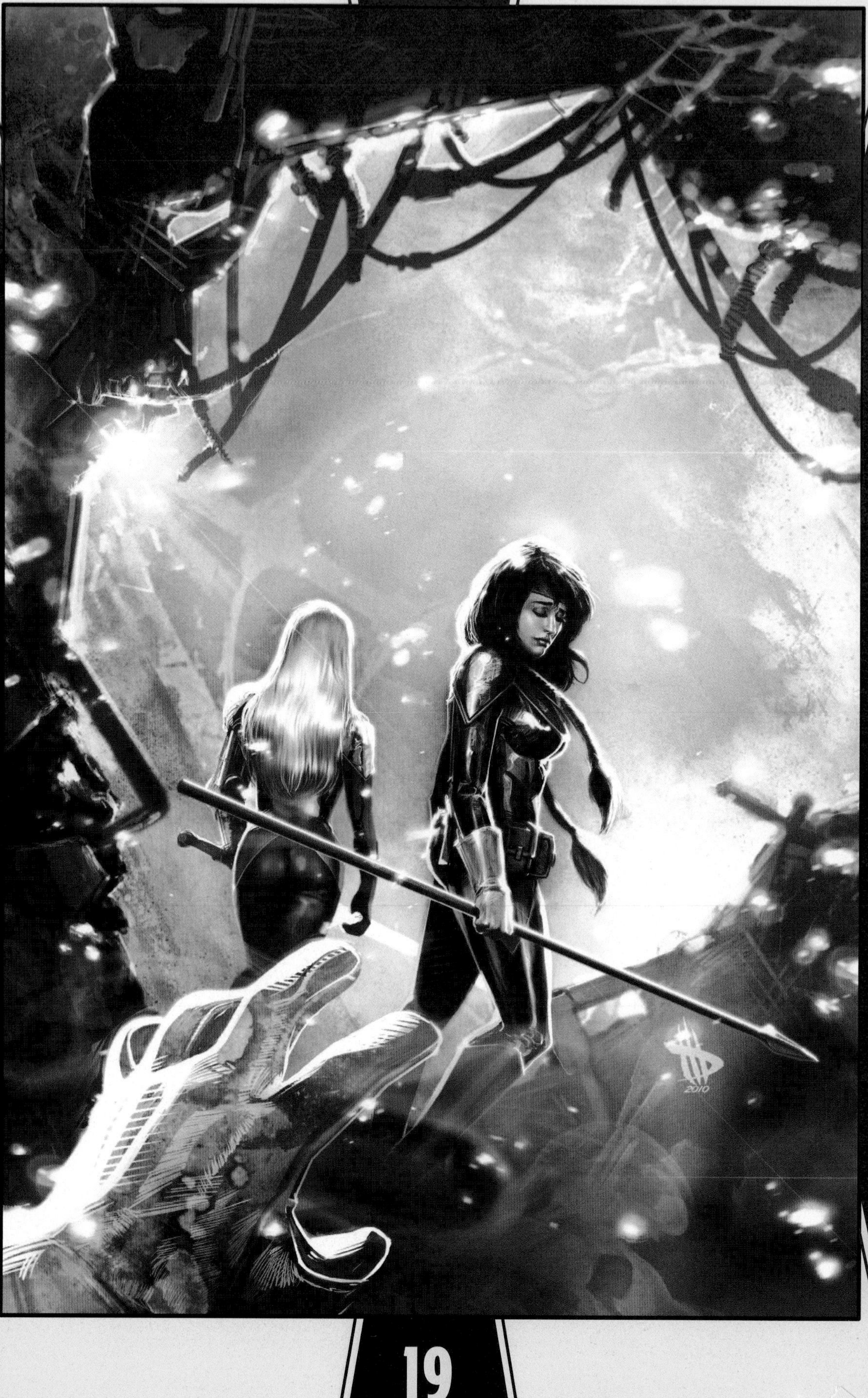
2010

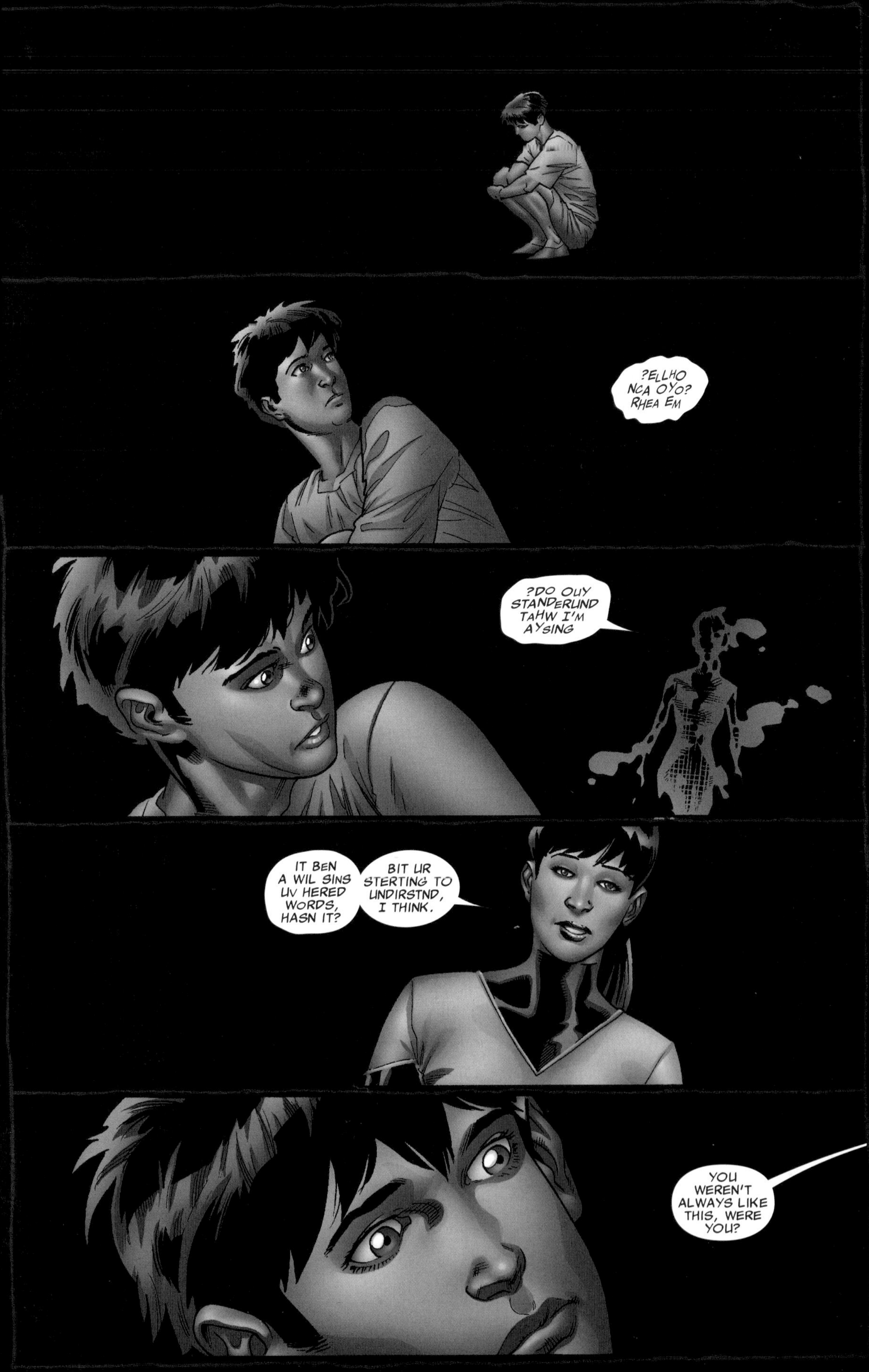
?ELLHO NCA OYO? RHEA EM
?DO OUY STANDERUND TAHW I'M AYSING
IT BEN A WIL SINS UV HERED WORDS, HASN IT?
BIT UR STERTING TO UNDIRSTND, I THINK.
YOU WEREN'T ALWAYS LIKE THIS, WERE YOU?

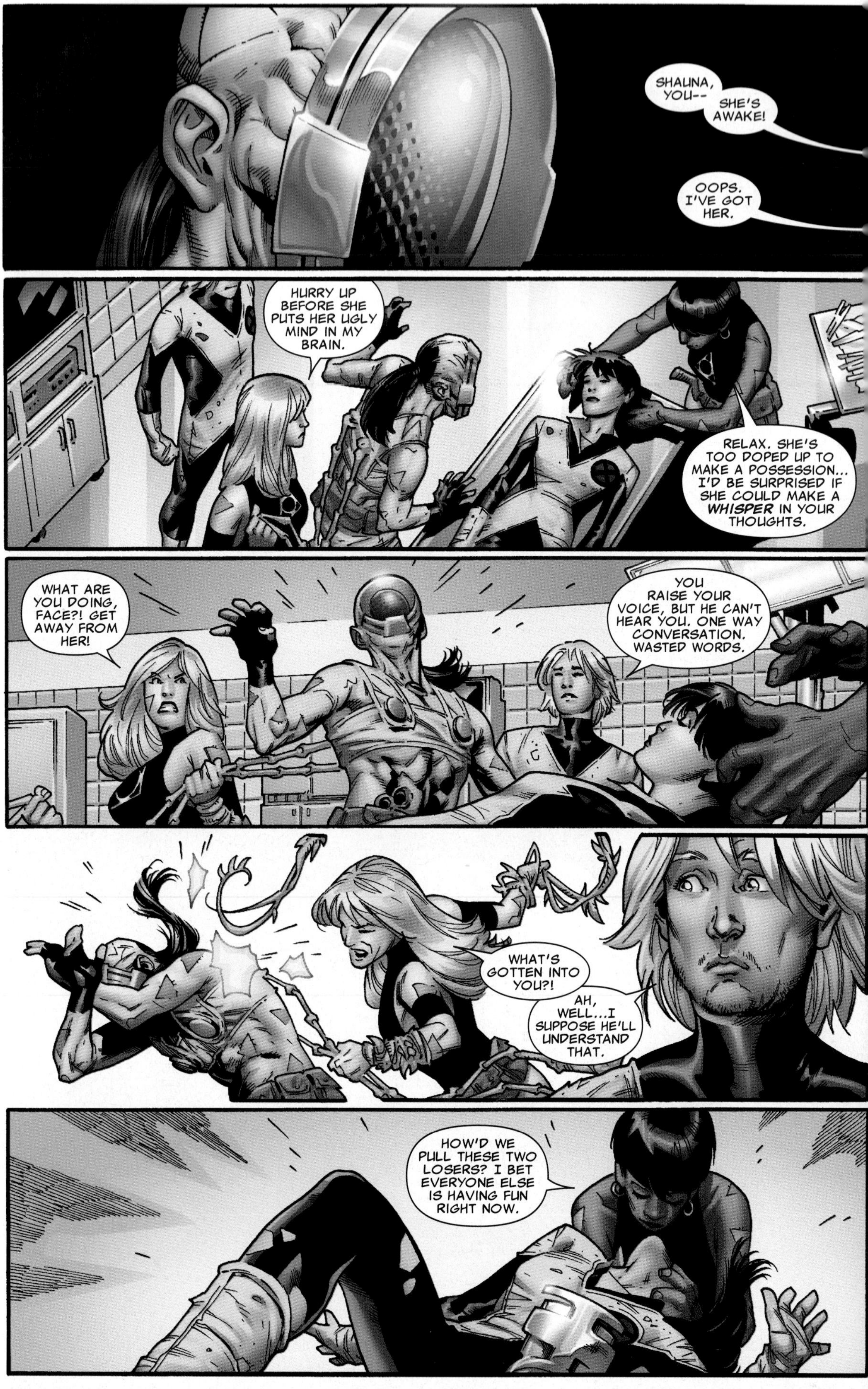
SHAUNA, YOU--
SHE'S AWAKE!
OOPS. I'VE GOT HER.
HURRY UP BEFORE SHE PUTS HER UGLY MIND IN MY BRAIN.
RELAX. SHE'S TOO DOPED UP TO MAKE A POSSESSION... I'D BE SURPRISED IF SHE COULD MAKE A WHISPER IN YOUR THOUGHTS.
WHAT ARE YOU DOING, FACE?! GET AWAY FROM HER!
YOU RAISE YOUR VOICE, BUT HE CAN'T HEAR YOU. ONE WAY CONVERSATION. WASTED WORDS.
WHAT'S GOTTEN INTO YOU?!
AH, WELL...I SUPPOSE HE'LL UNDERSTAND THAT.
HOW'D WE PULL THESE TWO LOSERS? I BET EVERYONE ELSE IS HAVING FUN RIGHT NOW.

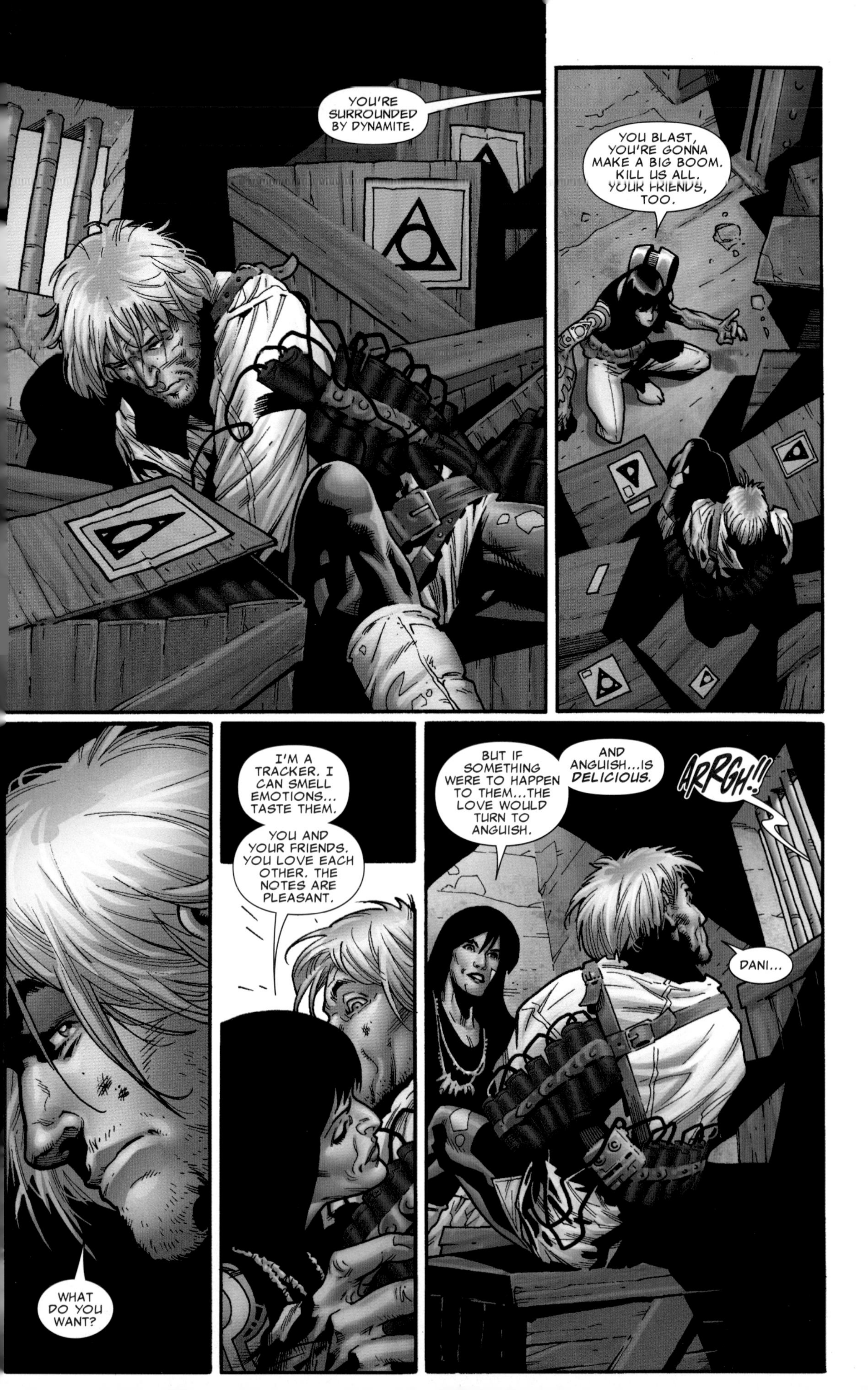
YOU'RE SURROUNDED BY DYNAMITE.
YOU BLAST, YOU'RE GONNA MAKE A BIG BOOM. KILL US ALL. YOUR FRIENDS, TOO.
WHAT DO YOU WANT?
I'M A TRACKER. I CAN SMELL EMOTIONS... TASTE THEM.
YOU AND YOUR FRIENDS. YOU LOVE EACH OTHER. THE NOTES ARE PLEASANT.
BUT IF SOMETHING WERE TO HAPPEN TO THEM...THE LOVE WOULD TURN TO ANGUISH.
AND ANGUISH...IS DELICIOUS.
ARRGH!!
DANI...

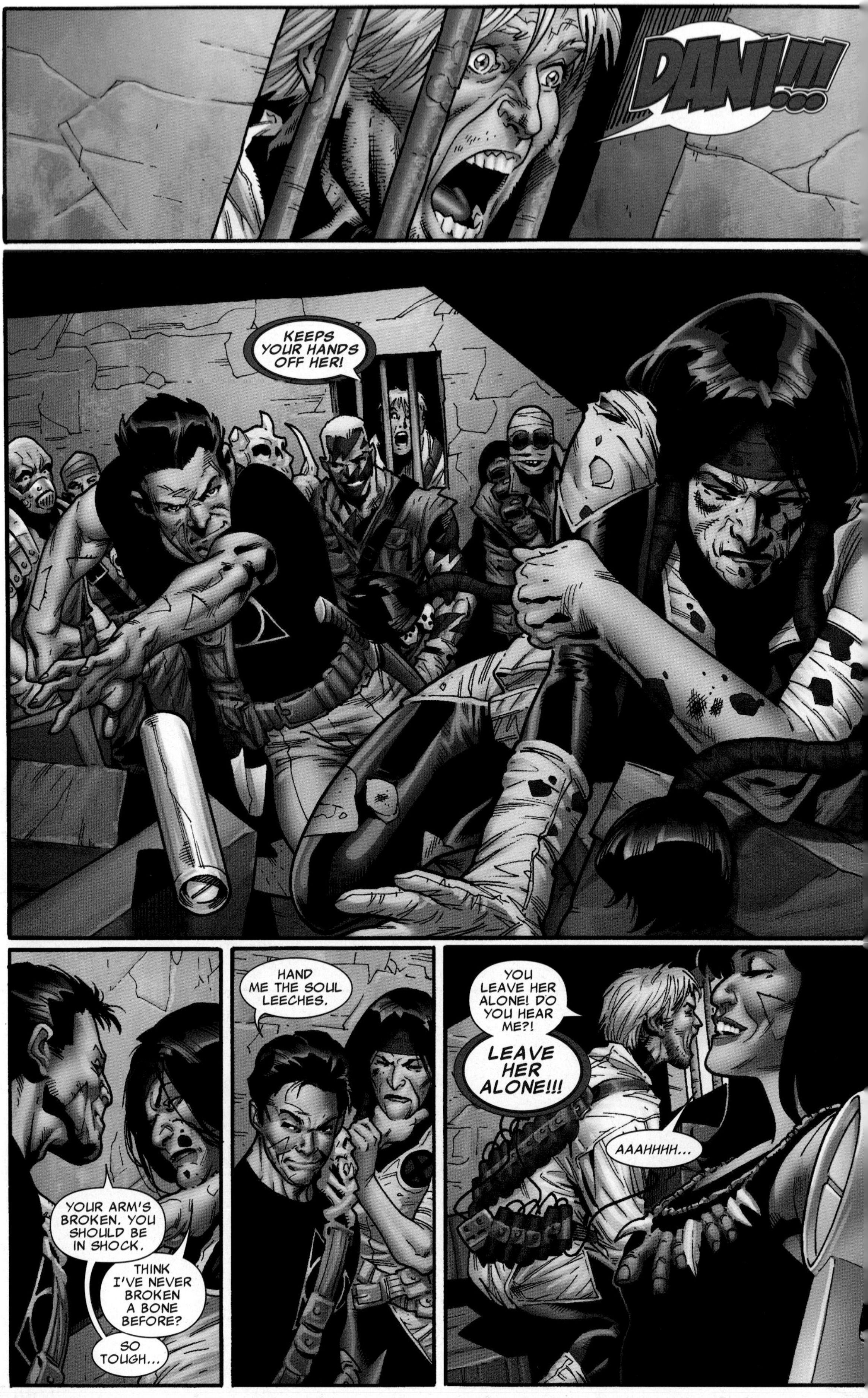
DANI!!!...
KEEPS YOUR HANDS OFF HER!
YOUR ARM'S BROKEN. YOU SHOULD BE IN SHOCK.
THINK I'VE NEVER BROKEN A BONE BEFORE?
SO TOUGH...
HAND ME THE SOUL LEECHES.
YOU LEAVE HER ALONE! DO YOU HEAR ME?!
LEAVE HER ALONE!!!
AAAHHHH...

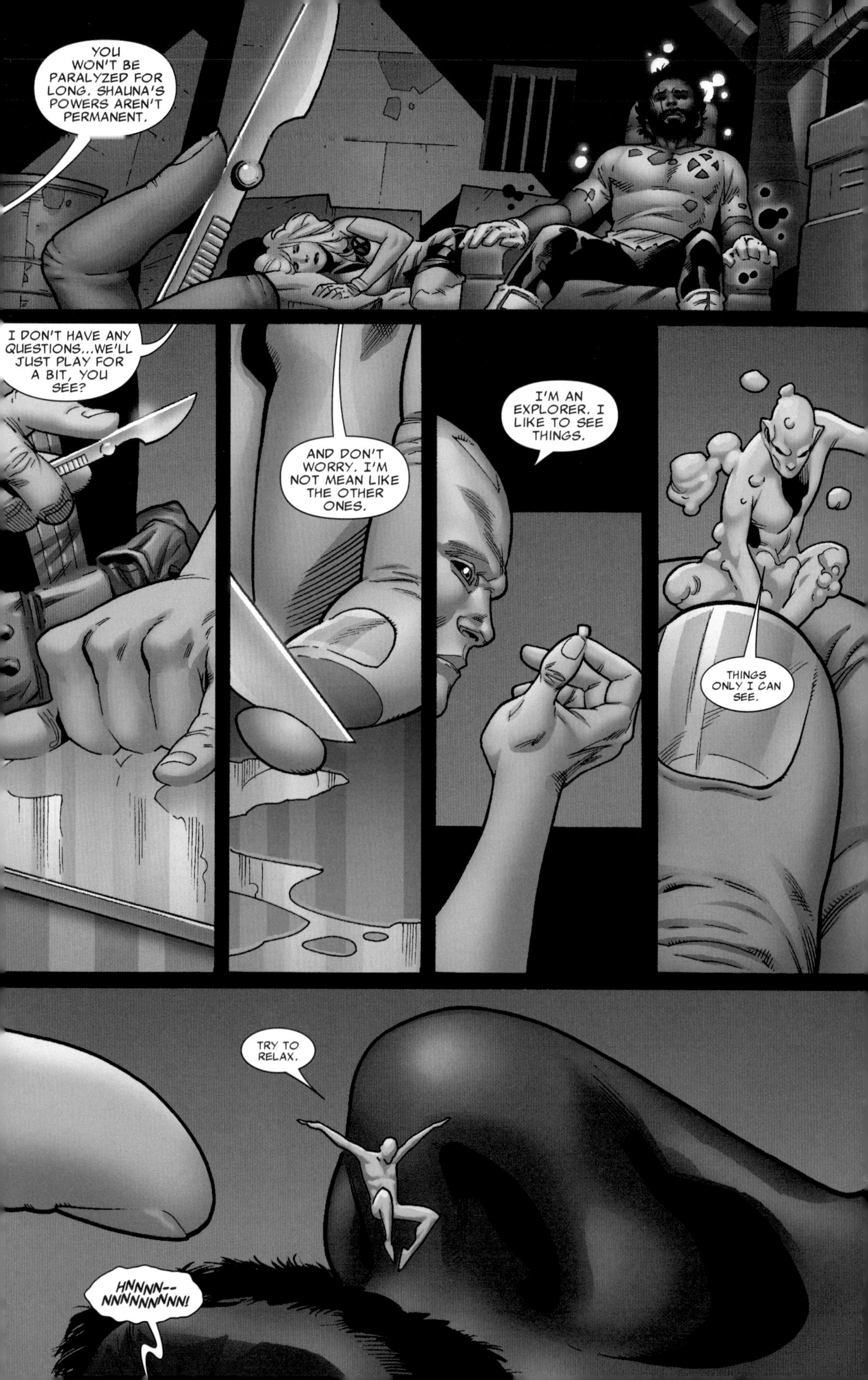
YOU WON'T BE PARALYZED FOR LONG. SHAUNA'S POWERS AREN'T PERMANENT.
I DON'T HAVE ANY QUESTIONS...WE'LL JUST PLAY FOR A BIT, YOU SEE?
AND DON'T WORRY. I'M NOT MEAN LIKE THE OTHER ONES.
I'M AN EXPLORER. I LIKE TO SEE THINGS.
THINGS ONLY I CAN SEE.
TRY TO RELAX.
HNNNN--NNNNNNNNN!

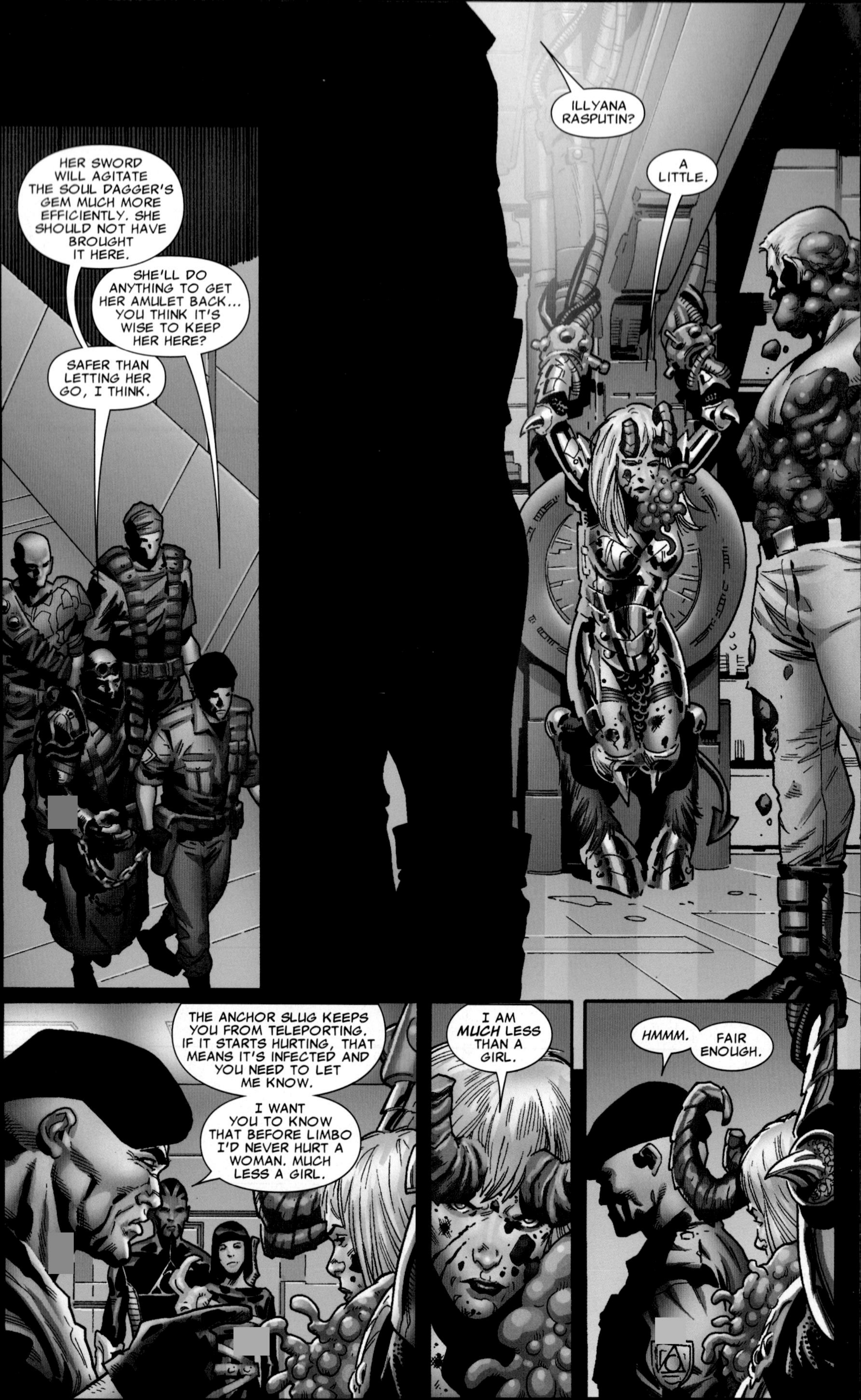
HER SWORD WILL AGITATE THE SOUL DAGGER'S GEM MUCH MORE EFFICIENTLY. SHE SHOULD NOT HAVE BROUGHT IT HERE.
SHE'LL DO ANYTHING TO GET HER AMULET BACK... YOU THINK IT'S WISE TO KEEP HER HERE?
SAFER THAN LETTING HER GO, I THINK.
ILLYANA RASPUTIN?
A LITTLE.
THE ANCHOR SLUG KEEPS YOU FROM TELEPORTING. IF IT STARTS HURTING, THAT MEANS IT'S INFECTED AND YOU NEED TO LET ME KNOW.
I WANT YOU TO KNOW THAT BEFORE LIMBO I'D NEVER HURT A WOMAN. MUCH LESS A GIRL.
I AM *MUCH* LESS THAN A GIRL.
HMMM.
FAIR ENOUGH.

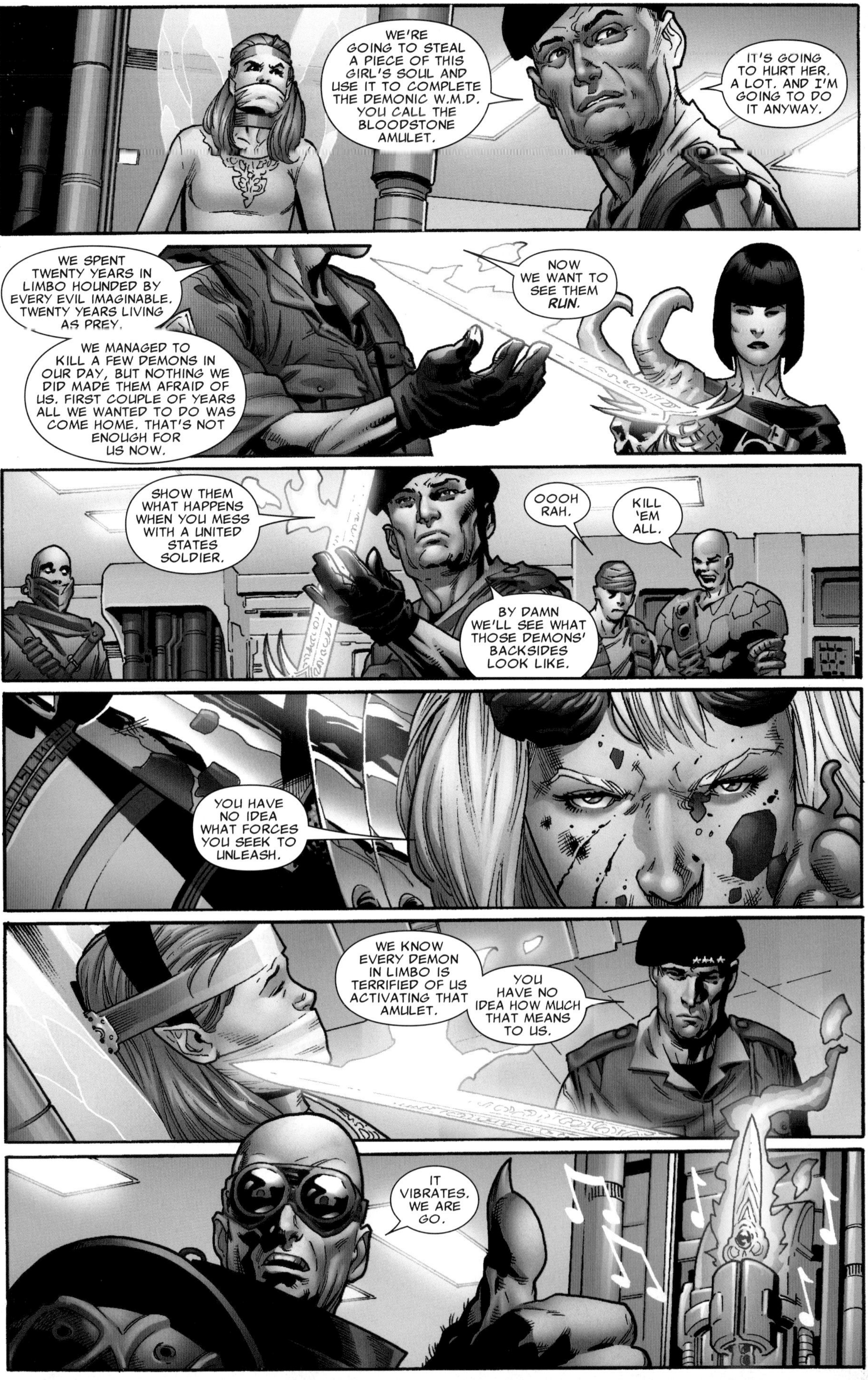
WE'RE GOING TO STEAL A PIECE OF THIS GIRL'S SOUL AND USE IT TO COMPLETE THE DEMONIC W.M.D. YOU CALL THE BLOODSTONE AMULET.
IT'S GOING TO HURT HER. A LOT. AND I'M GOING TO DO IT ANYWAY.
WE SPENT TWENTY YEARS IN LIMBO HOUNDED BY EVERY EVIL IMAGINABLE. TWENTY YEARS LIVING AS PREY.
WE MANAGED TO KILL A FEW DEMONS IN OUR DAY, BUT NOTHING WE DID MADE THEM AFRAID OF US. FIRST COUPLE OF YEARS ALL WE WANTED TO DO WAS COME HOME. THAT'S NOT ENOUGH FOR US NOW.
NOW WE WANT TO SEE THEM RUN.
SHOW THEM WHAT HAPPENS WHEN YOU MESS WITH A UNITED STATES SOLDIER.
BY DAMN WE'LL SEE WHAT THOSE DEMONS' BACKSIDES LOOK LIKE.
OOOH RAH.
KILL 'EM ALL.
YOU HAVE NO IDEA WHAT FORCES YOU SEEK TO UNLEASH.
WE KNOW EVERY DEMON IN LIMBO IS TERRIFIED OF US ACTIVATING THAT AMULET.
YOU HAVE NO IDEA HOW MUCH THAT MEANS TO US.
IT VIBRATES. WE ARE GO.

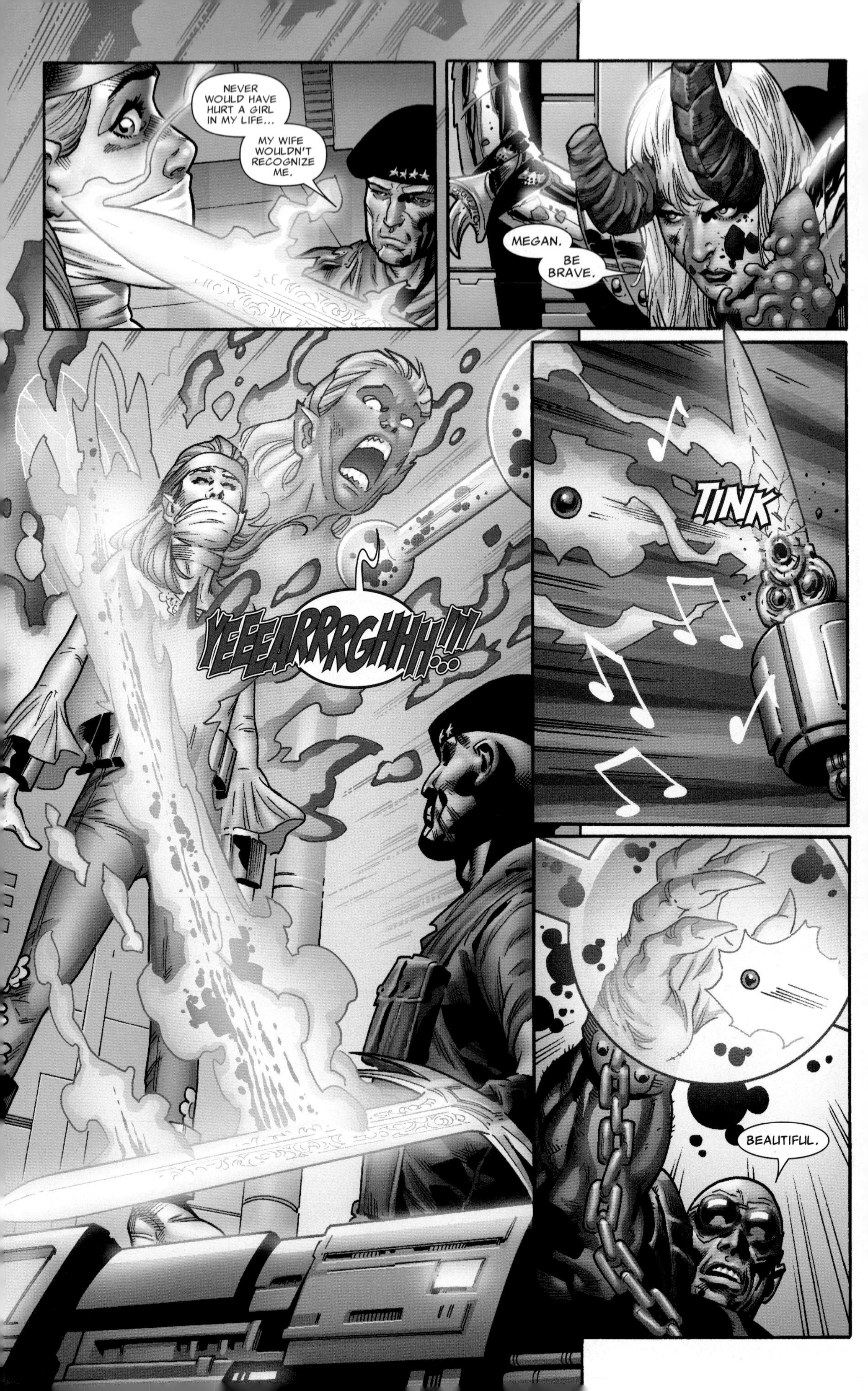
NEVER WOULD HAVE HURT A GIRL IN MY LIFE...
MY WIFE WOULDN'T RECOGNIZE ME.
MEGAN.
BE BRAVE.
YEEEARRRGHHH!!!
TINK
BEAUTIFUL.

SO WHEN YOU AND TRISTA...YOU KNOW...

HOW DO YOU KNOW SHE'S NOT USING HER VOICE TO MAKE YOU DO THINGS?

WHAT THE #@$% DO I CARE?

AND DON'T PICK YOURSELF IN FRONT OF ME, IT'S DISGUSTING.

COME ON, BOB. WE GOT THE GEM. WE'RE MOVING.

OH, CAN I HAVE A FEW MORE SECONDS? I HAVEN'T RETRIEVED MY OTHER SELF FROM--

SHUT UP.

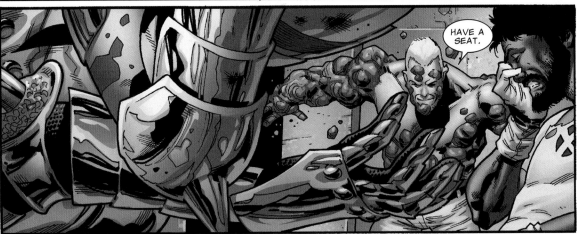

HAVE A SEAT.

I THINK HE GOT LOST IN THERE...IF I CAN TALK HIM OUT, MAYBE--

MOVE.

SEE YOU, LADIES...

AMARA HASN'T WOKEN UP, BUT I CAN SEE HER BREATHING. SHE'S STILL AL--

I KNOW.

I KNOW YOU KNOW.

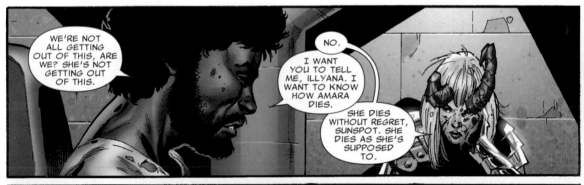

WE'RE NOT ALL GETTING OUT OF THIS, ARE WE? SHE'S NOT GETTING OUT OF THIS.

NO.

I WANT YOU TO TELL ME, ILLYANA. I WANT TO KNOW HOW AMARA DIES.

SHE DIES WITHOUT REGRET, SUNSPOT. SHE DIES AS SHE'S SUPPOSED TO.

TELL ME HOW, ILLYANA... I HAVEN'T ASKED YOU FOR ANYTHING. I FOLLOWED YOU INTO LIMBO AND DIDN'T SAY A WORD.

AMARA TOLD ME YOU HOLD HER AS SHE DIES. HOW DOES IT HAPPEN?

SHE DOESN'T LOVE YOU, YOU KNOW.

NOT AS YOU LOVE HER.

I DON'T CARE.

LISTEN CAREFULLY.

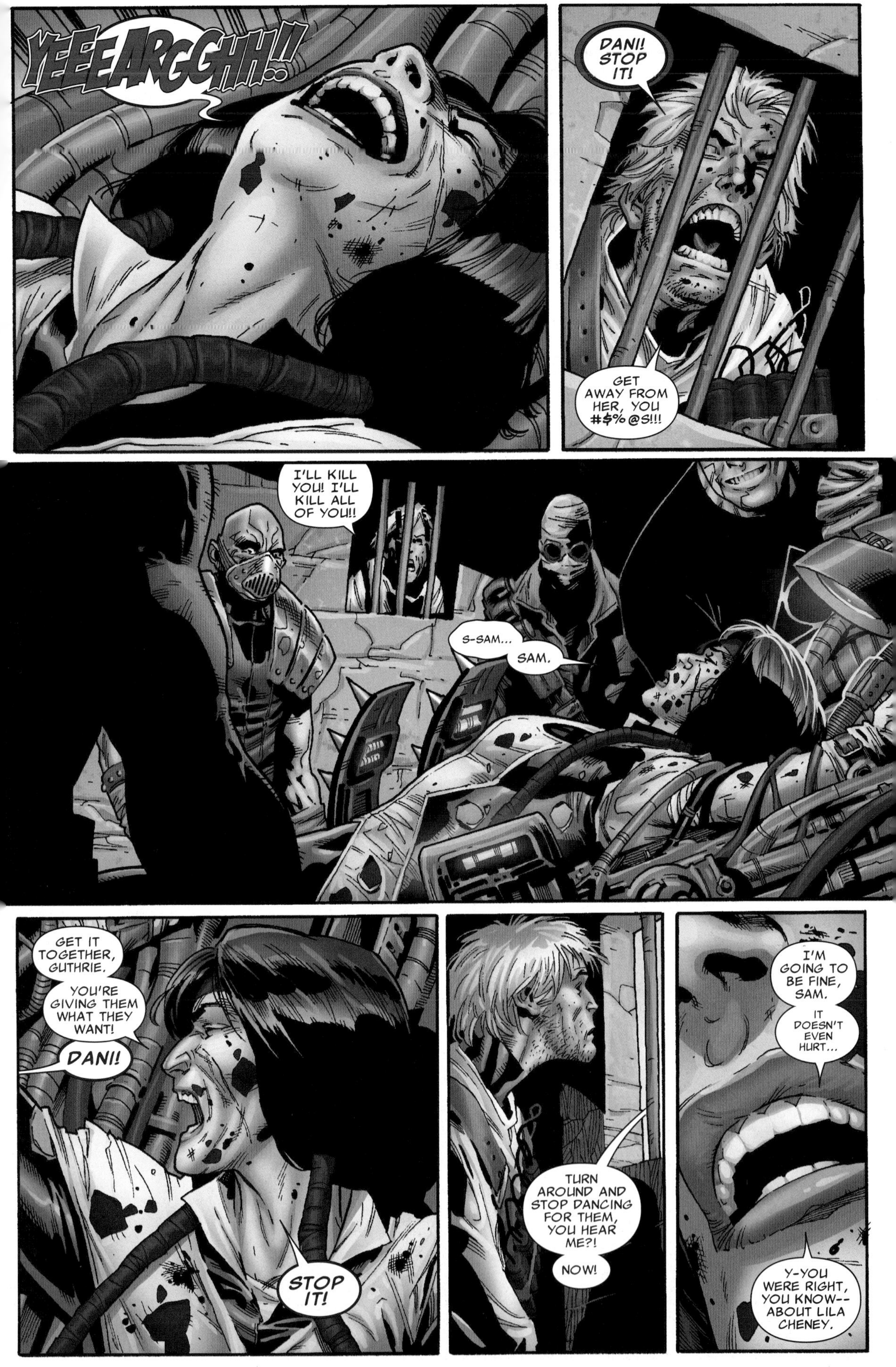

YEEEARGGHH!!
DANI! STOP IT!
GET AWAY FROM HER, YOU #$%@S!!!
I'LL KILL YOU! I'LL KILL ALL OF YOU!!
S-SAM...
SAM.
GET IT TOGETHER, GUTHRIE.
YOU'RE GIVING THEM WHAT THEY WANT!
DANI!
STOP IT!
TURN AROUND AND STOP DANCING FOR THEM, YOU HEAR ME?!
NOW!
I'M GOING TO BE FINE, SAM.
IT DOESN'T EVEN HURT...
Y-YOU WERE RIGHT, YOU KNOW--ABOUT LILA CHENEY.

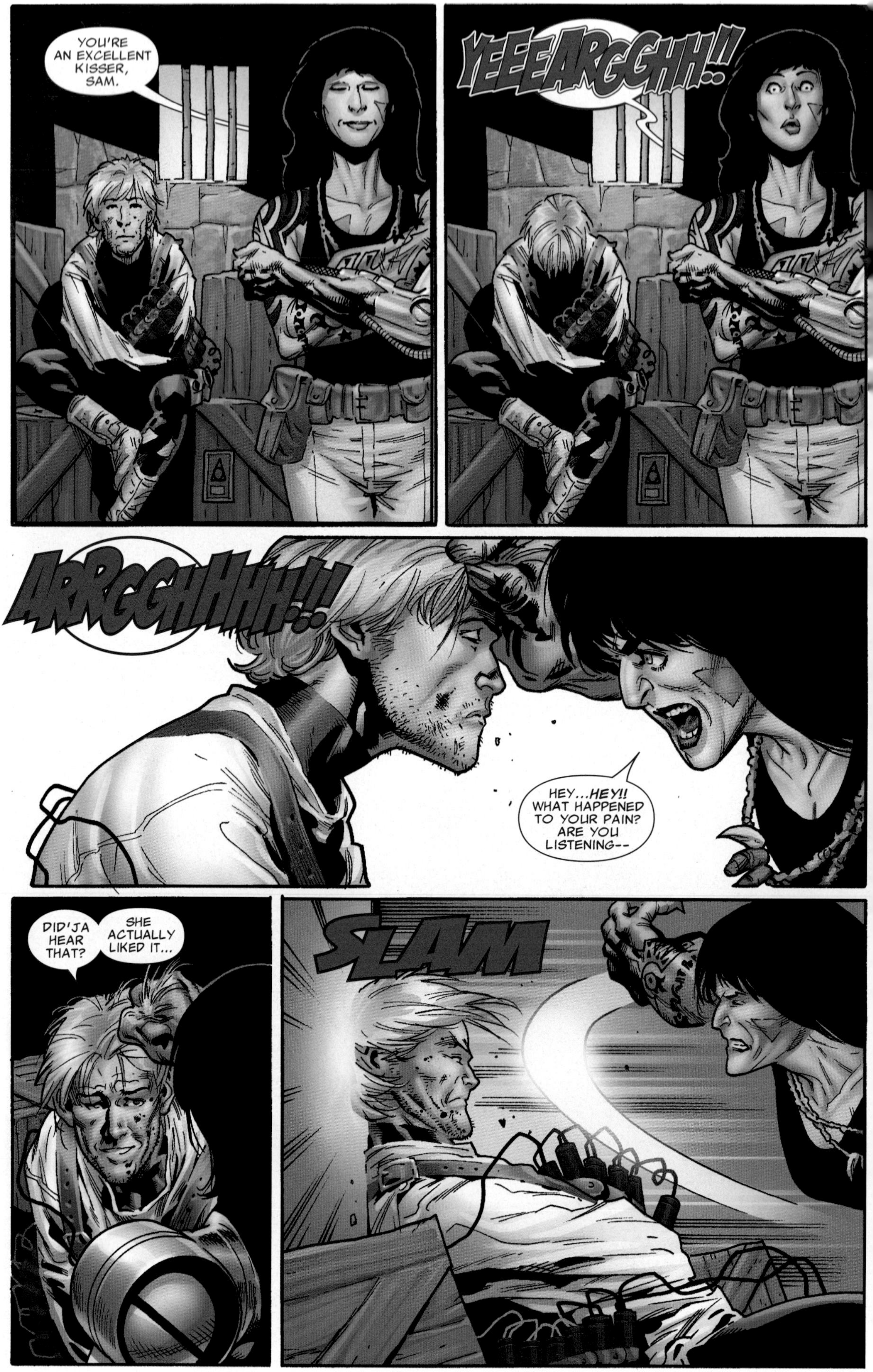

YOU'RE AN EXCELLENT KISSER, SAM.
YEEEARGGHH!!
ARRGGHHHH!!!
HEY...HEY!! WHAT HAPPENED TO YOUR PAIN? ARE YOU LISTENING--
DID'JA HEAR THAT?
SHE ACTUALLY LIKED IT...
SLAM

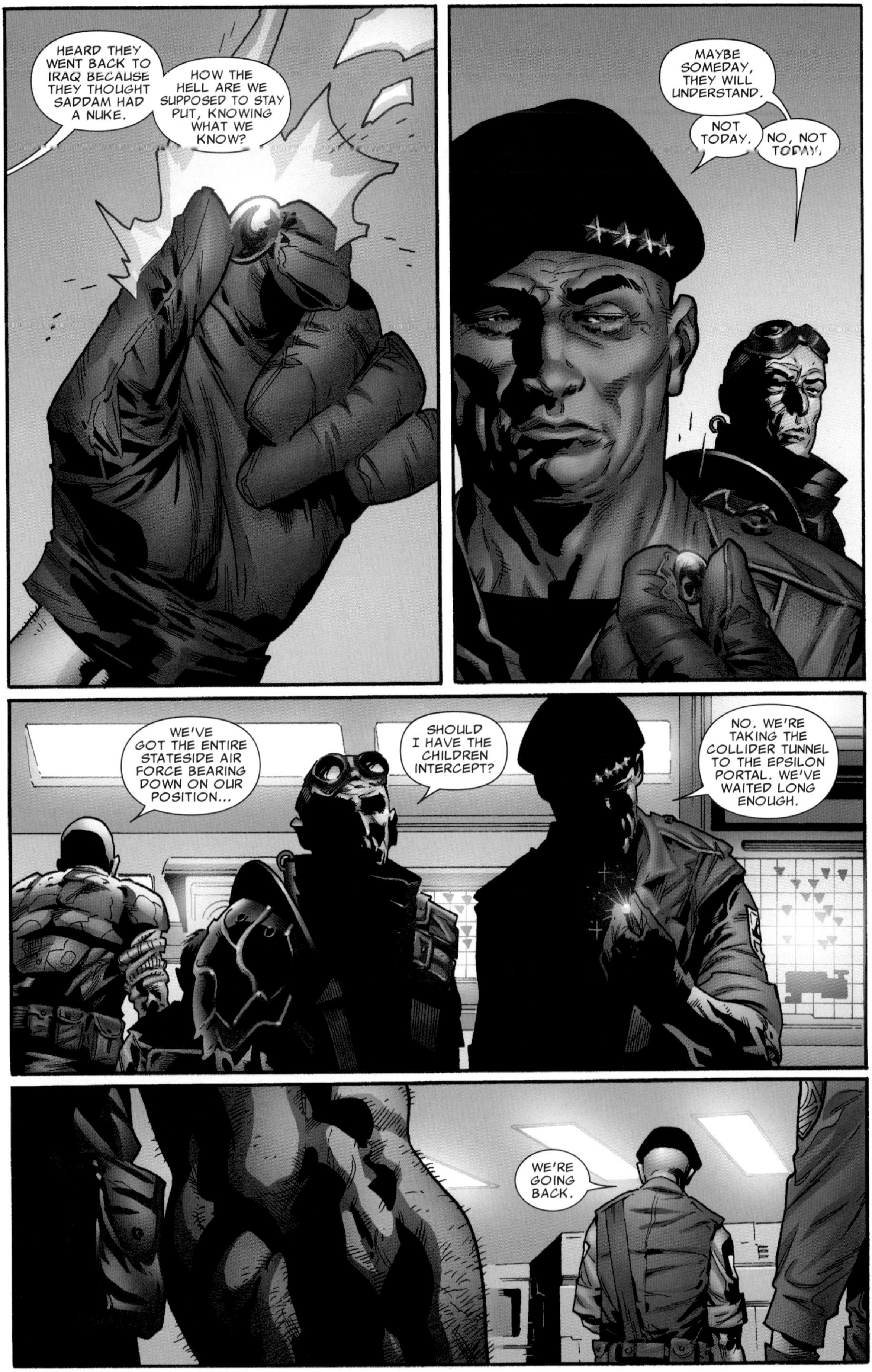
HEARD THEY WENT BACK TO IRAQ BECAUSE THEY THOUGHT SADDAM HAD A NUKE.
HOW THE HELL ARE WE SUPPOSED TO STAY PUT, KNOWING WHAT WE KNOW?
MAYBE SOMEDAY, THEY WILL UNDERSTAND.
NOT TODAY.
NO, NOT TODAY.
WE'VE GOT THE ENTIRE STATESIDE AIR FORCE BEARING DOWN ON OUR POSITION...
SHOULD I HAVE THE CHILDREN INTERCEPT?
NO. WE'RE TAKING THE COLLIDER TUNNEL TO THE EPSILON PORTAL. WE'VE WAITED LONG ENOUGH.
WE'RE GOING BACK.

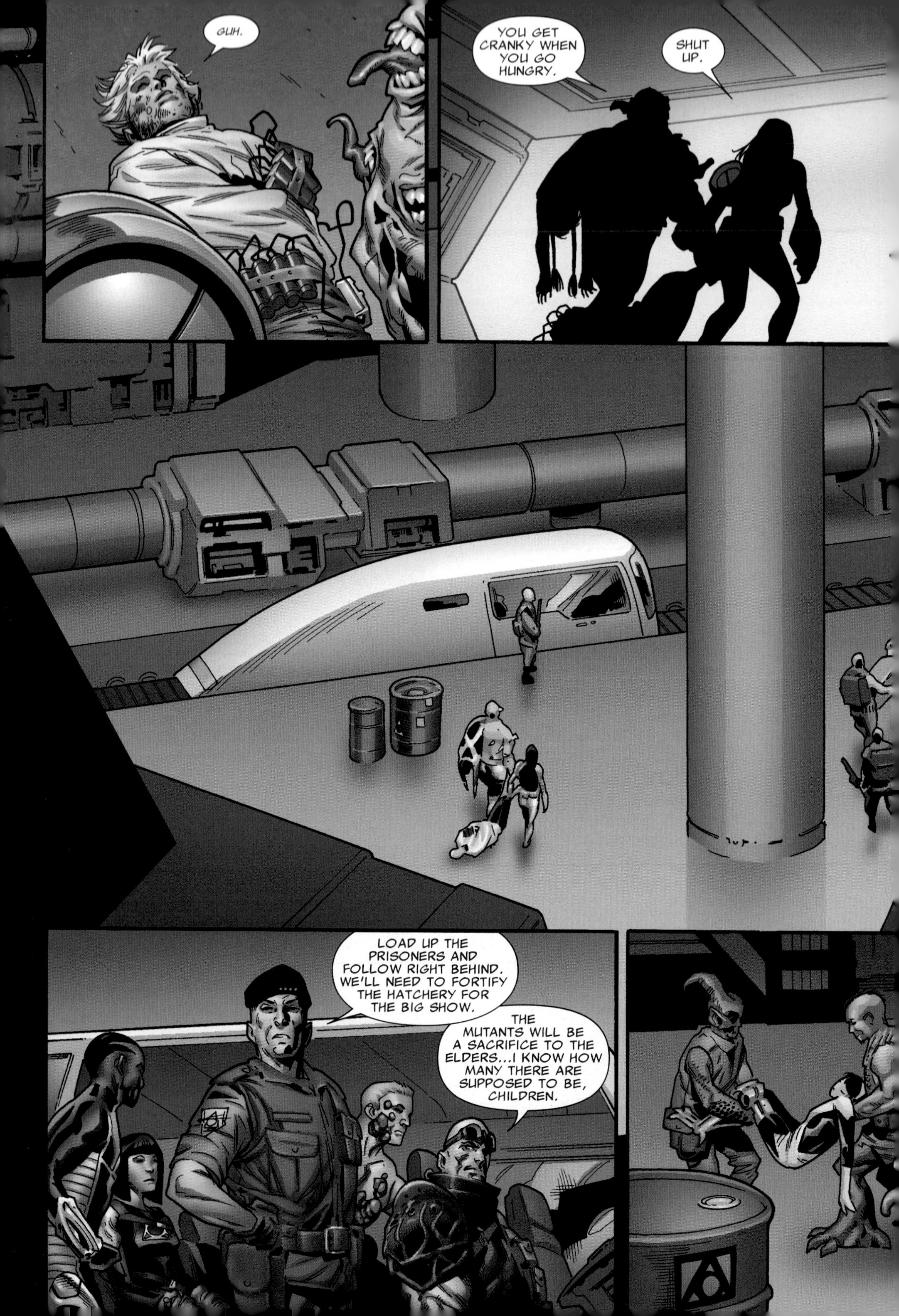
GUH.
YOU GET CRANKY WHEN YOU GO HUNGRY.
SHUT UP.
LOAD UP THE PRISONERS AND FOLLOW RIGHT BEHIND. WE'LL NEED TO FORTIFY THE HATCHERY FOR THE BIG SHOW.
THE MUTANTS WILL BE A SACRIFICE TO THE ELDERS...I KNOW HOW MANY THERE ARE SUPPOSED TO BE, CHILDREN.

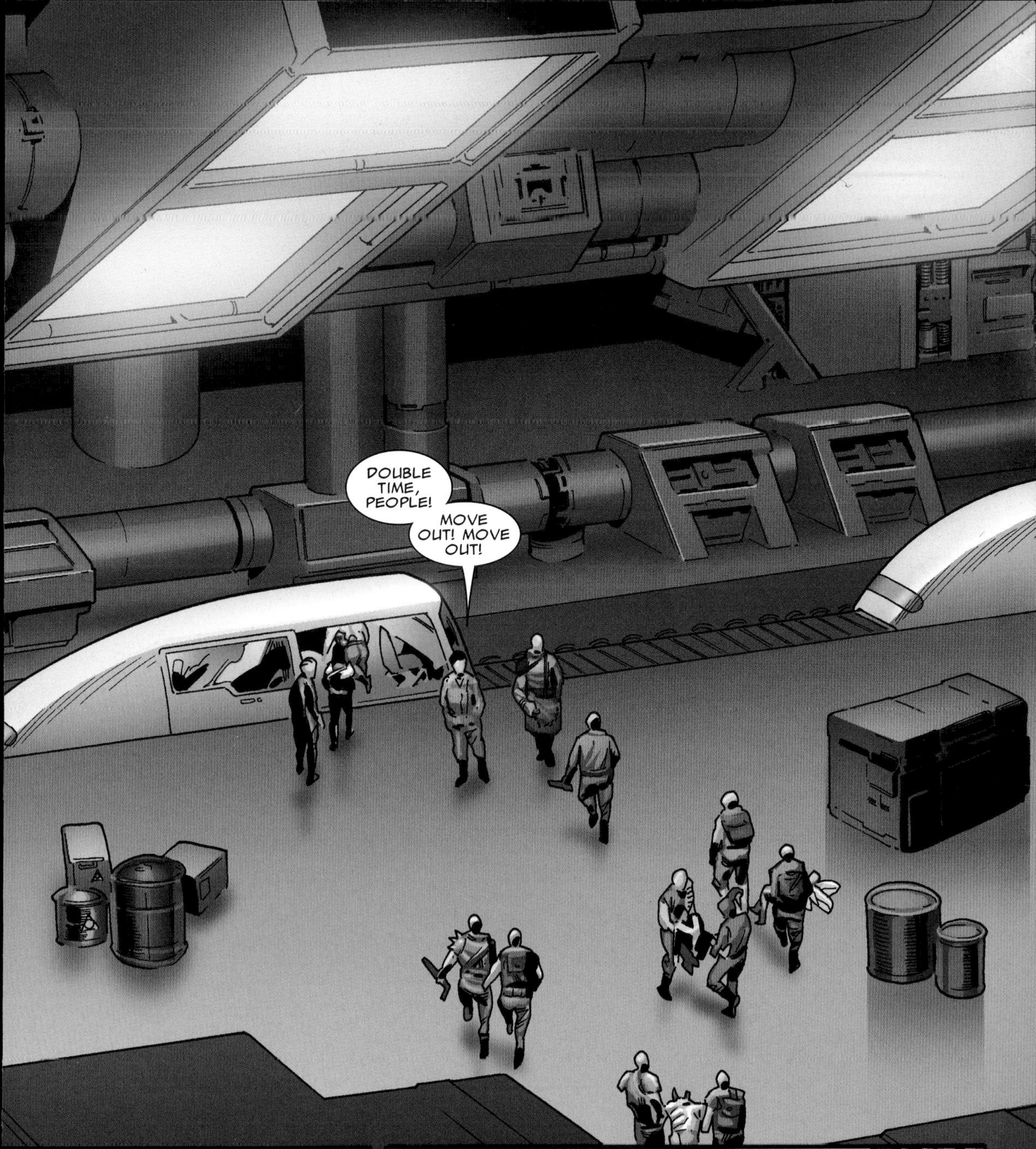
DOUBLE TIME, PEOPLE!
MOVE OUT! MOVE OUT!

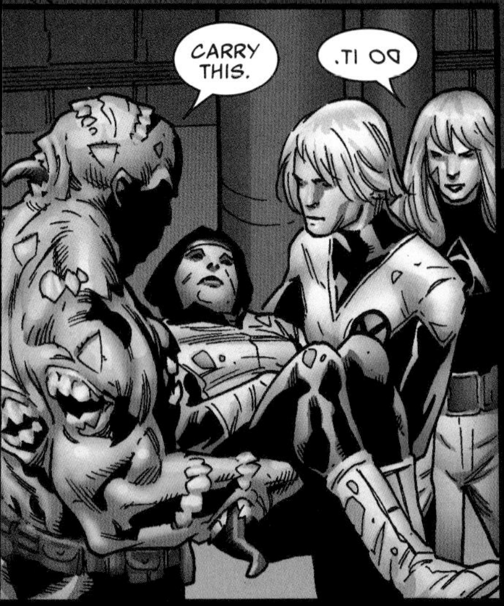
CARRY THIS.
DO IT.

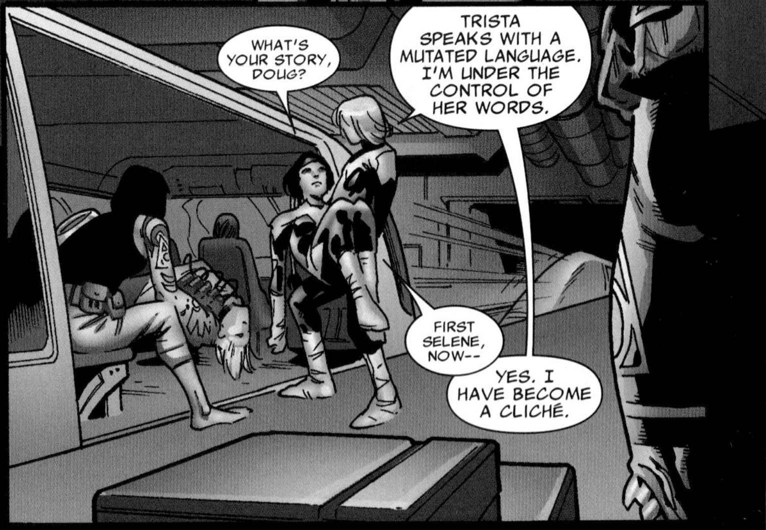
WHAT'S YOUR STORY, DOUG?
TRISTA SPEAKS WITH A MUTATED LANGUAGE. I'M UNDER THE CONTROL OF HER WORDS.
FIRST SELENE, NOW--
YES. I HAVE BECOME A CLICHÉ.

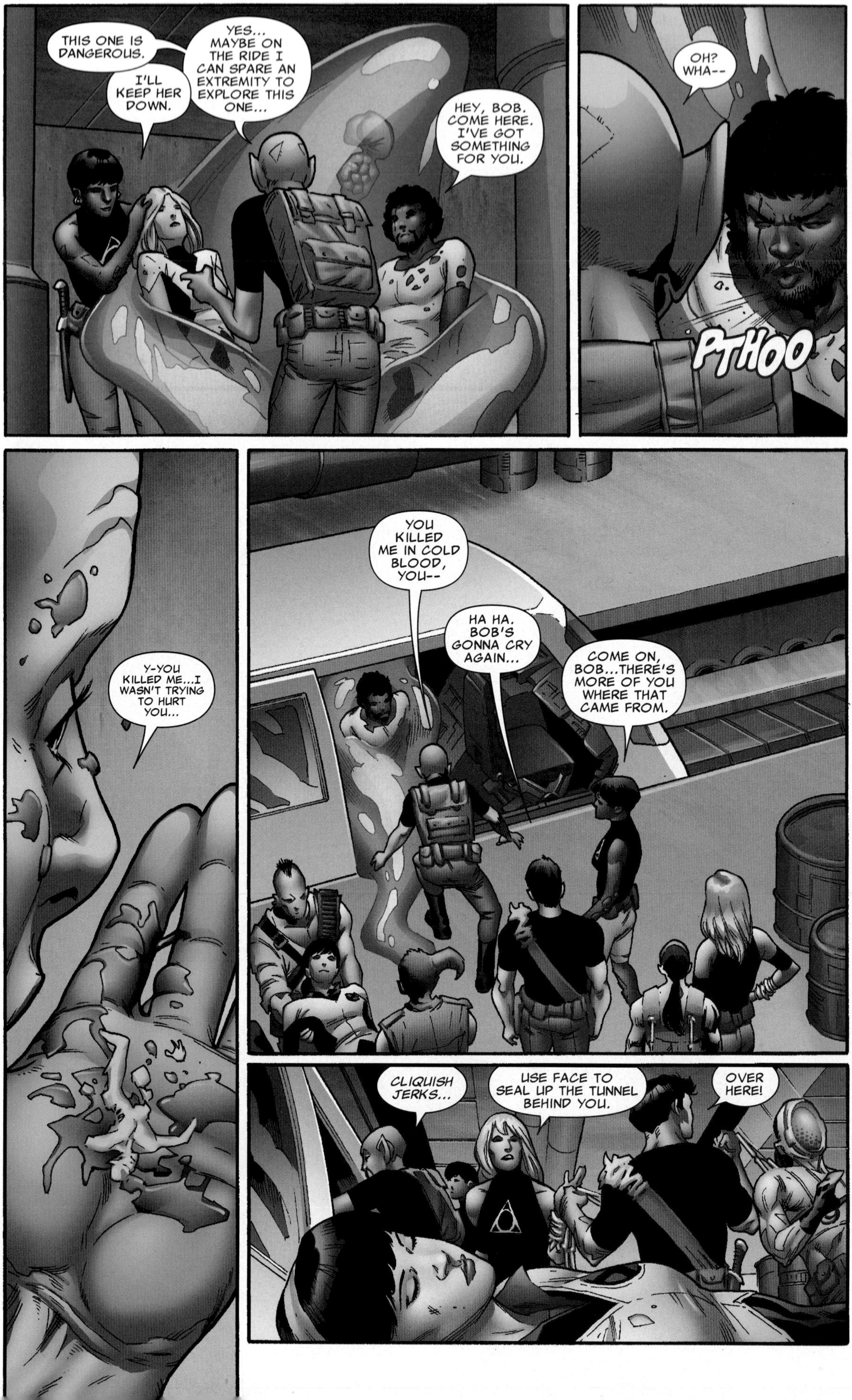

THIS ONE IS DANGEROUS.
I'LL KEEP HER DOWN.
YES... MAYBE ON THE RIDE I CAN SPARE AN EXTREMITY TO EXPLORE THIS ONE...
HEY, BOB. COME HERE. I'VE GOT SOMETHING FOR YOU.
OH? WHA--
PTHOO
Y-YOU KILLED ME...I WASN'T TRYING TO HURT YOU...
YOU KILLED ME IN COLD BLOOD, YOU--
HA HA. BOB'S GONNA CRY AGAIN...
COME ON, BOB...THERE'S MORE OF YOU WHERE THAT CAME FROM.
CLIQUISH JERKS...
USE FACE TO SEAL UP THE TUNNEL BEHIND YOU.
OVER HERE!

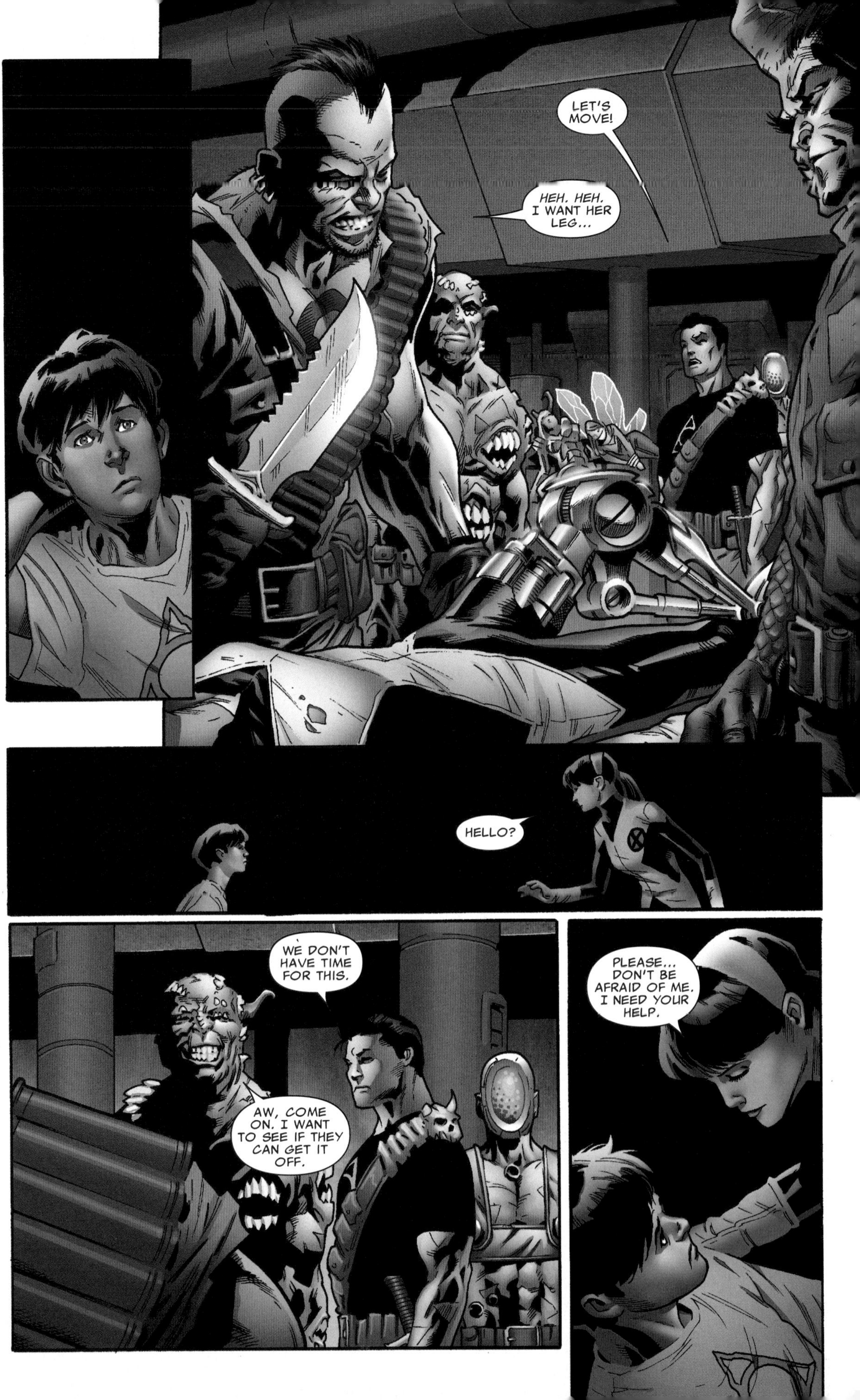
LET'S MOVE!
HEH. HEH. I WANT HER LEG...
HELLO?
WE DON'T HAVE TIME FOR THIS.
AW, COME ON. I WANT TO SEE IF THEY CAN GET IT OFF.
PLEASE... DON'T BE AFRAID OF ME. I NEED YOUR HELP.

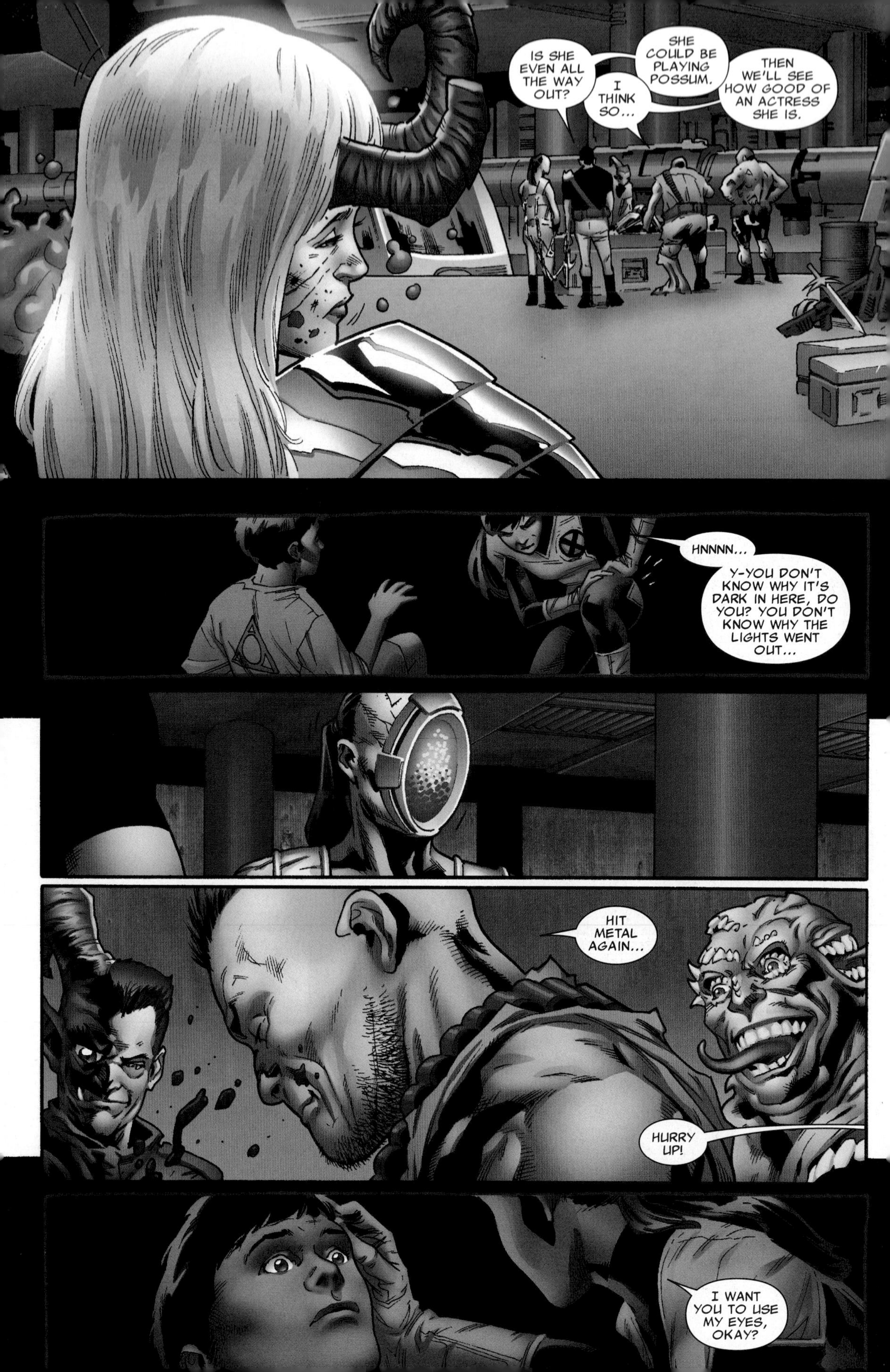
IS SHE EVEN ALL THE WAY OUT?
SHE COULD BE PLAYING POSSUM.
I THINK SO...
THEN WE'LL SEE HOW GOOD OF AN ACTRESS SHE IS.
HNNNN...
Y-YOU DON'T KNOW WHY IT'S DARK IN HERE, DO YOU? YOU DON'T KNOW WHY THE LIGHTS WENT OUT...
HIT METAL AGAIN...
HURRY UP!
I WANT YOU TO USE MY EYES, OKAY?

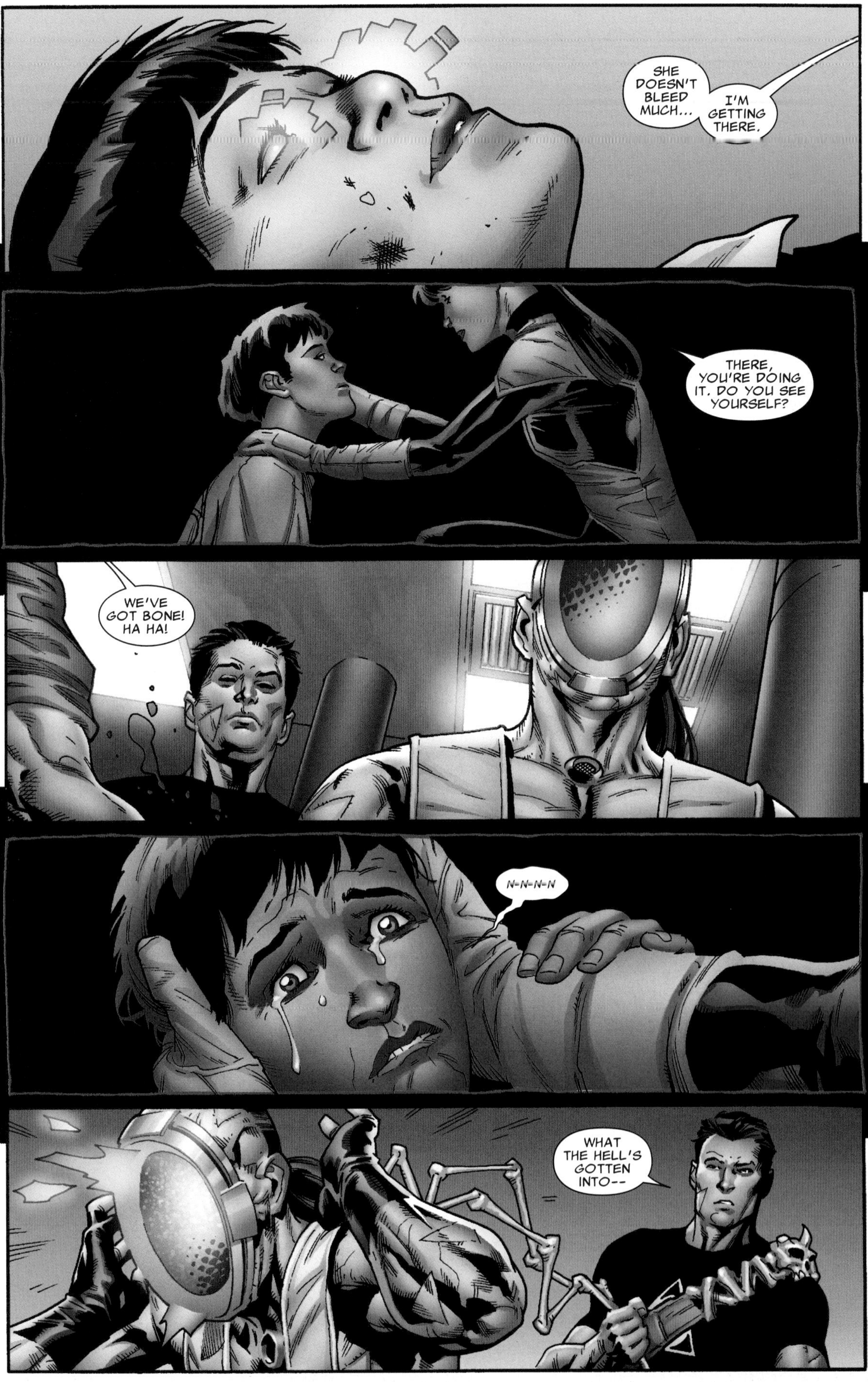
SHE DOESN'T BLEED MUCH...
I'M GETTING THERE.
THERE, YOU'RE DOING IT. DO YOU SEE YOURSELF?
WE'VE GOT BONE! HA HA!
N-N-N-N
WHAT THE HELL'S GOTTEN INTO--

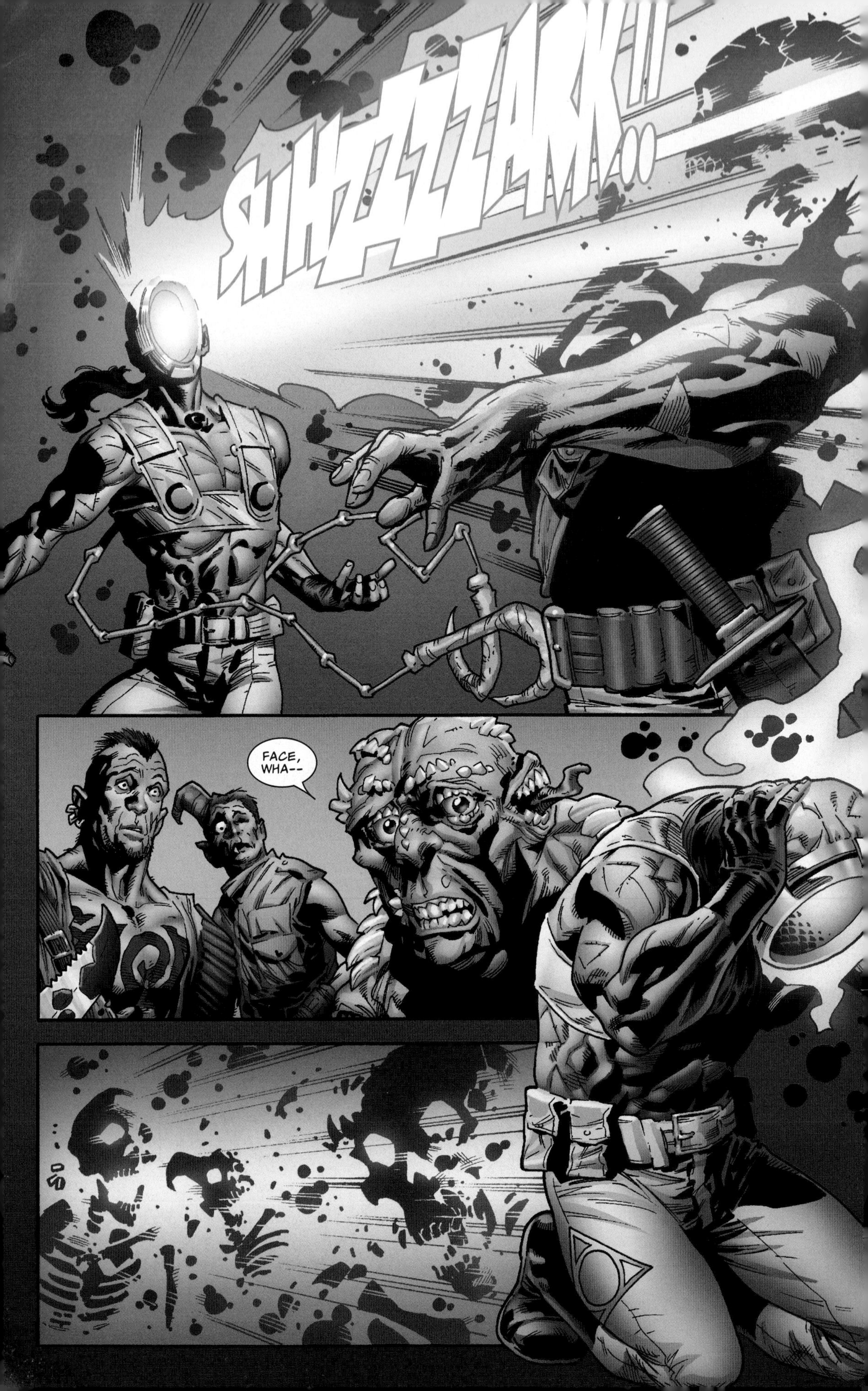
SHHZZZZARK!!
FACE, WHA--

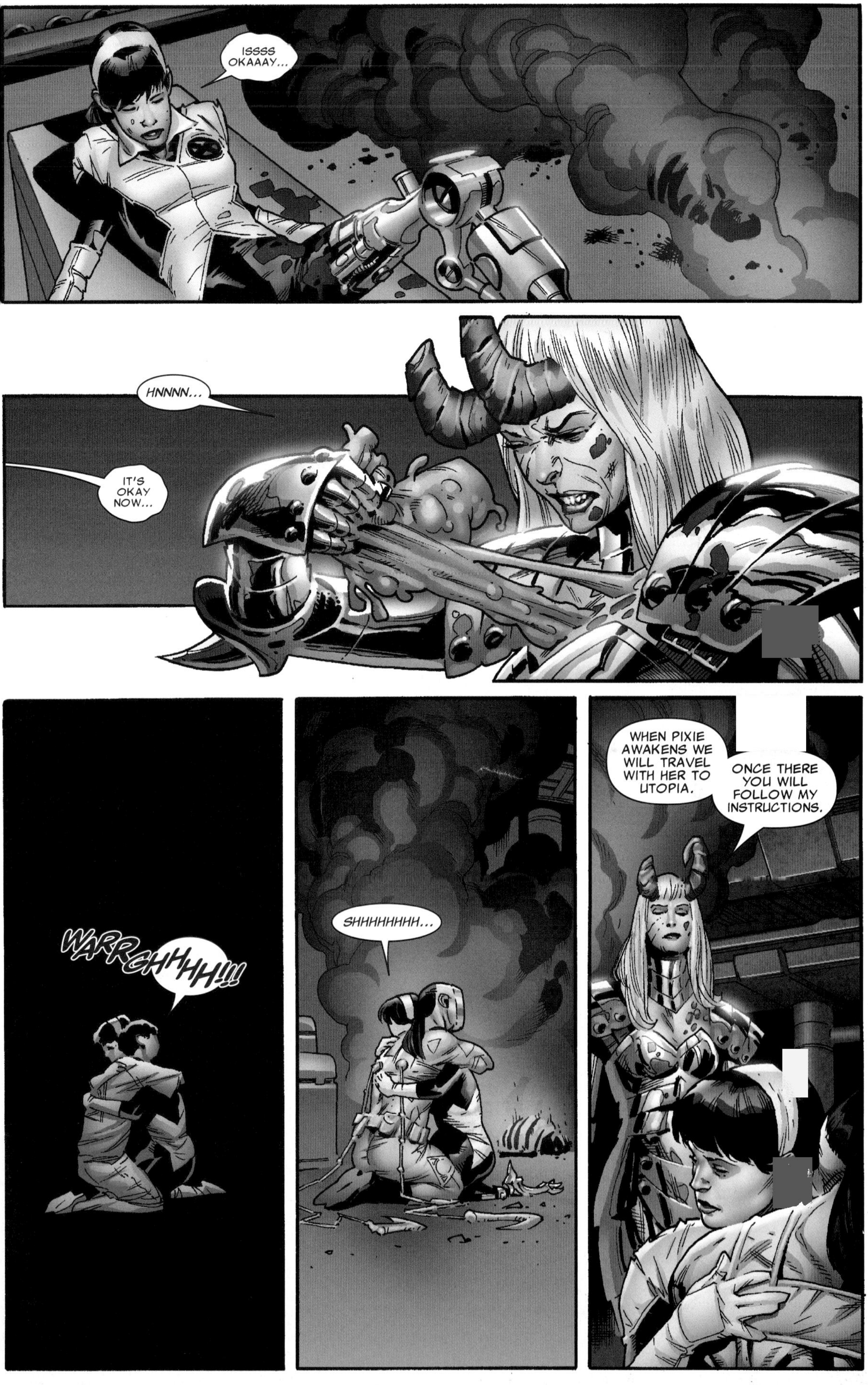
ISSSS OKAAAY...
HNNNN...
IT'S OKAY NOW...
WARRGHHHH!!!
SHHHHHHHH...
WHEN PIXIE AWAKENS WE WILL TRAVEL WITH HER TO UTOPIA.
ONCE THERE YOU WILL FOLLOW MY INSTRUCTIONS.

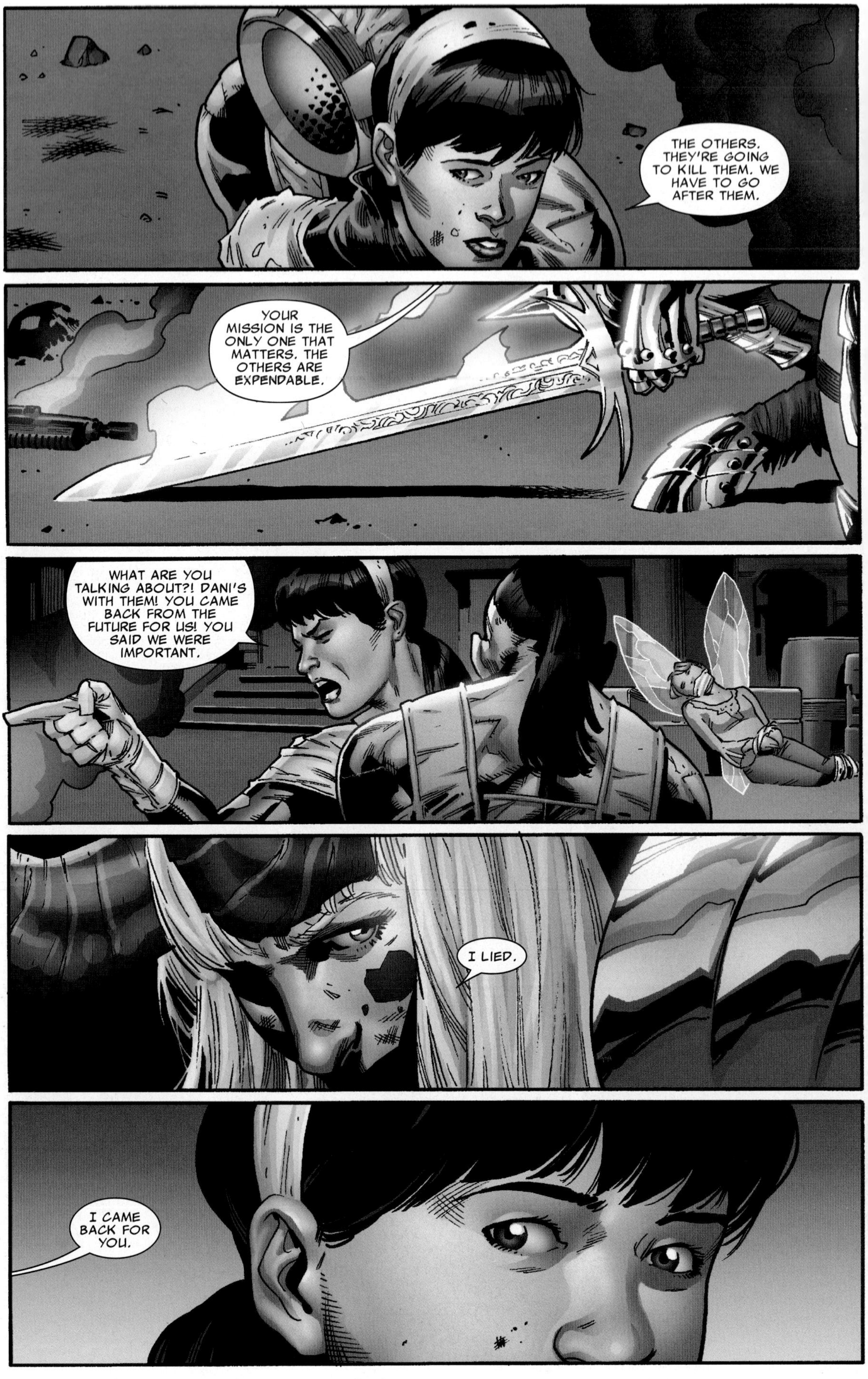
THE OTHERS. THEY'RE GOING TO KILL THEM. WE HAVE TO GO AFTER THEM.
YOUR MISSION IS THE ONLY ONE THAT MATTERS. THE OTHERS ARE EXPENDABLE.
WHAT ARE YOU TALKING ABOUT?! DANI'S WITH THEM! YOU CAME BACK FROM THE FUTURE FOR US! YOU SAID WE WERE IMPORTANT.
I LIED.
I CAME BACK FOR YOU.

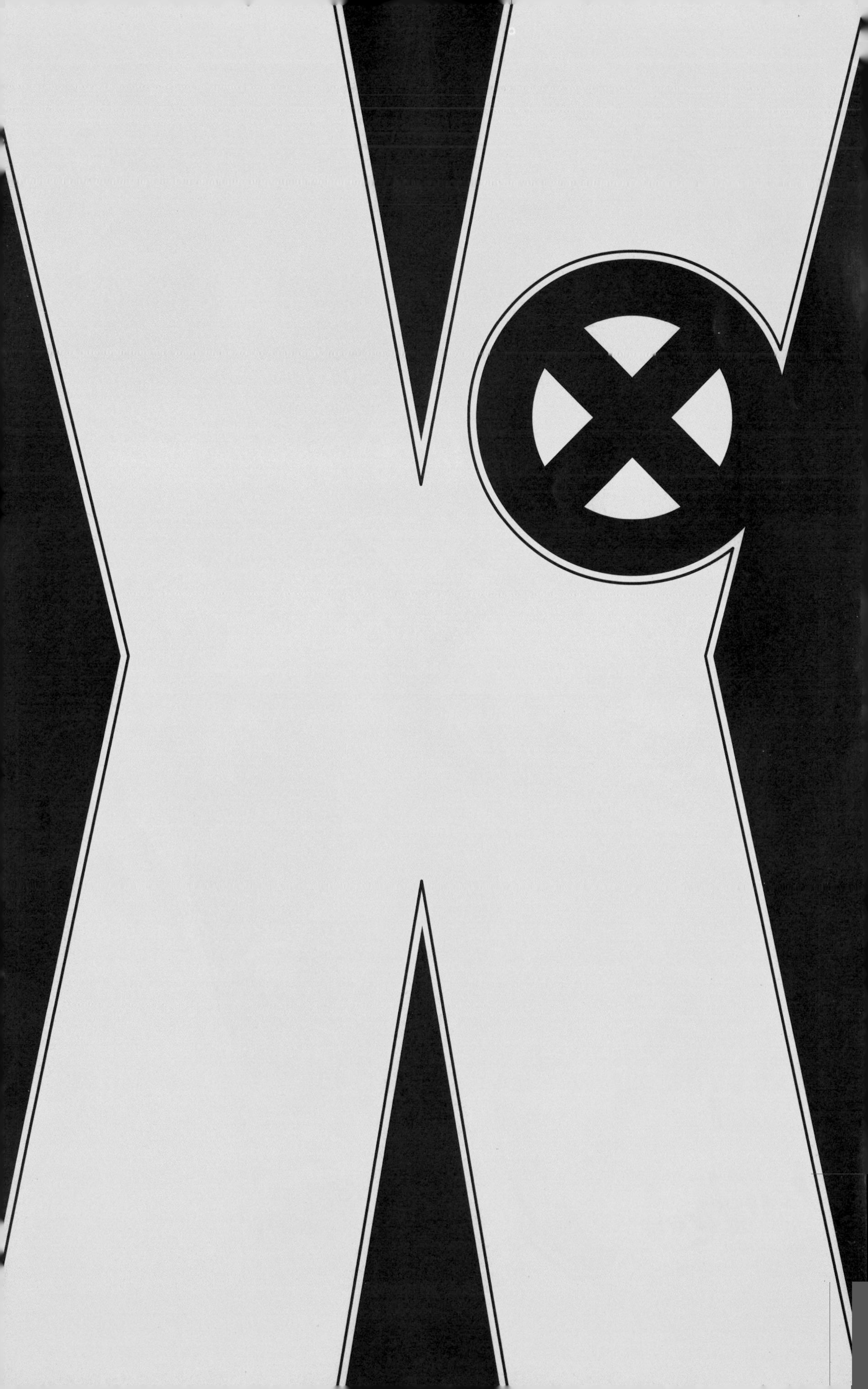

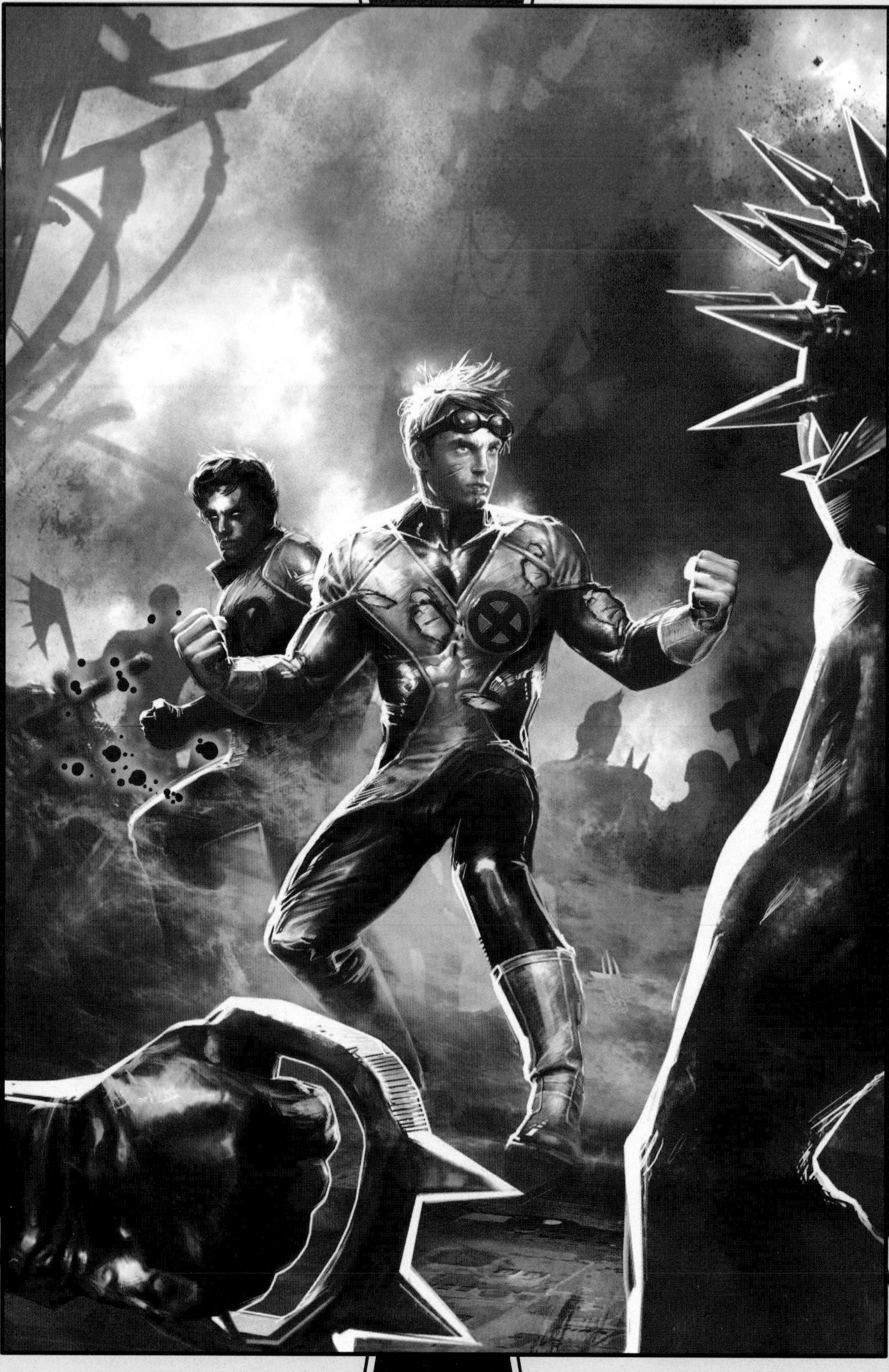

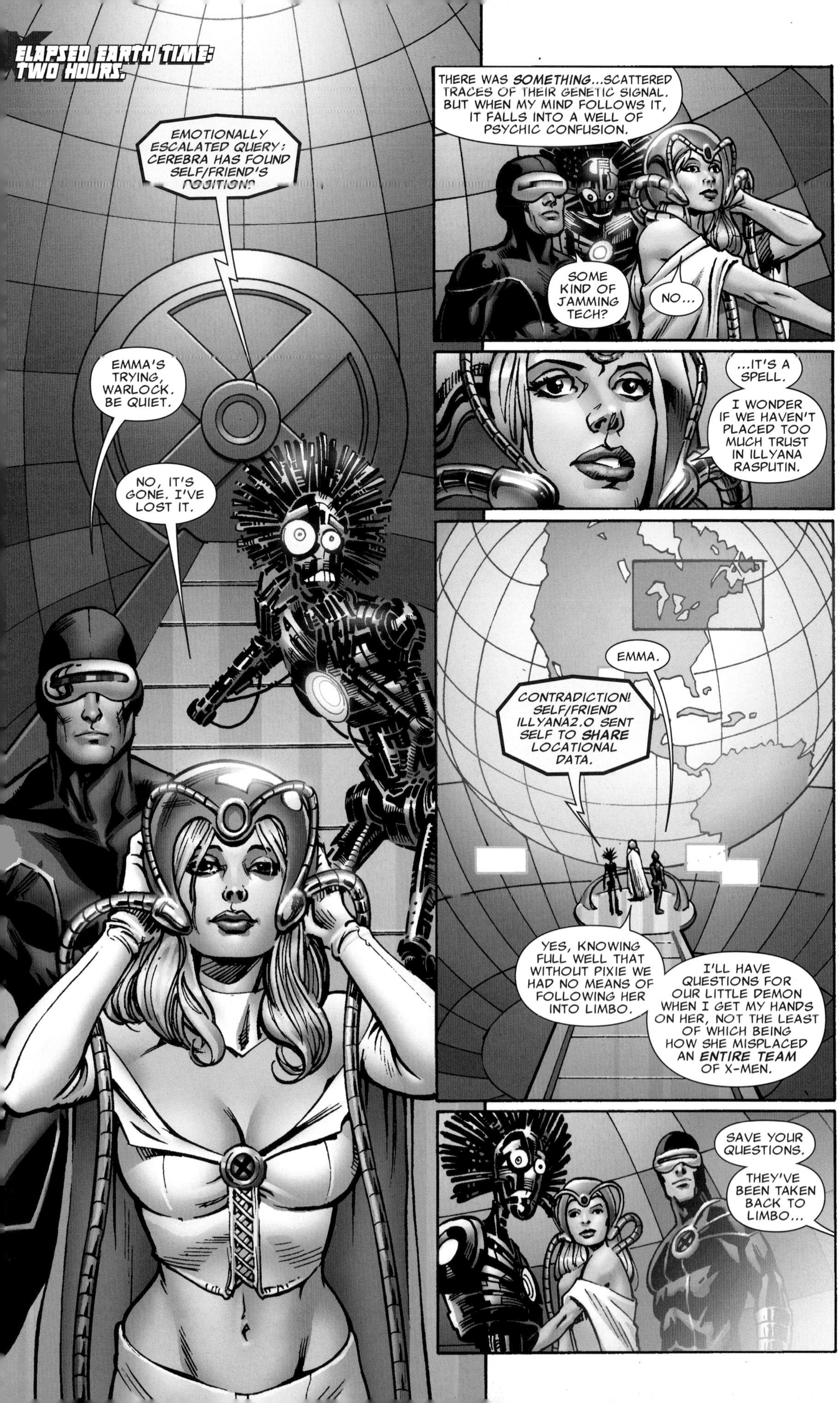
ELAPSED EARTH TIME: TWO HOURS.
EMOTIONALLY ESCALATED QUERY: CEREBRA HAS FOUND SELF/FRIEND'S POSITION?
EMMA'S TRYING, WARLOCK. BE QUIET.
NO, IT'S GONE. I'VE LOST IT.
THERE WAS SOMETHING...SCATTERED TRACES OF THEIR GENETIC SIGNAL. BUT WHEN MY MIND FOLLOWS IT, IT FALLS INTO A WELL OF PSYCHIC CONFUSION.
SOME KIND OF JAMMING TECH?
NO...
...IT'S A SPELL.
I WONDER IF WE HAVEN'T PLACED TOO MUCH TRUST IN ILLYANA RASPUTIN.
EMMA.
CONTRADICTION! SELF/FRIEND ILLYANA2.0 SENT SELF TO SHARE LOCATIONAL DATA.
YES, KNOWING FULL WELL THAT WITHOUT PIXIE WE HAD NO MEANS OF FOLLOWING HER INTO LIMBO.
I'LL HAVE QUESTIONS FOR OUR LITTLE DEMON WHEN I GET MY HANDS ON HER, NOT THE LEAST OF WHICH BEING HOW SHE MISPLACED AN ENTIRE TEAM OF X-MEN.
SAVE YOUR QUESTIONS.
THEY'VE BEEN TAKEN BACK TO LIMBO...

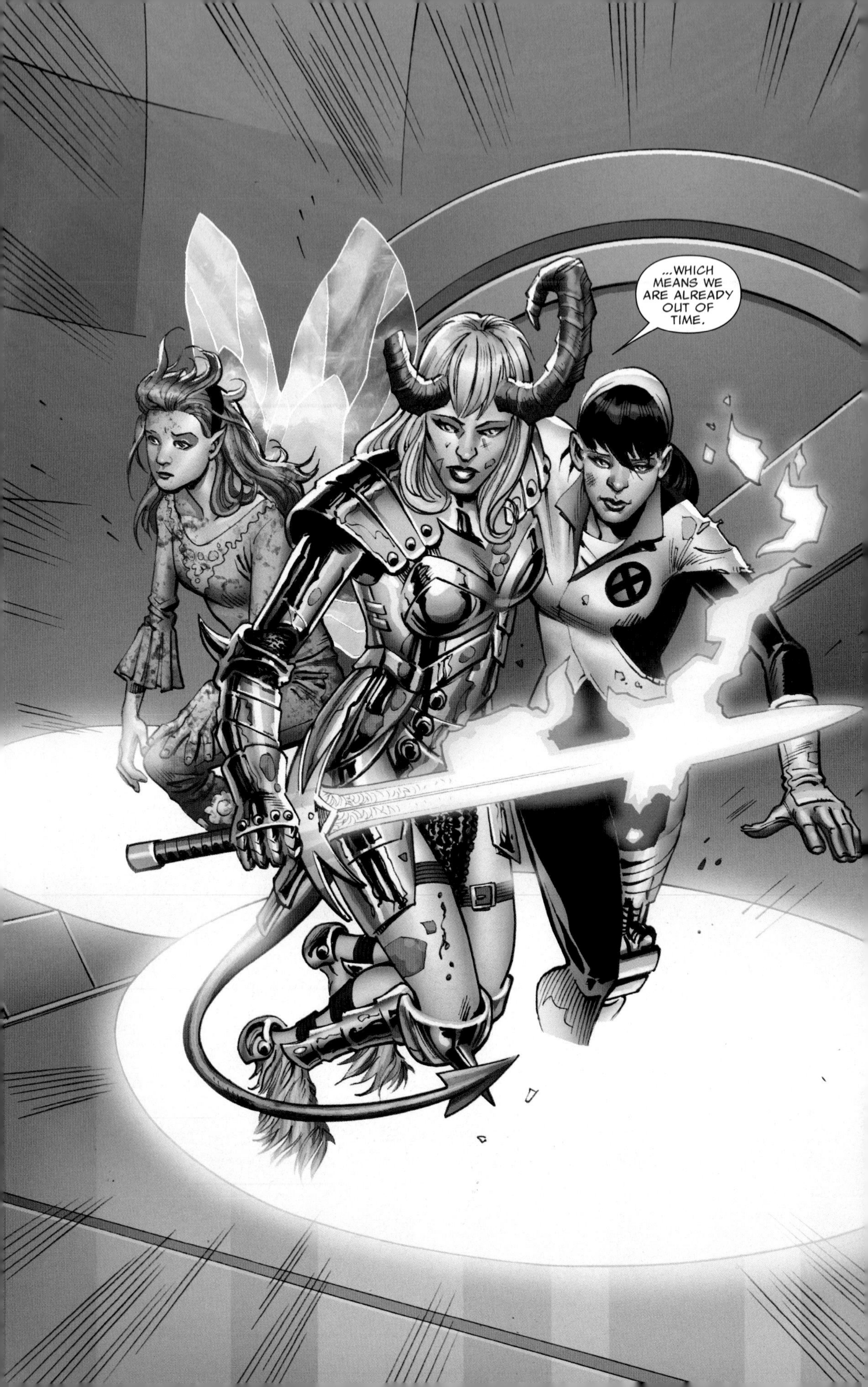
...WHICH MEANS WE ARE ALREADY OUT OF TIME.

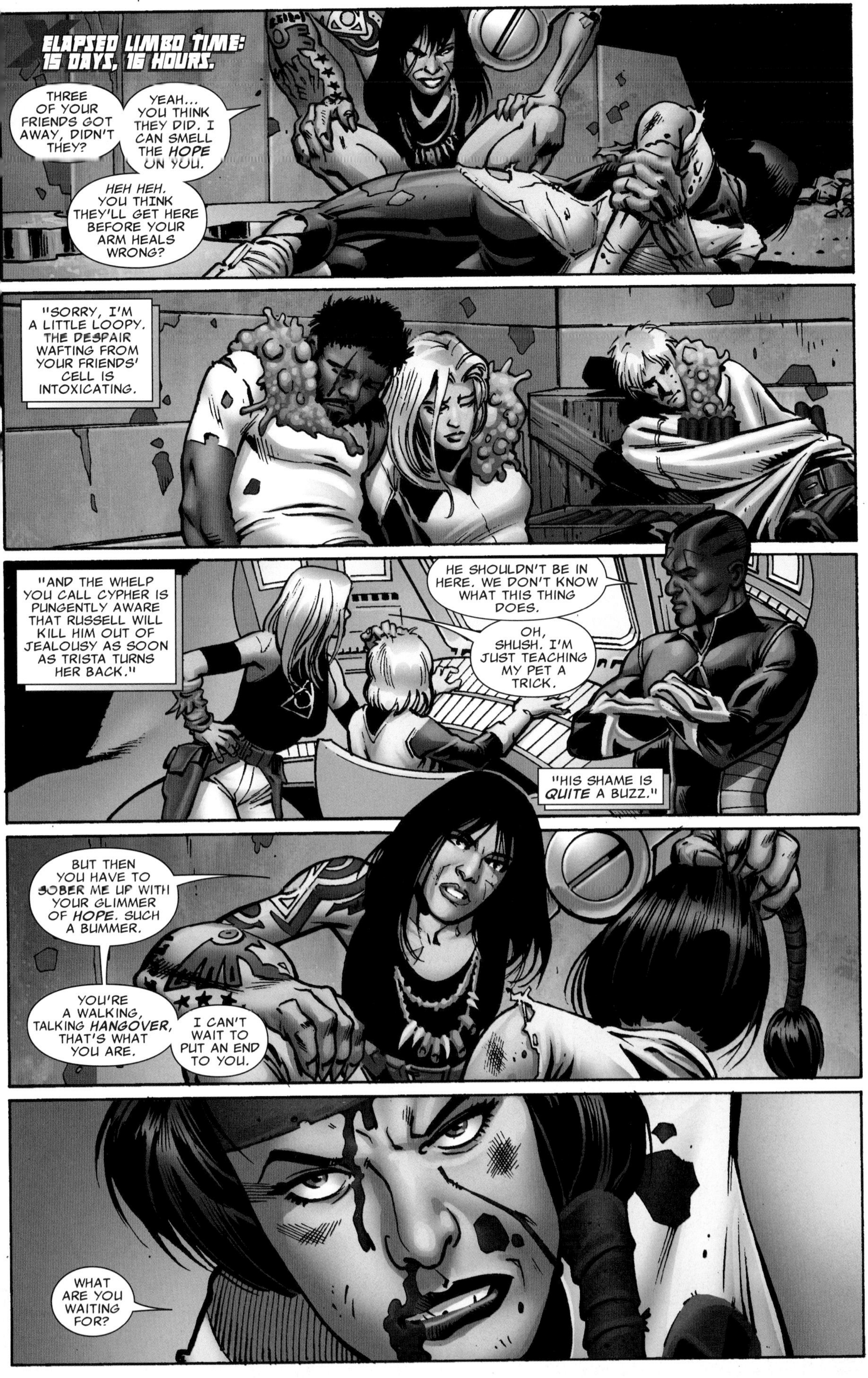
ELAPSED LIMBO TIME: 15 DAYS, 16 HOURS.
THREE OF YOUR FRIENDS GOT AWAY, DIDN'T THEY?
YEAH... YOU THINK THEY DID. I CAN SMELL THE HOPE ON YOU.
HEH HEH. YOU THINK THEY'LL GET HERE BEFORE YOUR ARM HEALS WRONG?
"SORRY, I'M A LITTLE LOOPY. THE DESPAIR WAFTING FROM YOUR FRIENDS' CELL IS INTOXICATING.
"AND THE WHELP YOU CALL CYPHER IS PUNGENTLY AWARE THAT RUSSELL WILL KILL HIM OUT OF JEALOUSY AS SOON AS TRISTA TURNS HER BACK."
HE SHOULDN'T BE IN HERE. WE DON'T KNOW WHAT THIS THING DOES.
OH, SHUSH. I'M JUST TEACHING MY PET A TRICK.
"HIS SHAME IS QUITE A BUZZ."
BUT THEN YOU HAVE TO SOBER ME UP WITH YOUR GLIMMER OF HOPE. SUCH A BUMMER.
YOU'RE A WALKING, TALKING HANGOVER, THAT'S WHAT YOU ARE.
I CAN'T WAIT TO PUT AN END TO YOU.
WHAT ARE YOU WAITING FOR?

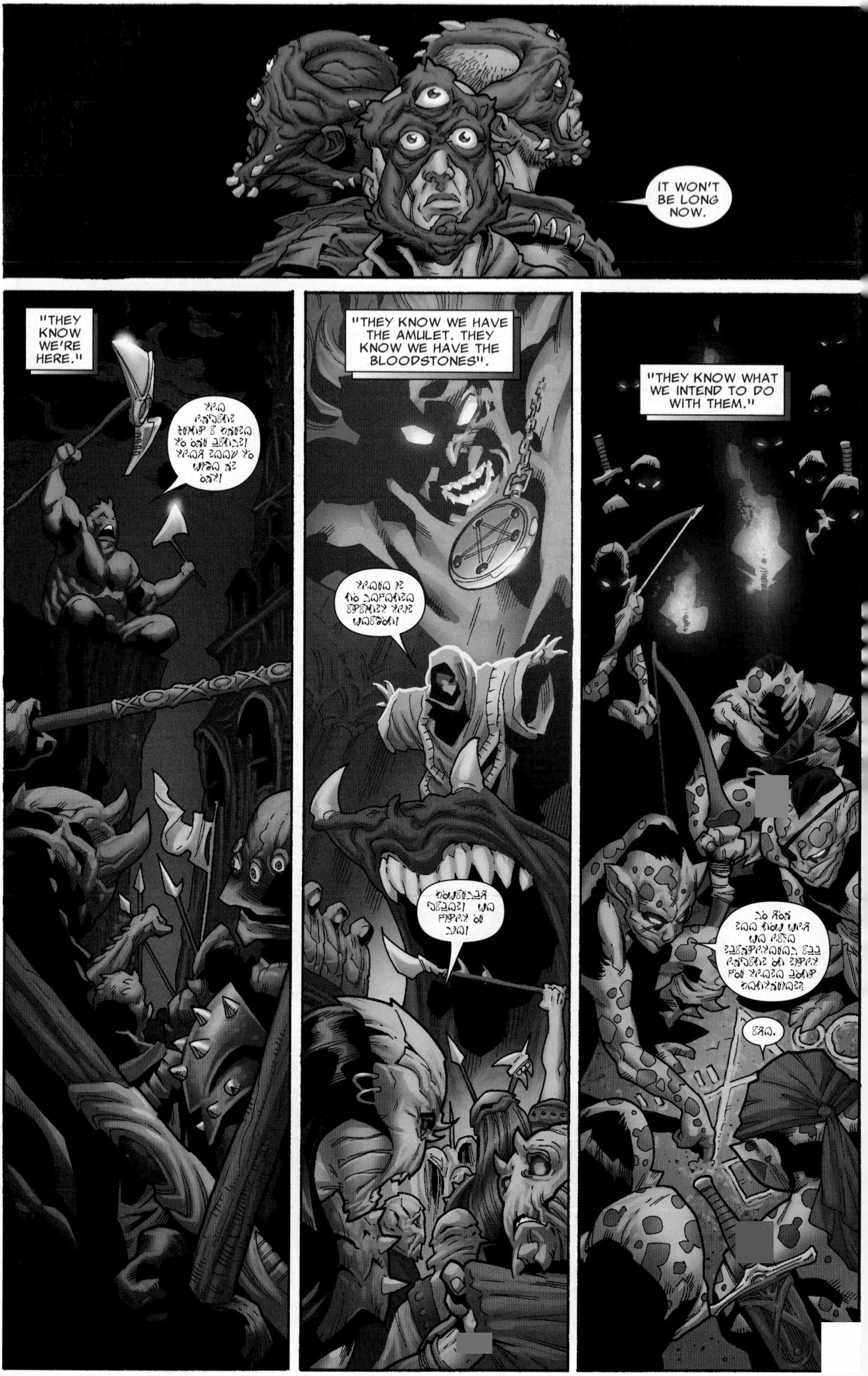
IT WON'T BE LONG NOW.
"THEY KNOW WE'RE HERE."
"THEY KNOW WE HAVE THE AMULET. THEY KNOW WE HAVE THE BLOODSTONES".
"THEY KNOW WHAT WE INTEND TO DO WITH THEM."

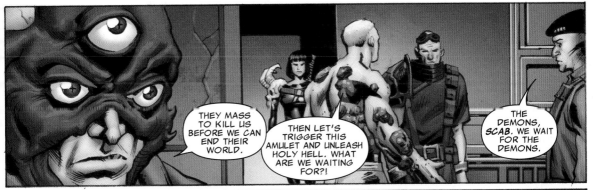

THEY MASS TO KILL US BEFORE WE CAN END THEIR WORLD.

THEN LET'S TRIGGER THIS AMULET AND UNLEASH HOLY HELL. WHAT ARE WE WAITING FOR?!

THE DEMONS, *SCAB*. WE WAIT FOR THE DEMONS.

MAW, TIMOTHY AND *FACE* HAVE NOT ARRIVED, GENERAL...WE MUST ASSUME THE DARKCHILDE HAS ESCAPED.

WE'RE IN LIMBO. WE HAVE THE TIME.

I WANT EVERY DEMON TOGETHER IN ONE MASSIVE PILE OF @#%$ SO I CAN STEP ON THEM ALL AT ONCE.

I WANT THEM TO KNOW I'VE GOT THEM BY THE @#%$.

I WANT THEM TO KNOW THEY MESSED WITH THE WRONG @#$% #$% MARINE.

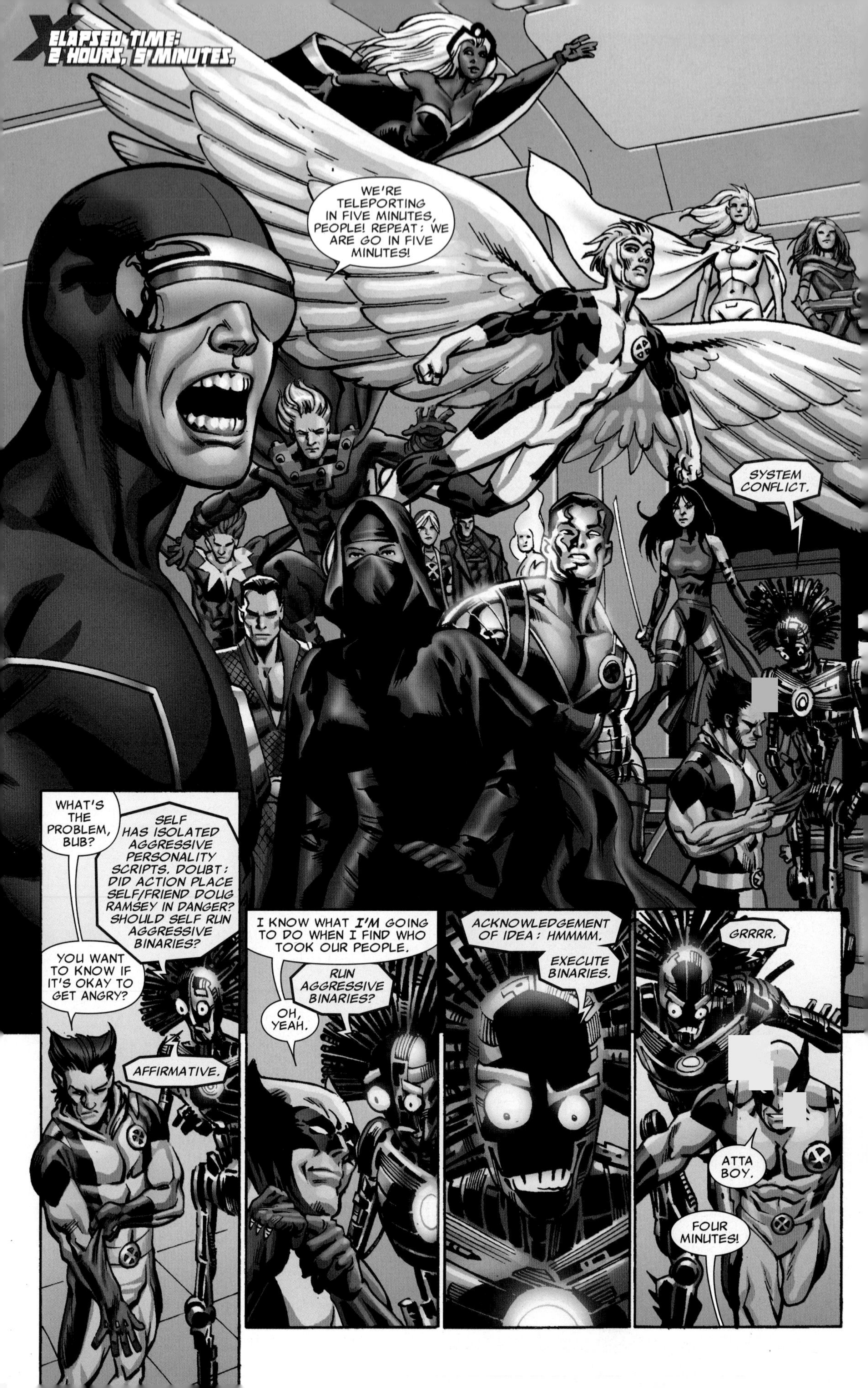

ELAPSED TIME: 2 HOURS, 5 MINUTES.
WE'RE TELEPORTING IN FIVE MINUTES, PEOPLE! REPEAT: WE ARE GO IN FIVE MINUTES!
SYSTEM CONFLICT.
WHAT'S THE PROBLEM, BUB?
SELF HAS ISOLATED AGGRESSIVE PERSONALITY SCRIPTS. DOUBT: DID ACTION PLACE SELF/FRIEND DOUG RAMSEY IN DANGER? SHOULD SELF RUN AGGRESSIVE BINARIES?
YOU WANT TO KNOW IF IT'S OKAY TO GET ANGRY?
AFFIRMATIVE.
I KNOW WHAT I'M GOING TO DO WHEN I FIND WHO TOOK OUR PEOPLE.
RUN AGGRESSIVE BINARIES?
OH, YEAH.
ACKNOWLEDGEMENT OF IDEA: HMMMMM.
EXECUTE BINARIES.
GRRRR.
ATTA BOY.
FOUR MINUTES!

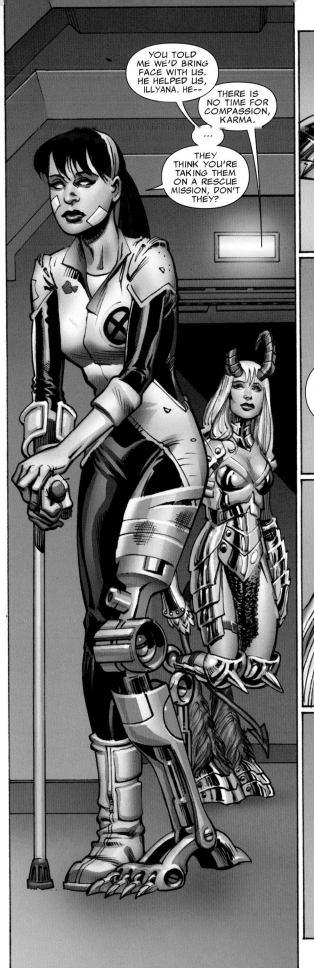

YOU TOLD ME WE'D BRING FACE WITH US. HE HELPED US, ILLYANA. HE--

THERE IS NO TIME FOR COMPASSION, KARMA.

...

THEY THINK YOU'RE TAKING THEM ON A RESCUE MISSION, DON'T THEY?

THERE IS NO NEED TO ASK QUESTIONS TO WHICH YOU KNOW THE ANSWER.

WHEN WE WERE IN LEGION'S MIND BEFORE... *THIS* IS WHY YOU LET ME USE THE SOULSWORD, ISN'T IT?

WHY YOU KEPT IT A SECRET...

I COULD NEVER HINT AT WHAT I PLANNED TO DO.

WHAT ARE YOU WAITING FOR?

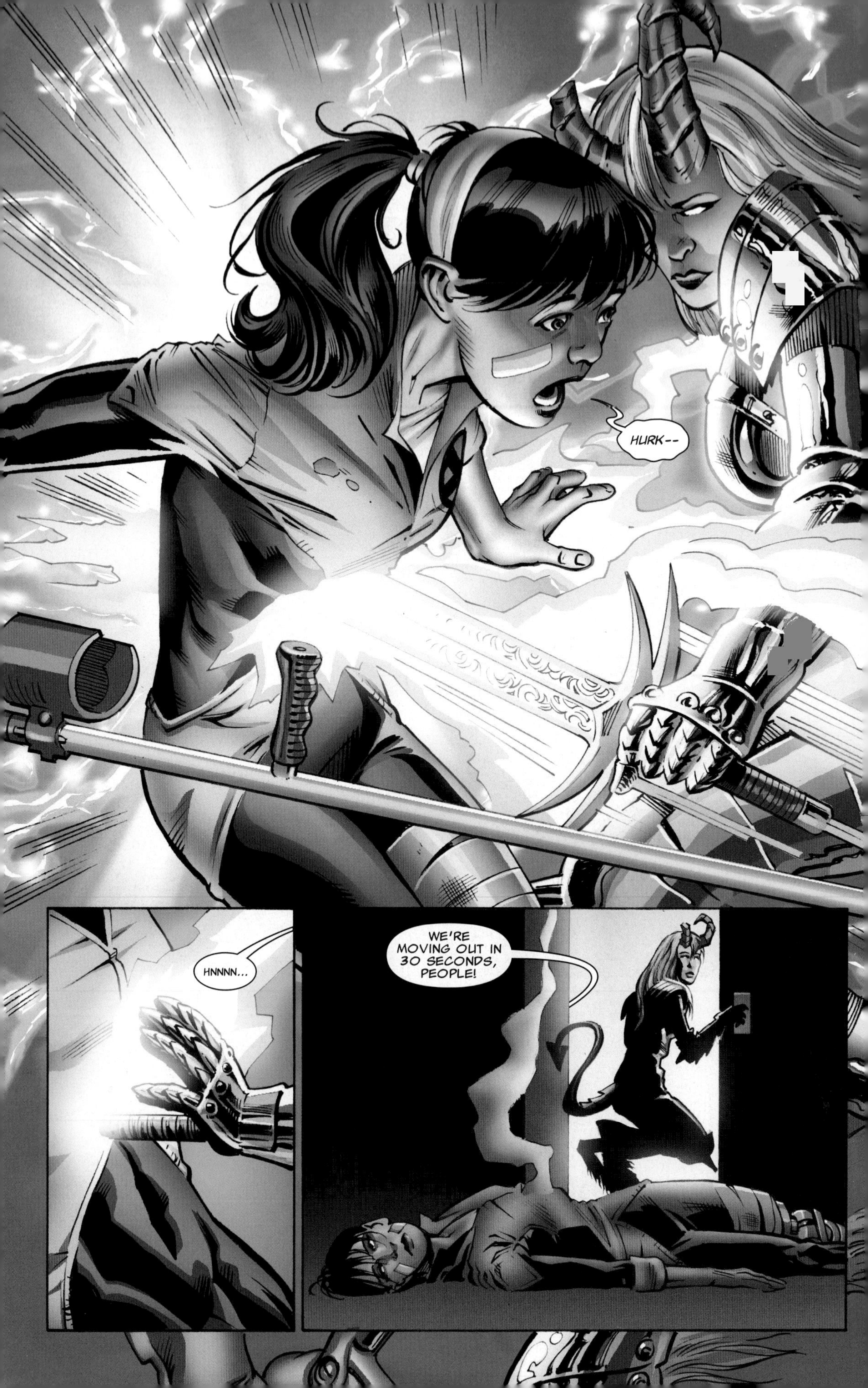
HURK--
HNNNN...
WE'RE MOVING OUT IN 30 SECONDS, PEOPLE!

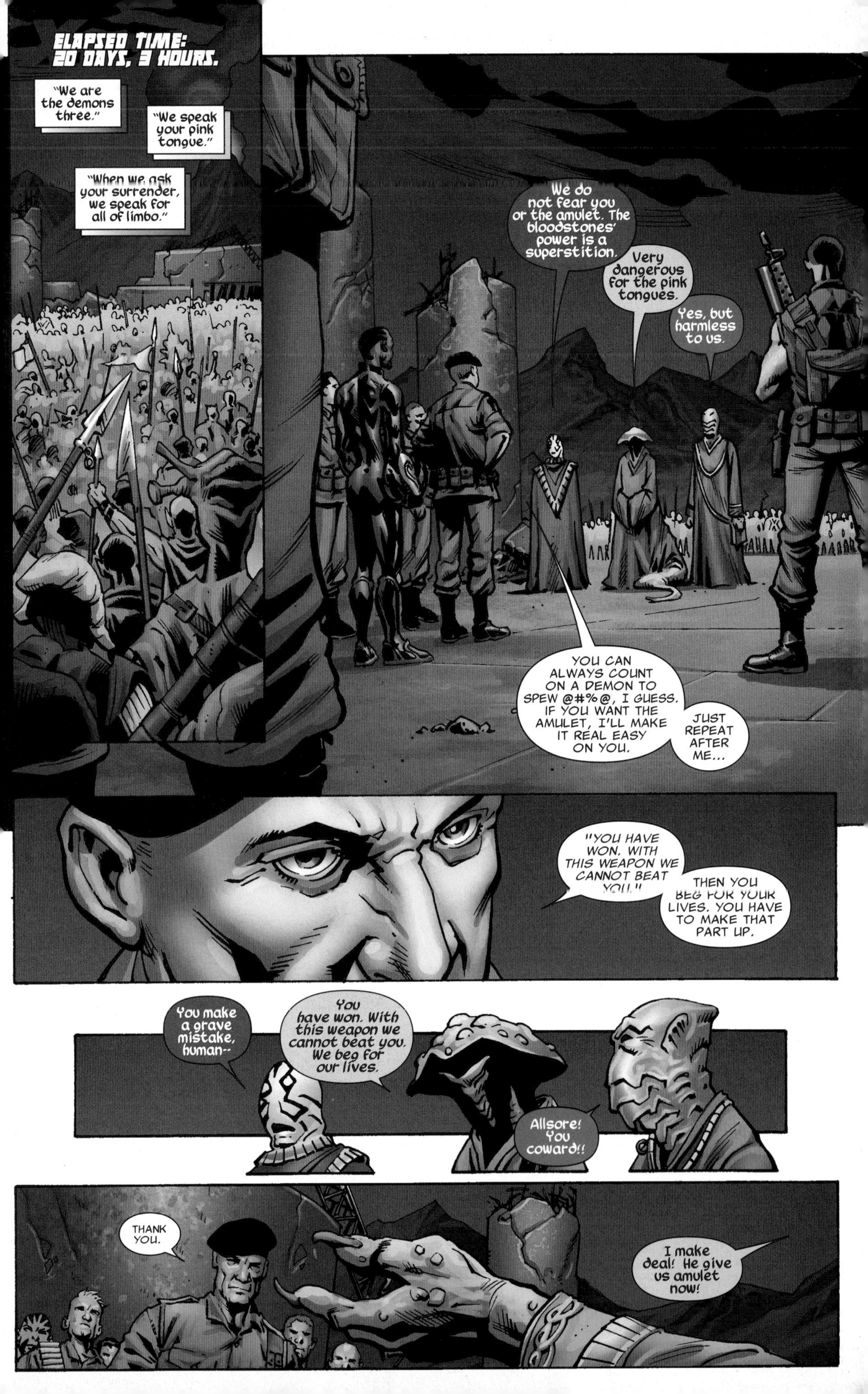
ELAPSED TIME:
20 DAYS, 3 HOURS.
"We are the demons three."
"We speak your pink tongue."
"When we ask your surrender, we speak for all of limbo."
We do not fear you or the amulet. The bloodstones' power is a superstition.
Very dangerous for the pink tongues.
Yes, but harmless to us.
YOU CAN ALWAYS COUNT ON A DEMON TO SPEW @#%@, I GUESS. IF YOU WANT THE AMULET, I'LL MAKE IT REAL EASY ON YOU.
JUST REPEAT AFTER ME...
"YOU HAVE WON. WITH THIS WEAPON WE CANNOT BEAT YOU."
THEN YOU BEG FOR YOUR LIVES. YOU HAVE TO MAKE THAT PART UP.
You make a grave mistake, human--
You have won. With this weapon we cannot beat you. We beg for our lives.
Allsore! You coward!!
THANK YOU.
I make deal! He give us amulet now!

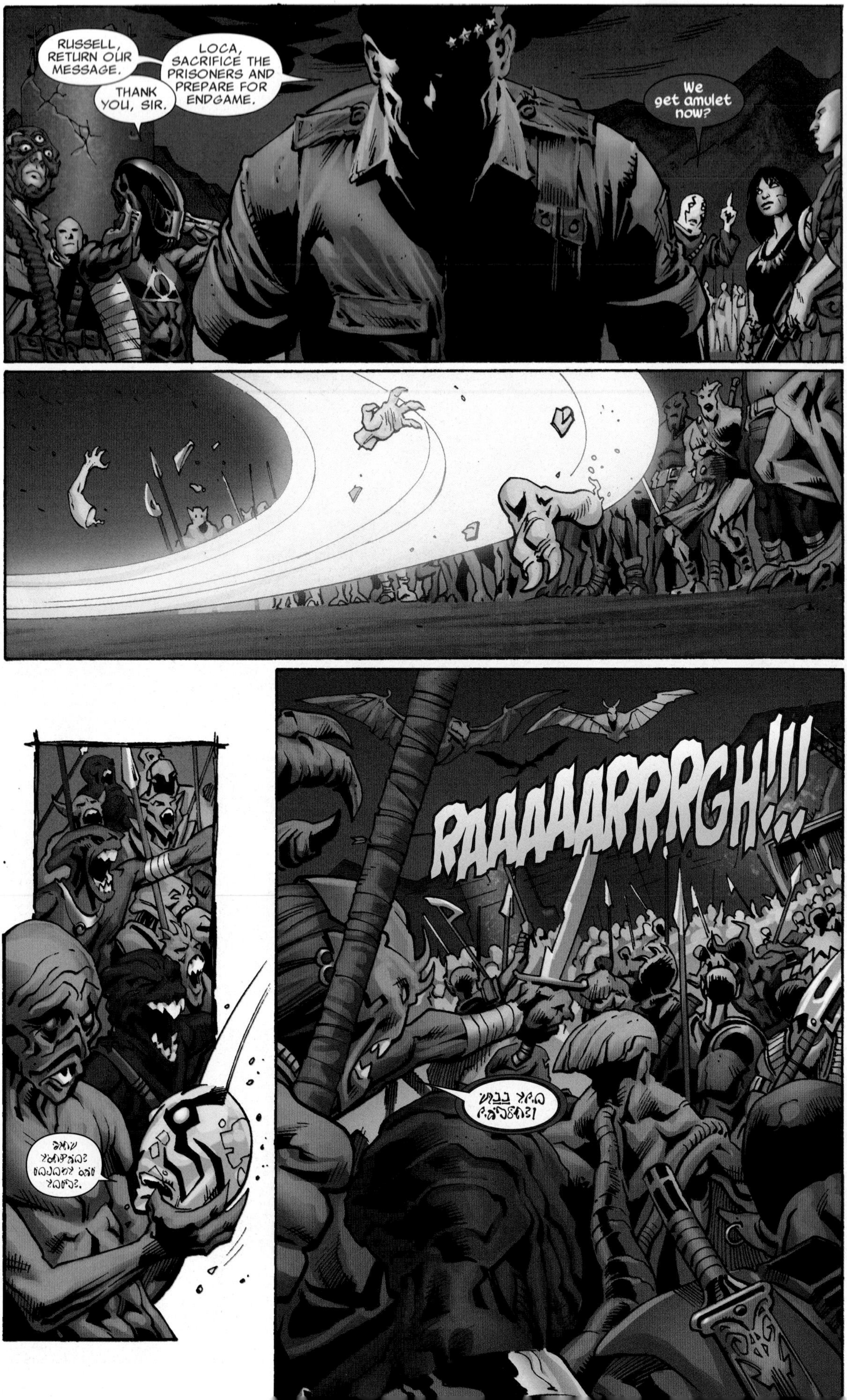
RUSSELL, RETURN OUR MESSAGE.
THANK YOU, SIR.
LOCA, SACRIFICE THE PRISONERS AND PREPARE FOR ENDGAME.
We get amulet now?
RAAAAARRRGH!!!

RARRRRRROOOOOOO!!!

RUMBLE

WHO'S THERE!

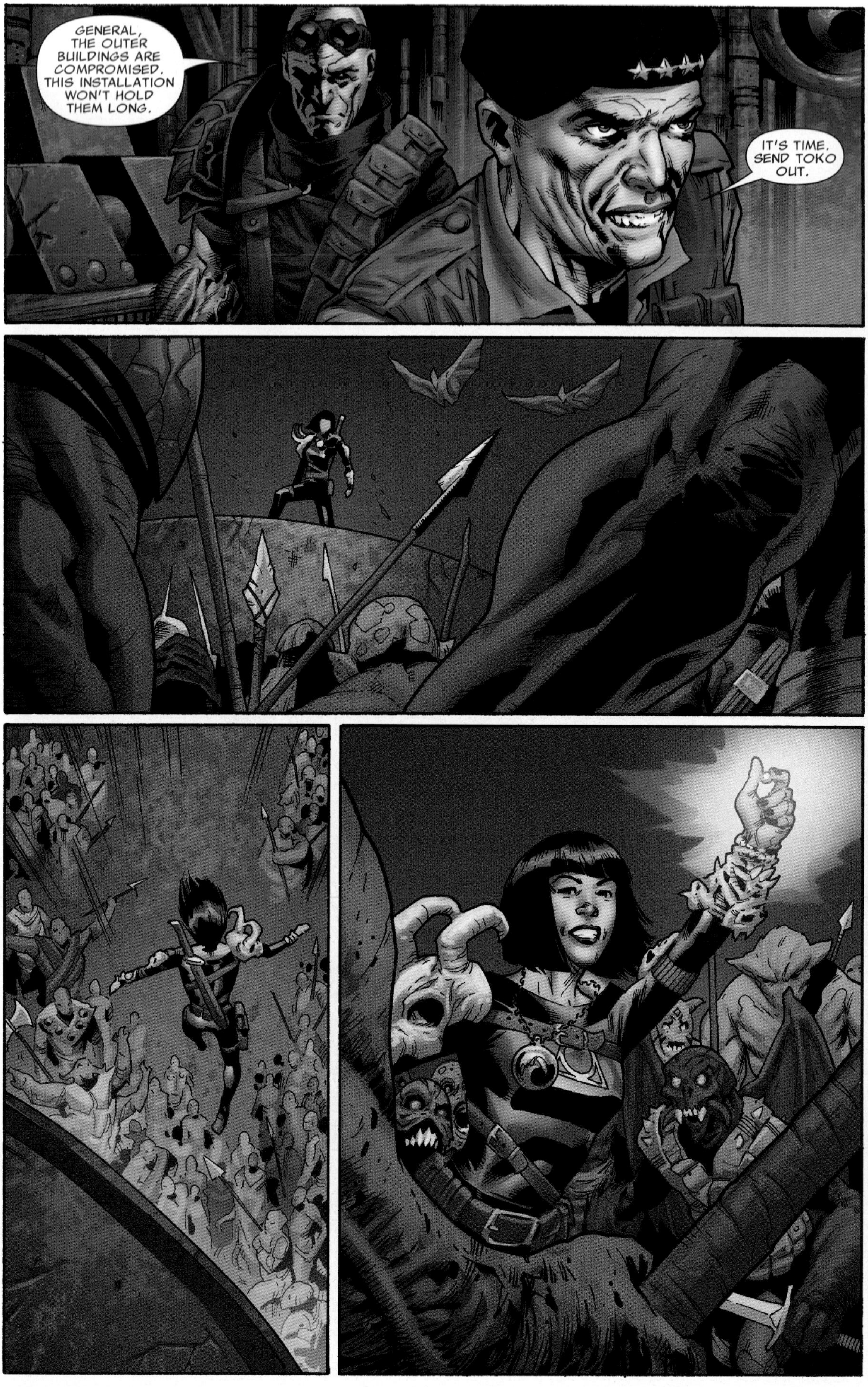
GENERAL, THE OUTER BUILDINGS ARE COMPROMISED. THIS INSTALLATION WON'T HOLD THEM LONG.
IT'S TIME. SEND TOKO OUT.

YOU DIE NEXT, MOONSTAR! DO YOU HEAR ME?

BAM!!

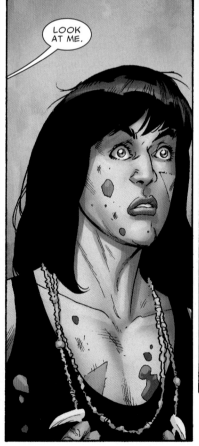

LOOK AT ME.

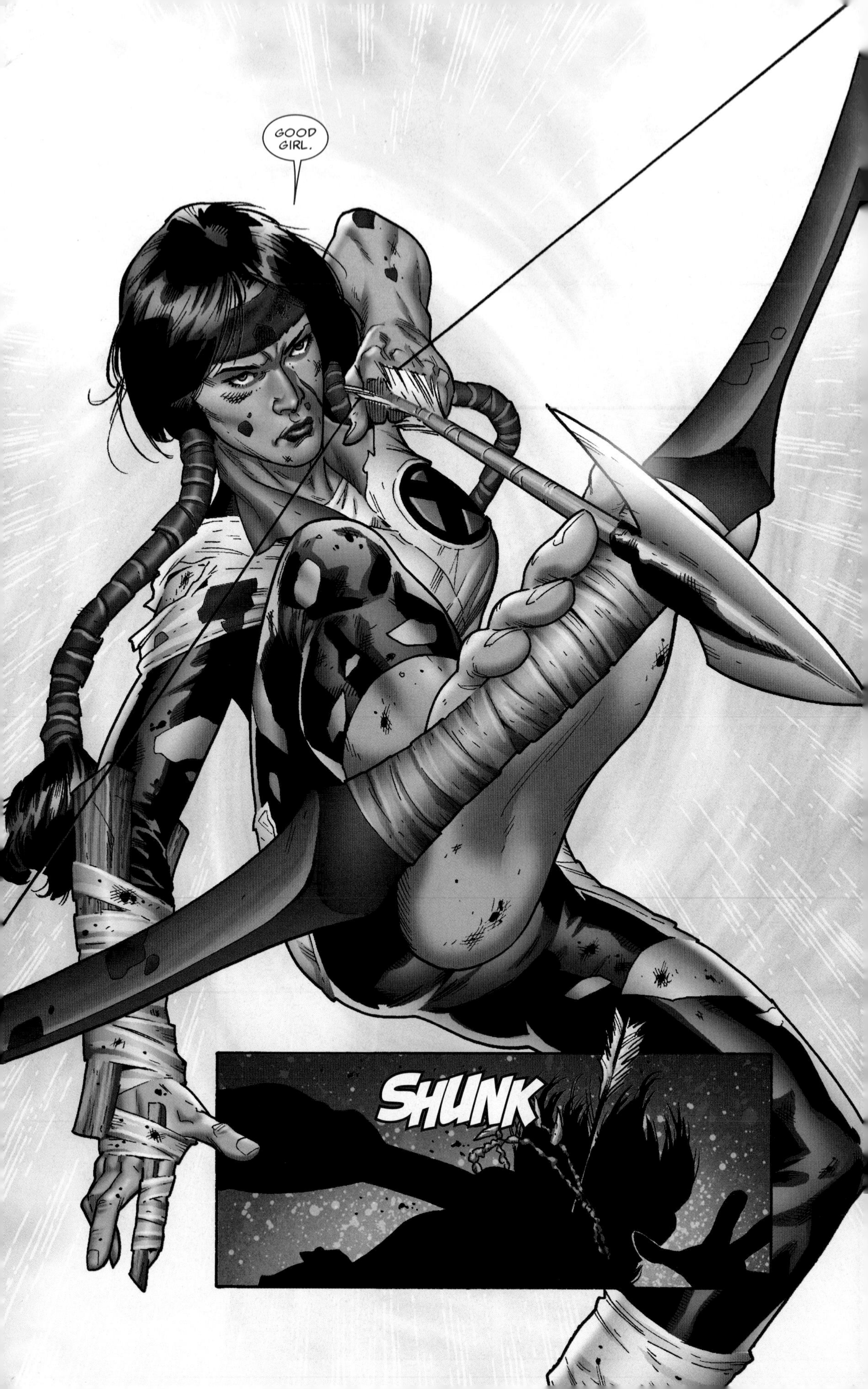
GOOD GIRL.
SHUNK

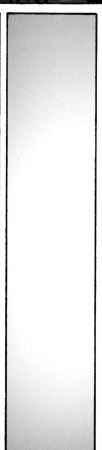

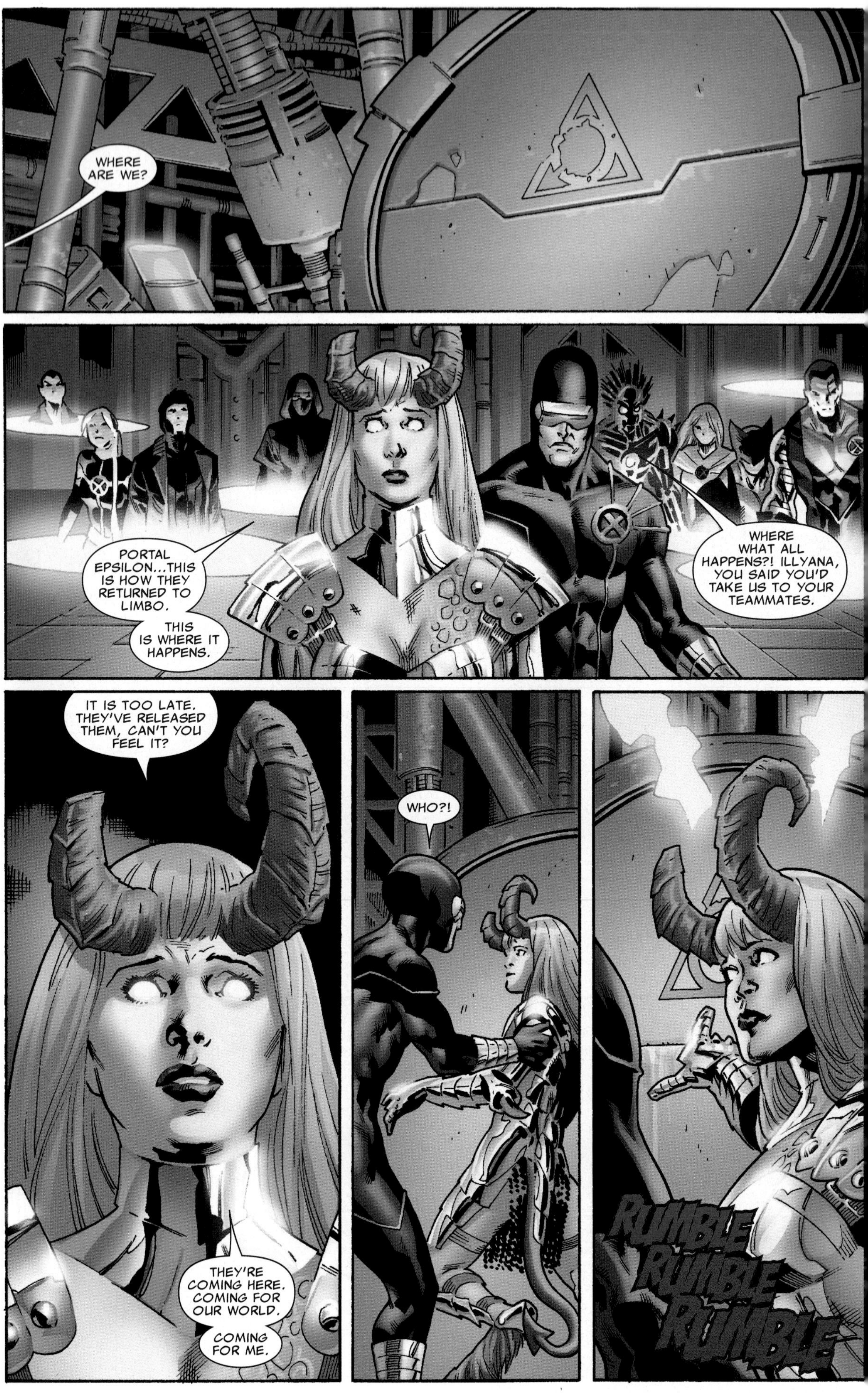
WHERE ARE WE?
PORTAL EPSILON...THIS IS HOW THEY RETURNED TO LIMBO.
THIS IS WHERE IT HAPPENS.
WHERE WHAT ALL HAPPENS?! ILLYANA, YOU SAID YOU'D TAKE US TO YOUR TEAMMATES.
IT IS TOO LATE. THEY'VE RELEASED THEM, CAN'T YOU FEEL IT?
THEY'RE COMING HERE. COMING FOR OUR WORLD.
COMING FOR ME.
WHO?!
RUMBLE RUMBLE RUMBLE

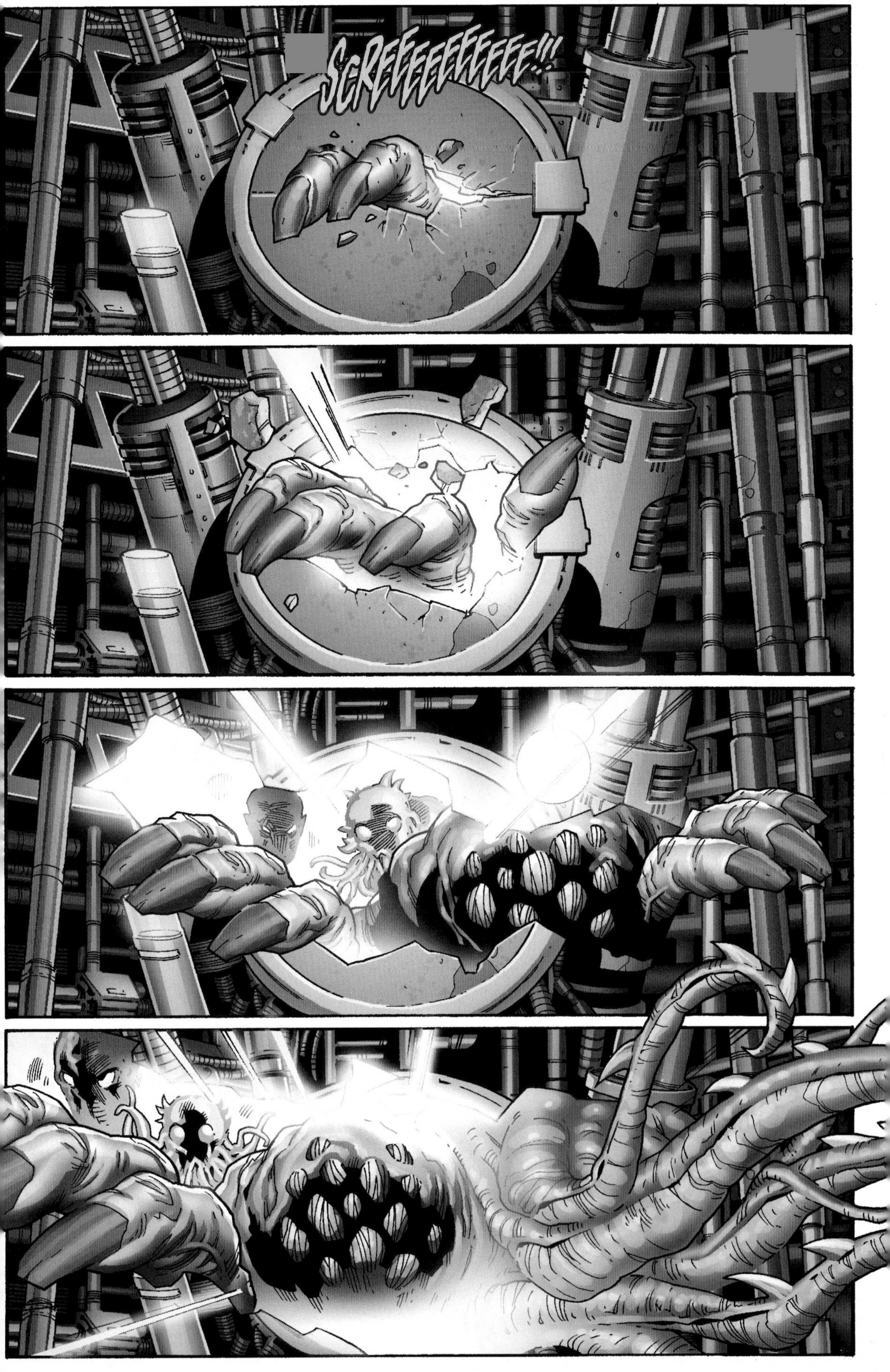
SCREEEEEEEEEE!!!

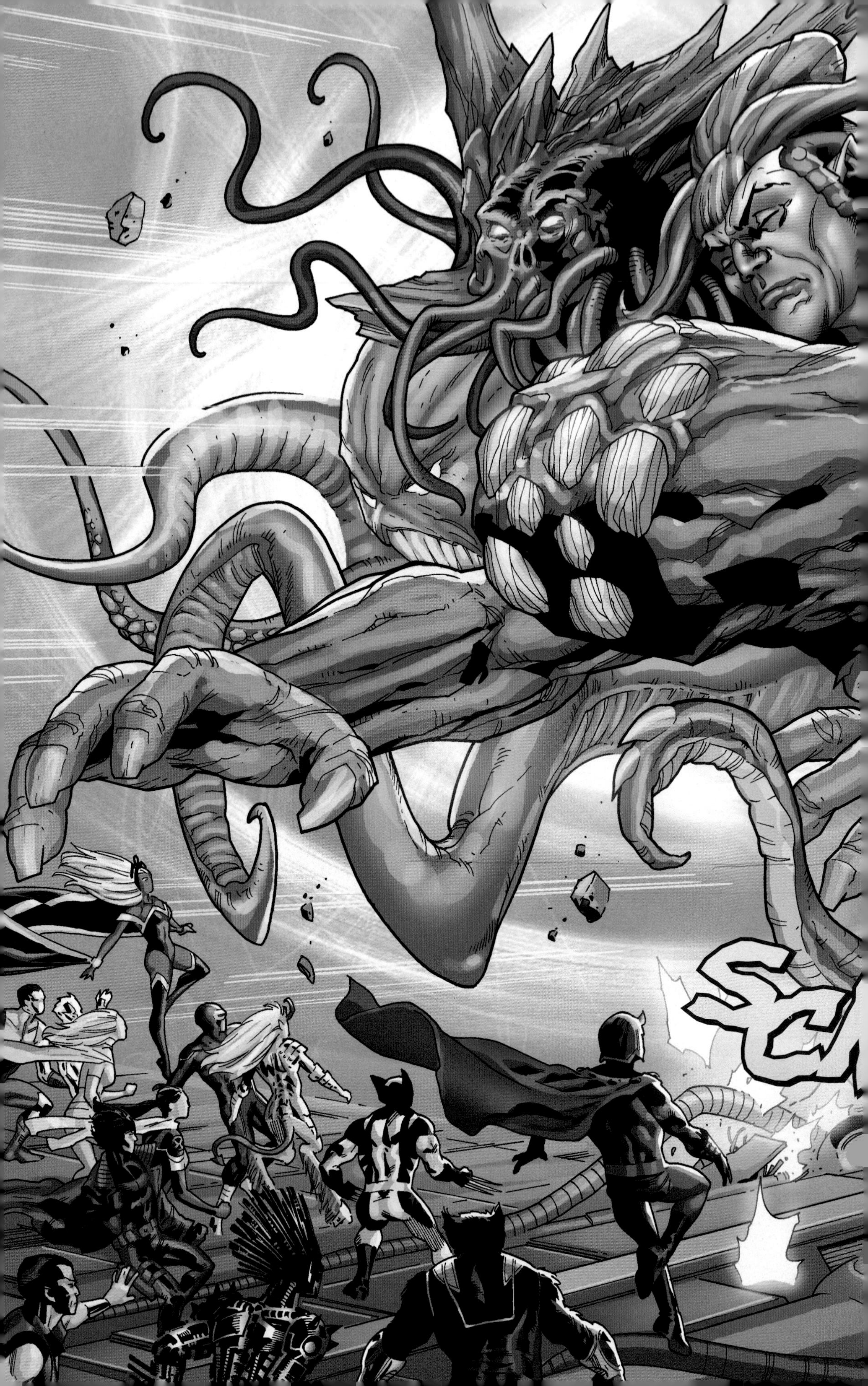

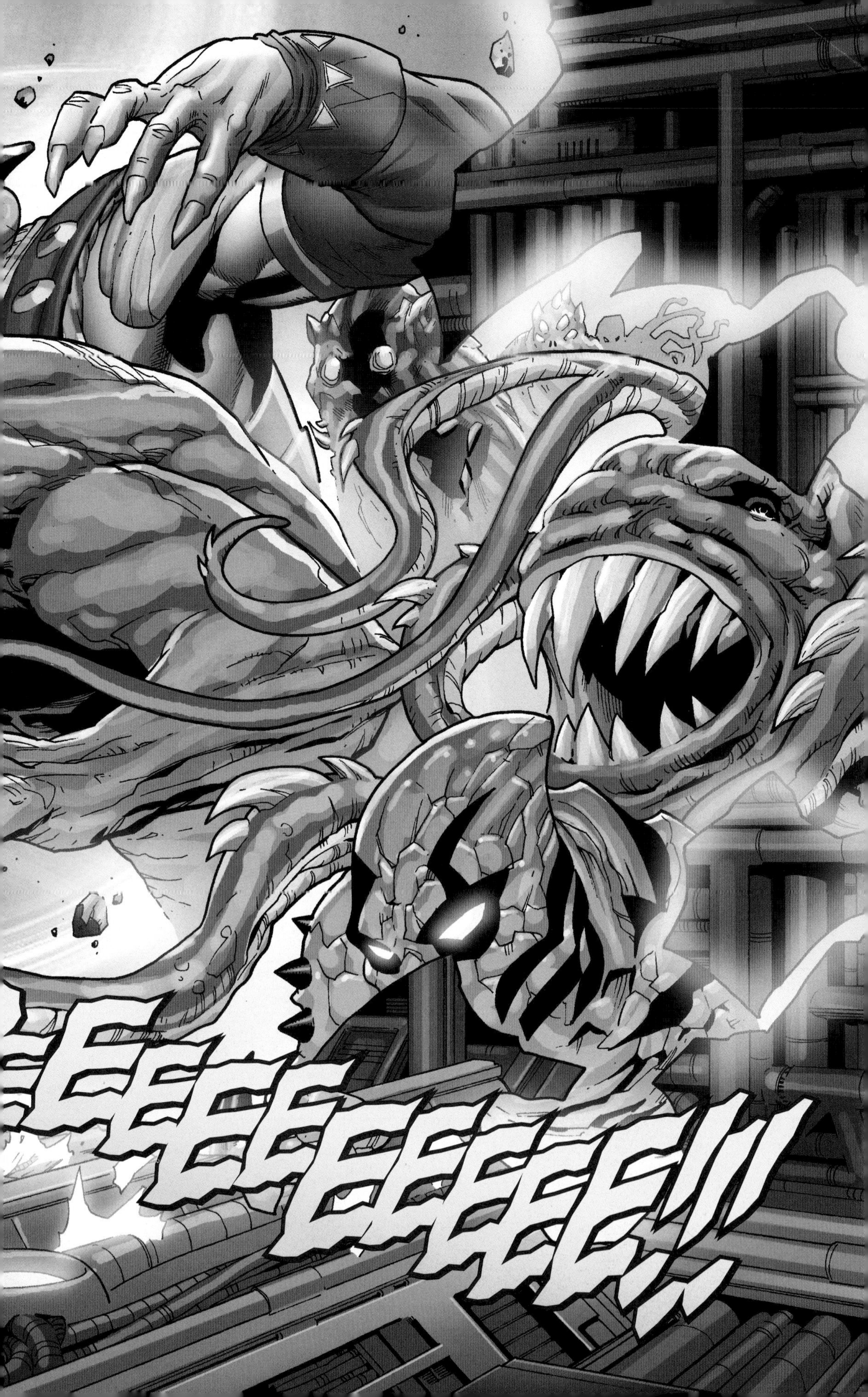
EEEEEEEEEE!!

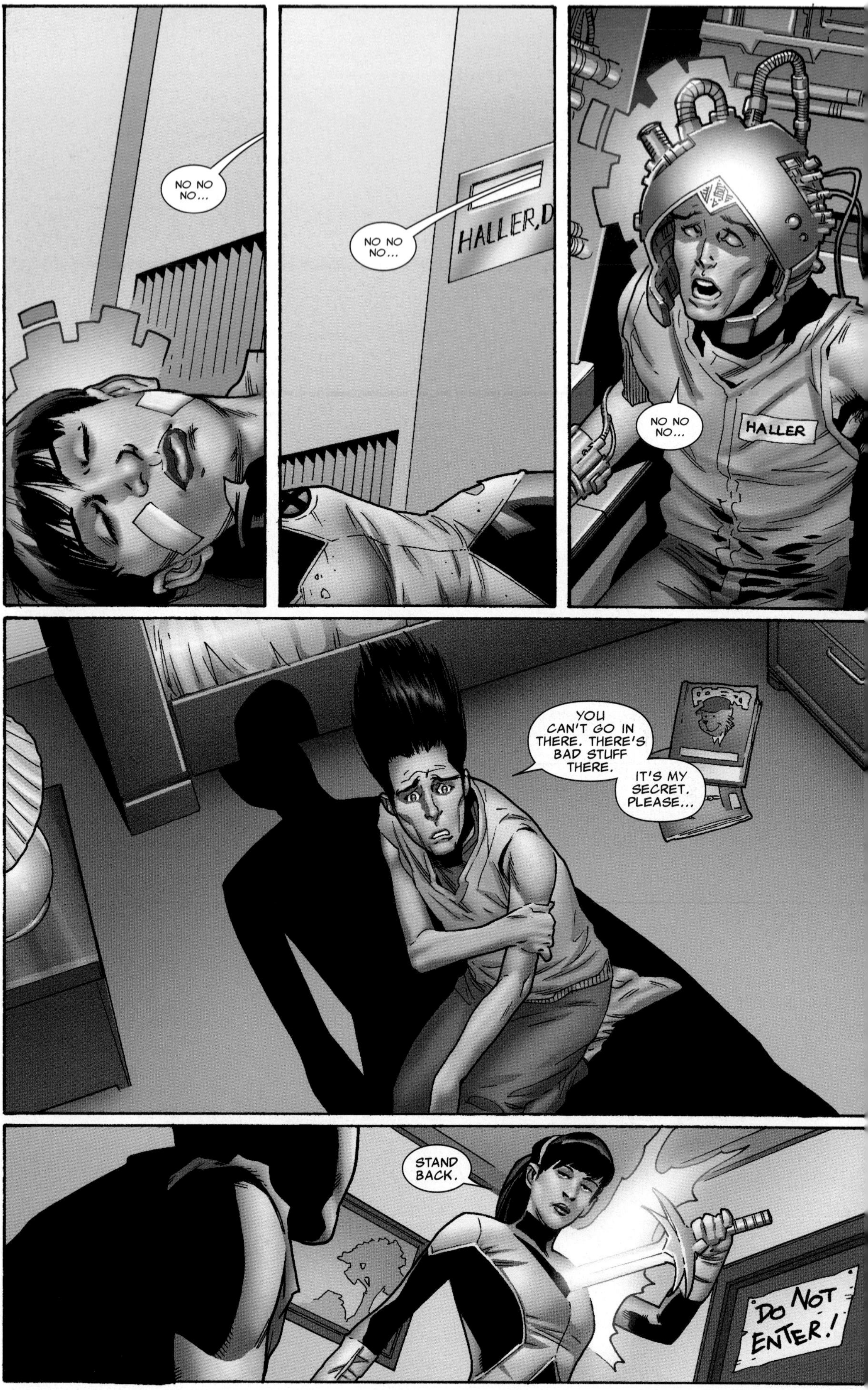
NO NO NO...
NO NO NO...
HALLER, D
NO NO NO...
HALLER
YOU CAN'T GO IN THERE. THERE'S BAD STUFF THERE.
IT'S MY SECRET. PLEASE...
STAND BACK.
DO NOT ENTER!

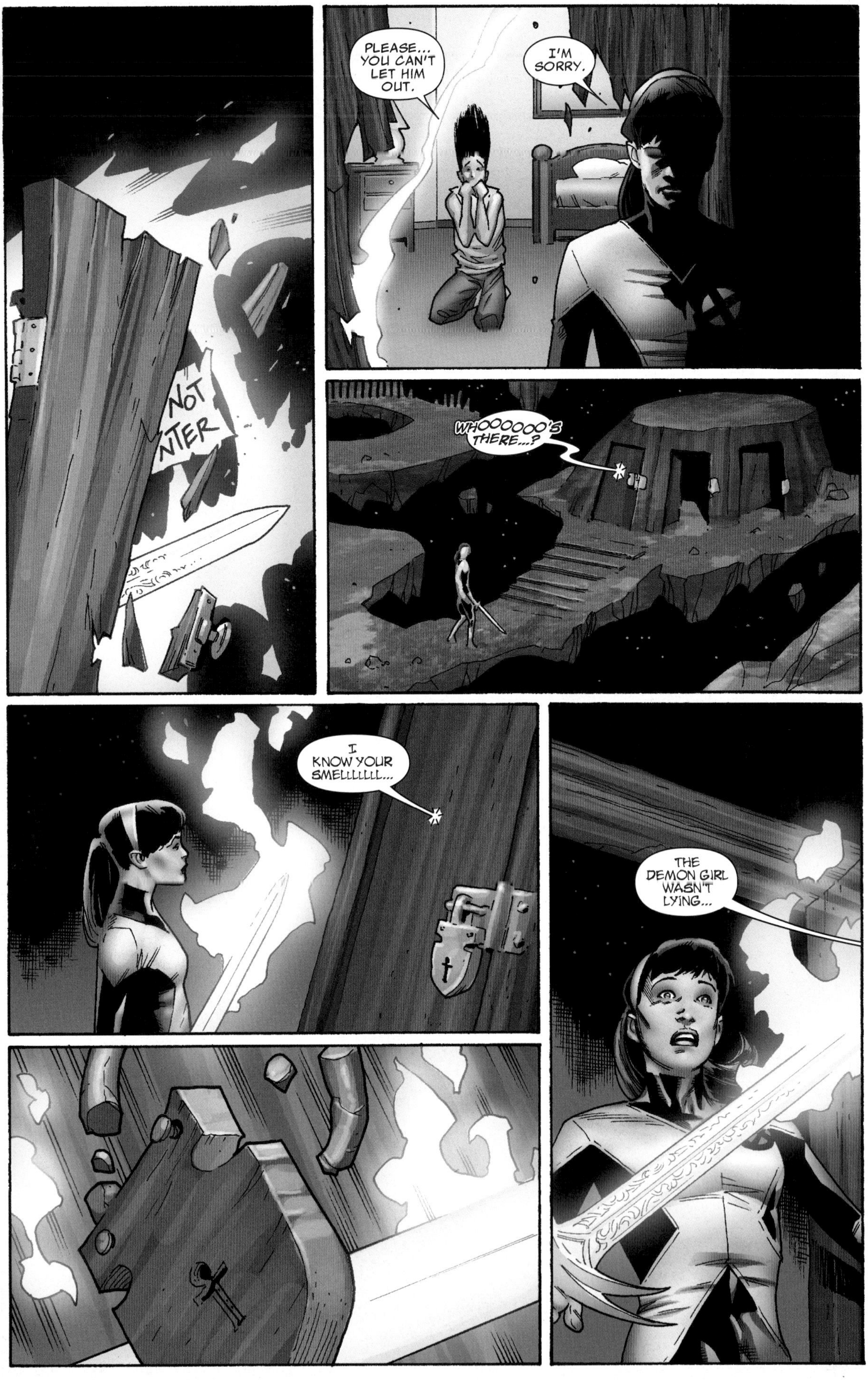
NOT
NTER
PLEASE... YOU CAN'T LET HIM OUT.
I'M SORRY.
WHOOOOOO'S THERE...?
I KNOW YOUR SMELLLLLLLL...
THE DEMON GIRL WASN'T LYING...

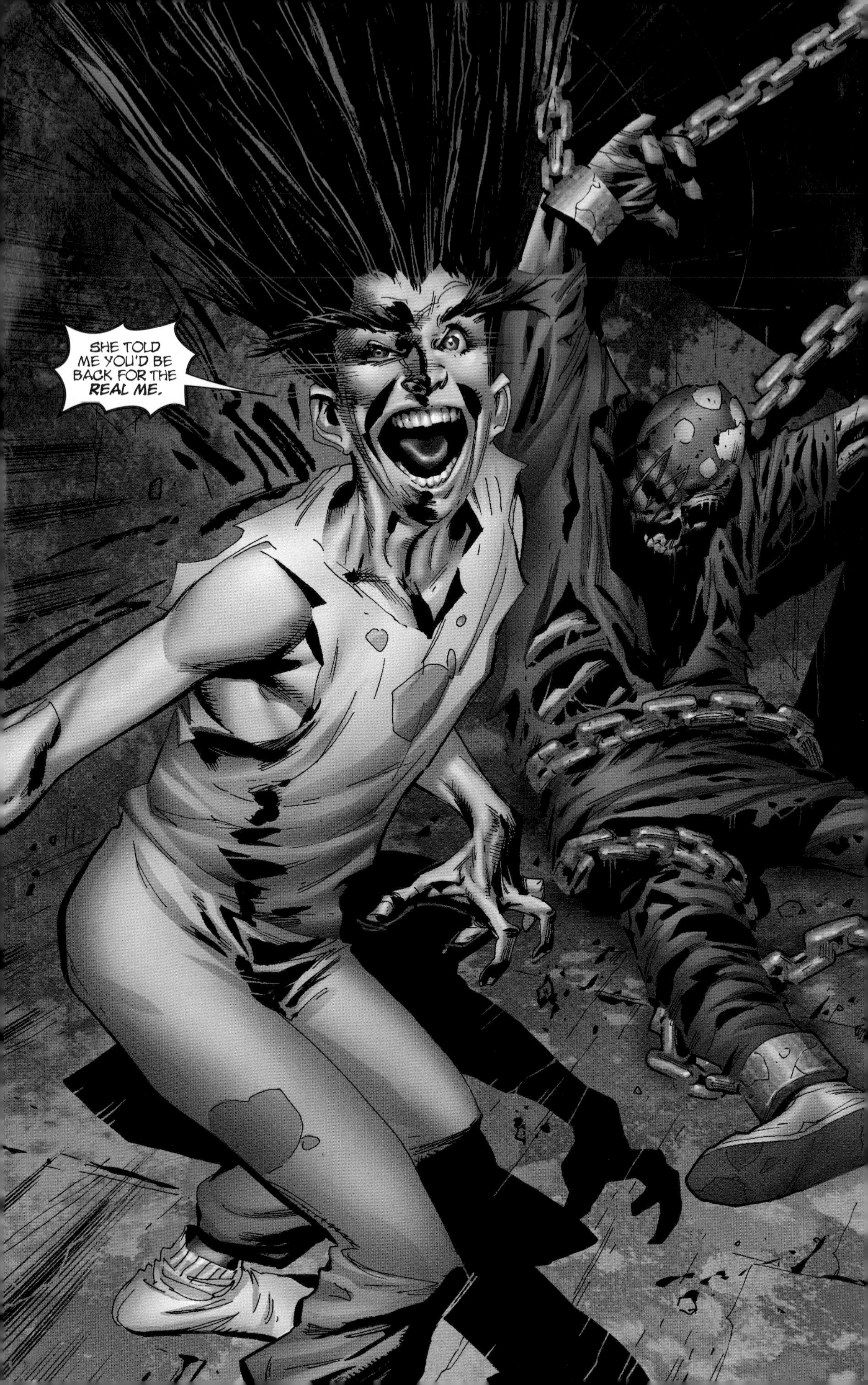
SHE TOLD ME YOU'D BE BACK FOR THE *REAL ME.*

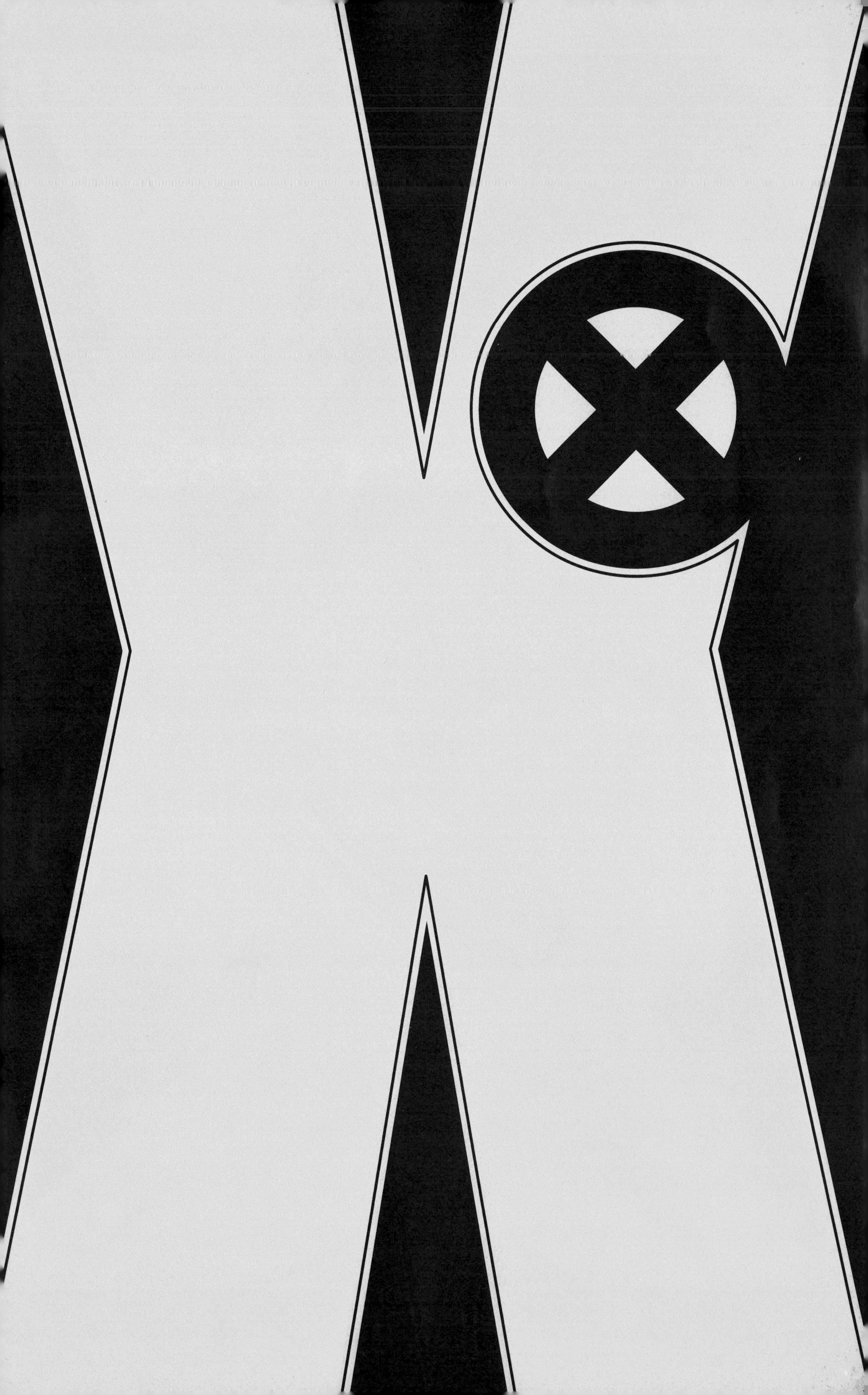

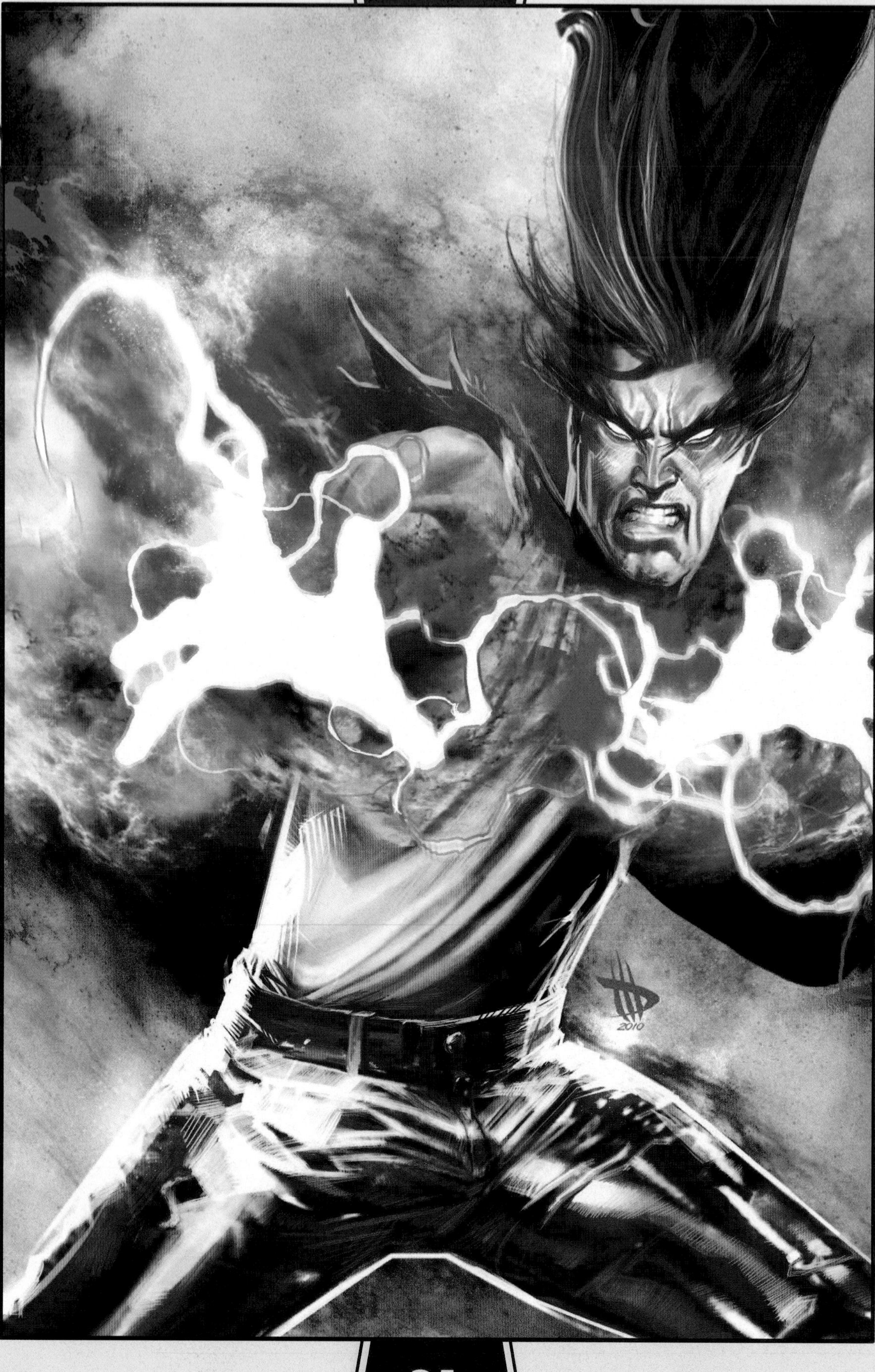
2010

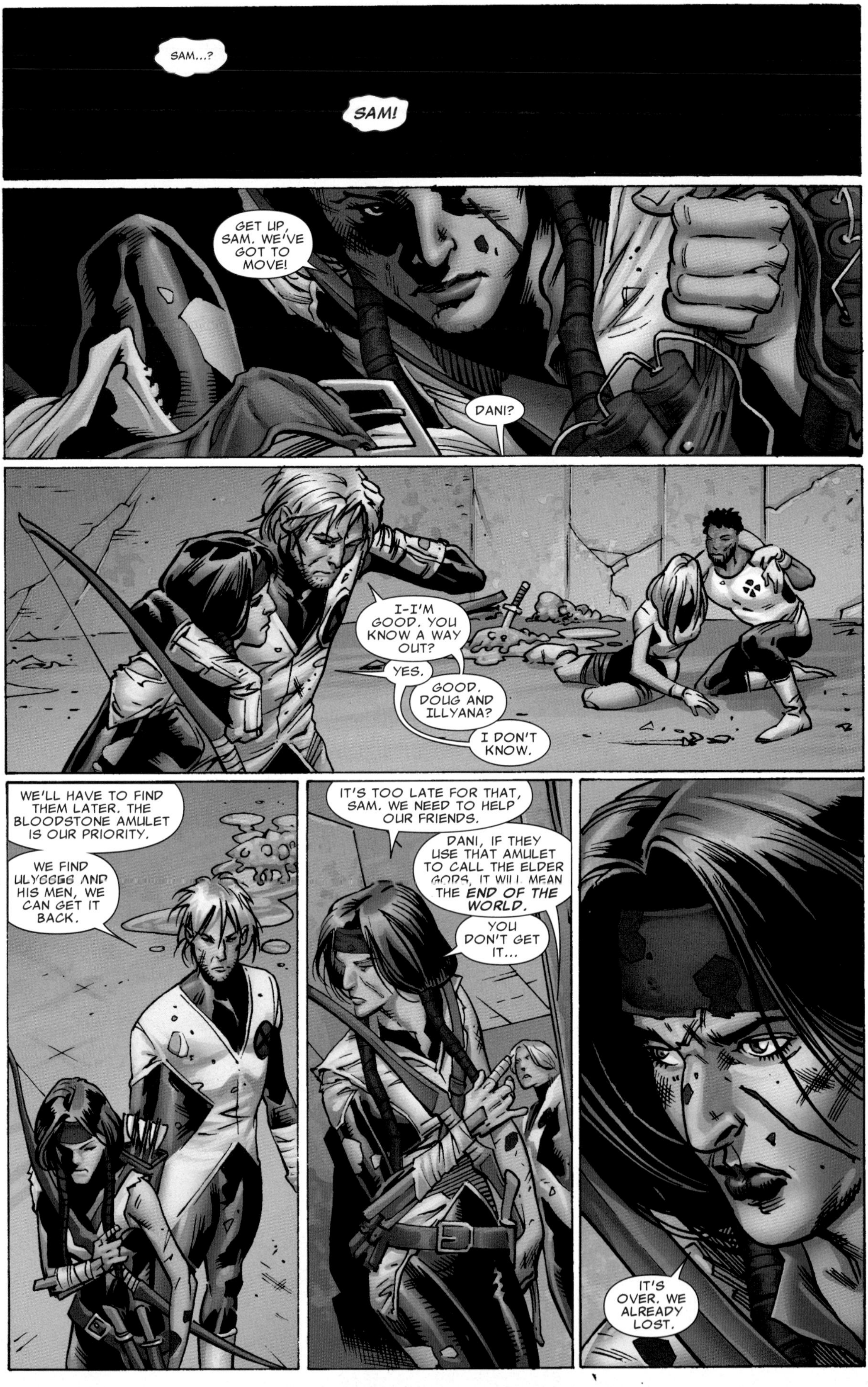

SAM...?
SAM!
GET UP, SAM. WE'VE GOT TO MOVE!
DANI?
I-I'M GOOD. YOU KNOW A WAY OUT?
YES.
GOOD. DOUG AND ILLYANA?
I DON'T KNOW.
WE'LL HAVE TO FIND THEM LATER. THE BLOODSTONE AMULET IS OUR PRIORITY.
WE FIND ULYSSES AND HIS MEN, WE CAN GET IT BACK.
IT'S TOO LATE FOR THAT, SAM. WE NEED TO HELP OUR FRIENDS.
DANI, IF THEY USE THAT AMULET TO CALL THE ELDER GODS, IT WILL MEAN THE END OF THE WORLD.
YOU DON'T GET IT...
IT'S OVER. WE ALREADY LOST.

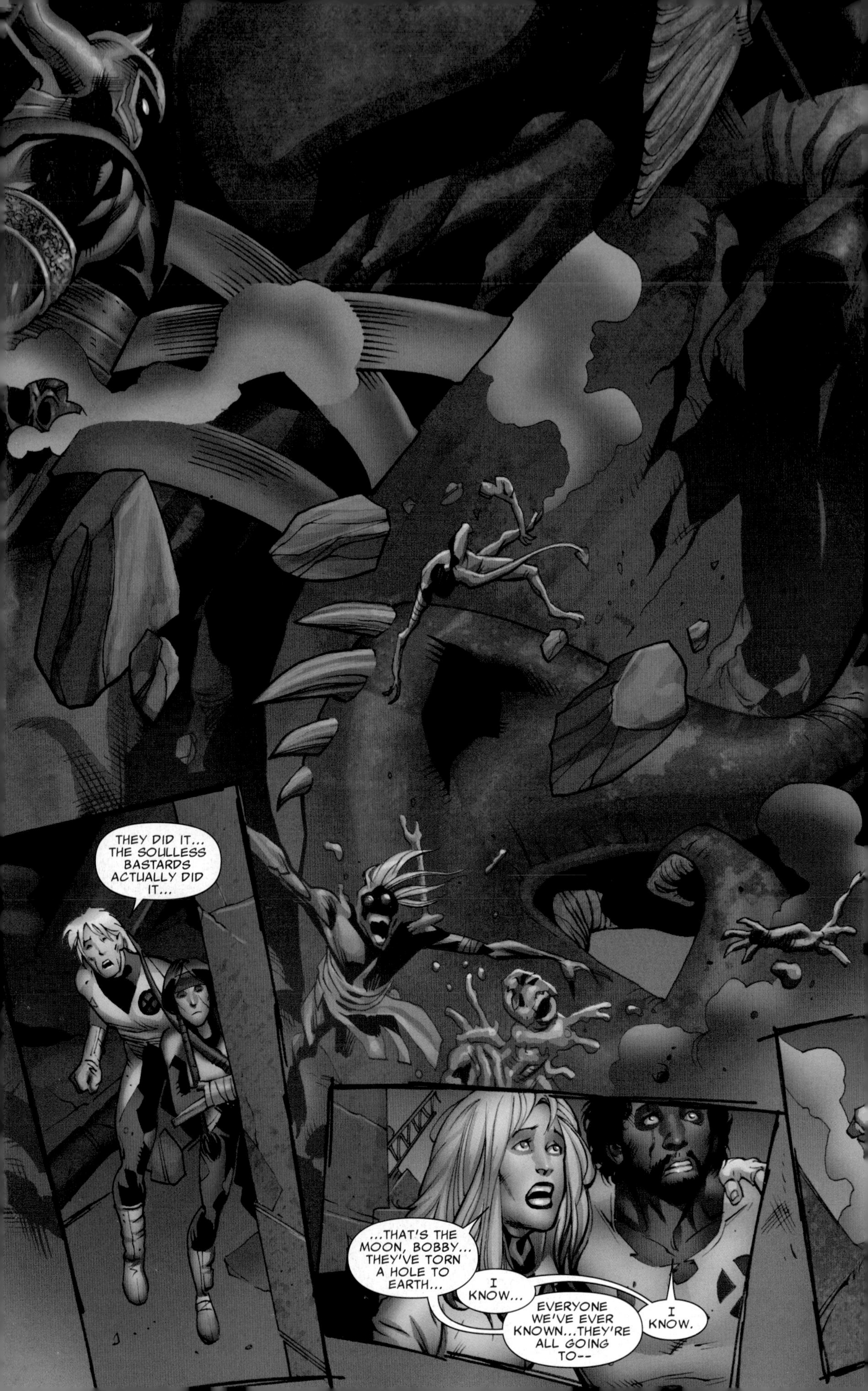
THEY DID IT... THE SOULLESS BASTARDS ACTUALLY DID IT...
...THAT'S THE MOON, BOBBY... THEY'VE TORN A HOLE TO EARTH...
I KNOW...
EVERYONE WE'VE EVER KNOWN...THEY'RE ALL GOING TO--
I KNOW.

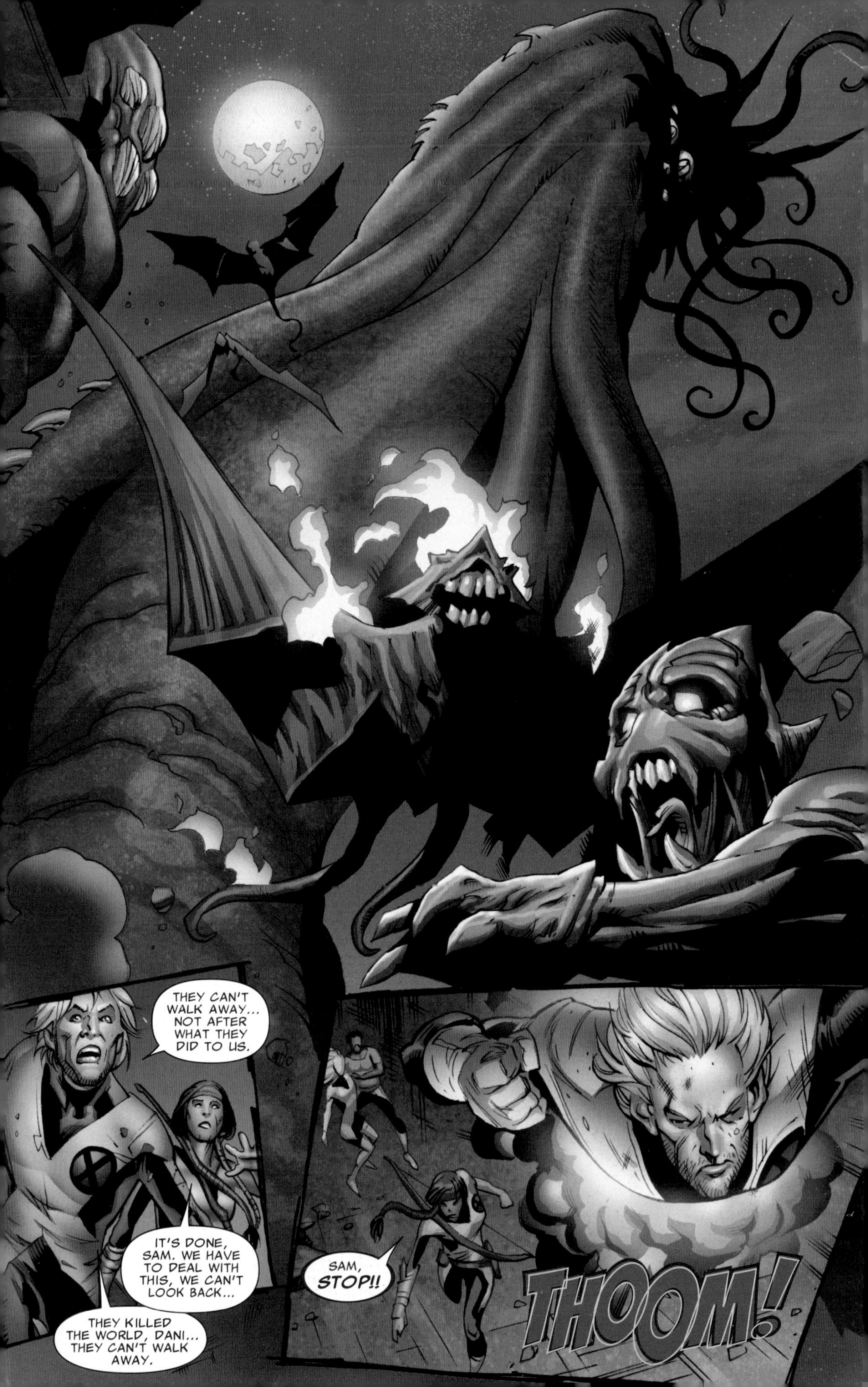
THEY CAN'T WALK AWAY... NOT AFTER WHAT THEY DID TO US.
IT'S DONE, SAM. WE HAVE TO DEAL WITH THIS, WE CAN'T LOOK BACK...
THEY KILLED THE WORLD, DANI... THEY CAN'T WALK AWAY.
SAM, STOP!!
THOOM!

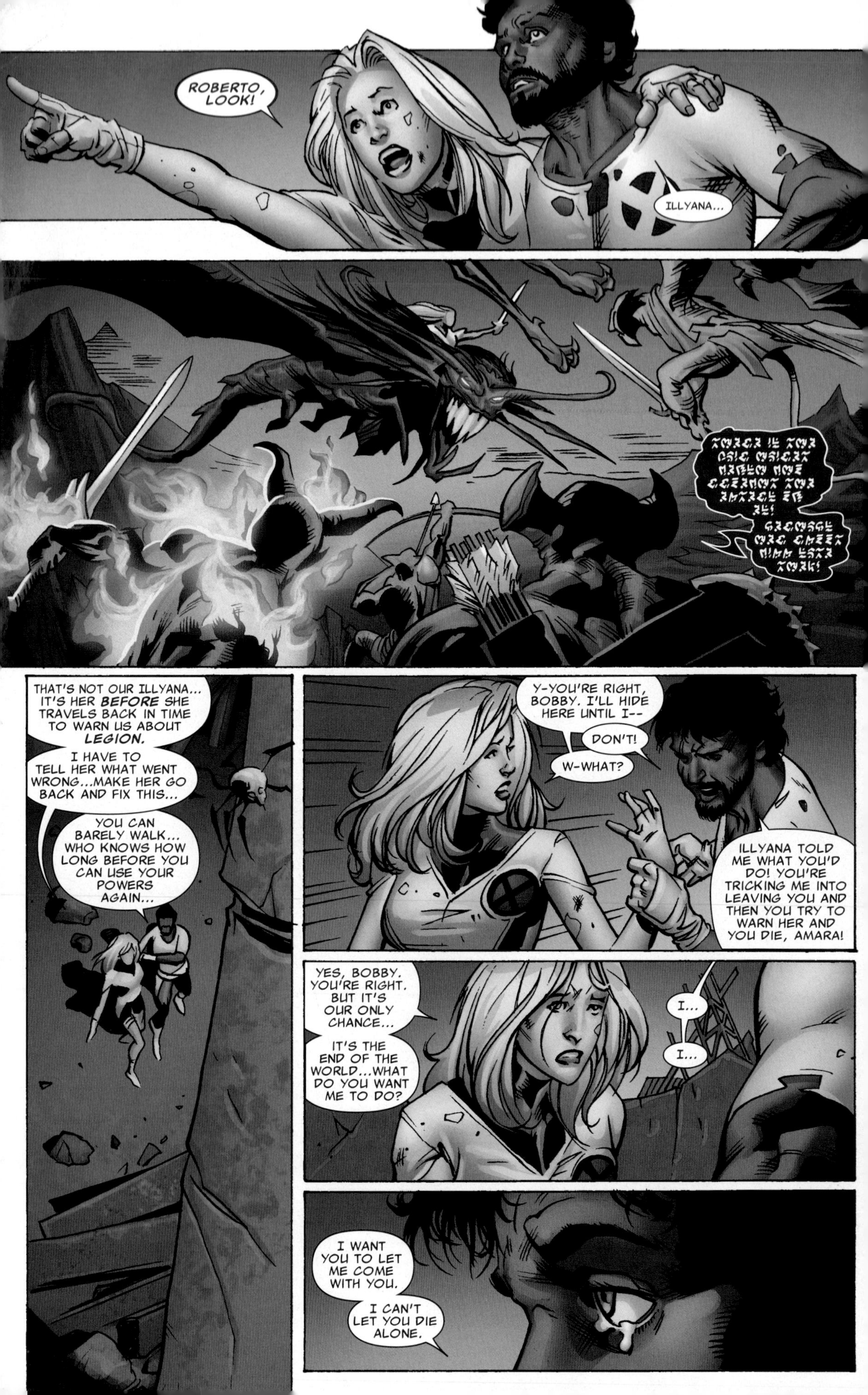
ROBERTO, LOOK!
ILLYANA...
THAT'S NOT OUR ILLYANA... IT'S HER BEFORE SHE TRAVELS BACK IN TIME TO WARN US ABOUT LEGION.
I HAVE TO TELL HER WHAT WENT WRONG...MAKE HER GO BACK AND FIX THIS...
YOU CAN BARELY WALK... WHO KNOWS HOW LONG BEFORE YOU CAN USE YOUR POWERS AGAIN...
Y-YOU'RE RIGHT, BOBBY. I'LL HIDE HERE UNTIL I--
DON'T!
W-WHAT?
ILLYANA TOLD ME WHAT YOU'D DO! YOU'RE TRICKING ME INTO LEAVING YOU AND THEN YOU TRY TO WARN HER AND YOU DIE, AMARA!
YES, BOBBY. YOU'RE RIGHT. BUT IT'S OUR ONLY CHANCE...
IT'S THE END OF THE WORLD...WHAT DO YOU WANT ME TO DO?
I...
I...
I WANT YOU TO LET ME COME WITH YOU.
I CAN'T LET YOU DIE ALONE.

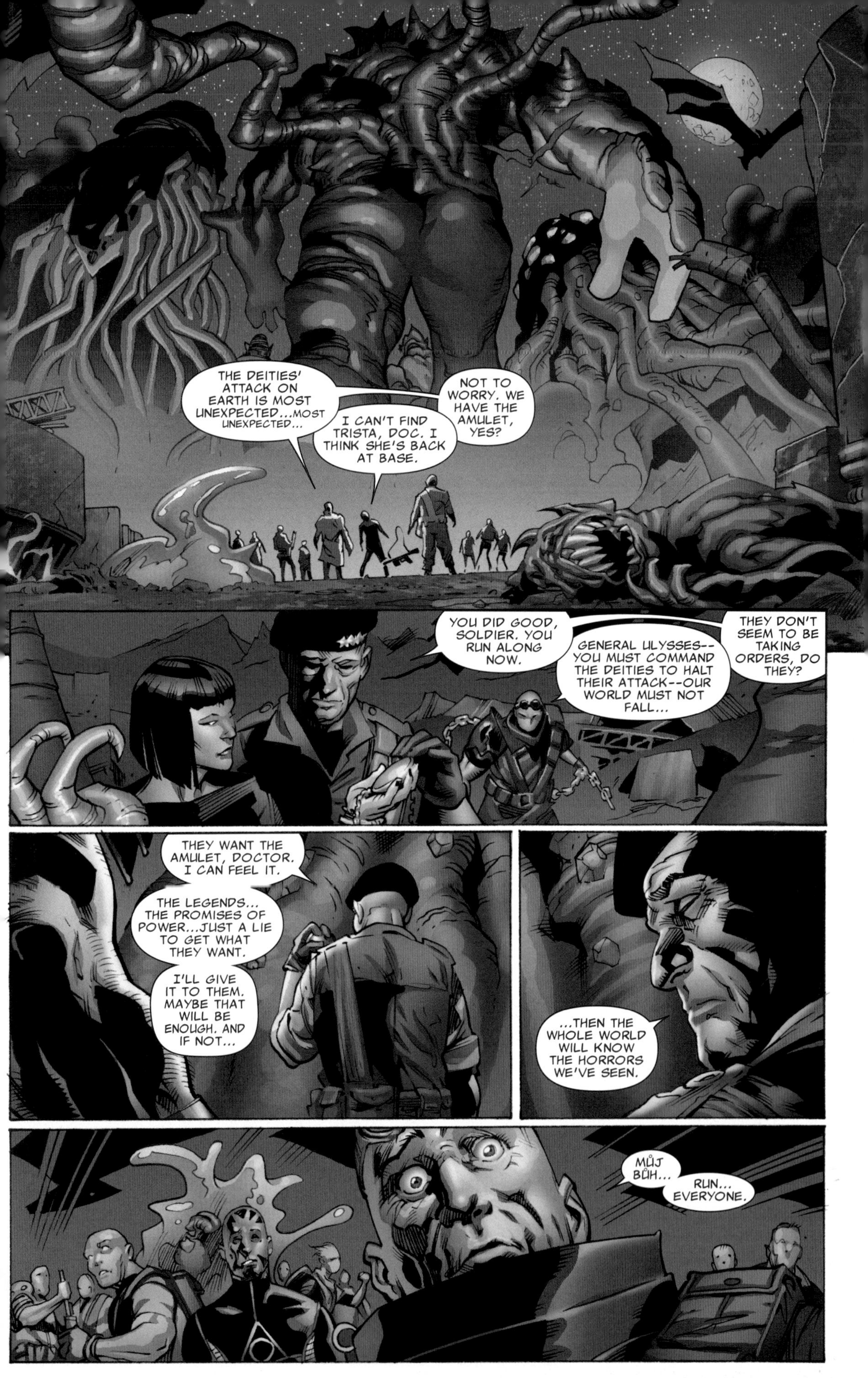
THE DEITIES' ATTACK ON EARTH IS MOST UNEXPECTED...MOST UNEXPECTED...
NOT TO WORRY. WE HAVE THE AMULET, YES?
I CAN'T FIND TRISTA, DOC. I THINK SHE'S BACK AT BASE.
YOU DID GOOD, SOLDIER. YOU RUN ALONG NOW.
THEY DON'T SEEM TO BE TAKING ORDERS, DO THEY?
GENERAL ULYSSES--YOU MUST COMMAND THE DEITIES TO HALT THEIR ATTACK--OUR WORLD MUST NOT FALL...
THEY WANT THE AMULET, DOCTOR. I CAN FEEL IT.
THE LEGENDS... THE PROMISES OF POWER...JUST A LIE TO GET WHAT THEY WANT.
I'LL GIVE IT TO THEM. MAYBE THAT WILL BE ENOUGH. AND IF NOT...
...THEN THE WHOLE WORLD WILL KNOW THE HORRORS WE'VE SEEN.
MŮJ BŮH...
RUN... EVERYONE.

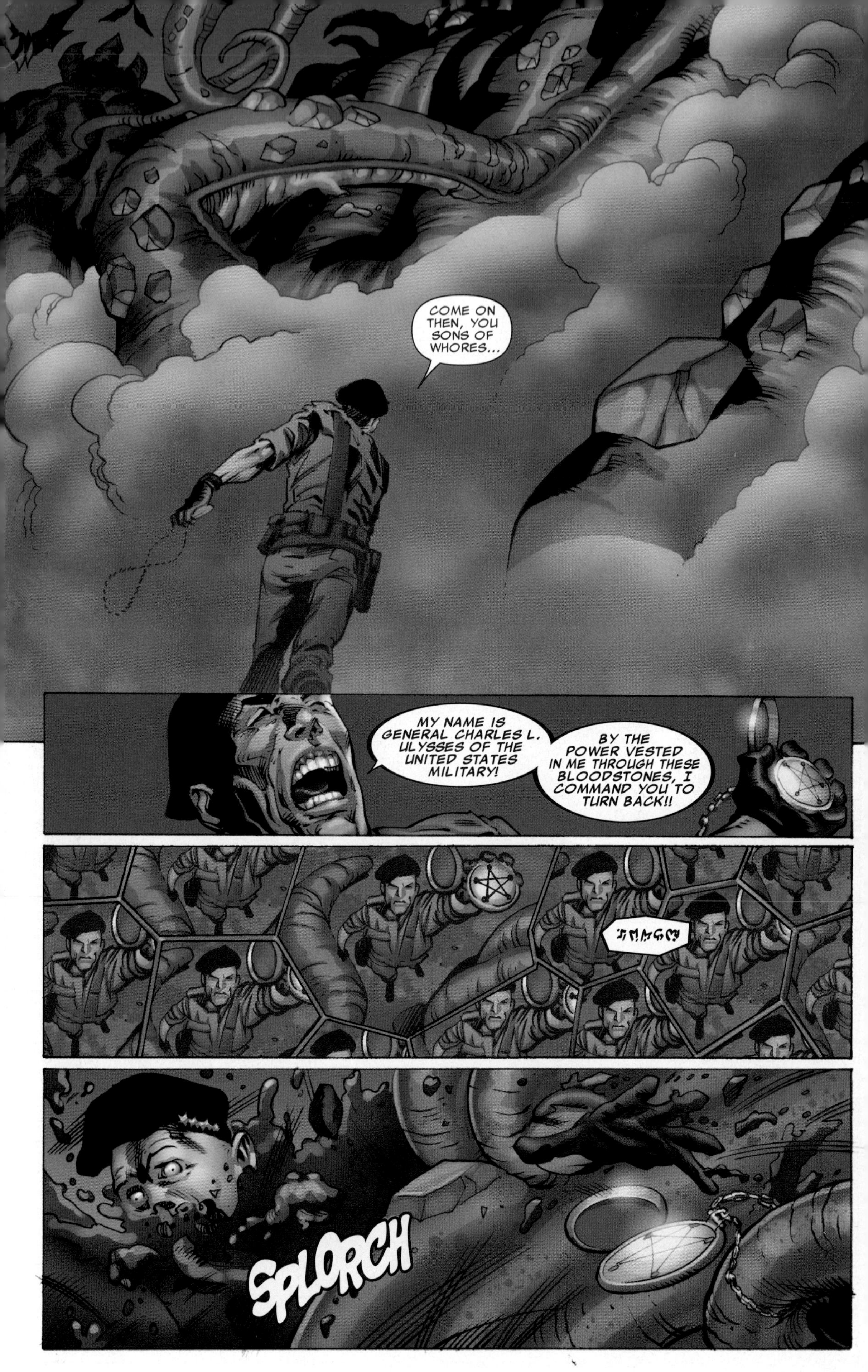
COME ON THEN, YOU SONS OF WHORES...
MY NAME IS GENERAL CHARLES L. ULYSSES OF THE UNITED STATES MILITARY!
BY THE POWER VESTED IN ME THROUGH THESE BLOODSTONES, I COMMAND YOU TO TURN BACK!!
SPLORCH

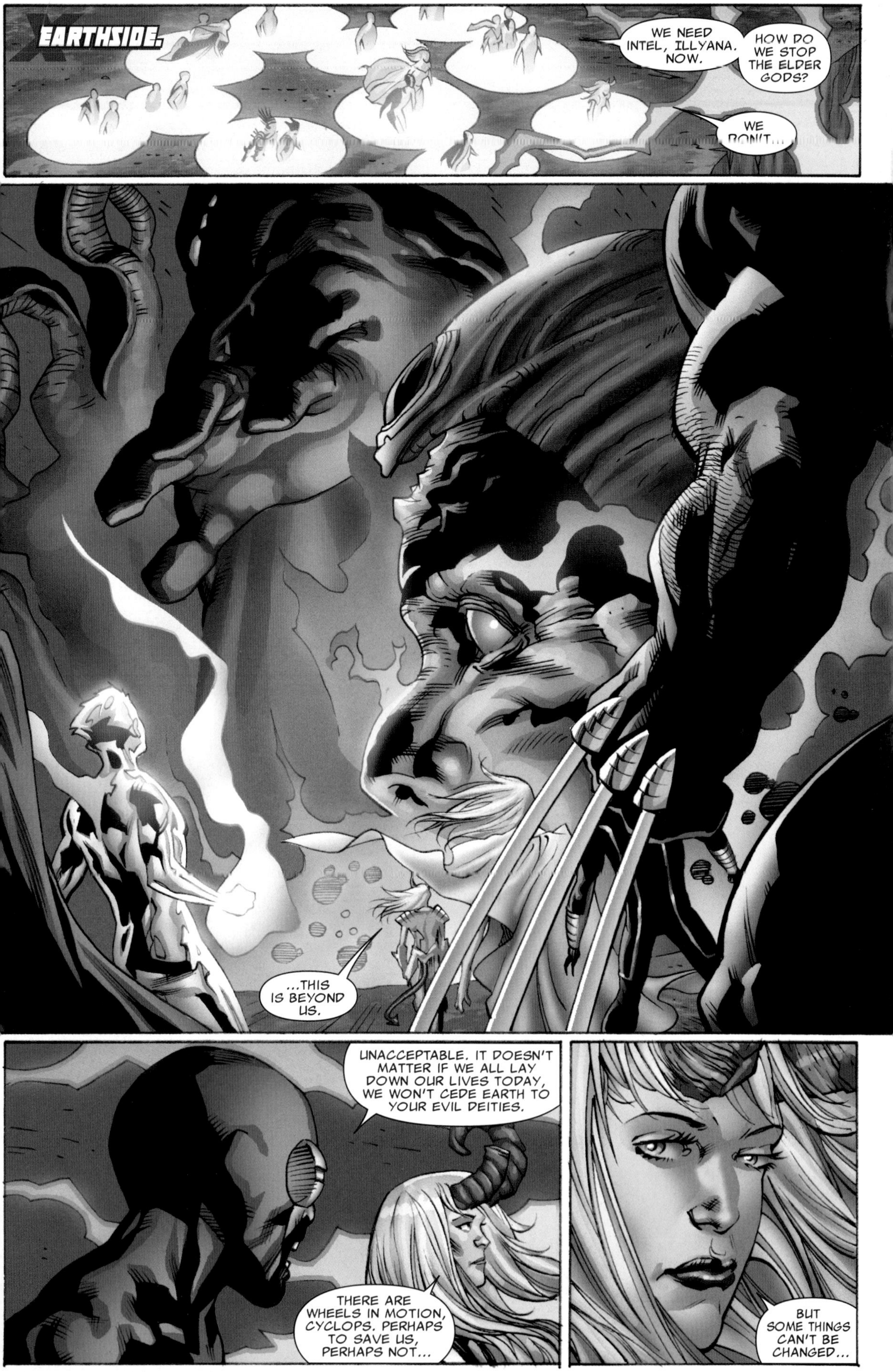
EARTHSIDE.
WE NEED INTEL, ILLYANA. NOW.
HOW DO WE STOP THE ELDER GODS?
WE DON'T...
...THIS IS BEYOND US.
UNACCEPTABLE. IT DOESN'T MATTER IF WE ALL LAY DOWN OUR LIVES TODAY, WE WON'T CEDE EARTH TO YOUR EVIL DEITIES.
THERE ARE WHEELS IN MOTION, CYCLOPS. PERHAPS TO SAVE US, PERHAPS NOT...
BUT SOME THINGS CAN'T BE CHANGED...

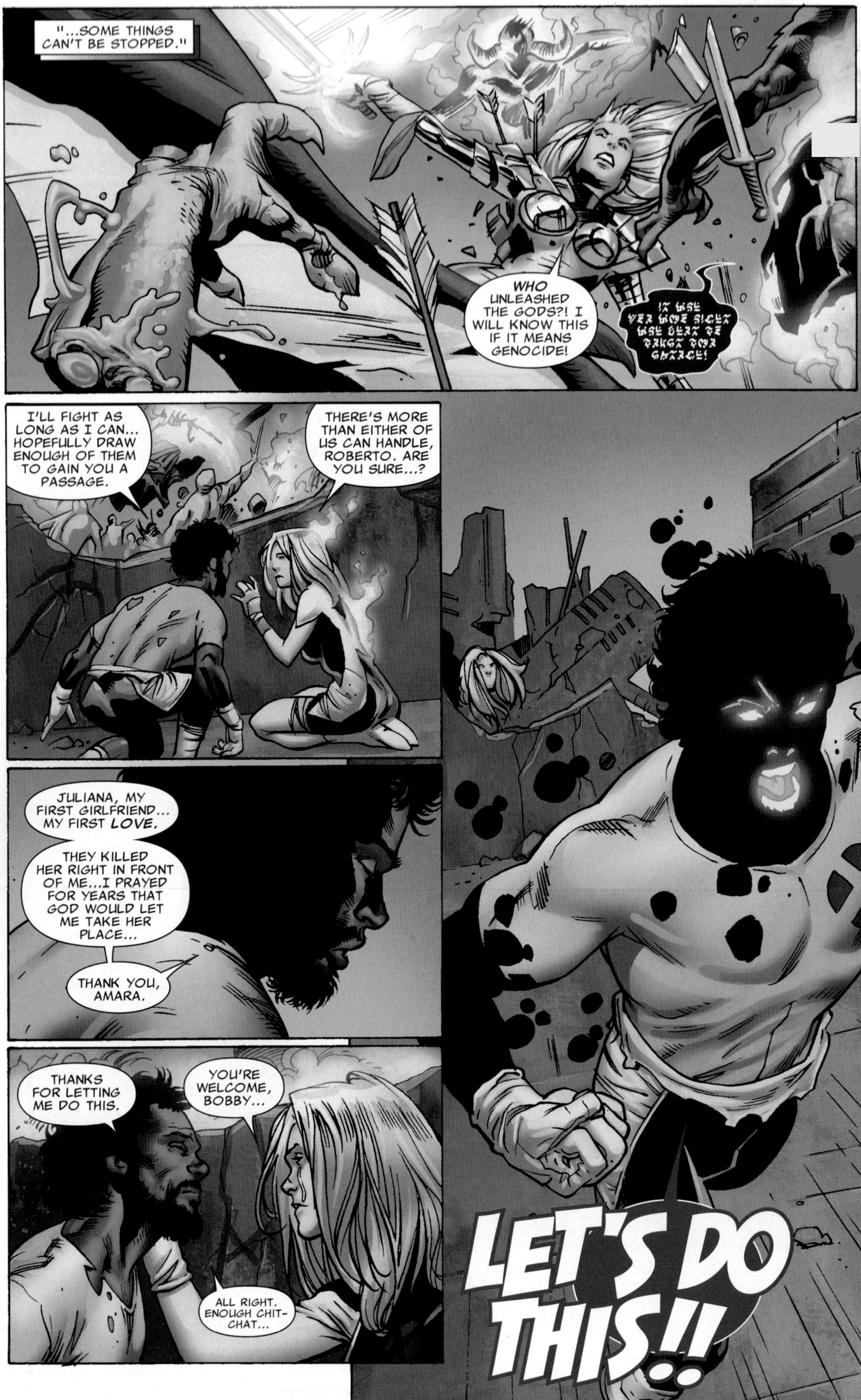
"...SOME THINGS CAN'T BE STOPPED."
WHO UNLEASHED THE GODS?! I WILL KNOW THIS IF IT MEANS GENOCIDE!
I'LL FIGHT AS LONG AS I CAN... HOPEFULLY DRAW ENOUGH OF THEM TO GAIN YOU A PASSAGE.
THERE'S MORE THAN EITHER OF US CAN HANDLE, ROBERTO. ARE YOU SURE...?
JULIANA, MY FIRST GIRLFRIEND... MY FIRST LOVE.
THEY KILLED HER RIGHT IN FRONT OF ME...I PRAYED FOR YEARS THAT GOD WOULD LET ME TAKE HER PLACE...
THANK YOU, AMARA.
THANKS FOR LETTING ME DO THIS.
YOU'RE WELCOME, BOBBY...
ALL RIGHT. ENOUGH CHIT-CHAT...
LET'S DO THIS!!

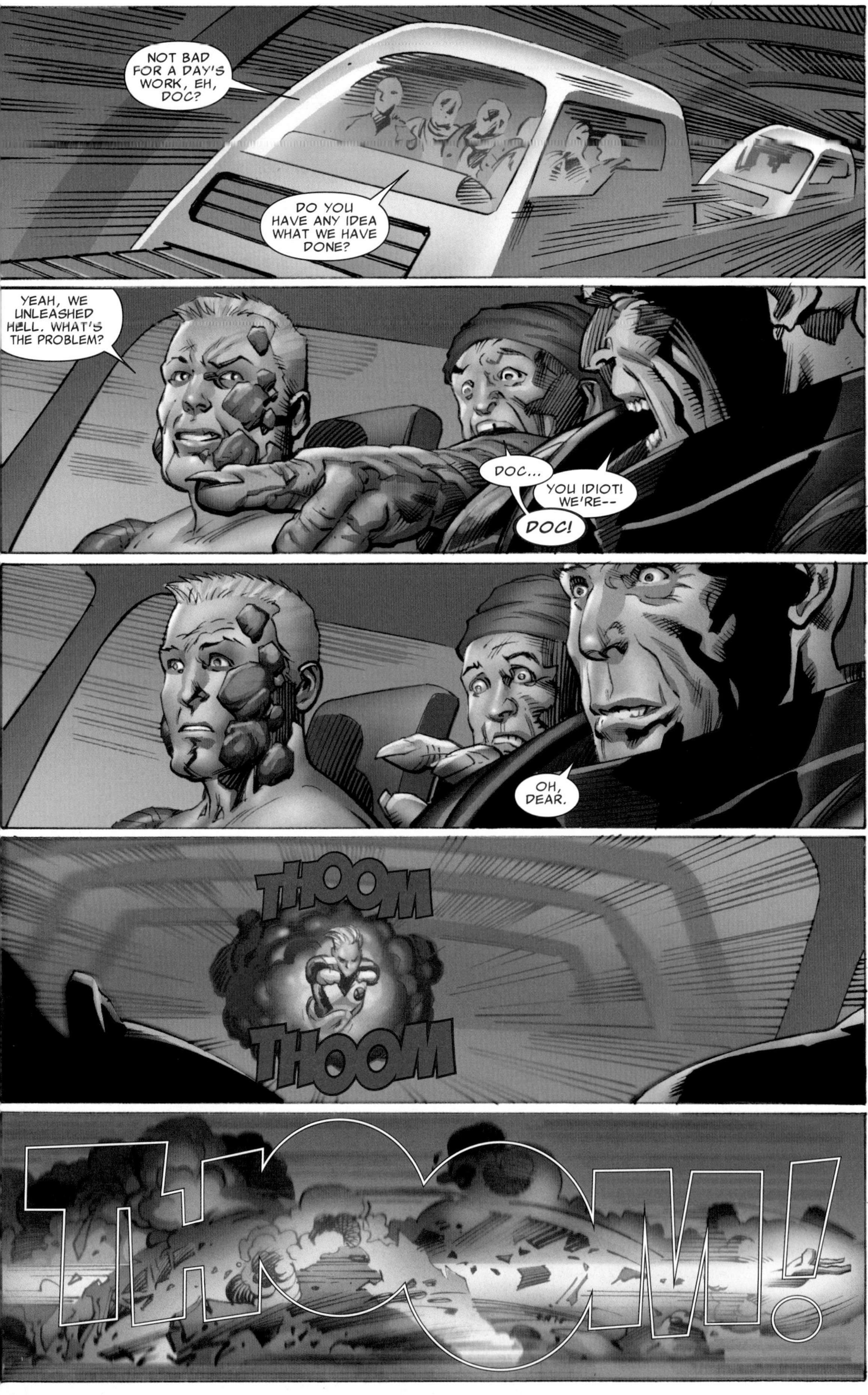
NOT BAD FOR A DAY'S WORK, EH, DOC?
DO YOU HAVE ANY IDEA WHAT WE HAVE DONE?
YEAH, WE UNLEASHED HELL. WHAT'S THE PROBLEM?
DOC...
YOU IDIOT! WE'RE--
DOC!
OH, DEAR.
THOOM
THOOM
THOOM!

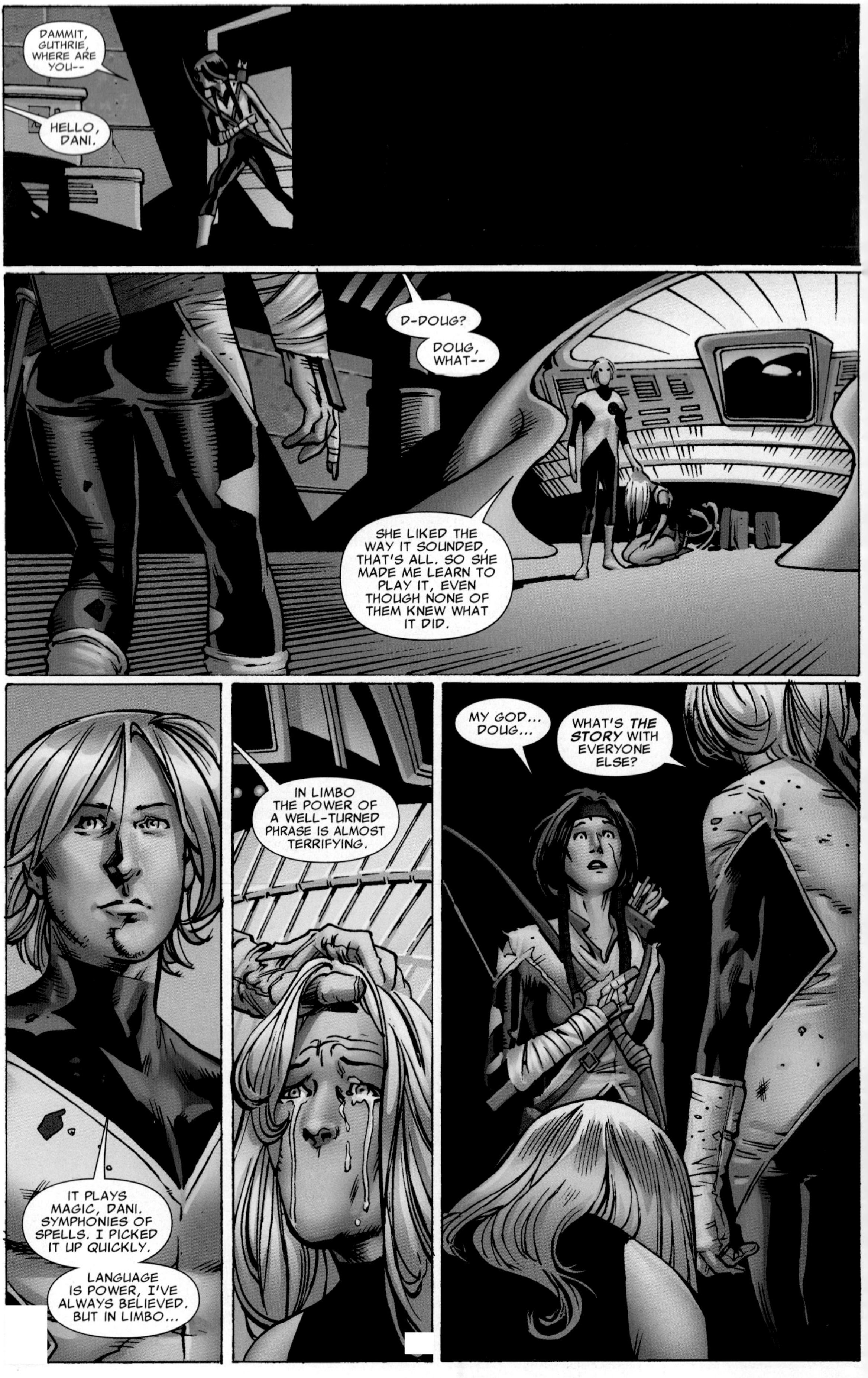
DAMMIT, GUTHRIE, WHERE ARE YOU--
HELLO, DANI.
D-DOUG?
DOUG, WHAT--
SHE LIKED THE WAY IT SOUNDED, THAT'S ALL. SO SHE MADE ME LEARN TO PLAY IT, EVEN THOUGH NONE OF THEM KNEW WHAT IT DID.
IT PLAYS MAGIC, DANI. SYMPHONIES OF SPELLS. I PICKED IT UP QUICKLY.
LANGUAGE IS POWER, I'VE ALWAYS BELIEVED. BUT IN LIMBO...
IN LIMBO THE POWER OF A WELL-TURNED PHRASE IS ALMOST TERRIFYING.
MY GOD... DOUG...
WHAT'S *THE STORY* WITH EVERYONE ELSE?

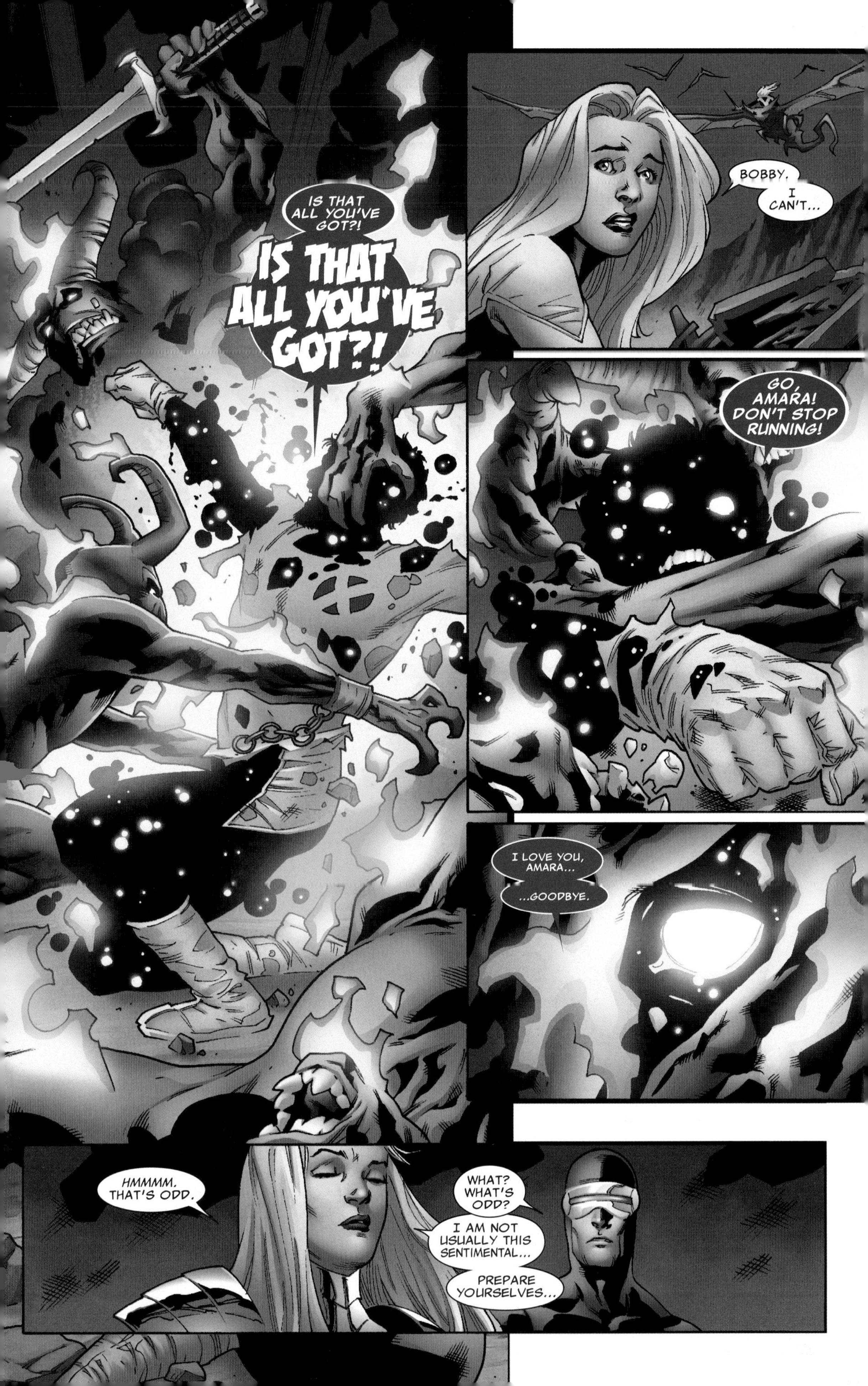
IS THAT ALL YOU'VE GOT?!
IS THAT ALL YOU'VE GOT?!
BOBBY, I CAN'T...
GO, AMARA! DON'T STOP RUNNING!
I LOVE YOU, AMARA...
...GOODBYE.
HMMMM. THAT'S ODD.
WHAT? WHAT'S ODD?
I AM NOT USUALLY THIS SENTIMENTAL...
PREPARE YOURSELVES...

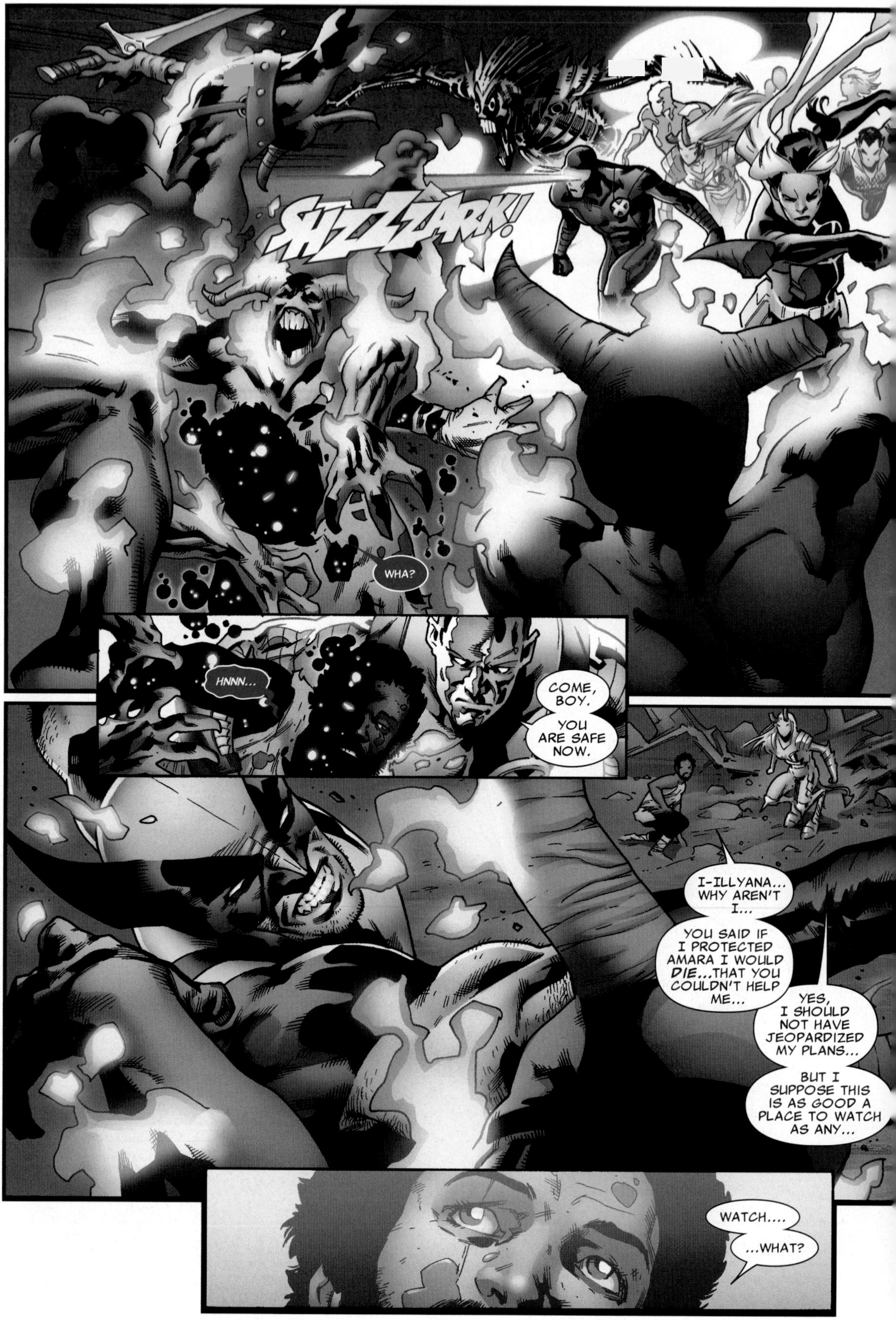
SHZZZARK!
WHA?
HNNN...
COME, BOY.
YOU ARE SAFE NOW.
I-ILLYANA... WHY AREN'T I...
YOU SAID IF I PROTECTED AMARA I WOULD DIE...THAT YOU COULDN'T HELP ME...
YES, I SHOULD NOT HAVE JEOPARDIZED MY PLANS...
BUT I SUPPOSE THIS IS AS GOOD A PLACE TO WATCH AS ANY...
WATCH....
...WHAT?

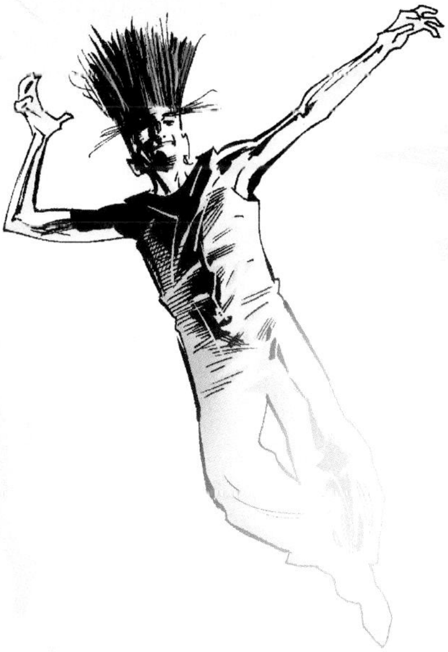

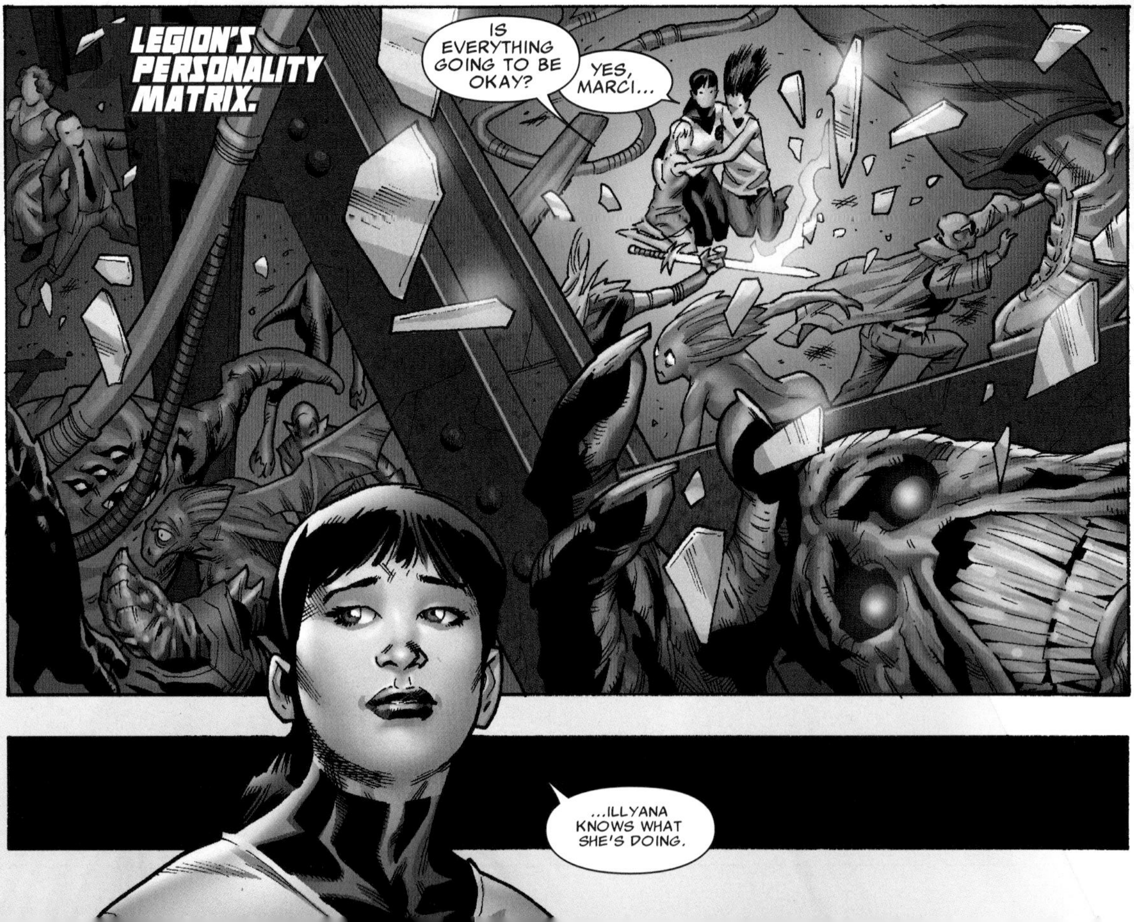
LEGION'S PERSONALITY MATRIX.
IS EVERYTHING GOING TO BE OKAY?
YES, MARCI...
...ILLYANA KNOWS WHAT SHE'S DOING.

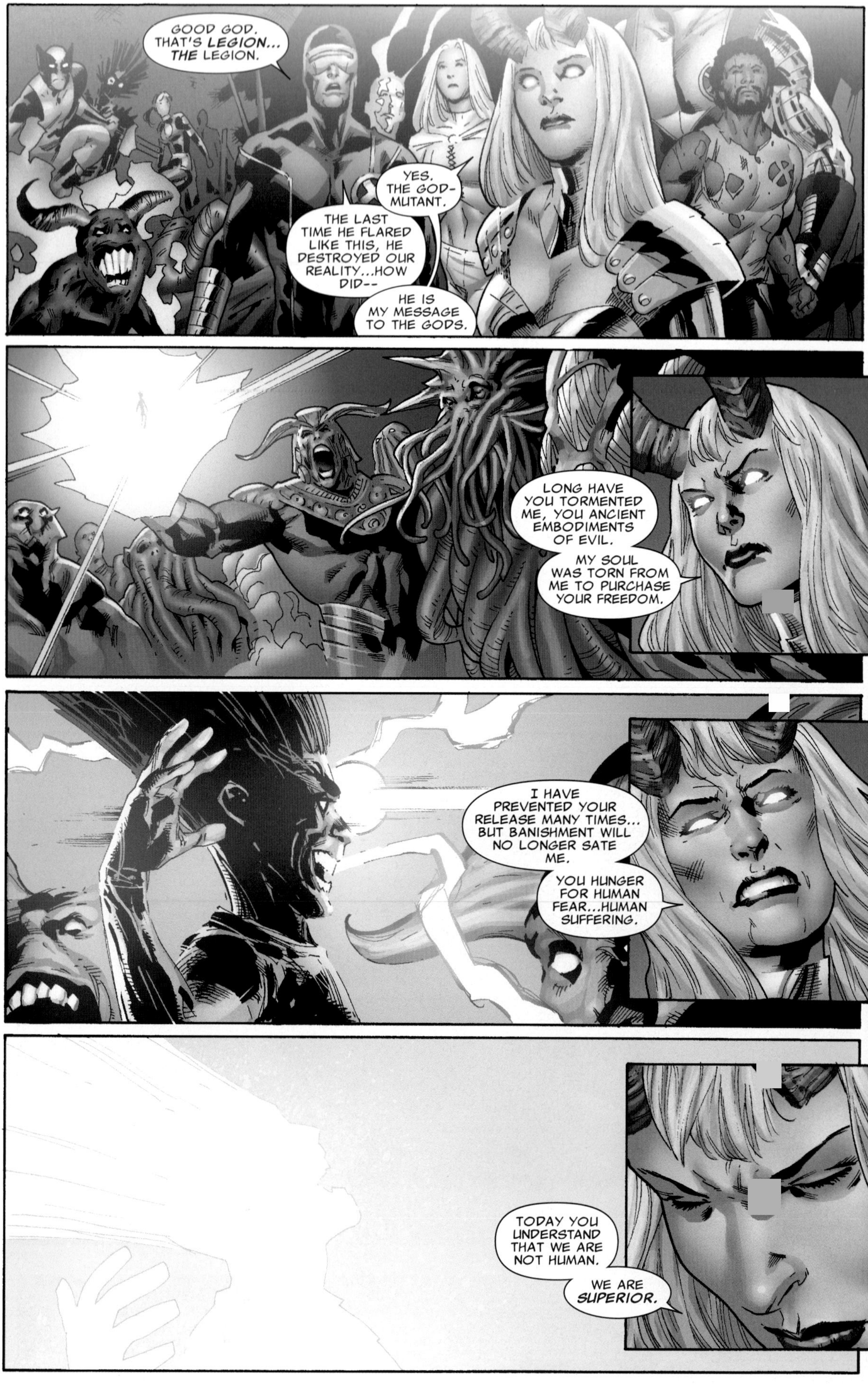
GOOD GOD. THAT'S LEGION... THE LEGION.
YES. THE GOD-MUTANT.
THE LAST TIME HE FLARED LIKE THIS, HE DESTROYED OUR REALITY...HOW DID--
HE IS MY MESSAGE TO THE GODS.
LONG HAVE YOU TORMENTED ME, YOU ANCIENT EMBODIMENTS OF EVIL.
MY SOUL WAS TORN FROM ME TO PURCHASE YOUR FREEDOM.
I HAVE PREVENTED YOUR RELEASE MANY TIMES... BUT BANISHMENT WILL NO LONGER SATE ME.
YOU HUNGER FOR HUMAN FEAR...HUMAN SUFFERING.
TODAY YOU UNDERSTAND THAT WE ARE NOT HUMAN.
WE ARE SUPERIOR.

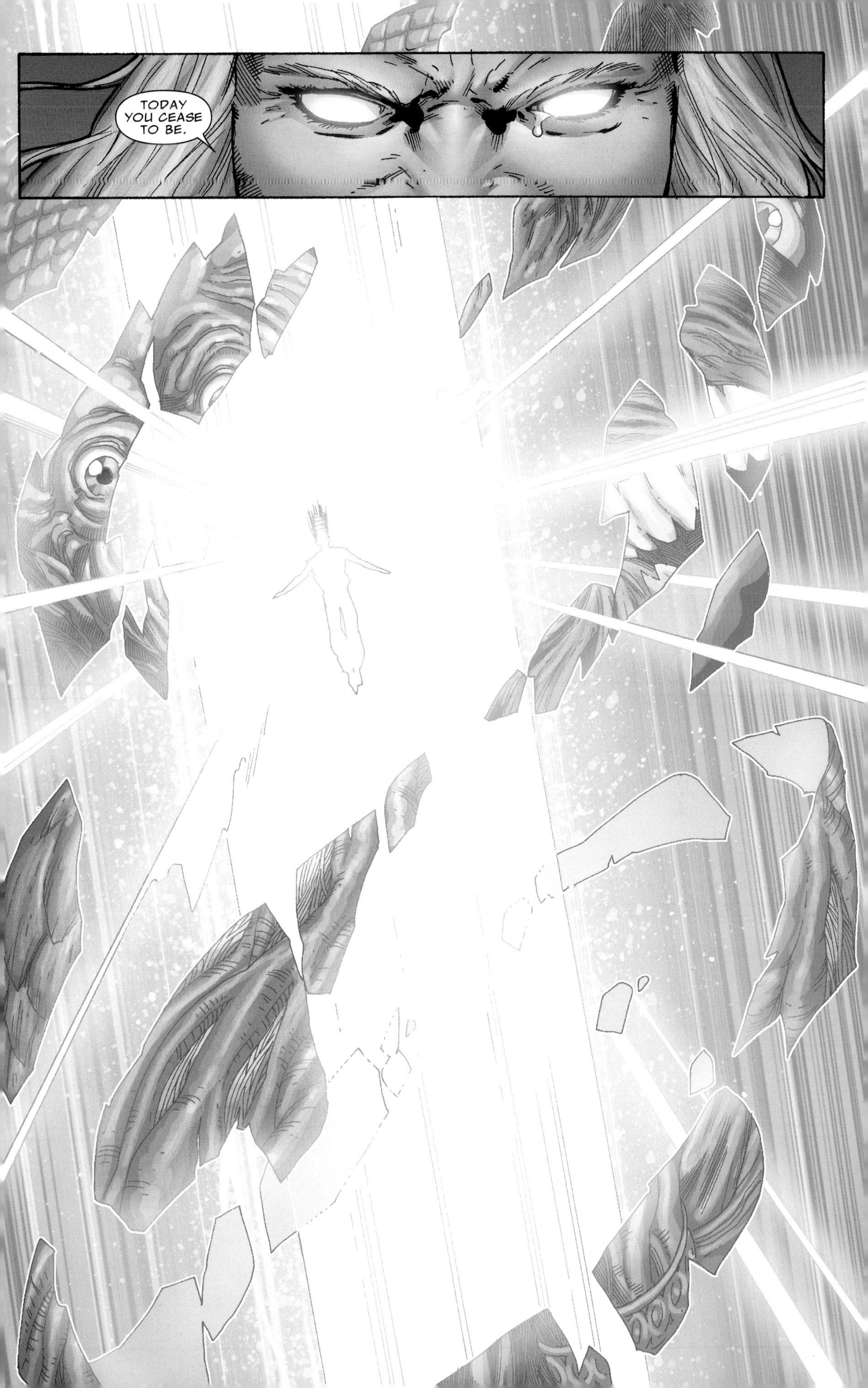
TODAY YOU CEASE TO BE.

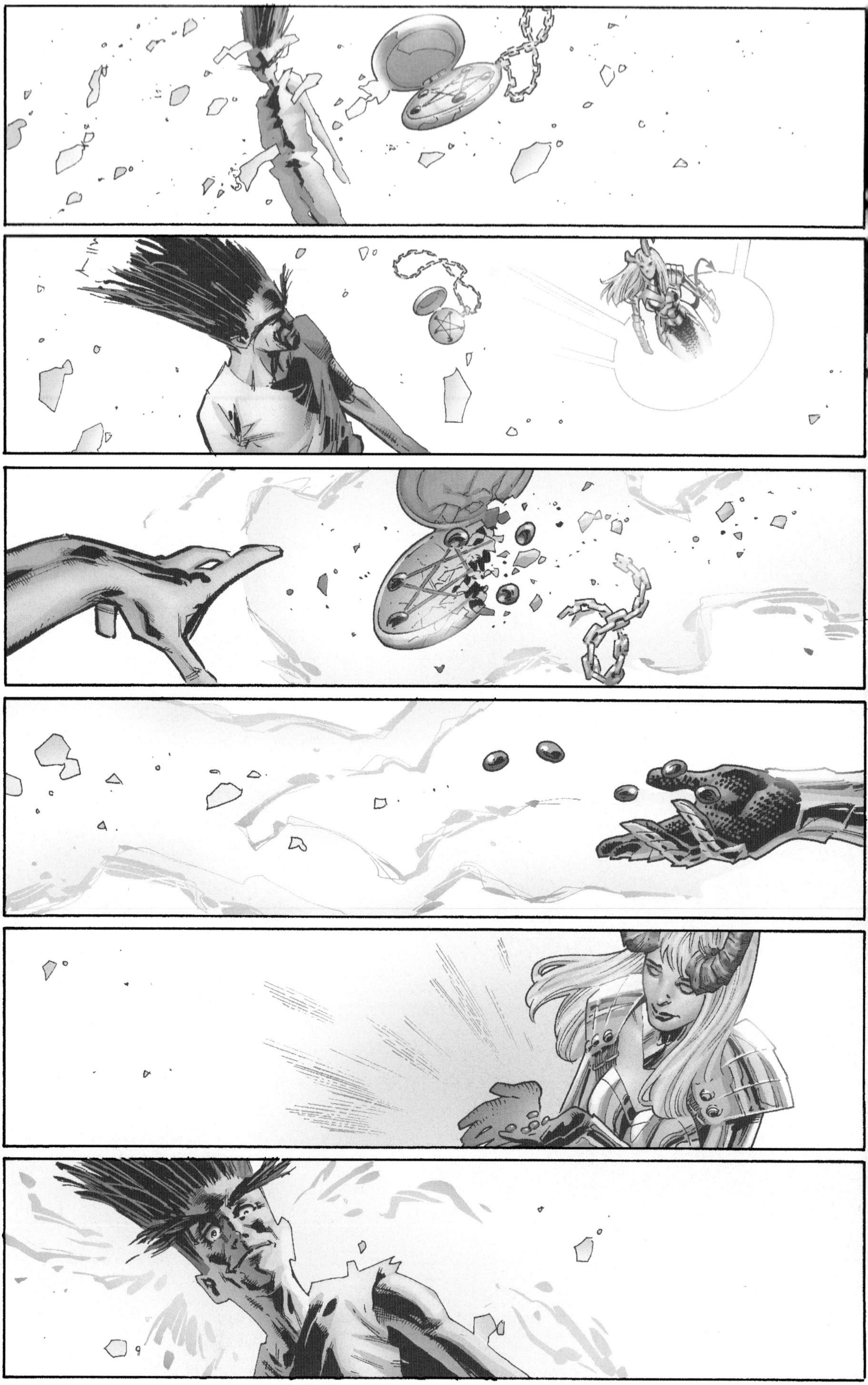

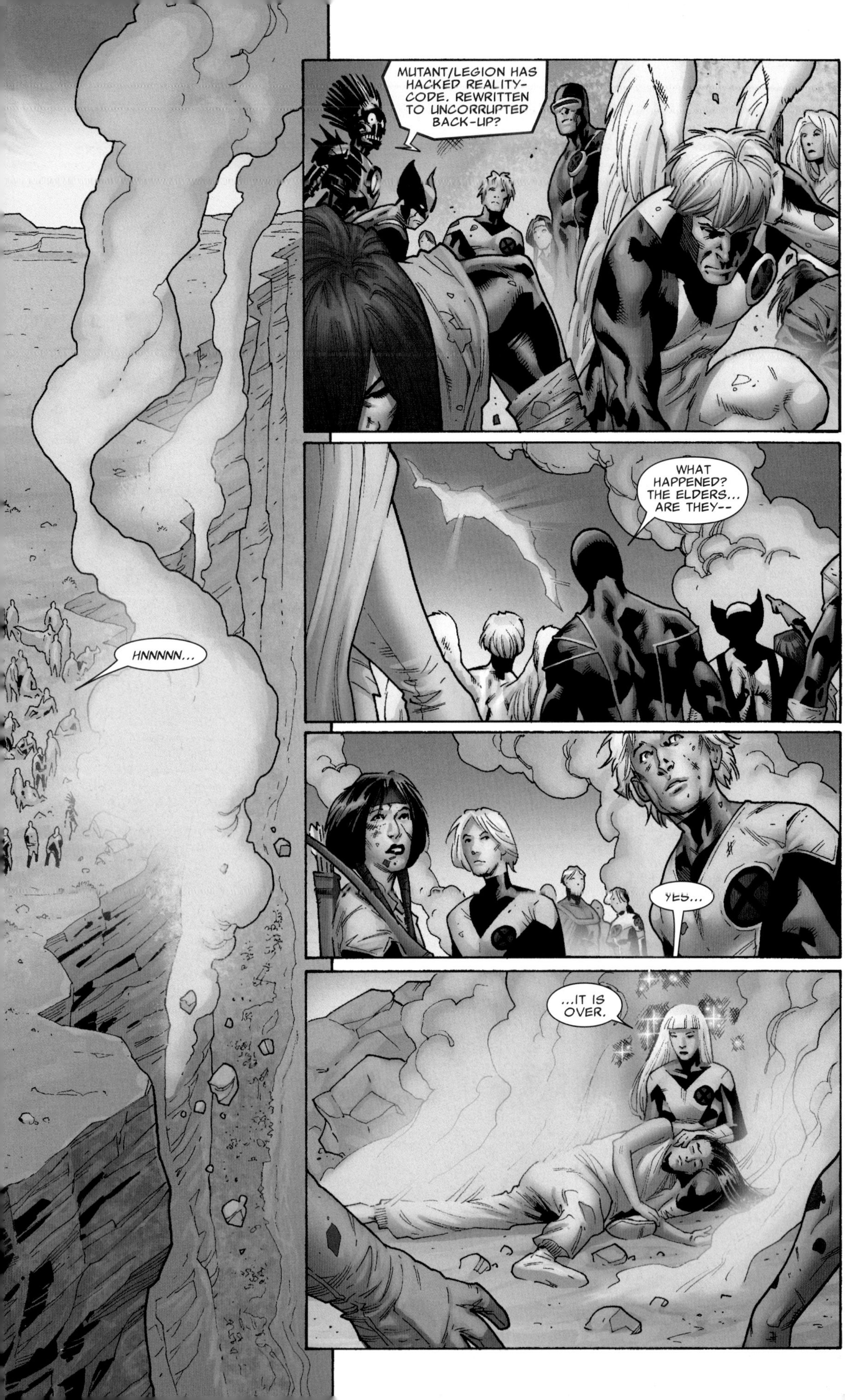
MUTANT/LEGION HAS HACKED REALITY-CODE. REWRITTEN TO UNCORRUPTED BACK-UP?
HNNNNN...
WHAT HAPPENED? THE ELDERS... ARE THEY--
YES...
...IT IS OVER.

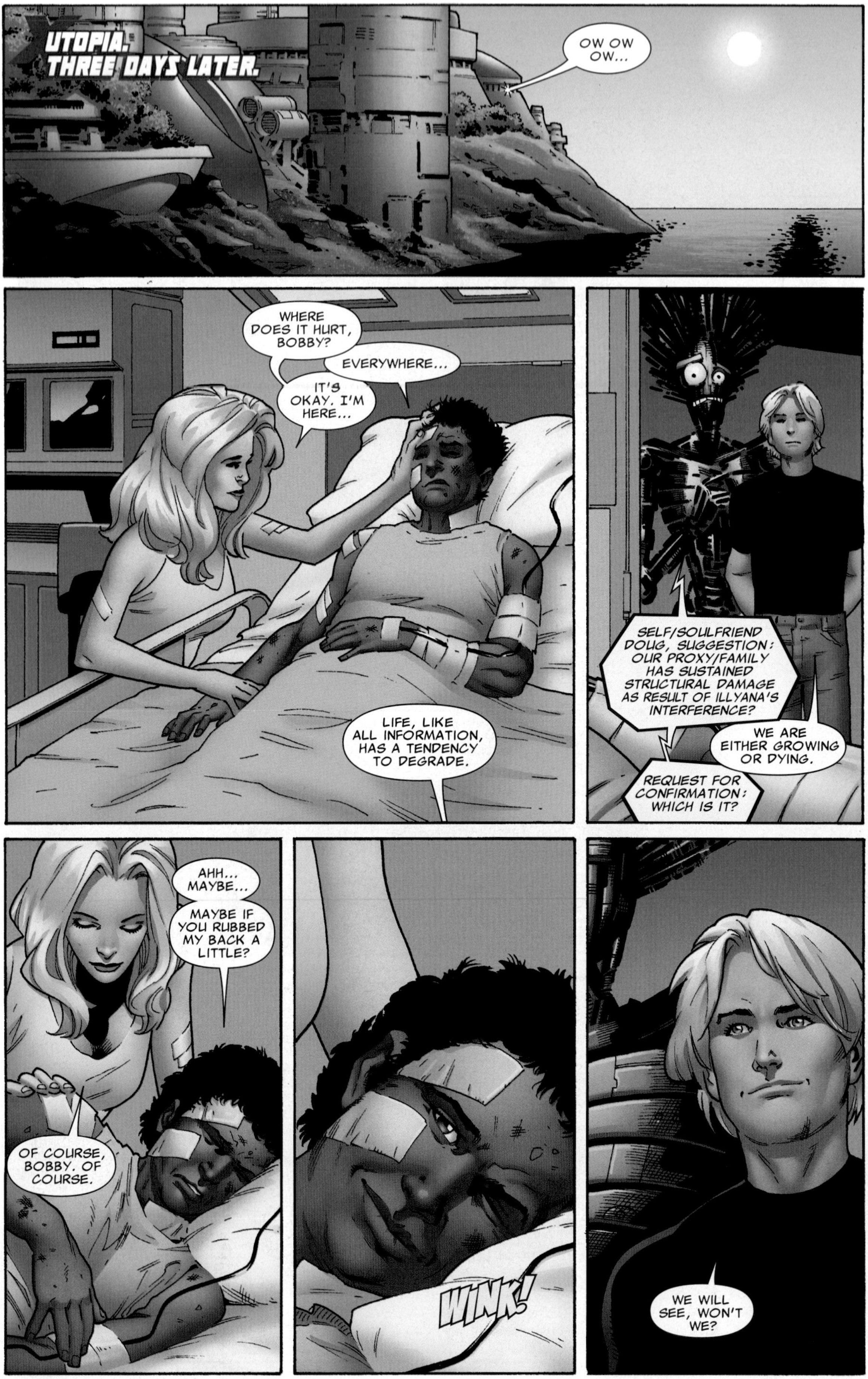
UTOPIA. THREE DAYS LATER.
OW OW OW...
WHERE DOES IT HURT, BOBBY?
EVERYWHERE...
IT'S OKAY. I'M HERE...
LIFE, LIKE ALL INFORMATION, HAS A TENDENCY TO DEGRADE.
SELF/SOULFRIEND DOUG, SUGGESTION: OUR PROXY/FAMILY HAS SUSTAINED STRUCTURAL DAMAGE AS RESULT OF ILLYANA'S INTERFERENCE?
WE ARE EITHER GROWING OR DYING.
REQUEST FOR CONFIRMATION: WHICH IS IT?
AHH... MAYBE...
MAYBE IF YOU RUBBED MY BACK A LITTLE?
OF COURSE, BOBBY. OF COURSE.
WINK!
WE WILL SEE, WON'T WE?

"WE WILL SEE..."

SAM.

DID YOU CATCH UP TO THEM, SAM?

DOCTOR NUO...THE BABIES?

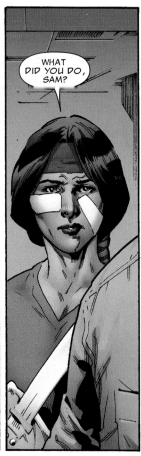

WHAT DID YOU DO, SAM?

"THEN THERE IS NOTHING MORE TO SAY..."

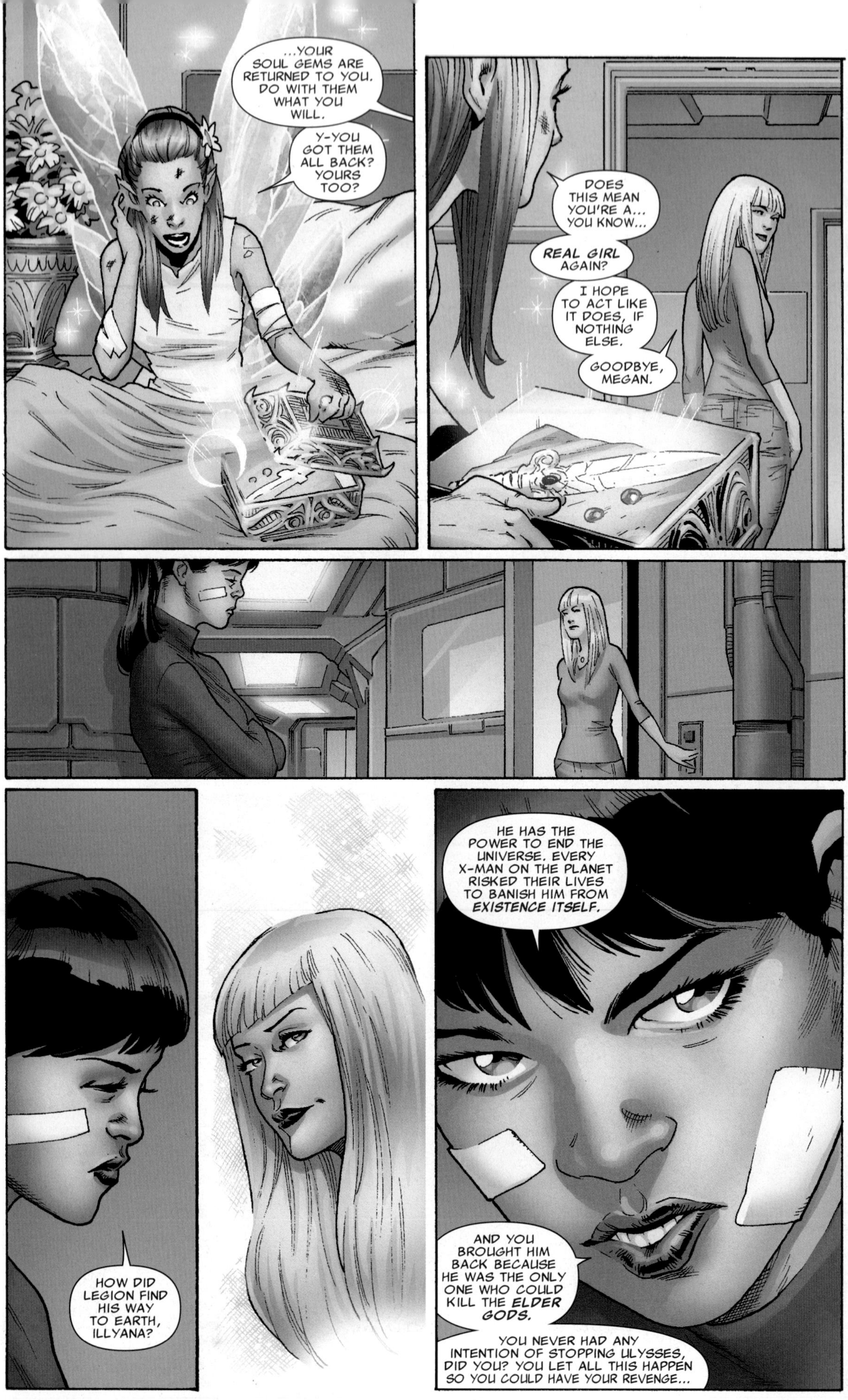
...YOUR SOUL GEMS ARE RETURNED TO YOU. DO WITH THEM WHAT YOU WILL.
Y-YOU GOT THEM ALL BACK? YOURS TOO?
DOES THIS MEAN YOU'RE A... YOU KNOW...
REAL GIRL AGAIN?
I HOPE TO ACT LIKE IT DOES, IF NOTHING ELSE.
GOODBYE, MEGAN.
HOW DID LEGION FIND HIS WAY TO EARTH, ILLYANA?
HE HAS THE POWER TO END THE UNIVERSE. EVERY X-MAN ON THE PLANET RISKED THEIR LIVES TO BANISH HIM FROM EXISTENCE ITSELF.
AND YOU BROUGHT HIM BACK BECAUSE HE WAS THE ONLY ONE WHO COULD KILL THE ELDER GODS.
YOU NEVER HAD ANY INTENTION OF STOPPING ULYSSES, DID YOU? YOU LET ALL THIS HAPPEN SO YOU COULD HAVE YOUR REVENGE...

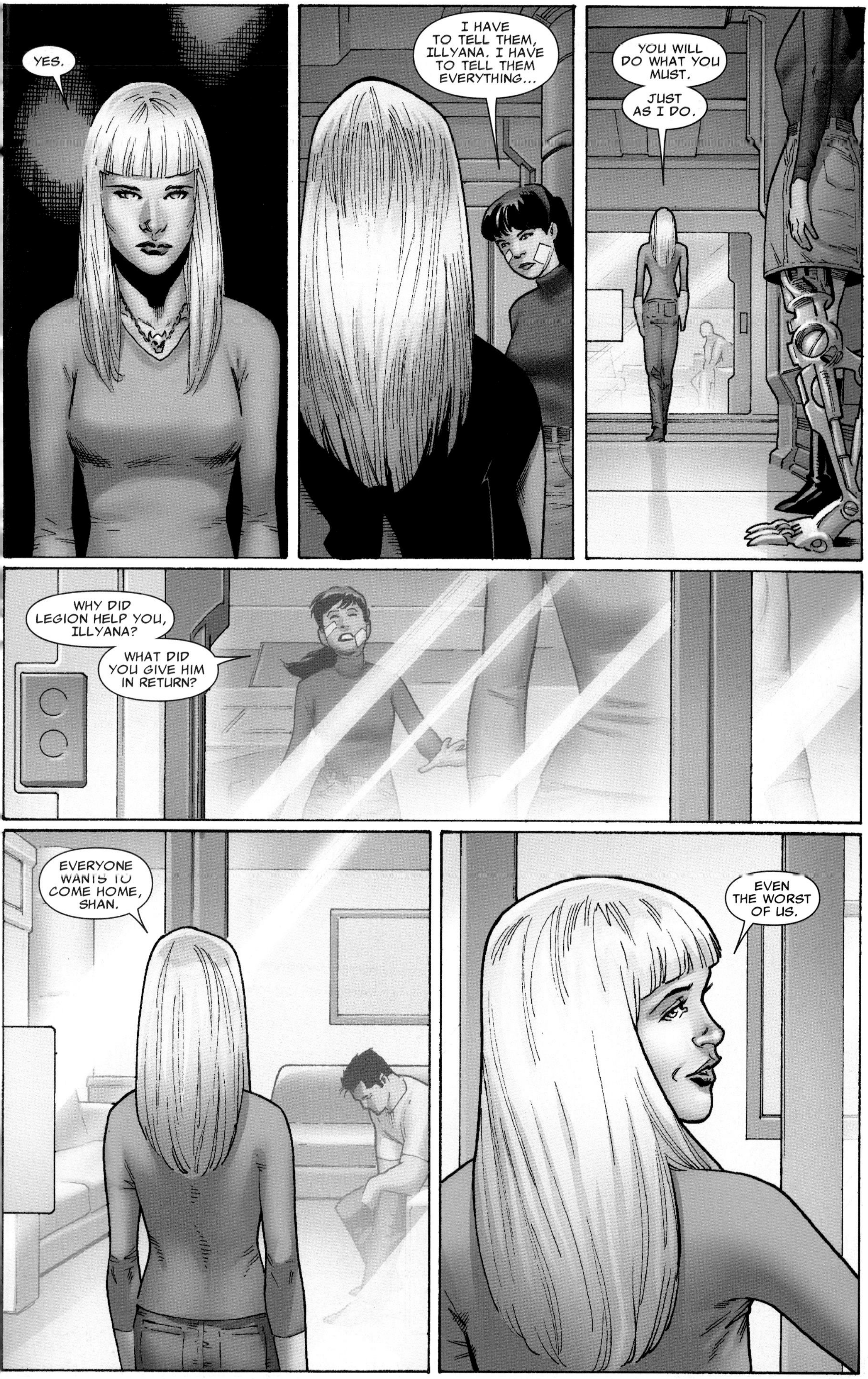
YES.
I HAVE TO TELL THEM, ILLYANA. I HAVE TO TELL THEM EVERYTHING...
YOU WILL DO WHAT YOU MUST.
JUST AS I DO.
WHY DID LEGION HELP YOU, ILLYANA?
WHAT DID YOU GIVE HIM IN RETURN?
EVERYONE WANTS TO COME HOME, SHAN.
EVEN THE WORST OF US.

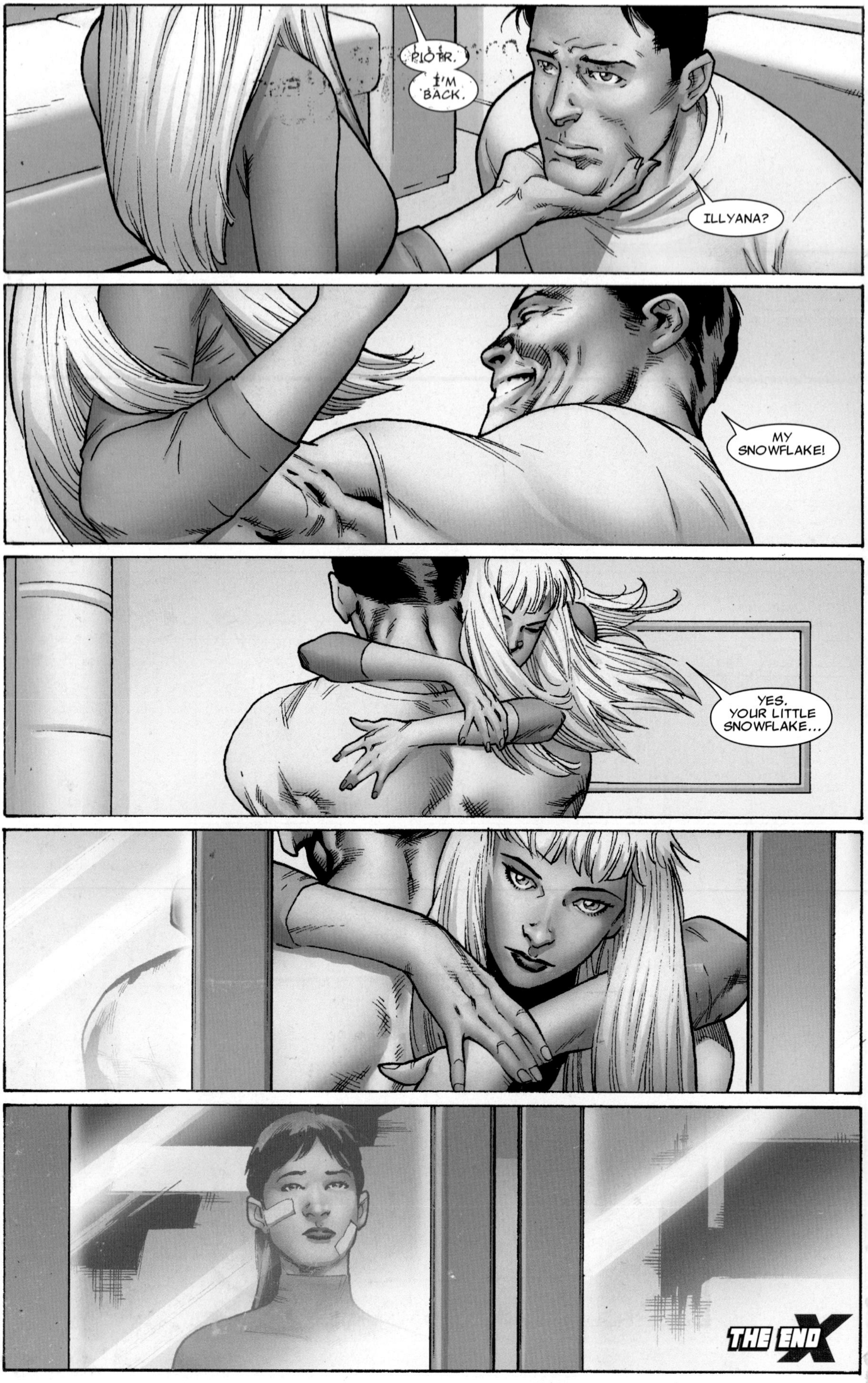
PIOTR.
I'M BACK.
ILLYANA?
MY SNOWFLAKE!
YES. YOUR LITTLE SNOWFLAKE...
THE END